OUT OF THE HITLER TIME

Anna was a German child when she had to flee from the Nazis before the war. By the time the bombs began to fall she was a stateless adolescent in London, and after it was all over she became a happily married young Englishwoman who had put the past behind her – or so she thought.

Judith Kerr's internationally acclaimed trilogy follows the story of Anna and her much-loved family: flight from Nazi Germany, the war, and Anna's eventual return to Berlin and confrontation with the past.

Judith Kerr was born in Berlin and left Germany with her family in 1933 to escape the Nazis. Her three novels are largely based on her own experience.

Also available from Collins

Street Child *Berlie Doherty*
Becky Bananas: This is Your Life *Jean Ure*
The Exiles *Hilary McKay*
Thursday's Child *Noel Streatfeild*
Blitz *Robert Westall*

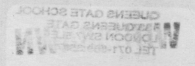

Judith Kerr

WHEN HITLER STOLE PINK RABBIT

·

THE OTHER WAY ROUND

·

A SMALL PERSON FAR AWAY

Collins

An *Imprint* of HarperCollins*Publishers*

When Hitler Stole Pink Rabbit, The Other Way Round,
and *A Small Person Far Away* were first published
in Great Britain in 1971, 1975 and 1978 by
William Collins Sons and Company Ltd.
First published in this edition in Lions in 1994
Reprinted in Collins in 1995
5 7 9 8 6

Collins is an imprint of
HarperCollins*Publishers* Ltd,
77-85 Fulham Palace Road,
Hammersmith, London W6 8JB.

Printed and bound in Great Britain by Caledonian
International Book Manufacturing Ltd, Glasgow, G64

ISBN 000 675077 X

WHEN HITLER STOLE
PINK RABBIT

Illustrated by the author

For my parents,
Julia and Alfred Kerr

Chapter One

Anna was walking home from school with Elsbeth, a girl in her class. A lot of snow had fallen in Berlin that winter. It did not melt, so the street cleaners had swept it to the edge of the pavement, and there it had lain for weeks in sad, greying heaps. Now, in February, the snow had turned into slush and there were puddles everywhere. Anna and Elsbeth skipped over them in their lace-up boots.

They both wore thick coats and woollen caps which kept their ears warm, and Anna had a muffler as well. She was nine but small for her age and the ends of the muffler hung down almost to her knees. It also covered up her mouth and nose, so the only parts of her that showed were her green eyes and a tuft of dark hair. She had been hurrying because she wanted to buy some crayons at the paper shop and it was nearly time for lunch. But now she was so out of breath that she was glad when Elsbeth stopped to look at a large red poster.

"It's another picture of that man," said Elsbeth. "My little sister saw one yesterday and thought it was Charlie Chaplin."

Anna looked at the staring eyes, the grim expression. She said, "It's not a bit like Charlie Chaplin except for the moustache."

They spelled out the name under the photograph.

Adolf Hitler.

"He wants everybody to vote for him in the elections and then he's going to stop the Jews," said Elsbeth. "Do you think he's going to stop Rachel Lowenstein?"

"Nobody can stop Rachel Lowenstein," said Anna. "She's form captain. Perhaps he'll stop me. I'm Jewish too."

"You're not!"

"I am! My father was talking to us about it only last week. He said we were Jews and no matter what happened my brother and I must never forget it."

"But you don't go to a special church on Saturdays like Rachel Lowenstein."

"That's because we're not religious. We don't go to church at all."

"I wish my father wasn't religious," said Elsbeth. "We have to go every Sunday and I get cramp in my seat." She looked at Anna curiously. "I thought Jews were supposed to have bent noses, but your nose is quite ordinary. Has your brother got a bent nose?"

"No," said Anna. "The only person in our house with a bent nose is Bertha the maid, and hers only got like that because she broke it falling off a tram."

Elsbeth was getting annoyed. "Well then," she said, "if you look the same as everyone else and you don't go to a special church, how do you know you *are* Jewish? How can you be sure?"

There was a pause.

"I suppose . . ." said Anna, "I suppose it's because my mother and father are Jews, and I suppose their mothers and fathers were too. I never thought about it much until Papa started talking about it last week."

"Well, I think it's silly!" said Elsbeth. "It's silly about Adolf Hitler and people being Jews and everything!" She started to run and Anna followed her.

They did not stop until they reached the paper shop. There was someone talking to the man at the counter and Anna's heart sank as she recognized Fräulein Lambeck who lived nearby. Fräulein Lambeck was making a face like a sheep and

9

saying, "Terrible times! Terrible times!" Each time she said "terrible times" she shook her head and her earrings wobbled.

The paper shop man said, "1931 was bad enough, 1932 was worse, but mark my words, 1933 will be worst of all." Then he saw Anna and Elsbeth and said, "What can I do for you, my dears?"

Anna was just going to tell him that she wanted to buy some crayons when Fräulein Lambeck spied her.

"It's little Anna!" cried Fräulein Lambeck. "How are you, little Anna? And how is your dear father? Such a wonderful man! I read every word he writes. I've got all his books and I always listen to him on the radio. But he hasn't written anything in the paper this week – I do hope he's quite well. Perhaps he's lecturing somewhere. Oh, we do need him in these terrible, terrible times!"

Anna waited until Fräulein Lambeck had finished. Then she said, "He's got 'flu."

This provoked another outburst. You would have thought that Fräulein Lambeck's nearest and dearest were lying at death's door. She shook her head until the earrings rattled. She suggested remedies. She recommended doctors. She would not stop talking until Anna had promised to give her father Fräulein Lambeck's best wishes for a speedy recovery. And then she turned back in the

10

doorway and said, "Don't say best wishes from Fräulein Lambeck, little Anna – just say from an admirer!" – before she finally swept out.

Anna bought her crayons quickly. Then she and Elsbeth stood together in the cold wind outside the paper shop. This was where their ways normally parted, but Elsbeth lingered. There was something she had wanted to ask Anna for a long time and it seemed a good moment.

"Anna," said Elsbeth, "is it nice having a famous father?"

"Not when you meet someone like Fräulein Lambeck," said Anna, absent-mindedly setting off for home while Elsbeth equally absent-mindedly followed her.

"No, but apart from Fräulein Lambeck?"

"I think it's quite nice. For one thing Papa works at home, so we see quite a lot of him. And sometimes we get free theatre tickets. And once we were interviewed by a newspaper, and they asked us what books we liked, and my brother said Zane Grey and the next day someone sent him a whole set as a present!"

"I wish my father was famous," said Elsbeth. "But I don't think he ever will be because he works in the Post Office, and that's not the sort of thing people get famous for."

"If your father doesn't become famous perhaps you will. One snag about having a famous father

11

is that you almost never become famous yourself."

"Why not?"

"I don't know. But you hardly ever hear of two famous people in the same family. It makes me rather sad sometimes." Anna sighed.

By this time they were standing outside Anna's white-painted gate. Elsbeth was feverishly trying to think of something she might become famous for when Heimpi, who had seen them from the window, opened the front door.

"Goodness!" cried Elsbeth, "I'll be late for lunch!" – and she rushed off up the street.

"You and that Elsbeth," grumbled Heimpi as Anna went inside. "You'd talk the monkeys off the trees!"

Heimpi's real name was Fräulein Heimpel and she had looked after Anna and her brother Max since they were babies. Now that they were older she did the house-keeping while they were at school, but she liked to fuss over them when they came back. "Let's have all this off you," she said, unwinding the muffler. "You look like a parcel with the string undone." As Heimpi peeled the clothes off her Anna could hear the piano being played in the drawing room. So Mama was home.

"Are you sure your feet aren't wet?" said Heimpi. "Then go quickly and wash your hands. Lunch is nearly ready."

12

Anna climbed up the thickly carpeted stairs. The sun was shining through the window and outside in the garden she could see a few last patches of snow. The smell of chicken drifted up from the kitchen. It was nice coming home from school.

As she opened the bathroom door there was a scuffle inside and she found herself staring straight at her brother Max, his face scarlet under his fair hair, his hands hiding something behind his back.

"What's the matter?" she asked, even before she caught sight of his friend Gunther who seemed equally embarrassed.

"Oh, it's you!" said Max, and Gunther laughed. "We thought it was a grown-up!"

"What have you got?" asked Anna.

"It's a badge. There was a big fight at school today – Nazis against Sozis."

"What are Nazis and Sozis?"

"I'd have thought even you would know that at your age," said Max, who was just twelve. "The Nazis are the people who are going to vote for Hitler in the elections. We Sozis are the people who are going to vote against."

"But you're none of you allowed to vote," said Anna. "You're too young!"

"Our fathers, then," said Max crossly. "It's the same thing."

"Anyway, we beat them," said Gunther. "You

should have seen those Nazis run! Max and I caught one of them and got his badge off him. But I don't know what my mum is going to say about my trousers." He looked dolefully down at a large tear in the worn cloth. Gunther's father was out of work and there was no money at home for new clothes.

"Don't worry, Heimpi will fix it," said Anna. "Can I see the badge?"

It was a small piece of red enamel with a black hooked cross on it.

"It's called a swastika," said Gunther. "All the Nazis have them."

"What are you going to do with it?"

Max and Gunther looked at each other.

"D'you want it?" asked Max.

Gunther shook his head. "I'm not supposed to have anything to do with the Nazis. My mum's afraid I might get my head cut open."

"They don't fight fair," agreed Max. "They use sticks and stones and everything." He turned the badge over with increasing dislike. "Well, I certainly don't want it."

"Put it down the what-not!" said Gunther. So they did. The first time they pulled the chain it would not flush away, but the second time, just as the gong went for lunch, it disappeared very satisfactorily.

They could still hear the piano as they went downstairs but it stopped while Heimpi was filling their plates and a moment later the door burst open and Mama came in.

"Hello, children, hello, Gunther," she cried, "how was school?"

Everybody immediately began to tell her and the room was suddenly filled with noise and laughter. She knew the names of all their teachers and always remembered what they had told her. So when Max and Gunther talked about how the geography master had flown into a rage she said, "No wonder, after the way you all played him up last week!" And when Anna told her that her essay had been read out in class she said, "That's marvellous – because Fräulein Schmidt hardly ever reads anything out, does she?"

When she listened she looked at whoever was talking with the utmost concentration. When she talked all her energy went into it. She seemed to do everything twice as hard as other people – even her eyes were a brighter blue than any Anna had ever seen.

They were just starting on the pudding (which was apple strudel) when Bertha the maid came in to tell Mama that there was someone on the telephone, and should she disturb Papa?

"What a time to ring up!" cried Mama and pushed her chair back so hard that Heimpi had to put out her hand to stop it falling over. "Don't any of you dare eat my apple strudel!" And she rushed out.

It seemed very quiet after she had gone, though Anna could hear her footsteps hurrying to the telephone and, a little later, hurrying even faster up the stairs to Papa's room. In the silence she asked, "How is Papa?"

"Feeling better," said Heimpi. "His temperature is down a bit."

Anna ate her pudding contentedly. Max and Gunther got through three helpings but still Mama had not come back. It was odd because she was particularly fond of apple strudel.

Bertha came to clear away and Heimpi took the boys off to see to Gunther's trousers. "No use mending these," she said, "they'd split again as soon as you breathed. But I've got an outgrown pair of Max's that will just do you nicely."

Anna was left in the dining-room wondering what to do. For a while she helped Bertha. They put the used plates through the hatch into the pantry. Then they brushed the crumbs off the table with a little brush and pan. Then, while they were folding the tablecloth, she remembered Fräulein Lambeck and her message. She waited until Bertha had the tablecloth safely in her hands and ran up to Papa's room. She could hear Papa and Mama talking inside.

"Papa," said Anna as she opened the door, "I met Fräulein Lambeck . . ."

"Not now! Now now!" cried Mama. "We're talking!" She was sitting on the edge of Papa's

16

bed. Papa was propped up against the pillows looking rather pale. They were both frowning.

"But Papa, she asked me to tell you . . ."

Mama got quite angry.

"For goodness' sake, Anna," she shouted, "we don't want to hear about it now! Go away!"

"Come back a little later," said Papa more gently. Anna shut the door. So much for that! It wasn't as though she'd ever wanted to deliver Fräulein Lambeck's silly message in the first place. But she felt put out.

There was no one in the nursery. She could hear shouts outside, so Max and Gunther were probably playing in the garden, but she did not feel like joining them. Her satchel was hanging on the back of a chair. She unpacked her new crayons and took them all out of their box. There was a good pink and quite a good orange, but the blues were best. There were three different shades, all beautifully bright, and a purple as well. Suddenly Anna had an idea.

Lately she had been producing a number of illustrated poems which had been much admired both at home and at school. There had been one about a fire, one about an earthquake and one about a man who died in dreadful agonies after being cursed by a tramp. Why not try her hand at a shipwreck? All sorts of words rhymed with sea and there was "save" to rhyme with "wave", and she could use the three new blue crayons for the illustration. She found some paper and began.

Soon she was so absorbed that she did not notice the early winter dusk creeping into the room, and she was startled when Heimpi came in and switched on the light.

"I've made some cakes," said Heimpi. "Do you want to help with the icing?"

"Can I just quickly show this to Papa?" asked Anna as she filled in the last bit of blue sea. Heimpi nodded.

This time Anna knocked and waited until Papa called "Come in". His room looked strange because only the bedside lamp was lit and Papa and his bed made an island of light among the shadows. She could dimly see his desk with the typewriter and the mass of papers which had, as usual, overflowed from the desk on to the floor. Because Papa often wrote late at night and did not want to disturb Mama his bed was in his workroom.

Papa himself did not look like someone who was feeling better. He was sitting up doing nothing at all, just staring in front of him with a kind of tight look on his thin face, but when he saw Anna he smiled. She showed him the poem and he read it through twice and said it was very good, and he also admired the illustration. Then Anna told him about Fräulein Lambeck and they both laughed. He was looking more like himself, so Anna said, "Papa, do you really like the poem?"

Papa said he did.

"You don't think it should be more cheerful?"

"Well," said Papa, "a shipwreck is not really a thing you can be very cheerful about."

"My teacher Fräulein Schmidt thinks I should write about more cheerful subjects like the spring and the flowers."

"And do you want to write about the spring and the flowers?"

"No," said Anna sadly. "Right now all I seem to be able to do is disasters."

Papa gave a little sideways smile and said perhaps she was in tune with the times.

"Do you think then," asked Anna anxiously, "that disasters are all right to write about?" Papa became serious at once.

"Of course!" he said. "If you want to write about disasters, that's what you must do. It's no use trying to write what other people want. The only way to write anything good is to try to please yourself."

Anna was so encouraged to hear this that she was just going to ask Papa whether by any chance Papa thought she might become famous one day, but the telephone by Papa's bed rang loudly and surprised them both.

The tight look was back on Papa's face as he lifted the receiver and it was odd, thought Anna, how even his voice sounded different. She listened to him saying, "Yes . . . yes . . ." and something about Prague before she lost interest. But the conversation was soon over.

"You'd better run along now," said Papa. He lifted his arms as though to give her a big hug. Then he put them down again. "I'd better not give you my 'flu," he said.

Anna helped Heimpi ice the cakes and then she and Max and Gunther ate them – all except three which Heimpi put in a paper bag for Gunther to take home to his mum. She had also found some more of Max's outgrown clothes to fit him, so he had quite a nice parcel to take with him when he left.

They spent the rest of the evening playing games. Max and Anna had been given a games compendium for Christmas and had not yet got over the wonder of it. It contained draughts, chess, Ludo, Snakes and Ladders, dominoes and six different card games, all in one beautifully made box. If you got tired of one game you could always play another. Heimpi sat with them in the nursery mending socks and even joined them for a game of Ludo. Bedtime came far too soon.

Next morning before school Anna ran into Papa's room to see him. The desk was tidy. The bed was neatly made.

Papa had gone.

Chapter Two

Anna's first thought was so terrible that she could not breathe. Papa had got worse in the night. He had been taken to hospital. Perhaps he . . . She ran blindly out of the room and found herself caught by Heimpi.

"It's all right!" said Heimpi. "It's all right! Your father has gone on a journey."

"A journey?" Anna could not believe it. "But he's ill – he had a temperature . . ."

"He decided to go just the same," said Heimpi firmly. "Your mother was going to explain it all to you when you came home from school. Now I suppose you'll have to hear straight away and Fräulein Schmidt will be kept twiddling her thumbs for you."

"What is it? Are we going to miss school?" Max appeared hopefully on the landing.

Then Mama came out of her room. She was still in her dressing-gown and looked tired.

"There's no need to get terribly excited," she said. "But there are some things I must tell you. Heimpi, shall we have some coffee? And I expect the children could eat some more breakfast."

Once they were all settled in Heimpi's pantry with coffee and rolls Anna felt much better, and was even able to calculate that she would miss the geography lesson at school which she particularly disliked.

"It's quite simple," said Mama. "Papa thinks Hitler and the Nazis might win the elections. If that happened he would not want to live in Germany while they were in power, and nor would any of us."

"Because we're Jews?" asked Anna.

"Not only because we're Jews. Papa thinks no one would be allowed to say what they thought any more, and he wouldn't be able to write. The Nazis don't like people to disagree with them." Mama drank some of her coffee and looked more cheerful. "Of course it may never happen and if it did it probably wouldn't last for long – maybe six months or so. But at the moment we just don't know."

"But why did Papa leave so suddenly?" asked Max.

22

"Because yesterday someone rang him up and warned him that they might be going to take away his passport. So I packed him a small suitcase and he caught the night train to Prague – that's the quickest way out of Germany."

"Who could take away his passport?"

"The police. There are quite a few Nazis in the police."

"And who rang him up to warn him?"

Mama smiled for the first time.

"Another policeman. One Papa had never met – but who had read his books and liked them."

It took Anna and Max some time to digest all this.

Then Max asked, "But what's going to happen now?"

"Well," said Mama, "it's only about ten days until the elections. Either the Nazis lose, in which case Papa comes back – or they win, in which case we join him."

"In Prague?" asked Max.

"No, probably in Switzerland. They speak German there – Papa would be able to write. We'd probably rent a little house and stay there until all this has blown over."

"Heimpi too?" asked Anna.

"Heimpi too."

It sounded quite exciting. Anna was beginning to imagine it – a house in the mountains . . . goats . . . or was it cows? . . . when Mama said,

"There is one thing more." Her voice was very serious.

"This is the most important thing of all," said Mama, "and we need you to help us with it. Papa does not want anyone to know that he has left Germany. So you must not tell anyone. If anyone asks you about him you must say that he's still in bed with 'flu."

"Can't I even tell Gunther?" asked Max.

"No. Not Gunther, nor Elsbeth, not anyone."

"All right," said Max. "But it won't be easy. People are always asking after him."

"Why can't we tell anyone?" asked Anna. "Why doesn't Papa want anyone to know?"

"Look," said Mama. "I've explained it all to you as well as I can. But you're both still children – you can't understand everything. Papa thinks the Nazis might . . . cause us some bother if they knew that he'd gone. So he does not want you to talk about it. Now are you going to do what he asks or not?"

Anna said, yes, of course she would.

Then Heimpi bundled them both off to school. Anna was worried about what to say if anyone asked her why she was late, but Max said, "Just tell them Mama overslept – she did, anyway!"

In fact, no one was very interested. They did high-jump in Gym and Anna jumped higher than anyone else in her class. She was so pleased about this that for the rest of the morning she almost forgot about Papa being in Prague.

When it was time to go home it all came back to her and she hoped Elsbeth would not ask her any awkward questions – but Elsbeth's mind was on more important matters. Her aunt was coming to take her out that afternoon to buy her a yo-yo. What kind did Anna think she should choose? And what colour? The wooden ones worked best on the whole, but Elsbeth had seen a bright orange one which, though made of tin, had so impressed her with its beauty that she was tempted. Anna only had to say Yes and No, and by the time she got home for lunch the day felt more ordinary than she would ever have thought possible that morning.

Neither Anna nor Max had any homework and it was too cold to go out, so in the afternoon they sat on the radiator in the nursery and looked out of the window. The wind was rattling the shutters and blowing great lumps of cloud across the sky.

"We might get more snow," said Max.

"Max," said Anna, "do you hope that we will go to Switzerland?"

"I don't know," said Max. There were so many things he would miss. Gunther . . . his gang with whom he played football . . . school . . . He said, "I suppose we'd go to a school in Switzerland."

"Oh yes," said Anna. "I think it would be quite fun." She was almost ashamed to admit it, but the more she thought about it the more she wanted to go. To be in a strange country where everything would be different – to live in a different house, go to a different school with different children – a huge urge to experience it all overcame her and though she knew it was heartless a smile appeared on her face.

"It would only be for six months," she said apologetically, "and we'd all be together."

The next few days passed fairly normally. Mama got a letter from Papa. He was comfortably installed in a hotel in Prague and was feeling much better. This cheered everyone up.

A few people inquired after him but were quite satisfied when the children said he had 'flu. There was so much of it about that it was not surprising. The weather continued very cold and the puddles caused by the thaw all froze hard again – but still there was no snow.

At last on the afternoon of the Sunday before the elections the sky turned very dark and then suddenly opened up to release a mass of floating, drifting, whirling white. Anna and Max were playing with the Kentner children who lived across the road. They stopped to watch the snow come down.

"If only it had started a bit earlier," said Max. "By the time it's thick enough for tobogganing, it will be too dark."

At five o'clock when Anna and Max were going

home it had only just stopped. Peter and Marianne Kentner saw them to the door. The snow lay thick and dry and crunchy all over the road and the moon was shining down on it.

"Why don't we go tobogganing in the moonlight?" said Peter.

"Do you think they'd let us?"

"We've done it before," said Peter, who was fourteen. "Go and ask your mother."

Mama said they could go provided they all stayed together and got home by seven. They put on their warmest clothes and set off.

It was only a quarter of an hour's walk to the Grunewald, where a wooden slope made an ideal run down to a frozen lake. They had tobogganed there many times before, but it had always been daylight and the air had been loud with the shouts of other children. Now all they could hear was the soughing of the wind in the trees, the crunching of the new snow under their feet, and the gentle whir of the sledges as they slid along behind them. Above their heads the sky was dark but the ground shone blue in the moonlight and the shadows of the trees broke like black bands across it.

At the top of the slope they stopped and looked down. Nobody had been on it before them. The shimmering path of snow stretched ahead, perfect and unmarked, right down to the edge of the lake.

"Who's going down first?" asked Max.

Anna did not mean to, but she found herself hopping up and down and saying. "Oh please – please . . .!"

Peter said, "All right – youngest first."

That meant her because Marianne was ten.

She sat on her sledge, held on to the steering rope, took a deep breath and pushed off. The sledge began to move, rather gently, down the hill.

"Go on!" shouted the boys behind her. "Give it another push!"

But she didn't. She kept her feet on the runners and let the sledge gather speed slowly. The powdery snow sprayed up all round her as the sledge struck it. The trees moved past, slowly at first, then faster and faster. The moonlight leapt all round her. At last she seemed to be flying through a mass of silver. Then the sledge hit the hump at the bottom of the slope, shot across it, and landed in a dapple of moonlight on the frozen lake. It was beautiful.

The others came down after her, squealing and shouting.

They went down the slope head first on their stomachs so that the snow sprayed straight into their faces. They went down feet first on their backs with the black tops of the fir trees rushing past above them. They all squeezed on to one sledge together and came down so fast that they shot on almost to the middle of the lake. After each ride they struggled back up the slope, panting and pulling the sledges behind them. In spite of the cold they were steaming inside their woollies.

Then it began to snow again. At first they hardly noticed it, but then the wind got up and blew the snow in their faces. All at once Max stopped in the middle of dragging his sledge up the slope and said, "What time is it? Oughtn't we to be getting back?"

Nobody had a watch and they suddenly realized that they had no idea how long they had been there. Perhaps it was quite late and their parents had been waiting for them at home.

"Come on," said Peter. "We'd better go quickly." He took off his gloves and knocked them together to shake the caked snow off them. His hands were red with cold. So were Anna's, and she noticed for the first time that her feet were frozen.

It was chilly going back. The wind blew through their damp clothes and with the moon hidden behind the clouds the path was black in front of them. Anna was glad when they were out of the trees and in a road. Soon there were street lamps, houses with lighted windows, shops. They were nearly home.

An illuminated clockface showed them the time. After all it was not yet quite seven. They heaved sighs of relief and walked more slowly. Max and Peter began to talk about football. Marianne tied two sledges together and scampered wildly ahead on the empty road, leaving a network of overlapping tracks in the snow. Anna lagged behind because her cold feet hurt.

She could see the boys stop outside her house, still talking and waiting for her, and was just going to catch them up when she heard the creak of a gate. Something moved in the path beside her and suddenly a shapeless figure loomed up. For a moment she was very frightened – but then she saw that it was only Fräulein Lambeck in some sort of furry cloak and with a letter in her hand.

"Little Anna!" cried Fräulein Lambeck. "Fancy meeting you in the dark of the night! I was just going to the post box but did not think to find a kindred spirit. And how is your dear Papa?"

"He's got 'flu," said Anna automatically.

Fräulein Lambeck stopped in her tracks.

"Still got 'flu, little Anna? You told me he had 'flu a week ago."

"Yes," said Anna.

"And he's still in bed? Still got a temperature?"

"Yes," said Anna.

"Oh, the poor man!" Fräulein Lambeck put a hand on Anna's shoulder. "Are they doing everything for him? Does the doctor come to see him?"

"Yes," said Anna.

"And what does the doctor say?"

"He says . . . I don't know," said Anna.

Fräulein Lambeck leaned down confidentially and peered into her face. "Tell me, little Anna," she said, "how high is your dear papa's temperature?"

"I don't know!" cried Anna, and her voice came out not at all as she had meant but in a sort of squeak. "I'm sorry but I must go home now!" – and she ran as fast as she could towards Max and the open front door.

"What's the matter with you?" said Heimpi in the hall. "Someone shoot you out of a cannon?"

Anna could see Mama through the half-open door in the drawing room.

"Mama!" she cried, "I hate lying to everybody about Papa. It's horrible. Why do we have to do it? I wish we didn't have to!"

Then she saw that mama was not alone. Onkel Julius (who was not really an uncle but an old friend of Papa's) was sitting in an armchair on the other side of the room.

"Calm yourself," said Mama quite sharply. "We all hate lying about Papa, but just now it's necessary. I wouldn't ask you to do it if it weren't necessary!"

"She got caught by Fräulein Lambeck," said Max who had followed Anna in. "You know

31

Fräulein Lambeck? She's ghastly. You can't answer her questions even when you're allowed to tell the truth!"

"Poor Anna," said Onkel Julius in his high voice. He was a gentle wispy man and they were all very fond of him. "Your father asked me to tell you that he misses you both very much and sends you lots of love."

"Have you seen him then?" asked Anna.

"Onkel Julius has just come back from Prague," said Mama. "Papa is fine, and he wants us to meet him in Zurich, in Switzerland, on Sunday."

"Sunday?" said Max. "But that's only a week. That's the day of the elections. I thought we were going to wait and see who won, first!"

"Your father has decided he'd rather not wait." Onkel Julius smiled at Mama. "I do think he's taking all this too seriously."

"Why?" asked Max. "What's he worried about?"

Mama sighed. "Ever since Papa heard of the move to take away his passport he's been worried that they might try to take away ours – then we wouldn't be able to leave Germany."

"But why should they?" asked Max. "If the Nazis don't like us, surely they'd be glad to get rid of us."

"Exactly," said Onkel Julius. He smiled at Mama again. "Your husband is a wonderful man with a wonderful imagination, but frankly in this matter I think he's off his head. Never mind, you'll all have a lovely holiday in Switzerland and when you come back to Berlin in a few weeks' time we'll all go to the Zoo together." Onkel Julius was a naturalist and went to the Zoo all the time. "Let me know if I can help with any of the arrangements. I'll see you again, of course." He kissed Mama's hand and went.

"Are we really leaving on Sunday?" asked Anna.

"Saturday," said Mama. "It's a long way to Switzerland. We have to spend a night in Stuttgart on the way."

"Then this is our last week at school!" said Max.

It seemed incredible.

Chapter Three

After that everything seemed to go very quickly, like a film that has been speeded up. Heimpi was busy sorting and packing all day long. Mama was nearly always out or on the telephone, arranging for the lease of the house or for the storage of furniture after they had gone. Every day when the children came home from school the house looked more bare.

One day Onkel Julius called while they were helping Mama to pack some books. He looked at the empty shelves and smiled. "You'll be putting them all back again, you know!"

That night the children were woken up by the sound of fire engines. Not just one or two but about a dozen were clanging their bells and racing along the main road at the end of their street. When they looked out of the window the sky above the centre of Berlin was brilliant orange. Next morning everyone was talking about the fire which had destroyed the Reichstag where the German Parliament met. The Nazis said that the fire had been started by revolutionaries and that the Nazis were the only people who could put a stop to that sort of thing – so everyone must vote for them at the elections. But Mama heard that the Nazis had started the fire themselves.

When Onkel Julius called that afternoon, for the first time he did not say anything to Mama about her being back in Berlin in a few weeks' time.

The last days Anna and Max spent at school were very strange. As they still were not allowed to tell anyone that they were leaving they kept forgetting about it themselves during school hours. Anna was delighted when she was given a part in the school play and only remembered afterwards that she would never actually appear in it. Max accepted an invitation to a birthday party which he would never be able to attend.

Then they would go home to the ever emptier rooms, the wooden crates and the suitcases, the endless sorting of possessions. Deciding which toys to take was the hardest part. They naturally wanted to take the games compendium but it was too big. In the end there was only room for some books and one of Anna's stuffed toys. Should she choose Pink Rabbit which had been her companion ever since she could remember, or a newly acquired woolly dog? It seemed a pity to leave the dog when she had hardly had time to play with it, and Heimpi packed it for her. Max took his football. They could always have more things sent on to them in Switzerland, said Mama, if it looked as though they were going to stay there a very long time.

When school was over on Friday Anna went up to her teacher and said quietly. "I shan't be coming to school tomorrow. We're going to Switzerland."

Fräulein Schmidt did not look nearly as surprised as Anna expected but only nodded and said, "Yes . . . yes . . . I wish you luck."

Elsbeth was not very interested either. She just said she wished she herself were going to Switzerland but that this was not likely to happen because her father worked in the Post Office.

Gunther was the hardest person to leave. Max brought him back to lunch after they had walked back from school together for the last time, though there were only sandwiches because Heimpi had not had time to cook. Afterwards they played hide-and-seek rather half-heartedly among the packing cases. It was not much fun because Max and Gunther were so gloomy and

Anna had a struggle to keep down her own excitement. She was fond of Gunther and sorry to leave him. But all she could think was, "This time tomorrow we'll be on the train . . . this time on Sunday we'll be in Switzerland . . . this time on Monday . . .?"

At last Gunther went home. Heimpi had sorted out a lot of clothes for his mum in the course of her packing and Max went with him to help him carry them. When he came back he seemed more cheerful. He had dreaded saying goodbye to Gunther more than anything. Now at least it was over.

Next morning Anna and Max were ready long before it was time to leave. Heimpi checked that their nails were clean, that they both had handkerchiefs – two for Anna because she had a bit of a cold – and that their socks were held up properly by elastic bands.

"Goodness knows what state you'll get into by yourselves," she grumbled.

"But you'll be with us again in a fortnight," said Anna.

"There's a lot of dirt can settle on a neck in a fortnight," said Heimpi darkly.

Then there was nothing more to do until the taxi came.

"Let's go right through the house for the last time," said Max.

They started at the top and worked down. Most of it no longer looked like itself. All the smaller things had been packed: some of the rugs had been rolled up and there were newspaper and packing cases everywhere. They ticked off the rooms as they went through them, shouting "Goodbye, Papa's bedroom . . . goodbye, landing . . . goodbye, stairs . . .!"

"Don't get too excited," said Mama as they passed her.

"Goodbye, hall . . . goodbye, drawing room . . .!"

They were getting through too quickly, so Max shouted, "Goodbye, piano . . . goodbye, sofa . . .!" and Anna took it up with, "Goodbye, curtains . . . goodbye, dining table . . . goodbye, hatch . . .!"

Just as she shouted, "Goodbye, hatch", its two small doors opened and Heimpi's head appeared looking through from the pantry. Suddenly something contracted in Anna's stomach. This was just what Heimpi had often done to amuse her when she was small. They had played a game called "peeping through the hatch" and Anna had loved it. How could she suddenly be going away? In spite of herself her eyes filled with tears and she cried, idiotically, "Oh Heimpi, I don't want to leave you and the hatch!"

"Well I can't pack it in my suitcase," said Heimpi, coming into the dining-room.

"You're sure you'll come to Switzerland?"

"I don't know what else I'd do," said Heimpi. "Your mama has given me my ticket and I've got it in my purse."

"Heimpi," said Max, "if you suddenly found you had a lot of room in your suitcase – only if, mind you – do you think you could bring the games compendium?"

"If . . . if . . . if . . ." said Heimpi. "If my grandmother had wheels she'd be a bus and we could all go for a ride in her." That was what she always said.

Then the doorbell rang to announce the arrival of the taxi and there was no more time. Anna hugged Heimpi. Mama said, "Don't forget the men are coming for the piano on Monday", and then she too hugged Heimpi. Max could not find his gloves but had them in his pocket all the time. Bertha wept, and the man who looked after the garden suddenly appeared and wished them all a pleasant journey.

Just as the taxi was about to drive off a small figure rushed up with something in his hand. It was Gunther. He thrust a parcel at Max through the window and said something about his mum which they could not understand because the taxi had started. Max shouted goodbye and Gunther waved. Then the taxi went up the street. Anna could still see the house, and Heimpi and Gunther waving . . . She could still see a bit of the house . . . At the top of the street they passed the

Kentner children on their way to school. They were talking to each other and did not look up . . . She could still see a tiny bit of the house through the trees . . . Then the taxi went round the corner and it all disappeared.

It was strange travelling on the train with Mama and without Heimpi. Anna was a little worried in case she felt sick. She had been train-sick a lot when she was small and even now that she had more or less outgrown it Heimpi always brought a paper bag just in case. Did Mama have a paper bag?

The train was crowded and Anna and Max were glad that they had window seats. They both looked out at the grey landscape tearing past until it began to rain. Then they watched the raindrops arrive with a splash and slowly trickle down the glass pane, but it became boring after a while. What now? Anna looked at Mama out of the corner of her eye. Heimpi usually had a few apples or some sweets about her.

Mama was leaning back in her seat. The corners of her mouth were pulled down and she was staring at the bald head of the man opposite without seeing him at all. On her lap was her big handbag with the picture of a camel on it which she had brought back from some journey with Papa. She was holding it very tight – Anna supposed because the tickets and passports were

40

in it. She was clutching it so hard that one of her fingers was digging right in the camel's face.

"Mama," said Anna, "you're squashing the camel."

"What?" said Mama. Then she realized what Anna meant and loosened her hold on the bag. The camel's face reappeared, to Anna's relief, looking just as foolish and hopeful as usual.

"Are you bored?" asked Mama. "We'll be travelling right through Germany, which you have never done. I hope the rain stops soon so that you can see it all."

Then she told them about the orchards in Southern Germany – miles and miles of them. "If only we were making this journey a little later in the year," she said, "you'd be able to see them all in blossom."

"Perhaps just a few of them might be out already," said Anna.

But Mama thought it was too early and the bald man agreed. Then they said how beautiful it was, and Anna wished she could see it.

"If the blossom isn't out this time," she said, "can we see it another time?"

Mama did not answer at once. Then she said, "I hope so."

The rain did not let up and they spent a lot of time playing guessing games at which Mama turned out to be very good. Though they could not see much of the country they could hear the change in people's voices every time the train stopped. Some were almost incomprehensible and Max hit on the idea of asking unnecessary questions like "Is this Leipzig?" or "What time is it?" just for the pleasure of hearing the strangely accented replies.

They had lunch in the dining car. It was very grand, with a menu to choose from, and Anna had frankfurters and potato salad which was her favourite dish. She did not feel train-sick at all.

Later in the afternoon she and Max walked through the train from end to end and then stood in the corridor. The rain was heavier than ever and dusk came very early. Even if the orchards had been in blossom they would not have been able to see them. For a while they amused themselves by watching the fleeing darkness through their reflections on the glass. Then Anna's head began to ache and her nose began to run as though to keep pace with the rain outside. She snuggled back into her seat and wished they would get to Stuttgart.

"Why don't you look at Gunther's book?" said Mama.

There had been two presents in Gunther's parcel. One, from Gunther to Max, was a puzzle – a little transparent box with a picture of an open-mouthed monster drawn on the bottom. You had to get three tiny balls into the monster's mouth. It was very difficult to do on a train.

The other was a book for both children from Gunther's mum. It was called *They Grew To Be Great* and she had written in it, "Thank you for all the lovely things – something to read on the journey." It described the early lives of various people who later became famous, and Anna, who had a personal interest in the subject, leafed through it eagerly at first. But the book was so dully written and its tone was so determinedly uplifting that she gradually became discouraged.

All the famous people had had an awful time. One of them had a drunken father. Another had a stammer. Another had to wash hundreds of dirty bottles. They had all had what was called a difficult childhood. Clearly you had to have one if you wanted to become famous.

Dozing in her corner and mopping her nose with her two soaked handkerchiefs, Anna wished that they would get to Stuttgart and that one day, in the long-distant future, she might become famous. But as the train rumbled through Germany in the darkness she kept thinking "difficult childhood . . . difficult childhood . . . difficult childhood . . ."

Chapter Four

Suddenly she found herself being gently shaken. She must have been asleep. Mama said, "We'll be in Stuttgart in a few minutes."

Anna sleepily put on her coat, and soon she and Max were sitting on the luggage at the entrance of Stuttgart station while Mama went to get a taxi. The rain was still pelting down, drumming on the station roof and falling like a shiny curtain between them and the dark square in front of them. It was cold. At last Mama came back.

"What a place!" she cried. "They've got some sort of a strike on – something to do with the elections – and there are no taxis. But you see that blue sign over there?" On the opposite side of the square there was a bluish gleam among the wet. "That's a hotel," said Mama. "We'll just take what we need for the night and make a dash for it."

With the bulk of the luggage safely deposited they struggled across the ill-lit square. The case Anna was carrying kept banging against her leg and the rain was so heavy that she could hardly see. Once she missed her footing and stepped into a deep puddle so that her feet were soaked. But at last they were in the dry. Mama booked rooms for them and then she and Max had something to eat. Anna was too tired. She went straight to bed and to sleep.

In the morning they got up while it was still dark. "We'll soon see Papa," said Anna as they ate their breakfast in the dimly-lit dining-room. Nobody else was up yet and the sleepy-eyed waiter seemed to grudge them the stale rolls and coffee which he banged down in front of them. Mama waited until he had gone back into the kitchen. Then she said, "Before we get to Zurich and see Papa we have to cross the frontier between Germany and Switzerland."

"Do we have to get off the train?" asked Max.

"No," said Mama. "We just stay in our compartment and then a man will come and look at our passports – just like the ticket inspector. But" – and she looked at both children in turn – "this is very important. When the man comes to look at our passports I want neither of you to say anything. Do you understand? Not a word."

"Why not?" asked Anna.

"Because otherwise the man will say 'What a horrible talkative little girl, I think I'll take away her passport'," said Max who was always bad-tempered when he had not had enough sleep.

"Mama!" appealed Anna. "He wouldn't really – take away our passports, I mean?"

"No . . . no, I don't suppose so," said Mama. "But just in case – Papa's name is so well known – we don't want to draw attention to ourselves in any way. So when the man comes – not a word. Remember – not a single, solitary word!"

Anna promised to remember.

The rain had stopped at last and it was quite easy walking back across the square to the station. The sky was just beginning to brighten and now Anna could see that there were election posters every-where. Two or three people were standing outside a place marked Polling Station, waiting for it to open. She wondered if they were going to vote, and for whom.

The train was almost empty and they had a whole compartment to themselves until a lady with a basket got in at the next station. Anna could hear a sort of shuffling inside the basket – there must be something alive in it. She tried to catch Max's eye to see if he had heard it too, but he was still feeling cross and was frowning out of the window. Anna began to feel bad-tempered too and to remember that her head ached and that her boots were still wet from last night's rain.

"When do we get to the frontier?" she asked.

"I don't know," said Mama. "Not for a while yet." Anna noticed that her fingers were squashing the camel's face again.

"In about an hour, d'you think?" asked Anna.

"You never stop asking questions," said Max, although it was none of his business. "Why can't you shut up?"

"Why can't you?" said Anna. She was bitterly hurt and cast around for something wounding to say. At last she came out with, "I wish I had a sister!"

"I wish I didn't!" said Max.

"Mama . . .!" wailed Anna.

"Oh, for goodness' sake, stop it!" cried Mama. "Haven't we got enough to worry about?" She was clutching the camel bag and peering into it every so often to see if the passports were still there.

Anna wriggled crossly in her seat. Everybody was horrible. The lady with the basket had produced a large chunk of bread with some ham and was eating it. No one said anything for a long time. Then the train began to slow down.

"Excuse me," said Mama, "but are we coming to the Swiss frontier?"

The lady with the basket munched and shook her head.

"There, you see!" said Anna to Max. "Mama is asking questions too!"

Max did not even bother to answer but rolled his eyes up to heaven. Anna wanted to kick him, but Mama would have noticed.

The train stopped and started again, stopped and started again. Each time Mama asked if it was the frontier, and each time the lady with the basket shook her head. At last when the train slowed down yet again at the sight of a cluster of buildings, the lady with the basket said, "I dare say we're coming to it now."

They waited in silence while the train stood in the station. Anna could hear voices and the doors of other compartments opening and shutting. Then footsteps in the corridor. Then the door of their own compartment slid open and the passport inspector came in. He had a uniform rather like a ticket inspector and a large brown moustache.

He looked at the passport of the lady with the basket, nodded, stamped it with a little rubber stamp, and gave it back to her. Then he turned to Mama. Mama handed him the passports and smiled. But the hand with which she was holding her handbag was squeezing the camel into terrible contortions. The man examined the passports. Then he looked at Mama to see if it was the same face as on the passport photograph, then at Max and then at Anna. Then he got out his rubber stamp. Then he remembered something and looked at the passports again. Then at last he stamped them and gave them back to Mama.

"Pleasant journey," he said as he opened the door of the compartment.

Nothing had happened. Max had frightened her all for nothing.

"There, you see . . .!" cried Anna, but Mama gave her such a look that she stopped.

The passport inspector closed the door behind him.

"We are still in Germany," said Mama.

Anna could feel herself blushing scarlet. Mama put the passports back in the bag. There was silence. Anna could hear whatever it was scuffling in the basket, the lady munching another piece of bread and ham, doors opening and shutting further and further along the train. It seemed to last for ever.

Then the train started, rolling a few hundred yards and stopped again. More opening and shutting of doors, this time more quickly. Voices saying, "Customs . . . anything to declare . . .?" A different man came into the compartment. Mama and the lady both said they had nothing to declare and he made a mark with chalk on all their luggage, even on the lady's basket. Another wait, then a whistle and at last they started again.

This time the train gathered speed and went on chugging steadily through the countryside.

After a long time Anna asked, "Are we in Switzerland yet?"

"I think so. I'm not sure," said Mama.

The lady with the basket stopped chewing. "Oh yes," she said comfortably, "this is Switzerland. We're in Switzerland now – this is my country."

It was marvellous.

"Switzerland!" said Anna. "We're really in Switzerland!"

"About time too!" said Max and grinned.

Mama put the camel bag down on the seat beside her and smiled and smiled.

"Well!" she said. "Well! We'll soon be with Papa."

Anna suddenly felt quite silly and light-headed. She wanted to do or say something extraordinary and exciting but could think of nothing at all – so she turned to the Swiss lady and said, "Excuse me, but what have you got in that basket?"

"That's my mogger," said the lady in her soft country voice.

For some reason this was terribly funny. Anna, biting back her laughter, glanced at Max and found that he too was almost in convulsions.

"What's a . . . what's a mogger?" she asked as the lady folded back the lid of the basket, and before anyone could answer there was a screech of "Meeee", and the head of a scruffy black tomcat appeared out of the opening.

At this Anna and Max could contain themselves no longer. They fell about with laughter.

"He answered you!" gasped Max. "You said, 'What's a mogger' and he said . . ."

"Meeee!" screamed Anna.

"Children, children!" said Mama, but it was no good – they could not stop laughing. They laughed at everything they saw, all the way to Zurich. Mama apologized to the lady but she said she did not mind – she knew high spirits when she saw them. Any time they looked like flagging Max only had to say, "What's a mogger?" and Anna cried, "Meeee!" and they were off all over again. They were still laughing on the platform in Zurich when they were looking for Papa.

Anna saw him first. He was standing by a book-stall. His face was white and his eyes were searching the crowds milling round the train.

"Papa!" she shouted. "Papa!"

He turned and saw them. And then Papa, who was always so dignified, who never did anything in a hurry, suddenly ran towards them. He put his arms round Mama and hugged her. Then he hugged Anna and Max. He hugged and hugged them all and would not let them go.

"I couldn't see you," said Papa. "I was afraid . . ."

"I know," said Mama.

Chapter Five

Papa had reserved rooms for them in the best hotel in Zurich. It had a revolving door and thick carpets and lots of gold everywhere. As it was still only ten o'clock in the morning they ate another breakfast while they talked about everything that had happened since Papa had left Berlin.

At first there seemed endless things to tell him, but after a while they found it was nice just being together without saying anything at all. While Anna and Max ate their way through two different kinds of croissants and four different kinds of jam, Mama and Papa sat smiling at each other. Every so often they would remember something and Papa would say, "Did you manage to bring the books?" or Mama would say, "The paper rang and they'd like an article from you this week if possible." But then they would relapse back into their contented, smiling silence.

At last Max drank the last of his hot chocolate, wiped the last crumbs of croissant off his lips and said, "What shall we do now?"

Somehow nobody had thought.

After a moment Papa said, "Let's go and look at Zurich."

They decided first of all to go to the top of a hill overlooking the city. The hill was so steep that you had to go by funicular – a kind of lift on wheels that went straight up at an alarming angle. Anna had never been in one before and spent her time between excitement at the experience and anxious scrutiny of the cable for signs of fraying. From the top of the hill you could see Zurich clustered below at one end of an enormous blue lake. It was so big that the town seemed quite small by comparison, and its far end was hidden by mountains. Steamers, which looked like toys from this height, were making their way round the edge of the lake, stopping at each of the villages scattered along the shores and then moving on to the next. The sun was shining and made it all look very inviting.

"Can anyone go on those steamers?" asked Max. It was just what Anna had been going to ask.

"Would you like to go?" said Papa. "So you shall – this afternoon."

Lunch was splendid, at a restaurant with a glassed-in terrace overlooking the lake below, but Anna could not eat much. Her head was feeling swimmy, probably from getting up so early, she thought, and though her nose had stopped running her throat was sore.

"Are you all right?" asked Mama anxiously.

"Oh yes!" said Anna, thinking of the steamer trip in the afternoon. Anyway, she was sure it was just tiredness.

There was a shop selling picture postcards next door to the restaurant and she bought one and sent it to Heimpi while Max sent one to Gunther.

"I wonder how they're getting on with the elections," said Mama. "Do you think the Germans will really vote for Hitler?"

"I'm afraid so," said Papa.

"They might not," said Max. "A lot of the boys at my school were against him. We might find tomorrow that almost no one had voted for Hitler and then we could all go home again, just as Onkel Julius said."

"It's possible," said Papa, but Anna could see that he didn't really think so.

The steamer trip in the afternoon was a great success. Anna and Max stayed on the open deck in spite of the cold wind and watched the other traffic on the lake. Apart from the steamers there were private motor launches and even a few rowing boats. Their steamer went chug-chugging along from village to village on one side of the lake. These all looked very pretty, with their neat houses nestling among the woods and the hills. Whenever the steamer was getting near a landing stage it hooted loudly to let everyone in the village know that it was coming, and quite a lot of people got on and off each time. After about an hour it suddenly steamed straight across the lake to a village on the other side and then made its way back to Zurich where it had started.

As she walked back to the hotel through the noise of cars and buses and clanging trams Anna found she was very tired, and her head felt swimmy again. She was glad to get back to the hotel room which she shared with Max. She still was not hungry and Mama thought she looked so weary that she tucked her into bed straightaway. As soon as Anna put her head down on the pillow her whole bed seemed to take off and float away in the darkness with a chug-chugging noise which might have been a boat, or a train, or a sound coming from her own head.

Anna's first impression when she opened her eyes in the morning was that the room was far too bright. She closed them again quickly and lay quite still, trying to collect herself. There was a murmur of voices at the other end of the room

55

and also a rustling sound which she could not identify. It must be quite late and everyone else must be up.

She opened her eyes again cautiously and this time the brightness heaved and swayed and finally rearranged itself into the room she knew, with Max, still in his pyjamas, sitting up in the other bed and Mama and Papa standing close by. Papa had a newspaper and this was what was making the rustling sound. They were talking quietly because they thought she was still asleep. Then the room gave another heave and she closed her eyes again and seemed to drift away somewhere while the voices went on.

Someone was saying ". . . so they've got a majority . . ." Then the voice faded away and another – (or was it the same one?) – said ". . . enough votes to do what he wants . . ." and then unmistakably Max, very unhappily, ". . . so we shan't be going back to Germany . . . so we shan't be going back to Germany . . ." Had he really said it three times? Anna opened her eyes with a great effort and said "Mama!" At once one of the figures detached itself from the group and came towards her and suddenly Mama's face appeared quite close to hers. Anna said "Mama!" again and then all at once she was crying because her throat was so sore.

After this everything became vague. Mama and Papa were standing by her bed looking at a thermometer. Papa had his coat on. He must have gone out to buy the thermometer specially. Someone said, "A hundred and four", but it couldn't be her temperature they were talking about because she couldn't remember having it taken.

Next time she opened her eyes there was a man with a little beard looking at her. He said, "Well, young lady," and smiled and as he smiled his feet left the ground and he flew to the top of the wardrobe where he changed into a bird and sat croaking, "Influenza" until Mama shooed him out of the window.

Then suddenly it was night and she asked Max to get her some water, but Max was not there, it was Mama in the other bed. Anna said, "Why are you sleeping in Max's bed?" Mama said, "Because you're ill," and Anna felt very glad because if she was ill it meant that Heimpi would be coming to look after her. She said, "Tell Heimpi . . ." but then she was too tired to remember the rest, and the next time she looked the man with the little beard was there again and she didn't like him because he was upsetting Mama by saying, "Complications" over and over again. He had done something to the back of Anna's neck and had made it all swollen and sore, and now he was feeling it with his hand. She said, "Don't do that!" quite sharply, but he took no notice and tried to make her drink something horrible. Anna was going to push it away, but then she saw that it was not the man with the beard after all but Mama, and her blue eyes looked so fierce and determined that it didn't seem worth resisting.

After this the world grew a little steadier. She began to understand that she had been ill for some time, that she still had a high temperature and that the reason she felt so awful was that all the glands in her neck were enormously swollen and tender.

"We must get the temperature down," said the doctor with the beard.

Then Mama said, "I'm going to put something on your neck to make it better."

Anna saw some steam rising from a basin.

"It's too hot!" she cried. "I don't want it!"

"I won't put it on too hot," said Mama.

"I don't want it!" screamed Anna. "You don't know how to look after me! Where's Heimpi? Heimpi wouldn't put hot steam on my neck!"

"Nonsense!" said Mama, and suddenly she was holding a steaming pad of cotton wool against her own neck. "There," she said, "if it's not too hot for me it won't be too hot for you" – and she clapped it firmly on Anna's neck and quickly wrapped a bandage round it.

It was terribly hot but just bearable.

"That wasn't so bad, was it?" said Mama.

Anna was much too angry to answer and the room was beginning to spin again, but as she drifted off into vagueness she could just hear

Mama's voice: "I'm going to get that temperature down if it kills me!"

After this she must have dozed or dreamed because suddenly her neck was quite cool again and Mama was unwrapping it.

"And how are you, fat pig?" said Mama.

"Fat pig?" said Anna weakly.

Mama very gently touched one of Anna's swollen glands.

"This is fat pig," she said. "It's the worst of the lot. The one next to it isn't quite so bad – it's called slim pig. And this one is called pink pig and this is baby pig and this one . . . what shall we call this one?"

"Fräulein Lambeck," said Anna and began to laugh. She was so weak that the laugh sounded more like a cackle but Mama seemed very pleased just the same.

Mama kept putting on the hot fomentations and it was not too bad because she always made jokes about fat pig and slim pig and Fräulein Lambeck, but though her neck felt better Anna's temperature still stayed up. She would wake up feeling fairly normal but by lunch time she would be giddy and by the evening everything would have become vague and confused. She got the strangest ideas. She was frightened of the wallpaper and could not bear to be alone. Once when Mama left her to go downstairs for supper she thought the room was getting smaller and smaller and cried because she thought she would be squashed. After this Mama had her supper on a tray in Anna's room. The doctor said, "She can't go on like this much longer."

Then one afternoon Anna was lying staring at the curtains. Mama had just drawn them because it was getting dark and Anna was trying to see what shapes the folds had made. The previous evening they had made a shape like an ostrich, and as Anna's temperature went up she had been able to see the ostrich more and more clearly until at last she had been able to make him walk all round the room. This time she thought perhaps there might be an elephant.

Suddenly she became aware of whispering at the other end of the room. She turned her head with difficulty. Papa was there, sitting with Mama, and they were looking at a letter together. She could not hear what Mama was saying, but she could tell from the sound of her voice that she was excited and upset. Then Papa folded the letter and put his hand on Mama's, and Anna thought he would probably go soon but he didn't – he just stayed sitting there and holding Mama's hand. Anna watched them for a while until her eyes became tired and she closed them. The whispering voices had become more quiet and even. Somehow it was a very soothing sound and after a while Anna fell asleep listening to it.

When she woke up she knew at once that she

had slept for a long time. There was something else, too, that was strange, but she could not quite make out what it was. The room was dim except for a light on the table by which Mama usually sat, and Anna thought she must have forgotten to switch it off when she went to bed. But Mama had not gone to bed. She was still sitting there with Papa just as they had done before Anna went to sleep. Papa was still holding Mama's hand in one of his and the folded letter in the other.

"Hello, Mama. Hello, Papa," said Anna. "I feel so peculiar."

Mama and Papa came over to her bed at once and Mama put a hand on her forehead. Then she popped the thermometer in Anna's mouth. When she took it out again she did not seem to be able to believe what she saw. "It's normal!" she said. "For the first time in four weeks it's normal!"

"Nothing else matters," said Papa and crumpled up the letter.

After this Anna got better quite quickly. Fat pig, slim pig, Fräulein Lambeck and the rest gradually shrank and her neck stopped hurting. She began to eat again and to read. Max came and played cards with her when he wasn't out somewhere with Papa, and soon she was allowed to get out of bed for a little while and sit in a chair. Mama had to help her walk the few steps across the room but she felt very happy sitting in the warm sunshine by the window.

Outside the sky was blue and she saw that the people in the street below were not wearing overcoats. There was a lady selling tulips at a stall on the opposite pavement and a chestnut tree at the corner was in full leaf. It was spring. She was amazed how much everything had changed during her illness. The people in the street seemed pleased with the spring weather too and several bought flowers from the stall. The lady elling tulips was round and dark-haired and ooked a little bit like Heimpi.

Suddenly Anna remembered something. Heimpi had been going to join them two weeks after they left Germany. Now it must be more than a month. Why hadn't she come? She was going to ask Mama, but Max came in first.

"Max," said Anna, "why hasn't Heimpi come?"

Max looked taken aback. "Do you want to go back to bed?" he said.

"No," said Anna.

"Well," said Max, "I don't know if I'm meant to tell you, but quite a lot happened while you were ill."

"What?" asked Anna.

"You know Hitler won the elections," said Max. "Well, he very quickly took over the whole government, and it's just as Papa said it would be

– nobody's allowed to say a word against him. If they do they're thrown into jail."

"Did Heimpi say anything against Hitler?" asked Anna with a vision of Heimpi in a dungeon.

"No, of course not," said Max. "But Papa did. He still does. And so of course no one in Germany is allowed to print anything he writes. So he can't earn any money and we can't afford to pay Heimpi any wages."

"I see," said Anna, and after a moment she added, "are we poor, then?"

"I think we are, a bit," said Max. "Only Papa is going to try to write for some Swiss papers instead – then we'll be all right again." He got up as though to go and Anna said quickly, "I wouldn't have thought Heimpi would mind about money. If we had a little house I think she'd want to come and look after us anyway, even if we couldn't pay her much."

"Yes, well, that's another thing," said Max. He hesitated before he added, "We can't get a house because we haven't any furniture."

"But . . ." said Anna.

"The Nazis have pinched the lot," said Max. "It's called confiscation of property. Papa had a letter last week." He grinned. "It's been rather like one of those awful plays where people keep rushing in with bad news. And on top of it all there were you, just about to kick the bucket . . ."

"I wasn't going to kick the bucket!" said Anna indignantly.

"Well, I knew you weren't, of course," said Max, "but that Swiss doctor has a very gloomy imagination. Do you want to go back to bed now?"

"I think I do," said Anna. She was feeling rather weak and Max helped her across the room. When she was safely back in bed she said, "Max, this . . . confiscation of property, whatever it's called – did the Nazis take everything – even our things?"

Max nodded.

Anna tried to imagine it. The piano was gone . . . the dining-room curtains with the flowers . . . her bed . . . all her toys which included her stuffed Pink Rabbit. For a moment she felt terribly sad about Pink Rabbit. It had had embroidered black eyes – the original glass ones had fallen out years before – and an endearing habit of collapsing on its paws. Its fur, though no longer very pink, had been soft and familiar. How could she ever have chosen to pack that character-less woolly dog in its stead? It had been a terrible mistake, and now she would never be able to put it right.

"I always knew we should have brought the games compendium," said Max. "Hitler's probably playing Snakes and Ladders with it this very minute."

"And snuggling my Pink Rabbit!" said Anna and laughed. But some tears had come into her eyes and were running down her cheeks all at the same time.

"Oh well, we're lucky to be here at all," said Max.

"What do you mean?" asked Anna.

Max looked carefully past her out of the window.

'Papa heard from Heimpi," he said with elaborate casualness. "The Nazis came for all our passports the morning after the elections."

Chapter Six

As soon as Anna was strong enough they moved out of their expensive hotel. Papa and Max had found an inn in one of the villages on the lake. It was called Gasthof Zwirn, after Herr Zwirn who owned it, and stood very near the landing stage, with a cobbled courtyard and a garden running down to the lake. People mostly came there to eat and drink, but Herr Zwirn also had a few rooms to let, and these were very cheap. Mama and Papa shared one room and Anna and Max another, so that it would be cheaper still.

Downstairs there was a large comfortable dining-room decorated with deers' antlers and bits of edelweiss. But when the weather became warmer tables and chairs appeared in the garden, and Frau Zwirn served everybody's meals under the chestnut trees, overlooking the water. Anna thought it was lovely.

At weekends musicians came from the village and often played till late at night. You could listen to the music and watch the sparkle of the water through the leaves and the steamers gliding past. At dusk Herr Zwirn pressed a switch and little lights came on in the trees so that you could still see what you were eating. The steamers lit coloured lanterns to make themselves visible to other craft. Some were amber, but the prettiest were a deep, brilliant purply blue. Whenever Anna saw one of these magical blue lights against the darker blue sky and more dimly reflected in the dark lake, she felt as though she had been given a small present.

The Zwirns had three children who ran about barefoot and, as Anna's legs began to feel less like cotton wool, she and Max went with them to explore the country round about. There were woods and streams and waterfalls, roads lined with apple trees and wild flowers everywhere. Sometimes Mama came with them rather than stay alone at the inn. Papa went to Zurich almost every day to talk to the editors of Swiss newspapers.

The Zwirn children, like everyone else living in the village, spoke a Swiss dialect which Anna and Max first found hard to understand. But they soon learned and the eldest, Franz, was able to teach Max to fish – only Max never caught anything – while his sister Vreneli showed Anna the local version of hopscotch.

In this pleasant atmosphere Anna soon recovered her strength and one day Mama announced that it was time for her and Max to start school again. Max would go to the Boys' High School in Zurich. He would travel by train, which was not as nice as the steamer but much quicker. Anna would go to the village school with the Zwirn children, and as she and Vreneli were roughly the same age they would be in the same class.

"You will be my best friend," said Vreneli. She had very long, very thin, mouse-coloured plaits and a worried expression. Anna was not absolutely sure that she wanted to be Vreneli's best friend but thought it would be ungrateful to say so.

On Monday morning they set off together, Vreneli barefoot and carrying her shoes in her hand. As they approached the school they met other children, most of them also carrying their shoes. Vreneli introduced Anna to some of the girls, but the boys stayed on the other side of the road and stared across at them without speaking. Soon after they had reached the school playground a teacher rang a bell and there was a mad scramble by everyone to put their shoes on. It was a school rule that shoes must be worn but most children left them off till the last possible minute.

Anna's teacher was called Herr Graupe. He was quite old with a greyish yellowish beard, and everyone was much in awe of him. He assigned Anna a place next to a cheerful fair-haired girl called Roesli, and as Anna walked down the centre aisle of the classroom to her desk there was a general gasp.

"What's the matter?" Anna whispered as soon as Herr Graupe's back was turned.

"You walked down the centre aisle," Roesli whispered back. "Only the boys walk down the centre aisle."

"Where do the girls go?"

"Round the sides."

It seemed a strange arrangement, but Herr Graupe had begun to chalk up sums on the blackboard, so there was no time to go into it. The sums were very easy and Anna got them done quickly. Then she took a look round the classroom.

The boys were all sitting in two rows on one side, the girls on the other. It was quite different from the school she had gone to in Berlin where they had all been mixed up. When Herr Graupe called for the books to be handed in Vreneli got up to collect the girls' while a big red-haired boy collected the boys'. The red-haired boy walked up the middle of the classroom while Vreneli walked round the side until they met, each with a pile of books, in front of Herr Graupe's desk. Even there they were careful not to look at each other, but Anna noticed that Vreneli had turned a very faint shade of pink under her mouse-coloured hair.

At break-time the boys played football and horsed about on one side of the playground while the girls played hopscotch or sat sedately gossiping on the other. But though the girls pretended to take no notice of the boys they spent a lot of time watching them under their carefully lowered lids, and when Vreneli and Anna walked home for lunch Vreneli became so interested in the antics of the red-haired boy on the opposite side of the road that she nearly walked into a tree. They went back for an hour's singing in the afternoon and then school was finished for the day.

"How do you like it?" Mama asked Anna when she got back at three o'clock.

"It's very interesting," said Anna. "But it's funny – the boys and girls don't even talk to each other and I don't know if I'm going to learn very much."

When Herr Graupe had corrected the sums he had made several mistakes and his spelling had not been too good either.

"Well, it doesn't matter if you don't," said Mama. "It won't hurt you to have a bit of a rest after your illness."

"I like the singing," said Anna. "They can all yodel and they're going to teach me how to do it too."

"God forbid!" said Mama and immediately dropped a stitch.

Mama was learning to knit. She had never done it before, but Anna needed a new sweater and Mama was trying to save money. She had bought some wool and some knitting needles and Frau Zwirn had shown her how to use them. But somehow Mama never looked quite right doing it. Where Frau Zwirn sat clicking the needles lightly with her fingers, Mama knitted straight from the shoulder. Each time she pushed the needle into the wool it was like an attack. Each time she brought it out she pulled the stitch so tight that it almost broke. As a result the sweater only grew slowly and looked more like heavy tweed than knitting.

"I've never seen work quite like it," said Frau Zwirn, astonished, when she saw it, "but it'll be lovely and warm when it's done."

One Sunday morning soon after Anna and Max had started school they saw a familiar figure get off the steamer and walk up the landing stage. It was Onkel Julius. He looked thinner than Anna remembered and it was wonderful and yet somehow confusing to see him – as though a bit of their house in Berlin had suddenly appeared by the edge of the lake.

"Julius!" cried Papa in delight when he saw him. "What on earth are you doing here?"

Onkel Julius gave a little wry smile and said. "Well, officially I'm not here at all. Do you know that nowadays it is considered very unwise even to visit you?" He had been to a naturalists' congress in Italy and had left a day early in order to come and see them on his way back to Berlin.

"I'm honoured and grateful," said Papa.

"The Nazis certainly are very stupid," said Onkel Julius. "How could you possibly be an enemy of Germany? You know of course that they burned all your books."

"I was in very good company," said Papa.

"What books?" asked Anna. "I thought the Nazis had just taken all our things – I didn't know they'd burned them."

"These were not the books your father owned," said Onkel Julius. "They were the books he has written. The Nazis lit big bonfires all over the country and threw on all the copies they could find and burned them."

"Along with the works of various other distinguished authors," said Papa, "such as Einstein, Freud, H. G. Wells . . ."

Onkel Julius shook his head at the madness of it all.

"Thank heavens you didn't take my advice," he said. "Thank heavens you left when you did. But of course," he added, "this situation in Germany can't go on much longer!"

Over lunch in the garden he told them the news. Heimpi had found a job with another family. It had been difficult because when people heard that she had worked for Papa they did not want to employ her. But it was not a bad job considering. Their house was still empty. Nobody had bought it yet.

It was strange, thought Anna, that Onkel Julius could go and look at it any time he liked. He could walk down the street from the paper shop at the corner and stand outside the white painted gate. The shutters would be closed but if he had a key Onkel Julius would be able to go through the front door into the dark hall, up the stairs to the nursery, or across into the drawing room, or along the passage to Heimpi's pantry . . . Anna remembered it all so clearly, and in her mind she walked right through the house from top to bottom while Onkel Julius went on talking to Mama and Papa.

"How are things with you?" he asked. "Are you able to write here?"

Papa raised an eyebrow. "I have no difficulty

in writing," he said, "only in getting my work published."

"Impossible!" said Onkel Julius.

"Unfortunately not," said Papa. "It seems the Swiss are so anxious to protect their neutrality that they are frightened of publishing anything by an avowed anti-Nazi like myself."

Onkel Julius looked shocked.

"Are you all right?" he asked. "I mean – financially?"

"We manage," said Papa. "Anyway, I'm trying to make them change their mind."

Then they began to talk about mutual friends. It sounded as though they were going through a long list of names. Somebody had been arrested by the Nazis. Somebody else had escaped and was going to America. Another person had compromised (what was "compromised"? wondered Anna) and had written an article in praise of the new regime. The list went on and on. All grown-up conversations were like this nowadays, thought Anna, while little waves lapped against the edge of the lake and bees buzzed in the chestnut trees.

In the afternoon they showed Onkel Julius round. Anna and Max took him up into the woods and he was very interested to discover a special kind of toad that he had never seen before. Later, they all went for a row on the lake in a hired boat.

Then they had supper together, and at last it was time for Onkel Julius to leave.

"I miss our outings to the Zoo," he said as he kissed Anna.

"So do I!" said Anna. "I liked the monkeys best."

"I'll send you a picture of one," said Onkel Julius.

They walked down to the landing stage together.

While they were waiting for the steamer Papa suddenly said, "Julius – don't go back. Stay here with us. You won't be safe in Germany."

"What – me?" said Onkel Julius in his high voice. "Who's going to bother about me? I'm only interested in animals. I'm not political. I'm not even Jewish unless you count my poor old grandmother!"

"Julius, you don't understand . . ." said Papa.

"The situation is bound to change," said Onkel Julius, and there was the steamer puffing towards them. "Goodbye, old friend!" He embraced Papa and Mama and both children.

As he walked across the gangplank he turned back for a moment.

"Anyway," he said, "the monkeys at the Zoo would miss me!"

Chapter Seven

As Anna went on attending the village school she
liked it more and more. She made friends with
other girls apart from Vreneli, and especially with
Roesli, who sat next to her in class and was a little
less sedate than the rest. The lessons were so easy
that she was able to shine without any effort, and
though Herr Graupe was not a very good teacher
of the more conventional subjects he was a
remarkable yodeller. Altogether what she liked
best about the school was that it was so different
from the one she had been to before. She felt
sorry for Max who seemed to be doing very much
the same things at the Zurich High School as he
had done in Berlin.

There was only one thing that bothered her.

She missed playing with boys. In Berlin she and Max had mostly played with a mixed group of both boys and girls and it had been the same at school. Here the girls' endless hopscotch began to bore her and sometimes in break she looked longingly at the more exciting games and acrobatics of the boys.

One day there was no one even playing hopscotch. The boys were turning cartwheels and all the girls were sitting demurely watching them out of the corner of their eyes. Even Roesli, who had cut her knee, was sitting with the rest. Vreneli was particularly interested because the big red-haired boy was trying to turn cartwheels and the others were trying to teach him, but he kept flopping over sideways.

"Would you like to play hopscotch?" Anna asked her, but Vreneli shook her head, absorbed. It really was too silly, especially as Anna loved turning cartwheels herself – and it wasn't as though the red-haired boy was any good at it.

Suddenly she could stand it no longer and without thinking what she was doing she got up from her seat among the girls and walked over to the boys.

"Look," she said to the red-haired boy, "you've got to keep your legs straight like this" – and she turned a cartwheel to show him. All the other boys stopped turning cartwheels and stood back, grinning. The red-haired boy hesitated.

"It's quite easy," said Anna. "You could do it if you'd only remember about your legs."

The red-haired boy still seemed undecided, but the other boys shouted, "Go on – try!" So he tried again and managed a little better. Anna showed him again, and this time he suddenly got the idea and turned a perfect cartwheel just as the bell went for the end of break.

Anna walked back to her own group and all the boys watched and grinned but the girls seemed mostly to be looking elsewhere. Vreneli looked frankly cross and only Roesli gave her a quick smile.

After break it was history and Herr Graupe decided to tell them about the cavemen. They had lived millions of years ago, he said. They killed wild animals and ate them and made their fur into clothes. Then they learned to light fires and make simple tools and gradually became civilized. This was progress, said Herr Graupe, and one way it was brought about was by pedlars who called at the cavemen's caves with useful objects for barter.

"What sort of useful objects?" asked one of the boys.

Herr Graupe peered indignantly over his beard. All sorts of things would be useful to a caveman, he said. Things like beads, and coloured wools, and safety pins to fasten their furs together. Anna was very surprised to hear about the pedlars and the safety pins. She longed to ask Herr Graupe whether he was really sure about them but thought perhaps it would be wiser not to. Anyway the bell went before she had the chance.

She was still thinking about the cavemen so much on the way home to lunch that she and Vreneli had walked nearly halfway before she realized that Vreneli was not speaking to her.

"What's the matter, Vreneli?" she asked.

Vreneli tossed her thin plaits and said nothing.

"What is it?" asked Anna again.

Vreneli would not look at her.

"You know!" she said. "You know perfectly well!"

"No, I don't," said Anna.

"You do!" said Vreneli.

"No, honestly I don't!" said Anna. "Please tell me."

But Vreneli wouldn't. She walked the rest of the way home without giving Anna a single glance, her nose in the air and her eyes fixed on some distant point. Only when they had reached the inn and were about to separate, did she look at her briefly, and Anna was surprised to see that she was not only angry but nearly in tears.

"Anyway," Vreneli shouted over her shoulders as she ran off, "anyway, we all saw your knickers!"

During lunch with Mama and Papa Anna was so quiet that Mama noticed it.

"Anything bother you at school?" she asked.

Anna considered. There were two things which had bothered her. One was Vreneli's extraordinary behaviour and the other was Herr Graupe's account of the cavemen. She decided that the business about Vreneli was too complicated to explain and said instead, "Mama, did the cavemen really pin their furs together with safety pins?" This produced such a flood of laughter, questions and explanations that they lasted until the end of lunch, and then it was time to go back to school. Vreneli had already left and Anna, feeling a little lonely, went on her own.

The afternoon lesson was singing again with a lot of yodelling which Anna enjoyed, and when it was over she suddenly found the red-haired boy standing in front of her.

"Hello, Anna!" he said boldly. Some of his friends who were with him laughed, and before Anna could answer they had all turned on their heel and marched out of the classroom.

"Why did he say that?" asked Anna.

Roesli smiled. "I think you're going to have an escort," she said and added, "Poor Vreneli!"

Anna would have liked to ask her what she meant, but the mention of Vreneli reminded her that she must be quick if she did not want to walk home alone. So she said, "See you tomorrow," and ran.

There was no sign of Vreneli in the playground. Anna waited for a while, in case she might be in the cloakroom, but she did not appear. The only people in the playground were the red-haired boy and his friends, who also seemed to be waiting for someone. Vreneli must have rushed off early specially to avoid her. Anna went on hoping a little longer, but at last she had to admit to herself that it was no use and set off on her own. The red-haired boy and his friends decided to leave at exactly the same time.

It was less than ten minutes' walk back to the Gasthof Zwirn and Anna knew the way well. Outside the school gates she turned right and walked down the road. After a few moments she noticed that the red-haired boy and his friends had also turned right outside the school. The road led to a steep path covered in gravel which joined another road and this in turn, after some twists and turns, led to the inn.

It was while Anna was walking down the gravel path that she first began to wonder whether everything was as it should be. The gravel was thick and very loose and her feet made a loud crunching sound at every step. Presently she became aware of similar, more muffled crunchings behind her. She listened to them for a few moments, then glanced over her shoulder. It was the red-haired boy and his friends again. Their shoes dangling from their hands and they were trudging through the gravel in their bare feet, apparently untroubled by the sharpness of the stones. Even Anna's brief glance had been enough to show her that they were all watching her.

She walked more quickly and the steps behind her quickened also. Then a little stone bounced off the gravel to one side of her. While she was still wondering where it had come from another little stone hit her leg. She turned round sharply and was just in time to see the red-haired boy pick up a bit of gravel and throw it at her.

"What are you doing?" she shouted. "Stop it!" But he just grinned and threw another bit. Then his friends began to throw some too. Most of it missed her and any stones that did hit her were too small to hurt, but it was horrid just the same.

Then she saw, a small bandy-legged boy hardly bigger than herself pick up a whole handful of gravel.

"Don't you dare throw that at me!" she shouted so fiercely that the bandy-legged boy automatically took a step backwards. He threw the gravel in her direction but deliberately aimed short. Anna glared at him. The boys stood staring back at her.

Suddenly the red-haired boy took a step forward and shouted something. The others took it up in a sort of chant. "An-na! An-na!" they chanted. Then the red-haired boy threw another bit of gravel and hit her squarely on the shoulder. It was too much. She turned and fled.

Down the path, bits of gravel bouncing all

round her, peppering her back, her legs. An-na! An-na! They were coming after her. Her feet slipped and slithered on the stones. If only she could get to the road at least they wouldn't be able to throw gravel at her. And there it was! Lovely smooth, hard asphalt under her feet. An-na! An-na! They were gaining ground. Now they were no longer stopping to pick up gravel they were coming on faster.

Suddenly a large object hurled past her. A shoe! They were throwing their shoes at her! At least they'd have to stop to pick them up. She rounded a bend and could see the Gasthof Zwirn at the end of the road. The last bit was downhill and she almost threw herself down the slope as with one final effort she reached the courtyard of the inn.

An-na! An-na! Boys right behind her, shoes raining all round . . . And there, like a miracle, like an avenging angle, was Mama! She shot out of the inn like a torpedo. She grabbed the red-haired boy and slapped him. She hit another one with his own shoe. She flung herself into the group and scattered them. All the time she was shouting, "Why are you doing this? What's the matter with you?" That was what Anna wanted to know too.

Then she saw that Mama had got hold of the bandy-legged boy and was shaking him. All the rest had fled.

"Why did you chase her?" Mama was asking. "Why did you all throw things at her? What had she done?"

The bandy-legged boy scowled and wouldn't say.

"I won't let you go!" said Mama. "I won't let you go until you tell me why you did it!"

The bandy-legged boy looked hopelessly at Mama. Then he blushed and mumbled something.

"What?" said Mama.

Suddenly the bandy-legged boy grew desperate.

"Because we love her!" he shouted at the top of his voice. "We did it because we love her!"

Mama was so surprised that she let go of him and he shot away from her, across the courtyard and away down the road. "Because they love you?" said Mama to Anna. Neither of them could understand it. But when, later, they consulted Max he did not seem very surprised.

"It's what they do here," he said. "When they're in love with anyone they throw things at them."

"But, good heavens, there were six of them!" said Mama. "Surely there must be other ways for them to express their love!"

Max shrugged. "It's what they do," he said and added, "Really Anna should feel honoured."

A few days later Anna saw him in the village, throwing unripe apples at Roesli.

Max was very adaptable.

Anna was not too sure about going back to school the next day. "Suppose they're still in love with me today?" she said. "I don't want to have more things thrown at me."

But she need not have worried. The boys had been so terrified by Mama that none of them dared so much as look at her. Even the red-haired boy kept his eyes carefully averted. So Vreneli forgave her and they were friends as before. Anna even managed to persuade her to try one cartwheel, secretly in a corner at the back of the inn. But in public, at school, they both stuck strictly to hopscotch.

Chapter Eight

On Anna's tenth birthday Papa was invited on
an outing by the Zurich Literary Society, and
when he mentioned Anna's birthday they invited
her and Max and Mama as well. Mama was
delighted.

"How lucky that it should just be on your
birthday," she said. "What a lovely way to
celebrate."

But Anna did not think so at all. She said,
"Why can't I have a party as usual?" Mama
looked taken aback.

"But it's not the same as usual," she said.
"We're not at home."

Anna knew this really, but she still felt that her
birthday ought to be something special for her –

not just an outing in which everyone else was included. She said nothing.

"Look," said Mama, "it'll be lovely. They're going to hire a steamer, just for the people on the outing. We're going nearly to the other end of the lake and having a picnic on an island, and we won't be home till late!" But Anna was not convinced.

She did not feel any better when the day arrived and she saw her presents. There was a card from Onkel Julius, some crayons from Max, a small pencil box and a wooden chamois from Mama and Papa. That was all. The chamois was very pretty, but when Max was ten his birthday present had been a new bicycle. The card from Onkel Julius had a picture of a monkey on it and he had written on the back in his meticulous hand-writing, "A happy birthday, and many more even happier ones to come." Anna hoped he was right about the birthdays to come, because this one certainly did not look very promising.

"It's a funny sort of birthday for you this year," said Mama, seeing her face. "Anyway you're really getting too big to bother much with presents." But she hadn't said that to Max when he was ten. And it wasn't as though it were just any birthday, thought Anna. It was her first birthday with double figures.

* * *

As the day wore on she felt worse and worse. The outing was not really a success. The weather was lovely but it became very hot on the steamer and the members of the literary society all talked like Fräulein Lambeck. One of them actually addressed Papa as "dear Master". He was a fat young man with lots of small sharp teeth, and he interrupted just as Anna and Papa were starting a conversation.

"I was so sorry about your article, dear Master," said the fat young man.

"I was sorry too," said Papa. "This is my daughter Anna who is ten today."

"Happy birthday," said the young man briefly and at once went back to talking to Papa. It was such a pity that he hadn't been able to print Papa's article, especially as it was so splendid. The young man had admired it enormously. But the dear Master had such strong opinions . . . the policy of the paper . . . the feelings of the government . . . the dear Master must understand . . .

"I understand entirely," said Papa, turning away, but the fat young man held on.

Such difficult times, said the young man. Fancy the Nazis burning Papa's books – Papa must have felt terrible. The young man knew just how terrible Papa must have felt because as it happened he had just had his own first book published and could imagine . . . Had the dear Master by any chance seen the young man's first book? No? Then the young man would tell him about it . . .

He talked and talked with his little teeth clicking away and Papa was too polite to stop him. At last Anna could stand it no longer and wandered off.

The picnic, too, proved a disappointment. It consisted largely of bread rolls with rather grown-up fillings. The rolls were hard and a bit stale so that only the fat young man with the teeth, thought Anna, could have chewed his way through them. For drink there was ginger beer which she hated but Max liked. It was all right for him. He had brought his fishing rod and was quite content to sit on the edge of the island and fish. (Not that he caught anything – but then he was using bits of stale rolls for bait and it was not surprising that the fish did not like them either.) There was nothing for Anna to do. There were no other children to play with and after lunch it was even worse because there were speeches. Mama had not told her about the speeches. She should have warned her. They went on for what seemed like hours and Anna sat through them miserably in the heat, thinking of what she would have been doing if they had not had to leave Berlin.

Heimpi would have made a birthday cake with strawberries. She would have had a party with at least twenty children and each of them would have brought her a present. About now they would all be playing games in the garden. Then there would be tea, and candles round the cake . . . She could imagine it all so clearly that she hardly noticed when the speeches finally came to an end.

Mama appeared beside her. "We're going back to the boat now," she said. Then she whispered, "The speeches were dreadfully dull, weren't they?" with a conspiratorial smile. But Anna did not smile back. It was all very well for Mama – after all it wasn't her birthday.

Once back on the boat she found a place by the side and stood there alone, staring into the water. That was it, she thought as the boat steamed back towards Zurich. She'd had her birthday – her tenth birthday – and not a single bit of it had been nice. She folded her arms on the railings and rested her head on them, pretending to look at the view so that no one should see how miserable she was. The water rushed past below her and the warm wind blew through her hair, and all she could think of was that her birthday had been spoilt and nothing would ever be any good again.

After a while she felt a hand on her shoulder. It was Papa. Had he noticed how disappointed she was? But Papa never noticed things like that – he was too absorbed in his own thoughts.

"So now I have a ten-year-old daughter," he said and smiled.

"Yes," said Anna.

"As a matter of fact," said Papa, "I don't think you are quite ten years old yet. You were born at six o'clock in the evening. That's not for another twenty minutes."

"Really?" said Anna. For some reason the fact that she was not quite ten yet made her feel better.

"Yes," said Papa, "and to me it doesn't seem so very long ago. Of course we didn't know then that we'd be spending your tenth birthday steaming about Lake Zurich as refugees from Hitler."

"Is a refugee someone who's had to leave their home?" asked Anna.

"Someone who seeks refuge in another country," said Papa.

"I don't think I'm quite used to being one yet," said Anna.

"It's an odd feeling," said Papa. "You live in a country all your life. Then suddenly it is taken over by thugs and there you are, on your own in a strange place, with nothing."

He looked so cheerful as he said this that Anna asked, "Don't you mind?"

"In a way," said Papa. "But I find it very interesting."

The sun was sinking in the sky. Every so often it disappeared behind the top of a mountain, and then the lake darkened and everything on the boat became dull and flat. Then it reappeared in a gap between two peaks and the world turned rosy-gold again.

"I wonder where we'll be on your eleventh birthday," said Papa, "and on your twelfth."

"Won't we be here?"

"Oh, I don't think so," said Papa. "If the Swiss won't print anything I write for fear of upsetting the Nazis across the border we may as well live in another country altogether. Where would you like to go?"

"I don't know," said Anna.

"I think France would be very nice," said Papa. He considered it for a while. "Do you know Paris at all?" he asked.

Until Anna became a refugee the only place she had ever gone to was the seaside, but she was used to Papa's habit of becoming so interested in his own thoughts that he forgot whom he was talking to. She shook her head.

"It's a beautiful city," said Papa. "I'm sure you'd like it."

"Would we go to a French school?"

"I expect so. And you'd learn to speak French. On the other hand," said Papa, "we might live in England – that's very beautiful too. But a bit damp." He looked at Anna thoughtfully. "No," he said, "I think we'll try Paris first."

The sun had now disappeared completely and

it was dusk. It was hard to see the water as the boat sped through it, except for the foam which flashed white in what little light was left.

"Am I ten yet?" asked Anna. Papa looked at his watch.

"Ten years old exactly." He hugged her. "Happy, happy birthday, and very many happy returns!"

And just as he said it the boat's lights came on. There was only a sprinkling of white bulbs round the rails which left the deck almost as dark as before, but the cabin suddenly glowed yellow and at the back of the boat the ship's lantern shone a brilliant purply-blue.

"Isn't it lovely!" cried Anna and somehow, suddenly, she no longer minded about her birthday and her presents. It seemed rather fine and adventurous to be a refugee, to have no home and not to know where one was going to live. Perhaps at a pinch it might even count as a difficult childhood like the ones in Gunther's book and she would end up by being famous.

As the boat steamed back to Zurich she snuggled up to Papa and they watched the blue light from the ship's lantern trailing through the dark water behind them.

"I think I might quite like being a refugee," said Anna.

Chapter Nine

The summer wore on and suddenly it was the end of term. On the last day there was a celebration at school with a speech by Herr Graupe, an exhibition of needlework by the girls, a gym display by the boys and much singing and yodelling by everyone. At the end of the afternoon each child was presented with a sausage and a hunk of bread, and they wandered home through the village chewing and laughing and making plans for the next day. The summer holidays had begun.

Max did not finish until a day or two later. At the High School in Zurich the term did not end with yodelling and sausages but with reports. Max brought home his usual quota of comments like "Docs not try" and "Shows no interest", and he and Anna sat through the usual gloomy lunch while Mama and Papa read them. Mama was particularly disappointed because, while she had got used to Max not trying and showing no interest in Germany, she had somehow hoped it might be different in Switzerland – because Max was clever, only he did not work. But the only difference was that whereas in Germany Max had neglected his work to play football, in Switzerland he neglected it in order to fish, and the results were much the same.

It was amazing, thought Anna, how he went on with his fishing even though he never caught anything. Even the Zwirn children had begun to tease him about it. "Bathing worms again?" they would say as they passed him and he would scowl at them furiously, unable to shout an insult back for fear of disturbing some fish that might just be going to bite.

When Max was not fishing he and Anna and the three Zwirn children swam in the lake and played together or went for walks in the woods. Max got on well with Franz, and Anna had become quite fond of Vreneli. Trudi was only six, but she trailed along behind no matter what the others were doing. Sometimes they were joined by Roesli and once even by the red-haired boy who studiously ignored both Anna and Vreneli and only talked about football to Max.

Then one morning Anna and Max came down to find the Zwirn children playing with a boy and a girl they had never seen before. They were German, about their own ages, and were spending a holiday with their parents at the inn.

"Which part of Germany do you come from?" asked Max.

"Munich," said the boy.

"We used to live in Berlin," said Anna.

"Gosh," said the boy, "Berlin must be marvellous."

They all played chase together. It had never been much fun before because there had only been four of them – (Trudi did not count because she could not run fast enough and always cried when anyone caught her). But the German children were both very quick on their feet and for the first time the game was really exciting. Vreneli had just caught the German boy, and he caught Anna, so now it was Anna's turn to catch someone and she chased after the German girl. They raced round and round the courtyard of the inn, doubling back and forth and leaping over things until Anna thought she was just going to catch her – but all at once her path was blocked by a tall thin lady with a disagreeable expression. The lady appeared so suddenly, apparently from nowhere, that Anna was barely able to stop and almost collided with her.

"Sorry," she said, but the lady did not reply.

"Siegfried!" she called shrilly. "Gudrun! I told you you were not to play with these children!" She grabbed hold of the German girl and pulled her away. The boy followed, but when his mother was not looking he made a funny face at Anna and waved his hands apologetically. Then the three of them disappeared into the inn.

"What a cross woman," said Vreneli.

"Perhaps she thinks we're badly brought up," said Anna.

They tried to go on playing chase without the German children, but it was no good and ended in the usual shambles, with Trudi in tears because she had been caught.

Anna did not see the German children again until the late afternoon. They must have been shopping in Zurich for they were each carrying a parcel and their mother had several large ones. As they were about to go into the inn Anna thought this was her chance to show that she was not badly brought up. She leapt forward and opened the door for them.

But the German lady did not seem at all pleased. "Gudrun! Siegfried!" she said and pushed her children quickly inside. Then, with a sour expression and keeping as far away from Anna as possible, she squeezed past herself. It was difficult because of the parcels which nearly stuck in the doorway, but at last she was through and disappeared. With never a word of thanks, thought Anna – the German lady was badly brought up herself!

The next day she and Max had arranged to go up into the woods with the Zwirn children, and the day after that it rained, and the day after that Mama took them to Zurich to buy them some socks – so they did not see the German children. But after breakfast on the following morning when Anna and Max went out into the yard, there they were again playing with the Zwirns. Anna rushed up to them.

"Shall we have a game of chase?" she said.

"No," said Vreneli, looking rather pink. "And any way you can't play."

Anna was so surprised that for a moment she could think of nothing to say. Was Vreneli upset about the red-haired boy again? But she hadn't seen him for ages.

"Why can't Anna play?" asked Max.

Franz was as embarrassed as his sister.

"Neither of you can," he said and indicated the German children. "They say they're not allowed to play with you."

The German children had clearly not only been forbidden to play but even to talk to them, for the boy looked as though he wanted to say something. But in the end he only made his funny apologetic face and shrugged.

Anna and Max looked at each other. They had

never met such a situation before. Then Trudi who had been listening suddenly sang out, "Anna and Max can't play! Anna and Max can't play!"

"Oh, shut up!" said Franz. "Come on!" and he and Vreneli ran off towards the lake with the German children following. For a moment Trudi was taken aback. Then she sang out one last defiant "Anna and Max can't play!" and scampered after them on her short legs.

Anna and Max were left standing.

"Why aren't they allowed to play with us?" asked Anna, but Max didn't know either. There seemed nothing to do but wander back to the dining-room where Mama and Papa were still finishing breakfast.

"I thought you were playing with Franz and Vreneli," said Mama.

Max explained what had happened.

"That's very odd," said Mama.

"Perhaps you could speak to the mother," said Anna. She had just noticed the German lady and a man who must be her husband sitting at a table in the corner.

"I certainly will," said Mama.

Just then the German lady and her husband got up to leave the dining-room and Mama went to intercept them. They met too far away for Anna to hear what they said, but Mama had only spoken a few words when the German lady answered something which caused Mama to flush with anger. The German lady said something more and made as though to move off. But Mama grabbed her arm.

"Oh no, it isn't!" shouted Mama in a voice which echoed right across the dining-room. "It's not the end of it at all!" Then she turned on her heel and marched back to the table while the German lady and her husband went out looking down their noses.

"The whole room could hear you," said Papa crossly as Mama sat down. He hated scenes.

"Good!" said Mama in such ringing tones that Papa whispered "Ssssh!" and made calming motions with his hands. Trying to speak quietly made Mama angrier than ever and she could hardly get the words out.

"They're Nazis," she said at last. "They've forbidden their children to play with ours because our children are Jewish!" Her voice rose higher in indignation. "And you want me to keep my voice down!" she shouted so that an old lady still finishing breakfast was startled into almost spilling her coffee.

Papa's mouth tightened. "I would not dream of allowing Anna and Max to play with the children of Nazis," he said, "so there is no difficulty."

"But what about Vreneli and Franz?" asked Max. "It means that if they're playing with the German children they can't play with us."

"I think Vreneli and Franz will have to decide

100

who their friends are," said Papa. "Swiss neutrality is all very well, but it can be taken too far." He got up from the table. "I'll have a word with their father now."

A little while later Papa returned. He had told Herr Zwirn that his children must choose whether they wished to play with Anna and Max or with the German visitors. They could not play with both. Papa has asked them not to decide in a hurry but to let him know that evening.

"I suppose they'll choose us," said Max. "After all we'll be here long after those other children have gone."

But it was difficult to know what to do with the rest of the day. Max went down to the lake with his fishing rod and his worms and his bits of bread. Anna could not settle to anything. At last she decided to write a poem about an avalanche which engulfed an entire city, but it did not turn out very well. When she came to do the illustration she was so bored at the thought of making it all white that she gave up. Max, as usual caught no fish, and by mid-afternoon they were both so depressed that Mama gave them half a franc to buy themselves some chocolate – although she had previously said it was too expensive.

On their way back from the sweet-shop they caught a glimpse of Vreneli and Franz talking earnestly in the doorway of the inn and walked past self-consciously, looking straight ahead. This made them feel worse than ever.

Then Max went back to his fishing and Anna decided to go for a bathe, to try and salvage something from the day. She floated on her back which she had only just learned to do, but it did not cheer her up. It all seemed so silly. Why couldn't she and Max and the Zwirns and the German children all play together? Why did they have to have all this business of decisions and taking sides?

Suddenly there was a splash in the water beside her. It was Vreneli. Her long thin plaits were tied in a knot on top of her head so as not to get wet and her long thin face looked pinker and more worried than ever.

"I'm sorry about this morning," said Vreneli breathlessly. "We've decided we'd rather play with you even if it does mean that we can't play with Siegfried and Gudrun."

Then Franz appeared on the bank. "Hello, Max!" he shouted. "Worms enjoying their swim?"

"I'd have caught a great big fish just then," said Max, "if you hadn't frightened it away." But he was very pleased just the same.

At supper that evening Anna saw the German children for the last time. They were sitting stiffly in the dining-room with their parents. Their mother was talking to them quietly and insistently, and even the boy never turned round once to look at Anna and Max. At the end of the meal he walked right past their table as though he could not see them.

The whole family left the next morning.

"I'm afraid we've lost Herr Zwirn some customers," said Papa.

Mama was triumphant.

"But it seems such a pity," said Anna. "I'm sure that boy really liked us."

Max shook his head. "He didn't like us any more at the end," he said. "Not by the time his mother had finished with him."

It was true, thought Anna. She wondered what the German boy was thinking now, what his mother had told him about her and Max, and what he would be like when he grew up.

Chapter Ten

Just before the end of the summer holidays Papa went to Paris. There were so many German refugees living there now that they had started their own newspaper. It was called the *Daily Parisian* and some of the articles Papa had written in Zurich had appeared in it. Now the editor wanted him to write for the paper on a more regular basis. Papa thought that if it worked out they might all go to Paris to live.

The day after he left Omama arrived. She was the children's grandmother and had come on a visit from the South of France.

"How funny," said Anna. "Omama might pass Papa in the train. They could wave to each other!"

"They wouldn't, though," said Max. "They don't get on."

"Why not?" asked Anna. It was true, now she came to think of it, that Omama only came to see them when Papa was away.

"One of those family things," said Max in an irritating would-be-grown-up voice. "She didn't want Mama and Papa to marry each other."

"Well, it's a bit late now!" said Anna with a giggle.

Anna was out playing with Vreneli when Omama arrived, but she knew at once that she had come because of the hysterical barking that issued from an open window of the inn. Omama never moved without her dachschund Pumpel. She followed the sound and found Omama with Mama.

"Darling Anna!" cried Omama. "How lovely to see you!" and she hugged Anna to her stout bosom. After a moment Anna thought the hug must be finished and wriggled, but Omama held on tight and hugged her a bit more. Anna remembered that Omama had always done this.

"It's been such a long time!" cried Omama. "That dreadful man Hitler . . .!" Her eyes, which were blue like Mama's but much paler, filled with tears and her chins – there were two – trembled gently. It was difficult to hear exactly what she was saying because of Pumpel's noise. Only a few

105

phrases like "torn from our homes" and "breaking up families" emerged above the frantic barks.

"What's the matter with Pumpel?" asked Anna.

"Oh Pumpel, my poor Pumpel! Just look at him!" cried Omama.

Anna had been looking at him. He was behaving very strangely. His brown hindquarters stuck straight up into the air and he kept flattening his head on his front paws as though he were bowing. Between bows he gazed beseechingly at something above Omama's wash basin. Since Pumpel was the same tubby shape as Omama the whole operation was very difficult for him.

"What does he want?" asked Anna.

"He's begging," said Omama. "Isn't he sweet? he's begging for that electric light bulb. Oh, but Pumpel, my darling Pumpel, I can't give it to you!"

Anna looked. Above the basin was a perfectly ordinary round bulb, painted white. It seemed an eccentric thing even for Pumpel to wish for.

"Why does he want it?" she asked.

"Well, of course he doesn't realize it's a bulb," Omama explained patiently. "He thinks it's a tennis ball and he wants me to throw it for him."

Pumpel, sensing that his needs were at last being taken seriously, bowed and barked with redoubled vigour.

Anna laughed. "Poor Pumpel," she said and

tried to stroke him – but he immediately snapped at her hand with his yellow teeth. She withdrew it quickly.

"We could unscrew the bulb," said Mama, but it was stuck fast in its socket and would not be moved.

"Perhaps if we had a real tennis ball . . ." said Omama, searching for her purse. "Anna darling, would you mind? I think the shops are still open."

"Tennis balls are quite expensive," said Anna. She had once wanted to buy one with her pocket money but had not had nearly enough.

"It doesn't matter," said Omama, "I can't leave poor Pumpel like this – he'll exhaust himself."

But when Anna returned Pumpel had lost interest in the whole business. He was lying on the floor growling, and when Anna placed the ball gingerly between his paws he gave it a look of utter loathing and sank his teeth straight into it. The tennis ball expired with a sigh. Pumpel got up, scratched the floor twice with his hind feet, and retired under the bed.

"He really is a horrible dog," Anna later told Max. "I don't know how Omama puts up with him."

"I wish we had the money for the tennis ball," said Max. "We could use it at the fair."

There was a fair coming to the village – an annual event which the local children were very excited about. Franz and Vreneli had been saving up their pocket money for months. Somehow Anna and Max had only just heard about it, and as they had no savings they did not see how they could go. Their combined assets would just about pay for one ride on the roundabout – and that, said Anna, would be worse than not going at all.

She had thought briefly of asking Mama for some money. This was after her first day back at school when no one had talked about anything except the fair and how much money they would have to spend. But Max had reminded her that Mama was trying to economize. If they were going to live in Paris they would need every penny for the move.

Meanwhile Pumpel, though no one could call him lovable, made life a lot more interesting. He had no sense at all. Even Omama, who was used to his ways, was surprised. When she took him on a steamer he made straight for the side and was only restrained with difficulty from throwing himself overboard. The next time she wanted to go to Zurich she tried to take him on the train, but he refused to get on it. However, as soon as the train pulled out of the station, leaving Omama and Pumpel on the platform, he tore himself free from his lead and pursued it, barking wildly, right down the line to the next village. He was brought back exhausted an hour later by a small boy and had to rest for the remainder of the day.

"Do you think there's something wrong with his eyesight?" asked Omama.

"Nonsense, Mother," said Mama who felt she had more important worries, what with possibly moving to Paris and having no money. "Anyway, even if there is you can't buy him spectacles!"

It was a shame because Omama, in spite of being silly about Pumpel, was really very kind. She too was a refugee but her husband was not famous like Papa. They had been able to move all their belongings out of Germany and now lived comfortably by the Mediterranean. Unlike Mama, she did not have to economize, and often devised little treats which Mama would not normally have been able to afford.

"I suppose we couldn't ask Omama to give us some money for the fair?" said Anna one day after Omama had bought them all éclairs at the local cake shop.

Max was horrified. "Anna! We couldn't!" he said quite sharply.

Anna had known really that they couldn't — only it was so tempting. The fair was only about a week away.

A few days before Omama was due to travel back to the South of France, Pumpel disappeared. He had escaped from Omama's room early in the morning and she had thought nothing of it. He often went for a sniff round the lake and usually came back quite quickly of his own accord. But by breakfast time he was still missing and she began to ask people whether they had seen him.

"Whatever has he got up to now?" asked Herr Zwirn. He did not like Pumpel who upset his other customers, chewed the furniture and had twice tried to bite Trudi.

"Sometimes he seems to act just like a puppy," said Omama fondly, though Pumpel was nine years old.

"It's more like his second childhood," said Herr Zwirn.

The children searched for him half-heartedly, but it was nearly time to go to school and they were sure that sooner or later he would turn up – probably accompanied by an angry victim whom he had either bitten or whose property he had destroyed. Vreneli came to call for Anna and they set off for school, and Anna promptly forgot all about him. When they returned at lunch-time they were met by Trudi with an air of great importance.

"They found your grandmother's dog," she said. "He's drowned."

"Nonsense!" said Vreneli. "You're making it up."

"I'm not making it up," said Trudi, outraged. "It's true – Pa found him in the lake. And I've seen him myself and he's quite dead. One reason I knew he was dead was because he didn't try to bite me."

Mama confirmed Trudi's story. Pumpel had been found at the bottom of a low wall at the edge of the lake. No one ever discovered how he got there – whether he had leapt down in a fit of madness or mistaken one of the large pebbles in the water for a tennis ball. Herr Zwirn suggested that it might have been suicide.

"I've heard of dogs doing that," he said, "when they're no good to themselves or to anyone else."

Poor Omama was dreadfully upset. She did not come down to lunch and only appeared, red-eyed and silent, for Pumpel's funeral in the afternoon. Herr Zwirn dug a little grave for him in a corner of the garden. Omama had wrapped Pumpel up in an old shawl and the children all stood by while she put him in his last resting place. Then, under Omama's direction, they each threw a shovelful of soil on top of him. Herr Zwirn briskly threw on a whole lot more and then flattened and shaped it into a low mound.

"Now for the decoration," said Herr Zwirn, and Omama tearfully placed a large plant-pot with a chrysanthemum on top.

Trudi watched her approvingly.

"Now your doggie can't get out!" she said with obvious satisfaction.

This was too much for Omama, and to the children's embarrassment she burst into tears and had to be led away by Herr Zwirn.

The rest of the day was rather gloomy. Nobody

really minded about poor Pumpel except Omama, but they all felt they owed it to her not to look too cheerful. After supper Max went off to do his homework while Anna and Mama kept Omama company.

She had hardly said a word all day, but now she suddenly could not stop talking. On and on she went about Pumpel and all the things he used to do. How could she face travelling back to the South of France without him? He had been such good company on the train. She even had his return ticket – both Mama and Anna had to inspect it. It was all the fault of the Nazis, cried Omama. If Pumpel had not had to leave Germany he would never have drowned in Lake Zurich. That dreadful man Hitler . . .

After this Mama gradually turned the talk into the usual list of people who had gone to live in different countries or had stayed behind and Anna began to read, but her book was not very interesting and bits of the conversation kept filtering through.

Somebody had got a job in films in England. Somebody else who had been rich was now very hard up in America and his wife had to go out cleaning. A famous professor had been arrested and sent to a concentration camp. (Concentration camp? Then Anna remembered that it was a special prison for people who were against Hitler.) The Nazis had chained him to a dog kennel.

What a silly thing to do, thought Anna, as Omama, who seemed to see some connection between this and Pumpel's death, talked more and more excitedly. The dog kennel was right by the entrance to the concentration camp and every time anyone went in or out the famous professor had to bark. He was given scraps to eat out of a dog dish and was not allowed to touch them with his hands.

Anna suddenly felt sick.

At night the famous professor had to sleep in the dog kennel. The chain was too short for him ever to stand up straight. After two months – two months . . .! thought Anna – the famous professor had gone mad. He was still chained to the dog kennel and having to bark but he no longer knew what he was doing.

A black wall seemed suddenly to have risen up in front of Anna's eyes. She could not breathe. She clutched her book in front of her, pretending to read. She wanted not to have heard what Omama had said, to be rid of it, to be sick.

Mama must have sensed something, for there was a sudden silence and Anna could feel Mama looking at her. She stared down fiercely at her book and deliberately turned a page as though absorbed. She did not want Mama and especially Omama to speak to her.

After a moment the conversation started up again. This time Mama was talking rather loudly

113

not about concentration camps but about how cold it had been lately.

"Enjoying your book, dear?" said Omama.

"Yes, thank you," said Anna and managed to make her voice sound quite normal. As soon as possible she got up and went to bed. She wanted to tell Max what she had heard but could not bring herself to talk about it. It was better not even to think about it.

In future she would try never to think about Germany at all.

The next morning Omama packed her bags. She had no heart to stay the last few days, now that Pumpel was gone. But there was one good thing that came of her visit. Just before she left she handed Anna and Max an envelope. She had written on it, "A present from Pumpel" and when they opened it they found that it contained a little over eleven Swiss francs.

"I want you to use this money in any way that gives you pleasure," said Omama.

"What is it?" asked Max, overcome by her generosity.

"It's Pumpel's return ticket to the South of France," said Omama with tears in her eyes. "I got it refunded."

So Anna and Max had enough money after all to go to the fair.

Chapter Eleven

Papa arrived back from Paris on a Sunday, so Anna and Max went to meet him in Zurich with Mama. It was a cool, bright day in early October and as they came back with him on the steamer they could see some new snow on the moutains.

Papa was very cheerful. He had enjoyed being in Paris. Although he had stayed in a scruffy little hotel to save money he had eaten delicious food and drunk lots of good wine. All these things were cheap in France. The editor of the *Daily Parisian* had been very nice and Papa had also spoken to the editors of several French papers. They too had said that they wanted him to write for them.

"In French?" asked Anna.

"Of course," said Papa. He had had a French governess when he was small and could speak French as well as he spoke German.

"Are we all going to live in Paris then?" asked Max.

"Mama and I must talk about it first," said Papa. But he clearly thought that they should.

"How lovely!" said Anna.

"Nothing's been decided yet," said Mama. "There may be possibilities in London too."

"But it's damp there," said Anna.

Mama got quite cross. "Nonsense," she said. "You don't know anything about it."

The trouble was that Mama did not speak much French. While Papa had learned French from his French governess Mama had learned English from an English governess. The English governess had been so nice that Mama had always wanted to see the country she came from.

"We'll talk about it," said Papa. Then he told them about the people he had met – old acquaintances from Berlin who had been distinguished writers, actors or scientists and were now trying to eke out a living in France.

"One morning I ran into that actor – you remember Blumenthal?" said Papa, and Mama knew at once whom he meant. "He's opened a cake shop. His wife bakes the cakes and he serves behind the counter. I met him delivering apple strudel to a special customer." Papa smiled. "The last time I'd seen him he was the guest of honour at a banquet at the Berlin Opera."

He had also met a French journalist and his wife who had invited him several times to their home.

"They're delightful people," said Papa, "and they have a daughter about Anna's age. If we go and live in Paris I'm sure you will like them enormously."

"Yes," said Mama, but she did not sound convinced.

For the next week or two Mama and Papa talked about Paris. Papa thought that he would be able to work there and that it would be a lovely place to live. Mama, who hardly knew Paris, had all sorts of practical considerations like the children's education and what sort of a home they would find, to which Papa had not given much thought. In the end they agreed that she must go back to Paris with Papa and see for herself. After all, it was a very important decision.

"What about us?" asked Max.

He and Anna were sitting on the bed in their parents' room where they had been summoned for a discussion. Mama had the only chair and Papa was perching like a rather elegant goblin on an upturned suitcase. It was a bit cramped but more private than downstairs.

"I think you're old enough to look after yourselves for a few weeks," said Mama.

"You mean we'd stay here on our own?" asked Anna. It seemed an extraordinary idea.

"Why not?" said Mama. "Frau Zwirn will keep an eye on you – she'll see that your clothes are clean and that you go to bed at the right time. I think you can manage the rest yourselves."

So it was settled. Anna and Max were to send their parents a postcard every other day, to let them know that everything was all right, and Mama and Papa would do the same. Mama asked them to remember to wash their necks and put on clean socks. Papa had something more serious to say to them.

"Remember that when Mama and I are in Paris you will be the only representatives of our family in Switzerland," he said. "It's a big responsibility."

"Why?" asked Anna. "What will we have to do?"

Once, at the Berlin Zoo with Onkel Julius, she had seen a small mouse-like creature with a notice on its cage claiming that it was the only representative of its species in Germany. She hoped no one was going to come and stare at her and Max.

But this was not what Papa had meant at all.

"There are Jews scattered all over the world," he said, "and the Nazis are telling terrible lies

118

about them. So it's very important for people like us to prove them wrong."

"How can we?" asked Max.

"By being better than other people," said Papa. "For instance, the Nazis say that Jews are dishonest. So it's not enough for us to be as honest as anyone else. We have to be more honest."

(Anna at once thought guiltily of the last time she had bought a pencil in Berlin. The man in the paper shop had not charged her quite enough and Anna had not pointed out the mistake. Suppose the Nazis had got to hear of this?)

"We have to be more hard-working than other people," said Papa, "to prove that we're not lazy, more generous to prove that we're not mean, more polite to prove that we're not rude."

Max nodded.

"It may seem like a lot to ask," said Papa, "but I think it's worth it because the Jews are wonderful people and it's rather splendid to be one. And when Mama and I come back I'm sure we'll be very proud of the way you have represented us in Switzerland."

It was funny, thought Anna. Normally she hated to be told that she must be extra good, but this time she did not really mind. She had not realized before that being a Jew was so important. Secretly she resolved really to wash her neck with soap each day while Mama was away so that at least the Nazis would not be able to say that Jews had dirty necks.

However, when Mama and Papa actually left for Paris she did not feel important at all – just rather small and forlorn. She managed not to cry while she watched their train pull out of the local station, but as she and Max walked back slowly to the inn she felt quite clearly that she was too young to be left in one country while her parents went off to a different one.

"Come on, little man," said Max suddenly, "cheer up!" – and it was so funny to be addressed as "little man", which was what people sometimes called Max, that she laughed.

After this things got better. Frau Zwirn had cooked her favourite lunch and it was rather grand for her and Max to eat it in the dining-room at a table all by themselves. Then Vreneli came to collect her for afternoon school and after school she and Max played with the three Zwirn children just as usual. Bedtime, which she had thought would be the worst bit, was actually very nice because Herr Zwirn came in and told them funny stories about some of the people who came to the inn. Next day she and Max were able to write quite a cheerful postcard to Mama and Papa, and one arrived for them from Paris the following morning.

After this life went along quite briskly. The postcards were a great help. Each day they either wrote to Mama and Papa or heard from them, and this made it feel as though Mama and Papa were not so far away. On Sunday Anna and Max and the three Zwirn children went into the woods to collect sweet chestnuts. They brought back great baskets full and Frau Zwirn roasted them in the oven. Then they all ate them for supper in the Zwirns' kitchen, spread thickly with butter. They were delicious.

At the end of the second week after Mama and Papa's departure Herr Graupe took Anna's class on an excursion into the mountains. They spent a night high up on a moutainside, sleeping on straw in a wooden hut, and in the morning Herr Graupe got them up before it was light. He walked them along a narrow path up the mountain and suddenly Anna found that the ground under her feet had become cold and wet. It was snow.

"Vreneli, look!" she cried, and as they looked at it the snow which had been dimly grey in the darkness suddenly became brighter and pinker. It happened quite quickly and soon a rosy brilliance swept across the entire mountainside.

Anna looked at Vreneli. Her blue sweater had turned purple, her face was scarlet and even her mouse-coloured plaits glowed orange. The other children were equally transformed. Even Herr Graupe's beard had turned pink. And behind them was a huge empty expanse of deep pink snow and slightly paler pink sky. Gradually the pink faded a little and the light became brighter, the pink world behind Vreneli and the rest divided itself into blue sky and dazzling white snow, and it was fully daylight.

"You have now seen the sunrise in the Swiss mountains – the most beautiful sight in the world," said Herr Graupe as though he personally had caused it to happen. Then he marched them all down again.

It was a long walk and Anna was tired long before they got to the bottom. In the train on the way back she dozed and wished that Mama and Papa were not in Paris so that she could tell them about her adventure. But perhaps there would soon be news of their return. Mama had promised that they would only stay away three weeks at the most and it was now a little more than two.

They did not get back to the inn until evening. Max had held back the regular postcard of the day and, tired as she was, Anna managed to cram a lot on it about her excursion. Then, although it was only seven o'clock, she went to bed.

On her way upstairs she came upon Franz and Vreneli whispering together in the corridor. When they saw her they stopped.

"What were you saying?" asked Anna. She had caught her father's name and something about the Nazis.

"Nothing," said Vreneli.

"Yes, you were," said Anna. "I heard you."

"Pa said we weren't to tell you," said Vreneli unhappily.

"For fear of upsetting you," said Franz. "But it was in the paper. The Nazis are putting a price on your Pa's head."

"A price on his head?" asked Anna stupidly.

"Yes," said Franz. "A thousand German marks. Pa says it shows how important your pa must be. There was a picture of him and all."

How could you put a thousand marks on a person's head? It was silly. She determined to ask Max when he came up to bed but fell asleep long before.

In the middle of the night Anna woke up. It was quite sudden, like something being switched on inside her head, and she was immediately wide awake. And as though she had been thinking of nothing else all night, she suddenly knew with terrible clarity how you put a thousand marks on a person's head.

In her mind she saw a room. It was a funny-looking room because it was in France and the ceiling, instead of being solid, was a mass of criss-crossing beams. In the gaps between them something was moving. It was dark, but now the door opened and the light came on. Papa was coming to bed. He took a few steps towards the middle of the room – "Don't!" Anna wanted to cry – and then the terrible shower of heavy coins began. It came pouring down from the ceiling on to Papa's head. He called out but the coins kept coming. He sank to his knees under their weight and the coins kept falling and falling until he was completely buried under them.

So this was what Herr Zwirn had not wanted her to know. This was what the Nazis were going to do to Papa. Or perhaps, since it was in the paper, they had already done it. She lay staring into the darkness, sick with fear. In the other bed she could hear Max breathing quietly and regularly. Should she wake him? But Max hated being disturbed in the night – he would probably only be cross and say that it was all nonsense.

And perhaps it was all nonsense, she thought with a sudden lightening of her misery. Perhaps in the morning she would be able to see it as one of those silly night fears which had frightened her when she was younger – like the times when she had thought that the house was on fire, or that her heart had stopped. In the morning there would be the usual postcard from Mama and Papa, and everything would be all right.

Yes, but this was not something she had imagined – it had been in the paper . . . Her thoughts went round and round. One moment she was making complicated plans to get up, take a train to Paris and warn Papa. The next moment she thought how silly she'd look if Frau Zwirn should happen to catch her. In the end she must have

124

fallen asleep because suddenly it was daylight and Max was already half-dressed. She stayed in bed for a moment, feeling very tired and letting the thoughts of the previous night come creeping back. After all they seemed rather unreal now that it was morning.

"Max?" she said tentatively.

Max had an open textbook on the table beside him and was looking at it while he put on his shoes and socks.

"Sorry," said Max. "Latin exam today and I haven't revised." He went back to his book, murmuring verbs and tenses. Anyway, it didn't matter, thought Anna. She was sure everything was all right.

But at breakfast there was no postcard from Mama and Papa.

"Why do you think it hasn't come?" she asked Max.

"Postal delay," said Max indistinctly through a mouthful of bread. "Bye!" and he rushed to catch his train.

"I daresay it'll come this afternoon," said Herr Zwirn.

But she worried about it all day at school and sat chewing her pencil instead of writing a description of the sunrise in the mountains.

"What's the matter with you?" said Herr Graupe. (She usually wrote the best compositions in the class.) "It was beautiful. You should have been inspired by the experience!" And he walked away, personally offended by her lack of response to his sunrise.

There was still no postcard when she came home from school, nor was there anything in the last post at seven o'clock. It was the first time that Mama and Papa had not written. Anna managed to get through supper thinking cool thoughts about postal delays, but once she was in bed with the light out all the terror of the previous night came flooding back with such force that she felt almost choked by it. She tried to remember that she was a Jew and must not be frightened, otherwise the Nazis would say that all Jews were cowards – but it was no use. She kept seeing the room with the strange ceiling and the terrible rain of coins coming down on Papa's head. Even though she shut her eyes and buried her face in the pillow she could still see it.

She must have been making some noise in bed for Max suddenly said, "What's the matter?"

"Nothing," said Anna, but even as she said it she could feel something like a small explosion making its way up from her stomach towards her throat, and suddenly she was sobbing, "Papa . . . Papa . . ." and Max was sitting on her bed and patting her arm.

"Oh, you idiot!" he said when she had explained her fears. "Don't you know what is meant by a price on someone's head?"

"Not . . . not what I thought?" said Anna.

"No," said Max. "Not at all what you thought. Putting a price on a person's head means offering a reward to anyone who captures that person."

"There you are!" wailed Anna. "The Nazis are trying to get Papa!"

"Well, in a way," said Max. "But Herr Zwirn doesn't think it's very serious – after all there's not much they can do about it as Papa isn't in Germany."

"You think he's all right?"

"Of course he's all right. We'll have a postcard in the morning."

"But supposing they sent someone after him in France – a kidnapper or someone like that?"

"Then Papa would have the whole of the French police force to protect him." Max assumed what he imagined to be a French accent. "Go away, pleeze. Ees not allowed to keednap in France. We chop off your head with the guillotine, no?"

He was such an awful mimic that Anna had to laugh and Max looked surprised at his success.

"Better go to sleep now," he said, and she was so tired that very soon she did.

In the morning instead of a postcard they had a long letter. Mama and Papa had decided that they should all live in Paris together and Papa was coming to collect them.

★ ★ ★

127

"Papa," said Anna after the first excitement of seeing him safe and sound had worn off. "Papa, I was a bit upset when I heard about the price on your head."

"So was I!" said Papa. "Very upset."

"Were you?" asked Anna, surprised. Papa had always seemed so brave.

"Well, it's such a very small price," explained Papa. "A thousand marks goes nowhere these days. I think I'm worth a lot more, don't you?"

"Yes," said Anna, feeling better.

"No self-respecting kidnapper would touch it," said Papa. He shook his head sadly. "I've a good mind to write to Hitler and complain!"

Chapter Twelve

Frau Zwirn packed the children's clothes. They said goodbye to their friends and their teachers at school and then they were ready to leave Switzerland for their new life in France. But it wasn't a bit like leaving Berlin, said Anna, because they would be able to come back and see everyone at the Gasthof Zwirn any time they liked, and Herr Zwirn had already invited them for next summer. They were to live in a furnished flat in Paris which Mama was busy now getting ready. What was it like? Max wanted to know. Papa thought for a moment. If you stood on the balcony, he said at last, you could see the Eiffel Tower and the Arc de Triomphe both at the same time – these were famous Paris landmarks. But beyond this he seemed unable to remember much about it. It was a pity, thought the children, that Papa was sometimes so vague about practical matters. But the fact that the flat had a balcony made it sound rather grand.

The journey to Paris took the whole day and they almost did not get there at all. They had no trouble until Basle, but there they had to change trains because Basle is the frontier between Switzerland, France and Germany. Owing to some delay on the line they arrived very late and only had a few minutes to catch their Paris connection.

"We'll have to be very quick," said Papa as the train drew into the station.

Luckily there was a porter immediately at hand. He grabbed their luggage and flung it on to his wheelbarrow.

"The Paris train! Hurry!" cried Papa and the porter set off at a gallop with them all running behind him. Anna had trouble keeping the porter in sight as he turned and twisted through the crowds of people, and Max and Papa were already helping him to heave the luggage aboard the other train when she caught up with them. She stood for a moment, getting her breath back. The train must be just about to leave, for all along it people were leaning out of the windows saying goodbye to their friends on the platform. Immediately beside her a young man seemed in danger of

130

falling right out as he gave his girlfriend a passionate farewell embrace.

"Go on with you!" said the girl and gave him a little push back into the train. As he straightened up, the bottom of the window came into view. There was a printed notice stuck on it. It read STUTTGART.

"Papa!" screamed Anna. "This is the wrong train! It's going to Germany!"

"Good God!" said Papa. "Get the luggage off quick!"

He and Max dragged the suitcases off again as fast as they could. Then they heard the whistle.

"Never mind!" shouted Papa and pulled Max back, even though there was a suitcase still left on the train.

"That's our case!" shouted Max. "Please give us our case!" and just as the carriage began to move the young man with the girlfriend kindly pushed it on to the platform for them. It landed at Anna's feet and they stood there, with luggage littered all round them, and watched the train steam out of the station.

"I clearly told you the Paris train!" said Papa, angrily looking round for the porter. But there was no sign of him. He had disappeared.

"If we'd got on that train," asked Anna, "would we have been able to get off before it got to Germany?"

"Possibly," said Papa. "If we'd realized it was

the wrong train." He put an arm round her shoulders. "I'm certainly very glad you noticed before we ever got on it."

It took some time to find another porter and Papa was sure they had missed the Paris connection, but in fact they caught it with time to spare. Its departure time had been put back to fit in with the delay on the Swiss line. It was odd that the first porter had not known about this.

As they sat in their compartment waiting for the French train to start Max suddenly said, "Papa, do you think that porter took us to the wrong train on purpose?"

"I don't know," said Papa. "It could just have been a mistake."

"I don't think it was a mistake," said Max. "I think he was trying to earn the thousand marks on your head."

For a moment they sat thinking about it, and about what would have happened if they had travelled to Germany. Then the whistle went and the train started with a jolt.

"Well," said Papa, "if that porter really was trying to earn a thousand marks he certainly made a bad bargain. I never had time even to give him a tip." He smiled and settled back in his seat. "And in a few minutes, thanks to Anna, we'll be not in Germany but in France. And thanks to Max we've even got all our luggage." He lifted his hands in mock admiration "Psssh!" said Papa. "What clever children I have!"

They arrived in Paris after dark and very tired. Anna had already sensed something different in the train after leaving Basle. There has been more French voices talking quickly, sharply and incomprehensibly. The smells from the dining-car had been different too. But now that she was standing on the platform in Paris she was overwhelmed.

All round her there were people shouting, greeting each other, talking, laughing. Their lips moved quickly, their mobile faces keeping pace with them. They shrugged, embraced each other and waved their hands to emphasize what they were saying – and she could not understand a word. For a moment, in the dim light and the noise and the steam drifting back from the engine, she felt quite lost.. But then Papa was bundling her and Max into a taxi and they were charging through the crowded streets.

There were lights everywhere, people walking along wide pavements, eating and drinking in the glass-fronted cafés, reading newspapers, looking into shop windows. She had forgotten a big city was like this. The height of the buildings amazed her, and the noise. As the taxi swayed and turned in the traffic, unfamiliar cars and buses and coloured electric signs which she could not read loomed out of the darkness and disappeared again.

"There's the Eiffel Tower!" cried Max – but she turned too late and missed it.

Then they were driving round a huge open space with a floodlit arch in the middle. There were cars everywhere, most of them blowing their horns.

"That's the Arc de Triomphe," said Papa. "We're nearly there."

They turned into a quieter avenue and then off it into a little narrow street, and then the taxi stopped quite suddenly with a squeal of brakes. They had arrived.

Anna and Max stood in the cold outside a tall house while Papa paid the taxi driver. Then he opened the front door and pushed them into the hall where a lady was sitting half-asleep in what appeared to be a glass-fronted cage. As soon as she saw Papa the lady leapt into life. She rushed out of what turned out to be a door in her cage and shook him by the hand, talking very quickly in French all the time. Then, still talking, she shook hands with Max and Anna who, unable to understand, could only smile weakly in reply.

"This is Madame la concierge," said Papa. "She looks after the house."

The taxi driver came in with the luggage and Madame la concierge helped him to push some of it through a narrow door which she then held open for Anna and Max. They could hardly believe their eyes.

"Papa!" said Max. "You never told us there was a lift!"

"It's very, very grand," said Anna.

This made Papa laugh.

"I'd hardly call it that," he said. But Anna and Max were not convinced, even when the lift creaked and groaned horribly as it rose slowly up to the top floor. At last it stopped with a bang and a shudder, and even before they had all got out a door opposite them flew open and there was Mama.

Anna and Max rushed to her, and all became confusion while she hugged them and they both tried to tell her everything that had happened since they had last seen her, and Papa came in with the suitcase and kissed Mama, and then the concierge brought in the rest of the cases and all at once the tiny hall was crammed with luggage and no one could move.

"Come into the dining-room," said Mama. It was not much bigger but the table was laid for supper and it looked bright and inviting.

"Where can I hang my coat?" called Papa from the hall.

"There's a hook behind the door," Mama called back in the middle of a noisy description by Max of how they had nearly caught the wrong train. Then there was a crash as of someone falling over something. Anna heard Papa's polite voice saying, "Good evening", and the mild smell of burning which Anna had noticed ever since their arrival suddenly became intensified.

A small glum figure appeared in the doorway.

"Your fried potatoes have gone all black," it announced with obvious satisfaction.

"Oh, Grete . . .!" cried Mama. Then she said, "This is Grete from Austria. She is in Paris to learn French and is going to help me with the housework when she isn't studying."

Grete shook hands gloomily with Anna and Max.

"No," said Grete. "It's a very difficult language. Some people never manage to learn it at all." Then she turned to Mama. "Well, I think I'll be off to bed."

"But Grete . . ." said Mama.

"I promised my mother that no matter what happened, I'd always get my proper sleep," said Grete. "I've turned off the gas under the potatoes. Goodnight all." And she went.

"Really!" said Mama. "That girl is no use at all! Never mind, it'll be nice to have our first meal in Paris together on our own. I'll show you your room and then you can get settled in while I fry some more potatoes."

Their room was painted a rather ugly yellow and there were yellow bedspreads on the two beds. A wooden wardrobe stood in the corner.

There were yellow curtains, a yellow lampshade and two chairs – nothing else. There would have been no space for any more furniture anyway because, like the dining-room, the room was quite small.

"What's outside the window?" asked Max.

Anna looked. It was not a street, as she had expected, but an inner courtyard with walls and windows all round it. It was like a well. A clanging sound far below told her there must be dustbins at the bottom, but it was too far down for her to see. Above there were only the irregular outlines of rooftops and the sky. It was very different from the Gasthof Zwirn and from their house in Berlin.

They unpacked their pyjamas and toothbrushes and decided which yellow bed would belong to whom, and then they explored the rest of the flat. Next to their room was Papa's room. It had a bed, a wardrobe, a chair and a table with Papa's typewriter on it, and it overlooked the street. From Papa's room a communicating door led to what looked like a little sitting-room, but there were some of Mama's clothes strewn about.

"Do you think this is Mama's room?" asked Anna.

"It can't be – there's no bed," said Max. There was only a sofa, a little table and two armchairs. Then Max took a closer look at the sofa.

"It's one of those special ones," he said.

"Look" – and he lifted up the seat. In a cavity underneath were sheets, blankets and pillows. "Mama can sleep on it at night and then she can turn the room into a sitting-room during the day."

"It's very clever," said Anna. "It means you can use the room twice over."

Certainly it was important to make the best possible use of the space in the flat, for there was so little of it. Even the balcony, which had sounded so grand when Papa talked about it, was not much more than a ledge surrounded by wrought iron railings. Apart from the dining-room which they had already seen there remained only the tiny room where Grete slept, an even tinier bathroom and a small square kitchen where they found Mama and Papa.

Mama, flushed and excited, was stirring something in a bowl. Papa was leaning against the window. He looked bothered and disapproving and as the children came in they heard him say, "Surely all this trouble can't be necessary."

The kitchen was full of smoke.

"Of course it's necessary!" said Mama. "What are the children going to eat?"

"Cheese and a glass of wine," said Papa, and the children burst into laughter while Mama cried, "Oh, you are hopelessly impractical!"

"I didn't know you could cook," said Anna. She had never before seen Mama in the kitchen.

"It'll be ready in five minutes," cried Mama,

stirring excitedly. "Oh, my potatoes . . .!" They were going to burn again, but she just caught them in time. "I'm making fried potatoes and scrambled eggs – I thought you'd like that."

"Lovely," said Max.

"Now where's the dish . . . and some salt . . . oh!" cried Mama, "I've got another lot of potatoes to do!" She looked appealingly at Papa. "Dearest, can you pass me the colander?"

"Which is the colander?" said Papa.

By the time the meal was ready on the table it was nearly an hour later and Anna felt so tired that she no longer cared whether she ate anything or not. But she did not like to say so as Mama had gone to so much trouble. She and Max ate their supper quickly and sleepily and then fell into bed.

Through the thin walls of the flat they could hear the murmur of voices and a clattering of dishes. Mama and Papa must be clearing the table.

"You know, it's funny," said Anna just before she went to sleep. "I remember when we lived in Berlin Heimpi used to make us fried potatoes with scrambled egg. She used to say it was quick and easy."

"I expect Mama needs more practice," said Max.

Chapter Thirteen

When Anna woke up in the morning it was bright daylight. Through a gap in the yellow curtains she could see a patch of windy sky above the rooftops. There was a smell of cooking and a clicking sound which she could not at first identify, until she realized that it was Papa typing in the room next door. Max's bed was empty. He must have crept out while she was still asleep. She got up and wandered out into the hall without bothering to dress. Mama and Grete must have been busy, for all the luggage had been cleared away and through the open door she could see that Mama's bed had been turned back into a sofa. Then Mama herself appeared from the dining-room.

"There you are, my darling," she said. "Come and have some breakfast, even though it's nearly lunch-time."

Max was already installed at the dining-room table, drinking milky coffee and pulling pieces off a long and incredibly thin loaf of bread.

"It's called a *baguette*," explained Mama, "that means a stick" – which was exactly what it looked like.

Anna tried some and found it delicious. The coffee was good too. There was a red oilcloth on the table which made the cups and plates look very pretty, and the room was warm in spite of the blustery November day outside.

"It's nice here," said Anna. "We wouldn't have been able to have breakfast in our pyjamas at the Gasthof Zwirn."

"It's a bit small," said Mama. "But we'll manage."

Max stretched himself and yawned. "It's nice having our own place."

There was something more that was nice. Anna could not at first think what it was. She looked at Mama pouring coffee and at Max tilting back his chair as he had been told a hundred times not to. Through the thin walls she could hear Papa's typewriter. Then it came to her.

"I don't really mind where we are," she said – "as long as we're all together."

In the afternoon Papa took them out. They

went on the Underground which was called the Metro and had a peculiar smell. Papa said it was a mixture of garlic and French cigarettes and Anna rather liked it. They saw the Eiffel Tower (but did not go up it because it would have cost too much) and the place where Napoleon was buried, and at last the Arc de Triomphe which was quite near home. By this time it was getting late, but Max noticed that you could go up to the top and that it was quite cheap, probably because it was not nearly as high as the Eiffel Tower – so they went.

No one else wanted to go to the top of the Arc de Triomphe on this cold, dark afternoon and the lift was empty. When Anna stepped out at the top she was met by an icy blast of wind and a prickle of raindrops and she wondered whether it had been a good idea to come. Then she looked down. It was as though she were standing at the centre of a huge sparkling star. Its rays stretched out in all directions and each one was a road lined with lights. When she looked closer she could see other lights which were cars and buses crawling along the roads, and immediately below they formed a bright ring circling the Arc de Triomphe itself. In the distance were the dim shapes of domes and spires and the twinkling spot which was the top of the Eiffel Tower.

"Isn't it beautiful?" said Papa. "Isn't this a beautiful city?"

Anna looked at Papa. His overcoat had lost a button and the wind was blowing through it, but Papa did not seem to notice.

"Beautiful," said Anna.

It was nice to get back to the warm flat, and this time Grete had helped Mama with the supper and it was ready in good time.

"Have you learned any French yet?" asked Mama.

"Of course not," said Grete before anyone else could answer. "It takes months."

But Anna and Max found that they had picked up quite a few words just from listening to Papa and other people. They could say *"oui"* and *"non"* and *"merci"* and *"au revoir"* and *"bonsoir Madame"*, and Max was particularly proud of *"trois billets s'il vous plaît"* which was what Papa had said when he bought tickets for the Metro.

"Well, you'll know a lot more soon," said Mama. "I've arranged for a lady to come and give you French lessons, and she's starting tomorrow afternoon."

The lady's name was Mademoiselle Martel and the following morning Anna and Max tried to collect everything they would need for her lesson. Papa lent them an old French dictionary and Mama found them some paper to write on. The only thing neither of them had was a pencil.

"You'll have to go and buy some," said Mama. "There's a shop at the corner of the street."

"But we can't speak French!" cried Anna.

"Nonsense," said Mama. "Take the dictionary with you. I'll give you a franc each and you can keep the change."

"What's the French for pencil?" asked Max.

"*Un crayon*," said Mama. Her voice did not sound as French as Papa's but she knew quite a lot of words. "Now off you go – quickly."

By the time they had travelled down in the lift by themselves – and it was Anna's turn to press the button – Anna felt quite bold about the enterprise, and her courage did not falter even when she found that the shop was rather grand and sold more office equipment than stationery. Clutching the dictionary under her arm she marched through the door ahead of Max and said in ringing tones. "*Bonsoir Madame!*"

The owner of the shop looked astonished and Max nudged her.

"That's not a *Madame* – that's a *Monsieur*," he whispered. "And I think *bonsoir* means good evening."

"Oh!" said Anna.

But the man who owned the shop did not seem to mind. He smiled and said something in French which they could not understand. They smiled back.

Then Anna said hopefully, "*Un crayon*," and Max added, "*S'il vous plaît*."

The man smiled again, searched in a cardboard

box behind the counter and produced a beautiful red pencil which he handed to Anna.

She was so amazed at her success that she forgot to say *"Merci"* and just stood there with the pencil in her hand. This was easy!

Then Max said, *"Un crayon,"* because he needed one too.

"Oui, oui," said the man, smiling and nodding and pointing to the pencil in Anna's hand. He agreed with Max that it was a pencil.

"Non!" said Max. *"Un crayon!"* He sought about for a way to explain. *"Un crayon,"* he cried, pointing to himself. *"Un crayon!"*

Anna giggled because it looked as though Max were introducing himself.

"Aah!" said the man. He took another pencil out of the box and handed it to Max with a little bow.

"Merci," said Max, much relieved. He gave the man the two francs and waited for the change. After a while it appeared that there wasn't any. Anna was very disappointed. It would have been nice to have some money.

"Let's ask him if he has any other pencils," she whispered. "They might be cheaper."

"We can't!" said Max.

"Well, let's just try," said Anna who was sometimes very pig-headed. "Look up the French for other."

Max leafed through the dictionary while the

man watched him curiously. At last he found it. "It's '*autre*'," he said.

Anna smiled brightly and held out her pencil to the man. "*Un autre crayon?*" she said.

"*Oui, oui,*" said the man after a moment's hesitation. He gave her another pencil from the box. Now she had two.

"*Non,*" said Anna, handing one of the pencils back to him. His smile was getting a bit frozen. "*Un autre crayon . . .*" – she made a face and a shape with her fingers to suggest something infinitely small and unimportant.

The man stared at her to see if she was going to do anything else. Then he shrugged his shoulders and said something hopeless in French.

"Come on!" said Max, pink with embarrassment.

"No!" said Anna. "Give me the dictionary!" She turned the pages feverishly. At last she found it. Cheap . . . *bon-marché*.

"*Un bon-marché crayon!*" she cried triumphantly, startling two ladies who were examining a typewriter. "*Un bon-marché crayon, s'il vous plaît!*"

The man looked very tired. He found another cardboard box and took from it a thinner blue pencil. He gave it to Anna who nodded and gave him back the red one. Then the man gave her twenty centimes change. Then he looked questioningly at Max.

"Oui!" said Anna excitedly. *"Un autre bon-marché crayon!"* and the procedure was repeated with Max's pencil.

"Merci," said Max.

The man just nodded. He seemed worn out.

"We've got twenty centimes each," said Anna. "Think of what we'll be able to buy with that!"

"I don't think it's very much," said Max.

"Still, it's better than nothing," said Anna. She wanted to show the man that she was grateful, so as they went out of the shop she smiled at him again and said, *"Bonsoir Madame!"*

Mademoiselle Martel arrived in the afternoon – a French lady in a neat grey suit, with a shaggy pepper and salt bun. She had been a school teacher and spoke a little German, a fact which so far had been of little interest to anyone. But now Paris was suddenly crowded with refugees from Hitler, all eager to learn French, and she was run off her feet trying to give them all lessons. Perhaps, thought Anna, this was the reason for the perpetual expression of mild surprise on her slightly faded face.

She was a good teacher. Right from the beginning she spoke French to the children nearly the whole of the time, using sign language and mime when they did not understand.

"Le nez," she would say, pointing to her well powdered nose, *"la main"*, pointing to her hand,

and "*les doigts*", wiggling her fingers. Then she would write the words down for them and they would practise spelling and pronouncing them until they knew them. Occasionally there were misunderstandings, such as when she said "*les cheveux*", pointing to her hair. Max became convinced that *cheveux* meant bun and burst into embarrassed giggles when she asked him to point out his own *cheveux*.

On the days when she did not come to give them a lesson they did homework. At first they just learned new words but after quite a short time Mademoiselle Martel demanded that they write little stories in French.

How could they? asked Anna. They didn't know enough French.

Mademoiselle Martel tapped the dictionary with her finger. "*Le dictionnaire*," she said firmly.

It turned out to be a terrible struggle. They had to look up almost every word and it took Anna nearly all morning to write half a page. Then, when she showed it to Mademoiselle Martel at their next lesson, most of it was wrong anyway.

"Never mind, it will come," said Mademoiselle Martel in one of her rare excursions into German, and "Never mind, it will come!" Max said mockingly to Anna the following day, when she was still struggling after more than an hour to put down some boring incident between a dog and a cat.

148

"What about you? You haven't done yours yet, either," said Anna crossly.

"Yes I have," said Max. "A page and a bit."

"I don't believe it."

"Look for yourself!"

It was quite true. He had written more than a page and it all looked like French.

"What does it mean?" Anna asked suspiciously.

Max translated with a flourish.

"Once a boy had his birthday. Many people came. They had a big feast. They ate fish, meat, butter, bread, eggs, sugar, strawberries, lobsters, ice cream, tomatoes, flour . . ."

"They wouldn't eat flour," said Anna.

"You don't know what they ate," said Max. "Anyway I'm not sure that word is flour. I looked it up at the time but I've forgotten."

"Is all this a list of what they ate?" asked Anna, pointing to the page crawling with commas.

"Yes," said Max.

"What is this last bit?" There was just one sentence at the end which had no commas in it.

"That's the best part," said Max proudly. "I think it means 'then they all burst'."

Mademoiselle Martel read Max's composition without batting an eyelid. She said she could see it had increased his vocabulary. But she was less pleased when, for the following day's homework, he produced an almost identical piece. This one began "Once there was a wedding," and the food the wedding guests ate was different, but it ended with everyone bursting as before. Mademoiselle Martel frowned and drummed her fingers on the dictionary. Then she told Max very firmly that he must write something different next time.

Next morning the children were sitting at the dining-room table with their books spread out on the red oilcloth as usual. Anna was wrestling with a piece about a man who had a horse and a cat. The man liked the cat and the cat liked the horse and the horse liked the man but it did not like the cat . . . It was sickening stuff to be turning out when there were so many interesting things she could have written about if only she had been able to write in German.

Max was not writing anything at all, but staring into space. When Grete came in and told them to clear their things away because she wanted to lay the table for lunch his sheet of paper was still blank.

"But it's only twelve o'clock!" cried Anna.

"I shan't have time to do it later," said Grete crossly as usual.

"Well, there's nowhere else we can work – this is the only table," said Max – and they prevailed on her, with difficulty to let them keep it a little longer.

"What are you going to do?" asked Anna. "We want to go out this afternoon."

Max seemed to come to a decision. "Pass me the dictionary," he said.

As he leafed through it briskly (they were both becoming very practised at this) Anna heard him murmuring "funeral" under his breath.

When Mademoiselle Martel came to give them their next lesson she read Max's composition in silence. Max had done his best to introduce variety into his basic theme. The funeral guests in his story – no doubt carried away by grief – ate paper, pepper, penguins, pemmican and peaches in addition to less exotic foodstuffs, and after his usual punch line about how they all burst at the end Max had added the words, "So there were many more funerals."

Mademoiselle Martel did not speak at all for a few moments. Then she gave Max a long, hard look and said, "Young man, you need a change."

When Mama came in at the end of the lesson as she often did to ask how the children were getting on, Mademoiselle Martel made a little speech. She said she had taught them now for three weeks and that they had made good progress. But the time had come when they would learn more by being with other children and hearing French spoken all round them.

Mama nodded. Clearly she had been thinking the same thing.

"It's nearly Christmas," she said. "Perhaps you

would give them one or two more lessons before the holidays, and then they can start school."

Even Max worked hard during the remaining time. The prospect of going to a school where no one spoke anything but French was rather daunting.

And then Christmas was upon them. Grete went home to Austria for a holiday a few days before, and as Mama was busy cooking the flat soon became rather dusty. But it was so much pleasanter without Grete's grumpy presence that no one minded. Anna looked forward to Christmas and dreaded it all at the same time. She looked forward to it because you couldn't not look forward to Christmas, but she was also terribly afraid that it would make her think of Berlin and of what Christmas used to be like – what it had been like even the year before.

"Do you think we'll have a tree?" she asked Max. In Berlin there had always been a big tree in the hall, and one of the delights of Christmas had been to recognize the many coloured glass balls, the birds with the feathery tails and the trumpets which you could actually blow, as they reappeared each year to decorate it.

"I don't think the French go in for Christmas trees very much," said Max.

However, Mama managed to get one just the same. When Papa called the children at tea-time on Christmas Eve for the celebrations to begin and they rushed into the dining-room, it was the first thing Anna saw. It was only a little tree – about two feet high – and instead of glass ornaments Mama had hung it with tinsel and covered it with little candles. But it looked so pretty, shining green and silver above the red oil-cloth of the table, that Anna suddenly knew that Christmas would be all right.

Presents were modest compared with previous years, but perhaps because everyone needed them more they enjoyed them just as much. Anna had a new paint box and Max a fountain pen. Omama had sent some money and Mama had bought Anna new shoes with her share. Anna had had to try them on in the shop, so they were not a surprise – but Mama had hidden them away immediately afterwards so that they would still be new for Christmas. They were thick brown leather with gold buckles and she felt very grand in them. She also had a pencil sharpener in a little case and a pair of hand-knitted red socks from Frau Zwirn, and when she thought she had seen all her presents she found one more – a very small parcel from Onkel Julius.

Anna opened it carefully and gave an exclamation of delight. "It's lovely!" she cried. "What is it?"

Nestling in the tissue paper was a short silver chain hung with tiny animals. There were a lion, a horse, a cat, a bird, an elephant and of course a monkey.

"It's a charm bracelet," said Mama, fastening it round her wrist. "How nice of Julius!"

"There's a letter with it," said Max, handing it over. Anna read it out.

"Dear Anna," it said, "I hope this little present will remind you of our many visits to the Berlin Zoo. It is not nearly so nice going there without you. Please give my love to your dear Aunt Alice. I hope she is well. Tell her I think of her often, and of her good advice which I should perhaps have taken. My love to you all. Yours, Onkel Julius."

"What does it mean?" asked Anna. "We haven't got an Aunt Alice."

Papa took the letter from her. "I think he means me," he said. "He calls me Aunt Alice because the Nazis often open letters and he could get into bad trouble if they knew that he was writing to me."

"What advice did you give him?" asked Max.

"I told him to leave Germany," said Papa and added under his breath, "Poor Julius."

"I'll write and thank him," cried Anna, "and I'll paint him a picture with my new paint box."

"Yes," said Papa, "and tell him Aunt Alice sends her love."

Then suddenly Mama made a sound with which by now they were all familiar.

154

"My chicken!" she cried and rushed off to the kitchen. But it had not burned and soon they were sitting down to a real Christmas dinner, all cooked by Mama. As well as the chicken there were roast potatoes and carrots, and apple flan with cream to follow. Mama was becoming quite a good cook. She had even made gingerbread hearts because they belonged to a proper German Christmas. There was something wrong with them and they had gone soggy instead of being hard and crisp, but they tasted quite nice just the same.

At the end of the meal Papa poured them all some wine and they drank a toast.

"To our new life in France!" he said and they all repeated. "To our new life in France."

Mama did not actually drink any of the wine because she said it all tasted like ink to her, but Anna liked it and drank a whole glassful. Her head felt muzzy when she finally got to bed and she had to close her eyes to stop the yellow lampshade and the wardrobe from whirling round and round.

It had been a nice Christmas, she thought. And soon she would go to school and find out what living in France was really like.

Chapter Fourteen

Anna did not go to school quite as soon as she had expected. Mama had arranged for Max to start at a *lycée* for boys early in January – a *lycée* was a French high school – but there were only very few *lycées* for girls in Paris and these were all full, with long waiting lists.

"We can't afford a private school," said Mama, "and I don't think it would be a good idea for you to go to an *école communale*."

"Why not?" asked Anna.

"They're for children who are going to leave school very early and I don't think the education is as good," said Mama. "For instance, you wouldn't be taught Latin."

"I don't need to learn Latin," said Anna. "I'll

have my hands full trying to learn French. I'd just like to go to school!"

But Mama said, "There's no rush. Give me a little while to look around."

So Max went to school and Anna stayed at home. Max's school was almost on the other side of Paris. He had to take the Metro early in the morning and did not get back till after five. Mama had chosen it, although it was so far away, because the boys there played football twice a week. At most French schools there was no time for games – only work.

The flat seemed dull and empty on the first day without Max. In the morning Anna went with Mama to do the shopping. The weather was bright and cold and she had grown so much in the past year that there was a huge gap between the top of her knitted socks and the hem of her winter coat. Mama looked at Anna's goose-fleshy legs and sighed.

"I don't know what we're going to do about clothes for you," she said.

"I'm all right," said Anna. "I'm wearing the sweater you made me."

This sweater, owing to Mama's curious technique of knitting, had turned out so large and thick and dense that no cold could penetrate it, and was a most useful garment. The fact that only a few centimetres of Anna's skirt protruded below it did not seem to matter.

"Well, if you're sure you're warm enough we'll go to the market," said Mama. "Everything is cheaper there."

The market turned out to be some distance away and Anna carried Mama's string bag while they walked through a number of winding little streets, until at last they emerged into a bustling road lined with shops and stalls. The stalls sold everything from vegetables to haberdashery and Mama insisted on inspecting them all before she bought anything, so as to be sure of getting the best value for her money.

The owners of shops and stalls alike were crying their wares, holding them up for people to see, and sometimes it was quite difficult for Anna and Mama to walk past, as onions and beautifully clean-scrubbed carrots were thrust in front of them to admire. Some shops specialized in only a few foods. One sold nothing but cheese, and there must have been at least thirty different kinds, all carefully wrapped in muslin, displayed on a trestle table on the pavement.

Suddenly, just as Mama was about to buy a red cabbage, Anna heard a strange French voice addressing them. It belonged to a lady in a green coat. She carried a bag bulging with purchases and was smiling at Anna with very friendly brown eyes. Mama, still thinking about the cabbage, did not recognize her for a moment. Then she cried,

"Madame Fernand!" in a pleased voice and they all shook hands.

Madame Fernand did not speak any German but she and Mama talked in French to each other. Anna noticed that although Mama's voice still did not sound very French she was talking more fluently than when they had first arrived. Then Madame Fernand asked Anna whether she could speak French, pronouncing the words so slowly and clearly that Anna could understand.

"A little," said Anna, and Madame Fernand clapped her hands and cried, "Very good!" and told her that she had a perfect French accent.

Mama was still holding the red cabbage which she had been about to buy and Madame Fernand took it from her gently and put it back on the stall. Then she led Mama round the corner to another stall which they must have missed and which had much better red cabbages for less money. Prompted by Madame Fernand Mama bought not only a red cabbage but quite a lot of other vegetables and fruit, and before she left them Madame Fernand presented Anna with a banana, "To strengthen her for the walk home," as Mama translated.

Mama and Anna were both much cheered by the encounter. Mama had met Madame Fernand and her journalist husband when she had first come to Paris with Papa and liked them both very much. Now Madame Fernand had asked her to ring up if she needed help or advice on anything. Her husband was going away for a few weeks but as soon as he got back she wanted Mama and Papa to come to dinner. Mama seemed very pleased at the prospect. "They're such nice people," she said, "and it would be lovely to have some friends in Paris."

They finished their shopping and carried it home. Anna said *"Bonjour Madame,"* to the concierge, hoping that she would notice her perfect French accent, and chattered cheerfully to Mama on the way up in the lift. But as they entered the flat she remembered that Max was at school and the day suddenly felt dull again. She helped Mama unpack the shopping but after that she could think of nothing to do.

Grete was washing some clothes in the bathroom and for a moment Anna wondered whether to go and talk to her. But Grete was grumpier than ever since her holiday in Austria. She thought everything in France was awful. The language was impossible, the people were dirty, the food was too rich – nothing suited her. In addition Grete's mother had extracted several more promises from her during her stay at home. Apart from always having to get her proper sleep Grete had promised her mother to be careful of her back, which meant that she could only wash the floors very slowly and not at all in the corners, and not to strain her wrists. She had also promised always to have a good lunch, to rest when she was tired and never to catch cold.

Grete was very anxious to keep all these promises which were constantly being threatened by requests from Mama and the rest of the family, and they cropped up in her conversation almost as often as her disapproval of the French.

Anna did not feel she could face her just now and she wandered back to Mama in the kitchen and said, "What shall I do?"

"You could read some French," said Mama.

Mademoiselle Martel had left a book of stories for Anna to read, and she sat down in the dining-room and struggled with it for a while. But it was meant for children much younger than herself and it was depressing to sit working away with the dictionary by her side, only to discover that Pierre had thrown a stick at his little sister and that his mother had called him a naughty boy.

Lunch came as a relief and Anna helped to put the things on the table and to clear them away afterwards. Then she did some painting, but still the time passed terribly slowly until at last, well after five o'clock, the door bell rang to announce Max's return. Anna rushed to let him in and found Mama already at the door.

"Well, how was it?" cried Mama.

"All right," said Max, but he looked white and tired.

"Isn't it nice?" asked Anna.

"How do I know?" said Max crossly. "I can't understand a word anyone says."

He was silent and morose for the rest of the evening. Only after supper he suddenly said to Mama, "I've got to have a proper French briefcase." He kicked the German satchel which he normally carried strapped to his back. "If I go round carrying this I even *look* different from everyone else."

Anna knew that briefcases were expensive and without thinking she said, "But your satchel was only new last year!"

"What's that to do with you?" shouted Max. "You don't know anything about it, sitting at home all day!"

"It isn't my fault that I don't go to school!" Anna shouted back. "Just because Mama can't find one for me to go to."

"Well, until you do go you can shut up!" cried Max, and after this they did not speak to each other any more even though Mama, to Anna's surprise, promised to let Max have the briefcase.

It was miserable, thought Anna. She had been looking forward to Max coming home all day, and now they'd had a row. She was determined that next day should be different, but it turned out much the same. Max came home so tired and irritable that before long they had another quarrel.

* * *

162

Then, to make it worse, the weather turned wet and Anna got a cold so that she could not go out. She began to feel cooped up in the flat day after day, and by evening both she and Max were so bad-tempered that they could hardly say a civil word to each other. Max felt it was unfair that he should have to struggle through long difficult days at school while Anna stayed at home, and Anna felt that Max was making enormous headway in this new world they were going to live in and worried in case she might never catch up.

"If only I could go to school – just anywhere!" Anna said to Mama.

"You can't go just anywhere," said Mama crossly. She had looked at several schools but none of them had been any good. She had even asked Madame Fernand. It was a very depressing time.

Papa was tired too. He had been working hard and had caught Anna's cold, and now he had started having nightmares again. Mama said that he had had them before, but at the Gasthof Zwirn the children had not been aware of them. He always dreamt the same thing – that he was trying to get out of Germany and was being stopped by the Nazis at the frontier. Then he woke up shouting.

Max was such a heavy sleeper that Papa's nightmares did not disturb him, even though Papa's room was next door, but Anna always heard him and it distressed her dreadfully. If Papa had woken up quickly with one big shout it would not have been so bad. But the nightmares always started slowly with Papa moaning and making frightening grunting sounds until at last they exploded into a great cry.

The first time it happened Anna thought Papa must be ill. She ran into his room and stood helplessly by his bed, calling for Mama. But even when Mama had explained to her about the nightmares and Papa had told her not to worry, she felt just as bad about them. It seemed terrible to lie in bed listening to Papa and knowing that in his dreams awful things were happening to him.

One night after she had gone to bed Anna wished very hard that Papa could stop having nightmares.

"Please, please," she whispered – for though she did not exactly believe in God she always hoped that there might be someone who could arrange these things – "Oh please let me have nightmares instead of Papa!" Then she lay quite still, waiting to fall asleep, but nothing happened.

Max cuddled his pillow close to his face, sighed twice and immediately dropped off. But what seemed like hours later Anna was still lying there, staring at the dark ceiling and wide awake. She began to feel very cross. How could she have a nightmare if she could not even go to sleep? She had tried doing sums in her head and to think of all sorts of boring things, but nothing had been any use. Perhaps it would help if she got up for a drink of water? But her bed was so comfortable that she decided against it.

However, she must have got up after all in the end, for she suddenly found herself in the hall. She was no longer thirsty, so she thought she would go down in the lift to see what the street looked like in the middle of the night. To her surprise she found the concierge asleep in a hammock slung across the front door and had to ease her aside in order to get out. Then the door slammed behind her – she hoped the concierge would not wake up – and she was in the street.

It was very quiet and there was a curious brown glow over everything that she had never seen before. Two men hurried past, carrying a Christmas tree.

"Better get inside," said one of them. "It's coming!"

"What's coming?" asked Anna, but the men disappeared round the corner and at the same time she could hear a shuffling sound from the opposite direction. The brown glow became stronger and then a huge, long creature heaved into view at the top of the street. Although it was so vast there was something familiar about it and Anna suddenly realized that it was Pumpel, grown to gigantic proportions. The shuffling sound was made by his legs and he looked at Anna with his little spiteful eyes and licked his lips.

"Oh, no!" said Anna.

She tried to run away, but the air had become leaden and she could not move. Pumpel started towards her.

There was a flurry of wheels and a policeman shot past on his bicycle, his cape flying behind him.

"Count its legs!" he shouted as he passed her. "It's your only chance!"

How could she count Pumpel's legs? He was like a centipede – his legs were everywhere, moving in great ripples on either side of his long body.

"One, two, three . . ." Anna began hurriedly, but it was hopeless – Pumpel was still coming towards her, and now she could see his nasty sharp teeth.

She would have to guess.

"Ninety-seven!" she cried, but still Pumpel kept coming and suddenly she realized that since they were in Paris, of course he would expect her to count in French. What was the French for ninety-seven? Her mind was blank, panicked.

"*Quatre-vingts* . . ." she stammered as Pumpel was nearly upon her . . . "*Quatre-vingts dix-sept!*" she shouted triumphantly and found herself sitting bolt upright in bed.

Everything was quiet and she could hear Max breathing peacefully on the other side of the room. Her heart was thumping and her chest felt so tight that she could hardly move. But it was all right. She was safe. It had only been a dream.

Someone on the opposite side of the courtyard still had a light on and it made a pale golden rectangle on the curtains. She could see the dim outlines of her clothes piled on a chair ready for the morning. There was no sound from Papa's room. She lay basking in the beautiful familiarity of it all until she felt calm and sleepy. And then, with a surge of triumph, she remembered. She had had a nightmare! She had had a nightmare and Papa hadn't! Perhaps it had really worked! She snuggled down happily, and the next thing she knew it was morning and Max was getting dressed.

"Did you have any bad dreams last night?" she asked Papa at breakfast.

"Not a thing," said Papa. "I think I've got over them."

Anna never told anyone, but she always felt that it was she who had cured Papa's nightmares – and curiously enough, after that day, neither she nor Papa had any more of them.

One evening a few days later Anna and Max had a worse row than usual. Max had come home to find Anna's drawing things all over the dining-room table and there was no room for his homework.

"Get this rubbish out of the way!" he shouted, and Anna shouted back, "It's not rubbish! Just because you go to school, you're not the only person who matters in this house!"

Mama was talking on the telephone and she called to them through the door to be quiet.

"Well, I certainly matter a lot more than you," said Max in a fierce whisper. "You just sit about all day doing nothing!"

"I don't," whispered Anna. "I draw and I lay the table . . ."

"I draw and I lay the table," Max mimicked her in a particularly hateful way. "You're nothing but a parasite!"

This was too much for Anna. She was not sure what a parasite was but she had a vague impression that it was something disgusting that grew on trees. As Mama put down the receiver, she burst into tears.

Mama sorted things out briskly as usual. Max must not call Anna names – anyway it was silly to call her a parasite – and Anna must clear away her things and make room for Max's homework.

Then she added, "In any case, if Max called you a parasite just because he goes to school and you don't, there'll soon be an end to that."

Anna stopped in the middle of putting her crayons back in their box.

"Why?" she asked.

"That was Madame Fernand on the telephone," said Mama. "She says she has heard of a very good little *école communale* not too far from here. So with luck you'll be able to start next week."

Chapter Fifteen

On the following Monday Anna set off with
Mama to the *école communale*. Anna was carrying
her satchel and a cardboard case containing sandwiches for her lunch. Under her winter coat she
wore a black pleated overall which Mama had
bought her at the headmistress's suggestion. She
was very proud of this overall and thought how
lucky it was that her coat was too short to cover
it, so that everyone could see it.

They went on the Metro, but although it was
only a short distance they had to change twice.
"Next time I think we'll try walking," said Mama.
"It will be cheaper, too." The school was just off
the Champs Elysées, a beautiful wide avenue with
glittering shops and cafés, and it was surprising

to find the old-fashioned gate marked *Ecole de Filles* tucked away at the back of all this grandeur. The building was dark and had clearly been there a long time. They crossed the empty playground and the sound of singing drifted down from one of the classrooms. School had already begun. As Anna climbed up the stone stairs at Mama's side to meet the headmistress, she suddenly wondered what on earth it would all be like.

The headmistress was tall and brisk. She shook hands with Anna and explained something to Mama in French which Mama translated. She was sorry that there was no one who spoke German in the school but hoped that Anna would soon learn French. Then Mama said, "See you at four o'clock," and Anna could hear her heels clattering down the stairs while she was left standing in the headmistress's study.

The headmistress smiled at Anna. Anna smiled back. But it is difficult to smile at someone without talking and after a few moments her face began to feel stiff. The headmistress must have felt stiff too, for she suddenly switched her smile off. Her fingers were drumming on the desk and she seemed to be listening for something, but nothing happened, and Anna was just beginning to wonder whether they would be there all day when there was a knock at the door.

The headmistress called *"Entrez!"* and a small dark-haired girl of about Anna's own age appeared. The headmistress exclaimed something that Anna thought probably meant "at last!" and launched into a long, cross tirade. Then she turned to Anna and told her that the other girl's name was Colette and something else which might or might not have meant that Colette was going to look after her. Then she said something more and Colette started for the door. Anna, not knowing whether she was meant to follow or not, stayed where she was.

"*Allez! Allez!*" cried the headmistress, waving her hands at her as though she were shooing away a fly, and Colette took Anna's hand and led her out of the room.

As soon as the door closed behind them Colette made a face at it and said "*Ouf!*" Anna was pleased that she, too, found the headmistress a bit much. She hoped all the teachers were not going to be like her. Then she followed Colette along a passage and through various doors. She could hear the murmur of French voices from one of the classrooms. Others were silent – the children must be writing or doing sums. They came to a cloakroom and Colette showed her where to hang her coat, admired her German satchel and pointed out that Anna's black overall was exactly like her own – all in rapid French supplemented by sign language. Anna could not understand any of the words, but she guessed what Colette meant.

Then Colette led her through another door and Anna found herself in a large room crammed with desks. There must be at least forty girls, Anna thought. They were all wearing black overalls and this, combined with the gentle gloom of the classroom, gave the whole scene a mournful look.

The girls had been reciting something in unison, but when Anna came in with Colette they all stopped and stared at her. Anna stared back, but she was beginning to feel rather small and suddenly wondered, violently, whether she was really going to like this school. She held on tight to her satchel and her sandwich box and tried to look as though she did not care.

Then there was a hand on her shoulder. A faint smell of scent with just a tinge of garlic enveloped her and she found herself looking into a very friendly, wrinkled face surrounded by frizzy black hair.

"*Bonjour*, Anna," said the face slowly and clearly so that Anna could understand. "I am your teacher. I am called Madame Socrate."

"*Bonjour, Madame*," said Anna in a low voice.

"Very good!" cried Madame Socrate. She waved her hand towards the rows of desks and added slowly and clearly as before. "These girls are in your class," and something about "friends".

Anna removed her eyes from Madame Socrate and risked a quick glance sideways. The girls were no longer staring but smiling and she felt much better. Then Colette led her to a desk next to her own, Madame Socrate said something, and the girls – all except Anna – began to recite in unison again.

Anna sat and let the sound drone over her. She wondered what they were reciting. It was strange to be having a lesson at school without even knowing what it was about. As she listened she detected some numbers among the droning. Was it a multiplication table? No, there were not nearly enough numbers. She glanced at the book on Colette's desk. There was a picture of a king with a crown on the cover. Then it came to her, just as Madame Socrate clapped her hands for the recitation to stop. It was history! The numbers were dates and it had been a history lesson! For some reason this discovery made her feel very pleased.

The girls were now taking exercise books out of their desks and Anna was given a brand-new one. The next lesson was dictation. Anna recognized the word because once or twice Mademoiselle Martel had dictated a few simple words to her and Max. But this was a very different matter. There were long sentences and Anna had no idea what any of them meant. She did not know where one sentence ended and another began – not even where one word ended and another began. It seemed hopeless to embark on it – but it would look even worse if she just sat without writing at all. So she did what she could to translate the incomprehensible sounds into letters arranged in what seemed like possible groups. After she had covered most of a page in this strange manner the dictation came to an end, the books were collected, a bell rang and it was time for break.

Anna put on her coat and followed Colette into the playground – a paved rectangle surrounded by railings which was already filling up with other girls. It was a cold day and they were running and skipping about to keep warm. As soon as Anna appeared with Colette, a number of them crowded round and Colette introduced them. There were Claudine, Marcelle, Micheline, Françoise, Madeleine . . . it was impossible to remember all their names, but they all smiled and held out their hands to Anna and she felt very grateful for their friendliness.

Then they played a singing game. They linked arms and sang and skipped forwards, backwards and sideways in time to the tune. It looked rather tame at first, but as the game went on they went faster and faster until at last they got into such a tangel that they collapsed in a heap, laughing and out of breath. The first time they did this Anna stood and watched, but the second time Colette took her hand and led her to the end of the row. She linked arms with Françoise – or it might have been Micheline – and did her best to follow the steps. When she went wrong everybody laughed, but in a friendly way. When she got it right they were delighted. She became hot and excited, and as a result of her mistakes the game ended in an even bigger muddle than before. Colette was laughing so much that she had to sit down and Anna was laughing too. She suddenly realized how long it was since she had really played with other children. It was lovely to be back at school. By the end of break she was even singing the words of the song, though she had no idea what any of them meant.

When they went back into the classroom Madame Socrate had covered the blackboard with sums and Anna's spirits rose. At least for this she did not need to know French. She worked away at them until the bell went and morning school was over.

Lunch was eaten in a small, warm kitchen under the supervision of a large lady called Clothilde. Nearly all the children lived near enough to go home to eat and there was only one other, much younger girl who stayed, apart from a little boy of about three who seemed to belong to Clothilde.

Anna ate her sandwiches but the other girl had meat, vegetables and a pudding, all of which Clothilde cheerfully heated up for her on the stove. It looked a much nicer lunch than her own and Clothilde thought so too. She made a face at the sandwiches as though they were poison, crying, "Not good! Not good!" and gave Anna to understand, with much pointing to the cooker, that another time she should bring a proper lunch.

"*Oui*," said Anna and even ventured "*Demain*", which meant tomorrow, and Clothilde nodded her fat face and beamed.

Just as they were coming to the end of this exchange which had taken some time, the door opened and Madame Socrate came in.

"Ah," she said in her slow, clear voice. "You are speaking French. That is good."

Clothilde's little boy ran up to her. "I can speak French!" he cried.

"Yes, but you can't speak German," said Madame Socrate and tickled his little tummy so that he squealed with delight.

Then she beckoned to Anna to follow her. They went back to the classroom and Madame Socrate sat down at a desk with Anna. She spread the morning's work out in front of them and pointed to the arithmetic.

"Very good!" she said. Anna had got nearly all of it right. Then Madame Socrate pointed to the dictation, "Very bad!" she said, but made such a funny face as she said it that Anna did not mind. Anna looked at her book. Her dictation had disappeared under a sea of red ink. Nearly every word was wrong. Madame Socrate had had to write the whole piece out again. At the bottom of the page it said in red, "142 mistakes" and Madame Socrate pointed to the number looking amazed and impressed, as though it were a record – which it probably was. Then she smiled, patted Anna on the back and asked her to copy the corrected version. Anna did so very carefully, and though she still could only understand very little of what she had written it was nice to have something in her book that was not all crossed out.

In the afternoon there was art and Anna drew a cat which was much admired. She gave it to Colette for being so kind to her and Colette told her in her usual mixture of quick French and dumb-show that she would pin it up on the wall of her bedroom.

When Mama came to fetch her at four o'clock Anna was very cheerful.

"How was school?" asked Mama, and Anna said, "Lovely!"

She did not realize until she got home how tired she was, but that evening, for the first time in weeks, she and Max did not have a row. It was exhausting going back to school again the next day, and the day after that, but the following day was Thursday when no one goes to school in France and she and Max both had a whole day off.

"What shall we do?" asked Max.

"Let's take our pocket money to Prisunic,"

said Anna. This was a store she and Mama had discovered on one of their shopping expeditions. Everything in it was very cheap – in fact nothing in the whole store cost more than ten francs. There were toys, household goods, stationery and even some clothes. Anna and Max spent a happy hour finding all the different things they could afford, from a cake of soap to half a pair of socks, and finally emerged with two spinning tops. In the afternoon the played with them in a little square near home till it got dark.

"Do you like your school?" Max suddenly asked as they were walking back.

"Yes," said Anna. "Everybody is very nice, and they don't mind if I can't understand what they say. Why? Don't you like yours?"

"Oh yes," said Max. "They're nice to me too, and I'm even beginning to understand French."

They walked in silence a little way and then suddenly burst out with, "But there's one thing I absolutely hate!"

"What?" asked Anna.

"Well – doesn't it bother you?" said Max. "I mean – being so different from everyone else?"

"No," said Anna. Then she looked at Max. He was wearing a pair of outgrown shorts and had turned them up to make them even shorter. There was a scarf dashingly tucked into the collar of his jacket and his hair was brushed in an unfamiliar way.

"You look exactly like a French boy," said Anna.

Max brightened for a moment. Then he said, "But I can't speak like one."

"Well, of course you can't, after such a short time," said Anna. "I suppose sooner or later we'll both learn to speak French properly."

Max stumped along grimly.

Then he said, "Well, in my case it's definitely going to be sooner rather than later!"

He looked so fierce that even Anna who knew him well was surprised at the determination in his face.

Chapter Sixteen

One Thursday afternoon a few weeks after Anna
had started school she and Mama went to visit
Great-Aunt Sarah. Great-Aunt Sarah was Omama's sister but had married a Frenchman, now
deceased, and had lived in Paris for thirty years.
Mama, who had not seen her since she was a little
girl, put on her best clothes for the occasion. She
looked very young and pretty in her good coat
and her blue hat with the veil, and as they walked
towards the Avenue Foch where Great-Aunt
Sarah lived, several people turned round to look
at her.

Anna had put on her best clothes too. She was
wearing the sweater Mama had knitted, her new
shoes and socks, and Onkel Julius's bracelet, but

her skirt and coat were horribly short. Mama sighed, as always, at the sight of Anna in her outdoor things.

"I'll have to ask Madame Fernand to do something with your coat," she said. "If you grow any more it won't even cover your pants."

"What could Madame Fernand do?" asked Anna.

"I don't know – stitch a bit of material round the hem or something," said Mama. "I wish I knew how to do these things, like her!"

Mama and Papa had been to dinner with the Fernands the previous week and Mama had come back bursting with admiration. In addition to being a wonderful cook Madame Fernand made all her own and her daughter's clothes. She had re-upholstered a sofa and made her husband a beautiful dressing-gown. She had even made him some pyjamas when he could not find the colour he wanted in the shops.

"And she does it all so easily," said Mama, for whom sewing on a button was a major undertaking – "as though it weren't work at all."

Madame Fernand had offered to help with Anna's clothes, too, but Mama had felt perhaps that would be too much to accept. Now, however, seeing Anna stick out of her coat in all directions, she changed her mind.

"I will ask her," she said. "If she just showed

me how to do it perhaps I could manage it myself."

By this time they had arrived at their destination. Great-Aunt Sarah lived in a large house set back from the road. They had to cross a courtyard planted with trees to reach it and the concierge who directed them to her flat wore a uniform with gold buttons and braid. Great-Aunt Sarah's lift was made of plate glass and carried them swiftly upwards without any of the groans and shudders Anna was used to, and her front door was opened by a maid in a frilly white apron and cap.

"I'll tell Madam you're here," said the maid, and Mama sat on a little velvet chair while the maid went into what must be the drawing room. As she opened the door they could hear a buzz of voices and Mama looked worried and said, "I hope this is the right day . . ." But almost at once the door opened again and Great-Aunt Sarah ran out. She was a stout old lady but she moved at a brisk trot and for a moment Anna wondered whether she would be able to stop when she reached them.

"Nu," she cried, throwing her heavy arms round Mama. "So here you are at last! Such a long time I haven't seen you – and such dreadful things happening in Germany. Still, you're safe and well and that's all that matters." She relapsed into another velvet chair, overflowing on all sides, and said to Anna, "Do you know that the last time I saw your Mama she was only a little girl? And now she has a little girl of her own. What's your name?"

"Anna," said Anna.

"Hannah – how nice. A good Jewish name," said Great-Aunt Sarah.

"No, Anna," said Anna.

"Oh, Anna. That's a nice name too. You must excuse me," said Great-Aunt Sarah, leaning perilously towards her on the little chair, "but I'm a bit deaf." Her eyes took in Anna properly for the first time and she looked astonished. "Goodness child," she exclaimed. "Such long legs you have! Aren't they cold?"

"No," said Anna. "But Mama says if I grow any more my coat won't even cover my pants."

As soon as the words were out of her mouth, she wished she had not said them. It was not the sort of thing one said to a great-aunt one hardly knew.

"What?" said Great-Aunt Sarah.

Anna could feel herself blushing.

"A moment," said Great-Aunt Sarah and suddenly from somewhere about her person, she produced an object like a trumpet. "There," she said, putting the thin end not to her mouth as Anna had half-expected, but to her ear. "Now say it again, child – very loudly – into my trumpet."

Anna tried desperately to think of something

quite different that she could say instead and that would still make sense, but her mind remained blank. There was nothing for it.

"Mama says," she shouted into the ear trumpet, "that if I grow any more my coat won't even cover my pants!"

When she withdrew her face she could feel that she had gone scarlet.

Great-Aunt Sarah seemed taken aback for a moment. Then her face crumpled up and a noise somewhere between a wheeze and a chuckle escaped from it.

"Quite right!" she cried, her black eyes dancing. "Your mama is quite right! But what is she going to do about it, eh?" Then she added to Mama, "Such a funny child – such a nice funny child you have!" And rising from the chair with surprising agility she said, "So now you must come and have some tea. There are some old ladies here who have been playing bridge, but I'll soon get rid of them" – and she led the way, at a gentle gallop, into the drawing room.

The first thing that struck Anna about Great-Aunt Sarah's old ladies was that they all looked a good deal younger than Great-Aunt Sarah. There were about a dozen of them, all elegantly dressed with elaborate hats. They had finished playing bridge – Anna could see the card tables pushed back against the wall – and were now drinking tea and helping themselves to tiny biscuits which the maid was handing round on a silver tray.

"Every Thursday they come," whispered Great-Aunt Sarah in German. "Poor old things, they have nothing better to do. But they're all very rich and they give me money for my needy children."

Anna, who had only just got over her surprise at Great-Aunt Sarah's old ladies, found it even more difficult to imagine her with needy children – or indeed with any children at all – but she did not have time to ponder the problem for she was being loudly introduced along with Mama.

"My niece and her daughter have come from Germany," shouted Great-Aunt Sarah in French but with a strong German accent. "Say bong-shour!" she whispered to Anna.

"*Bonjour*," said Anna.

Great-Aunt Sarah threw up her hands in admiration. "Listen to the child!" she cried. "Only a few weeks she has been in Paris and already she speaks French better than I!"

Anna found it difficult to keep up this impression when one of the ladies tried to engage her in conversation, but she was saved from further efforts when Great-Aunt Sarah's voice boomed out again.

"I have not seen my niece for years," she shouted, "and I have been longing to have a talk with her."

At this the ladies hurriedly drank up their tea and began to make their farewells. As they shook hands with Great-Aunt Sarah they dropped some money into a box which she held out to them, and she thanked them. Anna wondered just how many needy children Great-Aunt Sarah had got. Then the maid escorted the ladies to the door and at last they had all disappeared.

It was nice and quiet without them, but Anna noticed with regret that the silver tray with the little biscuits had disappeared along with the ladies and that the maid was gathering up the empty cups and carrying them out of the room. Great-Aunt Sarah must have forgotten her promise of tea. She was sitting on the sofa with Mama and telling her about her needy children. It turned out that they were not her own after all but a charity for which she was collecting money, and Anna who had briefly pictured Great-Aunt Sarah with a secret string of ragged urchins felt somehow cheated. She wriggled restlessly in her chair, and Great-Aunt Sarah must have noticed for she suddenly interrupted herself.

"The child is bored and hungry," she cried and added to the maid, "Have the old ladies all gone?"

The maid replied that they had.

"Well then," cried Great-Aunt Sarah, "you can bring in the real tea!"

A moment later the maid staggered back under a tray loaded with cakes. There must have been five or six different kinds, apart from an assortment of sandwiches and biscuits. There was also a fresh pot of tea, chocolate and whipped cream.

"I like cakes," said Great-Aunt Sarah in answer to Mama's look of astonishment, "but it's no use offering them to those old ladies – they're much too careful of their diets. So I thought we'd have our tea after they'd gone." So saying she slapped a large portion of apple flan on to a plate, topped it with whipped cream and handed it to Anna. "The child needs feeding," she said.

During tea she asked Mama questions about Papa's work and about their flat, and sometimes Mama had to repeat her answers into the ear-trumpet. Mama talked about everything quite cheerfully, but Great-Aunt Sarah kept shaking her head and saying, "To have to live like this . . . such a distinguished man . . .!" She knew all Papa's books and bought the *Daily Parisian* specially to read his articles. Every so often she would look at Anna, saying, "And the child – so skinny!" and ply her with more cake.

At last, when no one could eat any more, Great-Aunt Sarah heaved herself out from behind the tea-table and set off at her usual trot towards the door, beckoning to Mama and Anna to follow. She led them to another room which seemed to be entirely filled with cardboard boxes.

"Look," she said. "All this I have been given for my needy children."

The boxes were filled with lengths of cloth in all sorts of different colours and thicknesses.

"One of my old ladies is married to a textile manufacturer," explained Great-Aunt Sarah. "So he is very rich and he gives me all the ends of material he does not want. Now I have an idea – why shouldn't the child have some of it? After all it is for needy children, and she is as needy as most."

"No, no," said Mama, "I don't think I could . . ."

"Ach – always so proud," said Great-Aunt Sarah. "The child needs new clothes. Why shouldn't she have some?"

She rummaged in one of the boxes and pulled out some thick woollen material in a lovely shade of green. "Just nice for a coat," she said, "and a dress she needs, and perhaps a skirt . . ."

In no time at all she had assembled a pile of cloth on the bed, and when Mama tried again to refuse she only cried, "Such nonsense! You want the police should arrest the child for going about with her pants showing?"

At this Mama, who had in any case not been protesting very hard, had to laugh and give in. The maid was asked to wrap it all up, and when it was time to leave Mama and Anna each had a big parcel to carry.

"Thank you very, very much!" Anna shouted

into Great-Aunt Sarah's ear-trumpet. "I've always wanted a green coat!"

"I wish you luck to wear it!" Great-Aunt Sarah shouted back.

Then they were outside, and as Anna and Mama walked back in the dark they talked all the way about the different pieces of material and what they could be made into. As soon as they got home Mama telephoned Madame Fernand who was delighted and said they must bring everything round the following Thursday for a great dress-making session.

"Won't it be lovely!" cried Anna. "I can't wait to tell Papa!" – and just then Papa came in. She told him excitedly what had happened. "And I'll be able to have a dress and a coat," she gabbled, "and Great-Aunt Sarah just gave it to us because it was meant for needy children and she said I was as needy as most, and we had a lovely tea and . . ."

She stopped because of the expression on Papa's face.

"What is all this?" he said to Mama.

"It's just as Anna told you," said Mama, and there was something careful about her voice. "Great-Aunt Sarah had a whole lot of cloth which had been given to her and she wanted Anna to have some."

"But it had been given to her for needy children," said Papa.

"That's only what it was called," said Mama. "She's interested in various charities – she's a very kind woman . . ."

"Charities?" asked Papa. "But we can't accept charity for our children."

"Oh, why must you always be so difficult?" shouted Mama. "The woman is my aunt and she wanted Anna to have some clothes – that's all there is to it!"

"Honestly, Papa, I don't think she meant it in any way you wouldn't like," Anna put in. She was feeling miserable and almost wished she had never seen the cloth.

"It's a present for Anna from a relative," said Mama.

"No," said Papa. "It's a present from a relative who runs a charity – a charity for needy children."

"All right then, we'll give it back!" shouted Mama. "If that's what you want! But will you tell me what the child is going to wear? Do you know the price of children's clothes in the shops? Look at her – just look at her!"

Papa looked at Anna and Anna looked back at him. She wanted the new clothes but she did not want Papa to feel so badly about them. She tugged at her skirt to make it look longer.

"Papa . . ." she said.

"You do look a bit needy," said Papa. His face looked very tired.

"It doesn't matter," said Anna.

191

"Yes, it does," said Papa. "It does matter." He fingered the stuff in the parcels. "Is this the cloth?"

She nodded.

"Well then, you'd better get it made up into some new clothes," said Papa. "Something warm," he said and went out of the room.

In bed that night Anna and Max lay talking in the dark.

"I didn't know we were needy," said Anna. "Why are we?"

"Papa doesn't earn a lot," said Max. "The *Daily Parisian* can't afford to pay him very much for his articles and the French have their own writers."

"They used to pay him a lot in Germany."

"Oh yes."

For a while they lay without talking. Then Anna said, "Funny, isn't it?"

"What?"

"How we used to think we'd be back in Berlin within six months. We've been away more than a year already."

"I know," said Max.

Suddenly, for no particular reason, Anna remembered their old house so vividly that she could almost see it. She remembered what it felt like to run up the stairs and the little patch on the carpet on the landing where she had once spilt some ink, and how you could see the pear tree in

192

the garden from the windows. The nursery curtains were blue and there was a white-painted table to write or draw on and Bertha the maid had cleaned it all every day and there had been a lot of toys . . . But it was no use going on thinking about it, so she closed her eyes and went to sleep.

Chapter Seventeen

The dress-making session at the Fernands was a great success. Madame Fernand was just as nice as Anna remembered her, and she cut out Great-Aunt Sarah's cloth so cleverly that there was enough for a pair of grey shorts for Max as well as a coat, a dress and a skirt for Anna. When Mama offered to help with the sewing Madame Fernand looked at her and laughed.

"You go and play the piano," she said, "I'll get on with this."

"But I've even brought some sewing things," said Mama. She dug in her handbag and produced an elderly reel of white cotton and a needle.

"My dear," said Madame Fernand quite

kindly, "I wouldn't trust you to hem a handkerchief."

So Mama played the piano at one end of the Fernands' pleasant sitting-room while Madame Fernand sewed at the other, and Anna and Max went off to play with the Fernand's daughter Francine.

Max had had grave doubts about Francine before they came.

"I don't want to play with a girl!" he had said, and even claimed that he could not come because of his homework.

"You've never been so keen on your homework before!" said Mama crossly, but it was not really fair because lately, in his efforts to learn French as fast as possible, Max had become much more conscientious about school. He was deeply offended and scowled at everyone until they arrived at the Fernand's flat and Francine opened the door for them. Then his scowl quickly disappeared. She was a remarkably pretty girl with long honey-coloured hair and large grey eyes.

"You must be Francine," said Max and added untruthfully but in surprisingly good French, "I have so much looked forward to meeting you!"

Francine had quite a lot of toys and a big white cat. The cat immediately took possession of Anna and sat on her lap while Francine searched for something in her toy cupboard. At last she found it.

"This is what I got for my birthday," she said and produced a games compendium very like the one Anna and Max had owned in Germany.

Max's eyes met Anna's over the cat's white fur.

"Can I see?" he asked and had it open almost before Francine agreed. He took a long time looking at the contents fingering the dice, the chessmen, the different kinds of playing cards.

"We used to have a box of games like this," he said at last. "Only ours had dominoes as well."

Francine looked a little put out at having her birthday present belittled.

"What happened to yours?" she asked.

"We had to leave it behind," said Max and added gloomily, "I expect Hitler plays with it now."

Francine laughed. "Well, you'll have to use this one instead," she said. "As I have no brothers or sisters I don't often have anyone to play with."

After this they played Ludo and Snakes and Ladders all afternoon. It was nice because the white cat sat on Anna's lap and there was no need for her to speak much French during the games. The white cat seemed quite happy to have dice thrown over its head and did not want to get down even when Madame Fernand called Anna to try on the new clothes. For tea it ate a bit of iced bun which Anna gave it, and afterwards it climbed straight back on to her lap and smiled at

196

her through its long white fur. When it was time to leave it followed her to the front door.

"What a pretty cat," said Mama when she saw it.

Anna was longing to tell her how it had sat on her lap while she had played Ludo but thought it would be rude to speak German when Madame Fernand could not understand it. So, very haltingly, she explained in French.

"I thought you told me Anna spoke hardly any French," said Madame Fernand.

Mama looked very pleased. "She is beginning to," she said.

"Beginning to!" exclaimed Madame Fernand. "I've never seen two children learn a language so fast. Max sounds almost like a French boy at times and as for Anna – only a month or two ago she could hardly say a word, and now she understands everything!"

It was not quite true. There were still a lot of things Anna could not understand – but she was delighted just the same. She had been so impressed with Max's rapid progress that she had not noticed how much she herself had improved.

Madame Fernand wanted them all to come again the following Sunday so that Anna could have a final fitting, but Mama said, no, next time all the Fernands must come to them – and thus began a series of visits which both families found so pleasant that it soon became a regular arrangement.

Papa especially enjoyed Monsieur Fernand's company. He was a large clever-looking man and often, while the children played in the dining-room at home, Anna could hear his deep voice and Papa's in the bedroom-turned-sitting-room next door. They seemed to have endless things to talk about and sometimes Anna could hear them laughing loudly together. This always pleased her because she had hated the tired look on Papa's face when he had heard about Great-Aunt Sarah's cloth. She had noticed since that this look occasionally returned – usually when Mama was talking about money. Monsieur Fernand was always able to keep the look at bay.

The new clothes were soon finished and turned out to be the nicest Anna had ever had. She went to show them to Great-Aunt Sarah the very first time she wore them and took with her a poem she had composed specially as a thanks offering. It described all the clothes in detail and ended with the lines.

"And so I am the happy wearer
Of all these nice clothes from Aunt Sarah."

"Goodness, child," said Great-Aunt Sarah when she read it. "You'll be such a writer yet, like your father!"

She seemed terribly pleased with it.

Anna was pleased too because somehow the

poem seemed to make it quite definite that the gift of cloth had not been charity – and also it was the first time she had ever managed to write a poem about anything other than a disaster.

Chapter Eighteen

In April it suddenly became spring, and though Anna tried to go on wearing the beautiful green coat which Madame Fernand had made for her she soon found it much too thick.

Walking to school became a delight on these bright, sunny mornings, and as the Parisians opened their windows to let in the warm air all sorts of interesting smells escaped and mingled with the scent of spring in the streets. Apart from the usual hot garlicky breath rising from the Metro she suddenly encountered delicious waftings of coffee, freshly baked bread, or onions being fried ready for lunch. As the spring advanced, doors were opened as well as windows, and while walking down the sunlit streets she could glimpse the dim interiors of cafés and shops which had been invisible all through the winter. Everyone wanted to linger in the sunshine, and the pavements in the Champs Elysées became a sea of tables and chairs amongst which white-coated waiters flew about, serving drinks to their customers.

The first of May was called the day of the lily-of-the-valley. Baskets piled high with the little green and white bunches appeared at every street corner and the cries of the vendors echoed everywhere. Papa had an early appointment that morning and walked part of the way to school with Anna. He stopped to buy a paper from an old man at a kiosk. The was a picture of Hitler on the front page, making a speech, but the old man folded the paper in half so that Hitler disappeared. Then he sniffed the air appreciatively and smiled, showing one tooth.

"It smells of spring!" he said.

Papa smiled back and Anna knew that he was thinking how lovely it was to be spending this spring in Paris. At the next corner they bought some lily-of-the-valley for Mama without even asking first how much they cost.

The school building seemed dark and chilly after the brightness outside, but Anna looked forward each morning to seeing Colette, who had become her special friend, and her teacher Madame Socrate. Though she still found the school day long and tiring she was beginning to understand more of what was going on. The mistakes in her dictations had gradually been reduced to fifties instead of hundreds. Madame Socrate continued to help her during the lunch break, and she now managed sometimes to answer a question in class.

At home Mama was becoming a really good cook, helped with advice from Madame Fernand, and Papa said he had never eaten so well in his life. The children learned to enjoy all sorts of food they had never even heard of before and to drink a mixture of wine and water with their meals, like French children. Even fat Clothilde in the schoo kitchen approved of the lunches Anna broug for her to reheat.

"Your mother knows how to do things," sl said, and Mama was delighted when Anna tol her.

Only Grete remained gloomy and discontented. No matter what Mama served up she always compared it unfavourably with some Austrian version of the same dish, and if it was something you could not get in Austria Grete did not think you should eat it at all. She had an amazing resistance to everything French and did not seem to get any better at speaking the language even though she went to classes every day. Since the promises she had made to her mother continued to prevent her from being of much help to Mama, everyone, including Grete, looked forward to the time when she would return to Austria for good.

"And the sooner the better," said Madame Fernand who had been able to observe Grete at close quarters, for the two families still spent most of their Sundays together. As spring turned into summer, instead of meeting at their homes they went out to the Bois de Boulogne which was a large park not too far away and the children played ball games on the grass. Once or twice Monsieur Fernand borrowed a friend's car and drove them all out to the country for a picnic. To Anna's joy the cat came too on these occasions. It did not seem to mind being put on a lead and, while Francine chàttered to Max, Anna proudly took charge of it, holding on to the lead when the cat wanted to climb a tree or a lamp-post and following with the lead held high above her head when the cat decided to walk along the top of some railings instead of along the bottom.

In July it became very hot – much hotter than it had ever been in Berlin. There seemed no air at all in the little flat even though Mama kept all the windows open all the time. The children's bedroom especially was stifling and the courtyard it overlooked seemed almost hotter than the inside. It was difficult to sleep at night and nobody could concentrate on lessons at school. Even Madame Socrate was tired. Her frizzy black hair went limp with the heat and everyone longed for the end of term.

On the fourteenth of July not only the schools but the whole of France had a holiday. It was the anniversary of the French Revolution, and there were flags everywhere and fireworks in the evening. Anna and Max went to see them with their parents and the Fernands. They took the Metro, which was packed with cheerful people, and among a crowd of other Parisians they climbed a long flight of steps up to a church on top of a hill. From here they could see right across Paris, and as the fireworks began to explode against the dark blue sky everyone shouted and cheered. At the end of the display someone started to sing the *Marseillaise*, then someone else joined in, and soon the whole huge crowd was singing together in the hot night air.

"Come on, children!" cried Monsieur Fernand, and Anna and Max joined in too. Anna thought it sounded wonderful, especially an unexpected slow bit that came in the middle of the song, and she was sorry when it ended.

The crowds began to leak away down the steps and Mama said, "Home to bed!"

"Good heavens, you can't send them to bed now. It's the fourteenth of July!" cried Monsieur Fernand. Mama protested that it was late, but the Fernands only laughed at her.

"It's the fourteenth of July," they said, as

though this explained everything. "The evening has hardly begun!"

Mama looked doubtfully at the children's excited faces. "But what . . .?" she began.

"First," said Monsieur Fernand, "we are going to eat."

Anna was under the impression that they had eaten already, for they had had boiled eggs before they came out – but clearly this was not the sort of eating Monsieur Fernand had in mind. He took them to a large busy restaurant where they sat at a table outside on the pavement and ordered a meal.

"Snails for the children!" cried Fernand. "They've never tried them."

Max stared at his portion in horror and could not bring himself to touch them. But Anna, encouraged by Francine, tried one and found that it tasted like a very delicious mushroom. In the end she and Francine ate Max's snails as well as their own. Towards the end of the meal, while they were spooning up cream puffs, an old man arrived with a stool and an accordion. He sat down and began to play, and soon some of the people left their tables to dance in the street. A cheerful looking sailor appeared at Mama's side and invited her to dance. Mama was surprised at first but then she accepted and Anna watched her being whirled round and round, still looking astonished but pleased. Then Monsieur Fernand danced with Francine, and Anna danced with Papa, and Madame Fernand said she did not feel like dancing just yet because she could see that Max would absolutely hate it, and after a while Monsieur Fernand said, "Let's move on."

It was cooler now and Anna did not feel at all tired as they wandered through the crowded streets. There were accordions and people dancing everywhere, and every so often they stopped and joined in. Some cafés were serving free wine to celebrate the occasion and when they felt like a rest the grown-ups stopped for a drink and the children had cassis, which was blackcurrant juice. They saw the river shining in the moonlight and the cathedral of Notre Dame squatting like a great dark creature in the middle. At one time they walked along the bank and under the bridges, and there were accordion players and people dancing here too. They went on and on until Anna lost all sense of time and just followed Monsieur Fernand in a happy daze.

Suddenly Max said, "What is that funny light in the sky?"

It was the dawn.

By this time they had reached the main Paris market, and carts loaded with fruit and vegetables were rumbling over the cobblestones all about them.

"Hungry?" asked Monsieur Fernand.

It was ridiculous since they had already eaten

two suppers, but everyone was starving. There was no accordion music here, only people getting ready for the day's work, and a woman in a small café was serving bowls of steaming onion soup. They ate great bowlfuls, sitting on wooden benches with the market people, and mopped up the remains with hunks of bread. When they came out of the café it was daylight.

"Now you can put the children to bed," said Monsieur Fernand. "They have seen the fourteenth of July."

After a sleepy farewell they rode home on the Metro among late revellers like themselves and people going to work, and collapsed into their beds.

"We never had a fourteenth of July in Germany," said Anna just before she fell asleep.

"Well, of course not," said Max. "We didn't have the French Revolution!"

"I know that," said Anna crossly and added, just as sleep was about to overtake her, "But wasn't it lovely!"

Then the summer holidays were upon them. Just as they were wondering how to spend them, a letter arrived from Herr Zwirn inviting the whole family to the Gasthof Zwirn as his guests – and just as they were wondering where to get the money for the fares, Papa was asked to write three articles for a French newspaper. This paper paid him so much more than his normal fees from the *Daily Parisian* that it solved the problem.

Everyone was delighted at the prospect, and to top it all on the last day of term Max brought home a good report. Mama and Papa could hardly believe their eyes when they saw it. There was not a single "Does not try" or "Shows no interest". Instead there were words like "intelligent" and "hard-working" and the headmaster's comment at the bottom of the sheet said that Max had made remarkable progress. This made Mama feel so cheerful that she absent-mindedly bade quite a fond farewell to Grete, who was going to Austria at last. They were all so pleased to get rid of her that they felt they must be extra nice to her, and Mama even gave her a small scarf.

"I don't know if this sort of thing is worn in Austria," said Grete glumly when she saw it, but she took it anyway. And then they themselves set off for Switzerland.

The Gasthof Zwirn was quite unchanged. Herr and Frau Zwirn were as kind and warm-hearted as ever, and after the heat in Paris the air by the lake was wonderfully fresh. It was nice to hear the familiar German-Swiss dialect and to be able to understand everything people said instead of only half, and Frànz and Vreneli were ready to pick up their friendships with Anna and Max exactly where they had left off. In no time at all

Vreneli was bringing Anna up to date about the red-haired boy who had apparently taken to looking at Vreneli in a certain way – a warm sort of way, said Vreneli – which she could not describe but which appeared to please her. Franz carried Max off to fish with the same old fishing rod, and they all played the same games and walked along the same paths in the woods which they had enjoyed so much the previous year. It was all exactly as it had been, and yet there was something about this very sameness that made Anna and Max feel a little like strangers. How could the Zwirns' lives have stayed so much the same when their own had become so different?

"You'd think just something would have changed," said Max, and Franz asked, "What sort of thing?" But Max did not know himself.

One day Anna was walking through the village with Vreneli and Roesli when they met Herr Graupe.

"Welcome back to our beautiful Switzerland!" he cried, shaking her hand enthusiastically, and soon he was asking her all sorts of questions about school in France. He was convinced that nothing could compare with his own village school and Anna found herself sounding almost apologetic when she explained that she liked it all very much.

"Really?" said Herr Graupe incredulously, while she described the work, and her lunches with Clothilde in the school kitchen, and Madame Socrate.

And then an odd thing happened to her. Herr Graupe was asking her something about the French school-leaving age which she did not know – but instead of telling him so in German she found herself suddenly shrugging her shoulders and saying "*Je ne sais pas*" in her best Parisian accent. She was horrified as soon as she had said it. She knew he would think that she was showing off. But she hadn't been. She could not even understand where the words had come from. It was as though somewhere inside her something were secretly thinking in French – and that was ridiculous. Since she had never been able to think in French in Paris, why should she suddenly start now?

"I see we're becoming quite French already," said Herr Graupe disapprovingly when they had both recovered from their surprise at her reply. "Well – I musn't keep you." And he hurried off.

Vreneli and Roesli were both unusually quiet when the three of them walked back together.

"I suppose you can speak French like anything now," said Vreneli at last.

"No," said Anna. "Max is much better."

"I can say *Oui* – I think that means Yes, doesn't it?" said Roesli. "Are there any mountains in France?"

"Not near Paris," said Anna.

Vreneli had been staring at Anna thoughtfully. Then she said, "You know, you're different somehow."

"I'm not!" said Anna indignantly.

"But you are," said Vreneli. "I don't know what it is but you've changed."

"Nonsense!" cried Anna. "Of course I haven't!" But she knew that Vreneli was right and suddenly, though she was only eleven, she felt quite old and sad.

The rest of the holidays passed happily enough. The children bathed and played with the Zwirns, and if it was not quite as it had been it was still very pleasant. After all, what did it matter, said Max, that they no longer quite belonged? They were sorry to leave at the end of the summer and took a long and affectionate farewell from their friends. But to both Anna and Max, going back to Paris felt more like going home than they would ever have thought possible.

Chapter Nineteen

When Anna went back to school she found that she had been moved up. Madame Socrate was still her teacher but the work was suddenly much harder. This was because her class was preparing for an examination called the *certificat d'études* which everyone except Anna was taking the following summer.

"I'm excused because I'm not French," Anna told Mama, "and anyway I couldn't possibly pass."

But she had to do the work just the same.

The girls in her class were expected to do at least an hour's homework each day after school, to learn whole pages of history and geography by heart, to write essays and study grammar – and

Anna had to do it all in a language which she still did not completely understand. Even arithmetic which had been her great stand-by now let her down. Instead of sums which needed no translation her class were doing problems – long complicated tangles in which people dug ditches and passed each other in trains and filled tanks with water at one rate while siphoning it off at another – and all this she had to translate into German before she could even begin to think about it.

As the weather became colder and the days darker she began to feel very tired. She dragged her feet walking home from school and then just sat and stared at her homework instead of getting on with it. She suddenly felt quite discouraged. Madame Socrate, mindful of the coming exam, no longer had so much time for her, and her work seemed to be getting worse rather than better. No matter what she did, she could not reduce the mistakes in her dictation below forty – lately they had even climbed up again into the fifties. In class, even though she often knew the answers, it took her so long to translate them into French in her mind that it was usually too late to give them. She felt that she would never be able to catch up and was getting tired of trying.

One day when she was sitting over her homework Mama came into the room.

"Have you nearly finished?" she asked.

213

"Not quite," said Anna, and Mama came and looked at her book.

It was arithmetic homework and all Anna had written was the date and "Problems" at the top of the page. She had drawn a little box-shape round "Problems" with a ruler and had followed this with a wavy line in red ink. Then she had decorated the wavy line with dots and surrounded it with a zigzag shape and more dots in blue. All this had taken her the best part of an hour.

At the sight of it Mama exploded.

"No wonder you can't do your homework!" she shouted. "You put it off and put it off until you're too tired to make any sense of it! You'll never learn anything at this rate!"

This was so exactly what Anna felt herself that she burst into tears.

"I do try!" she sobbed. "But I just don't seem to be able to do it. It's too difficult! I try and try and it isn't any use!"

And in another burst of weeping she dripped tears all over "Problems" so that the paper cockled and the wavy line spread and got mixed up with the zigzag.

"Of course you can do it!" said Mama, reaching for the book. "Look, if I help you . . ."

But Anna shouted "No!" quite violently and pushed the book away so that it shot off the table and on to the floor.

"Well, you're obviously in no condition to do

any homework today," said Mama after a moment's silence and walked out of the room.

Anna was just wondering what she ought to do when Mama came back again with her coat on.

"I have to buy some cod for supper," she said. "You'd better come with me and get some fresh air."

They walked down the street together without talking. It was cold and dark and Anna trudged along beside Mama with her hands in her pockets, feeling quite empty. She was no good. She would never be able to speak French properly. She would be like Grete who had never managed to learn, but unlike Grete she could not go home to her own country. At this thought she began to blink and sniff all over again, and Mama had to grab her arm to stop her bumping into an old lady.

The fish shop was some distance away in a brightly lit, busy street. There was a cake shop next to it, its window filled with creamy delicacies which you could either take away or sit down to eat at one of the little tables inside. Anna and Max had often admired it, but neither had ever set foot inside it because it was so expensive. This time Anna was too miserable even to look at it, but Mama stopped by the heavy glass door.

"We'll go in here," she said to Anna's surprise, and steered her through.

They were met by a wave of warm air and a delicious smell of pastries and chocolate.

"I'll have a cup of tea and you can have a cake," said Mama, "and then we'll have a talk."

"Isn't it too expensive?" asked Anna in a small voice.

"We can manage one cake," said Mama. "But you'd better not pick one of those absolutely enormous ones, otherwise we might not have enough money left for the cod."

Anna chose a pastry filled with sweet chestnut purée and whipped cream, and they sat down at one of the little tables.

"Look," said Mama as Anna sank her fork into the cake, "I know it's difficult for you at school and I know you've tried. But what are we to do? We're living in France and you have to learn French."

"I get so tired," said Anna, "and I'm getting worse instead of better. Perhaps I'm just one of those people who can't learn languages."

Mama was up in arms at once.

"Nonsense!" she said. "There's no such thing at your age!"

Anna tried a bit of her pastry. It was delicious.

"Would you like some?" she said.

Mama shook her head.

"You've done very well so far," she said after a moment. "Everyone tells me your French accent

216

is perfect, and you really know an awful lot considering that we've been here less than a year."

"It's just that now I don't seem to be able to get any further," said Anna.

"But you will!" said Mama.

Anna looked down at her plate.

"Look," said Mama, "these things don't always happen as you expect. When I was studying music I sometimes struggled with something for weeks without getting anywhere at all – and then suddenly, just when I felt it was quite hopeless, the whole thing became clear and I couldn't think why I hadn't seen it before. Perhaps it will be like that with your French."

Anna said nothing. She did not think it was very likely.

Then Mama seemed to come to a decision.

"I'll tell you what we'll do," she said. "It's only two months till Christmas. Will you try just once more? Then if by Christmas you really feel you still can't manage, we'll do something about it. I don't quite know what, because we have no money for school fees, but I promise you I'll think of something. All right?"

"All right," said Anna.

The cake really was remarkably good, and by the time she had finished the last lick of chestnut purée she felt a lot less like Grete than before. They stayed sitting at the little table for a while longer because it was such a pleasant place to be.

"Nice to go out to tea with my daughter," said Mama at last and smiled.

Anna smiled back.

The bill came to more than they had expected and there was not enough money left for the cod after all, but Mama bought mussels instead and it did not matter. In the morning she gave Anna a note to Madame Socrate to explain about the homework and she must have put something else in it as well, for Madame Socrate told Anna not to worry about school and also found time again to help her during the lunch break.

After this the work did not seem quite so bad. Whenever it threatened to overwhelm her, Anna remembered that if she really found it impossible she would not have to go on trying for ever, and then she usually discovered that she could manage after all.

And then, one day, her whole world changed.

It was a Monday morning and Colette met Anna at the school gates.

"What did you do on Sunday?" she called – and instead of mentally translating the question into German, deciding on an answer and then translating that back into French, Anna called back, "We went to see our friends."

The words just seemed to arrive from nowhere, in perfect French, without her having to think at all. She was so astonished that she stood quite still and did not even hear Colette's next question.

"I said," shouted Colette, "did you take the cat out?"

"No, it was too wet," said Anna – again in perfect French and without thinking.

It was like a miracle. She could not believe that it would last. It was as though she had suddenly found that she could fly, and she expected each moment to crash to the ground again. With her heart beating faster than usual she went into the classroom – but her new talent persisted.

In the first lesson she answered four questions correctly, so that Madame Socrate looked at her in surprise and said, "Well done!" She chattered and laughed with Colette in break and during lunch she explained to Clothilde how Mama cooked liver and onions. Once or twice she still hesitated, and of course she made mistakes. But most of the time she was able to speak French just as she spoke German – automatically and without thinking. By the end of the day she was almost light-headed with excitement but not at all tired, and when she woke up the next morning she had a moment of utter terror. Suppose her new gift had vanished as suddenly as it had come? But she need not have worried. When she got to school she found that she was even more fluent than before.

By the end of the week Mama looked at her in amazement.

"I've never seen such a change in anyone," she said. "A few days ago you looked green and miserable. Now it's as though you'd grown five centimetres and you look quite pink. What's happened to you?"

"I think I've learned to speak French," said Anna.

Chapter Twenty

There was even less money to spend at Christmas than the previous year, but it was more fun because of the Fernands. The main celebration in France is not at Christmas but on New Year's Eve when even the children are allowed to stay up till midnight, and they all had a special dinner and exchanged presents at the Fernands' flat. Anna had used some of her pocket money to buy some chocolate as a present for the white cat and after dinner, instead of playing with Max and Francine, she stayed behind in the living room to feed it small crumbs of chocolate on the floor. Mama and Madame Fernand were washing up the dishes in the kitchen and Papa and Monsieur Fernand were drinking brandy and having one of their endless conversations, deep in two armchairs.

Papa seemed very interested in what they were talking about, and Anna was pleased because ever since that morning when a postcard had arrived from Onkel Julius, he had been silent and depressed. There had been postcards from Onkel Julius at irregular intervals throughout the year and though there was never any real news in them hey were always full of affection. Sometimes there were little jokes and always there were messages for "Aunt Alice" to which Papa replied. This card had been addressed to Anna as usual but there was no mention of "Aunt Alice" – not even any good wishes for the New Year. Instead, on the back of a picture of some bears, Onkel Julius had simply written, "The more I see of men the more I love animals." He had not even initialled it as usual, but they knew it was from him because of his beautiful neat handwriting.

Papa had read it without a word and then had put it with the rest of Onkel Julius's cards and letters which he kept carefully in his table drawer. He had hardly spoken for the rest of the day, and now it was good to see him as animated as Monsieur Fernand.

"But you live in a free country," he was saying. "Nothing else matters!"

"Yes, but . . ." said Monsieur Fernand, and

Anna realized that he must be worrying about the Depression again.

The Depression was the only thing that ever got Monsieur Fernand down, and though Anna had asked several times what it was no one had been able to explain it to her. It was something that had happened in France, and it meant that there was less money for everyone and fewer jobs, and it had caused some of Monsieur Fernand's colleagues to be sacked from his paper. Whenever Monsieur Fernand talked about the Depression Papa reminded him that he lived in a free country and this time, perhaps because of Onkel Julius, Papa was more eloquent than usual.

Monsieur Fernand argued with him for a while and then he suddenly laughed. The white cat opened its mouth in surprise at the noise and a crumb of chocolate fell out. When Anna looked up Monsieur Fernand was refilling Papa's glass and patting him on the shoulder.

"It's a funny thing," he said, "you trying to point out the more cheerful aspects of the situation, when you've got more to worry about than any of the rest of us!"

Then Mama and Madame Fernand came back into the room and soon it was midnight and everyone, even the children, drank a toast to the New Year.

"Happy 1935!" cried Monsieur Fernand, and "Happy 1935!" echoed everyone.

"To us and to all our friends," said Papa quietly, and Anna knew that he was thinking of Onkel Julius.

In February Mama caught 'flu and just as she was getting better the concierge developed a bad leg, which was very unfortunate. Since Grete's departure Mama had done most of the cleaning herself, but the concierge had come up for an hour each morning to help with the rough work. Now Mama was left with the lot. She did not like housework at the best of times and was feeling gloomy, as people tend to do after 'flu, and the burden of all the cleaning and cooking and washing and ironing and mending seemed to her simply too heavy to be borne. Anna and Max helped by doing odd jobs like shopping and emptying the dustbin, but of course most of the work fell back on Mama and she grumbled about it incessantly.

"I don't mind cooking," she said, "but it's the endless washing and ironing and mending – it takes so long and it goes on for ever!"

Papa was no help at all. He had no idea what needed to be done in a household and when Mama complained how tired she got ironing the sheets he seemed genuinely astonished.

"But why do you bother?" he asked. "They get crumpled again anyway when people sleep in them."

"Oh, you don't understand anything!" cried Mama.

She felt extra bad about it because Omama was planning a visit to Great-Aunt Sarah and she wanted the flat to look nice when she came to see it. But while she cleaned the rooms – and Mama cleaned them with a kind of ferocity which they had never encountered from either Grete or the concierge – the washing accumulated, and while she cooked good and inexpensive meals the pile of mending grew and grew. Because Papa seemed quite unable to understand her difficulties she somehow felt that he was to blame and one evening they had a row.

Mama was trying to mend an old vest of Anna's and groaning a good deal because there was a pile of socks and pillow-cases waiting to be darned after she had finished, when Papa spoke.

"Surely this is quite unnecessary," he said. "There can be no real need to mend the children's underwear when no one ever sees it!"

He might have known, thought Anna, that this would cause an explosion.

"You have no idea – but no idea – " shouted Mama, "of the work I have to do. I get worn out washing and cooking and ironing and mending, and all you ever say is that it isn't necessary!"

"Only because you complain so much," said Papa. "After all other people seem to manage. Look at Madame Fernand."

This provoked another outburst.

"Madame Fernand loves housework!" shouted Mama. "Also she has a daily woman and a sewing machine. Look at this," she cried, waving a torn pillow slip. "She'd be able to mend this in two minutes, whereas it'll take me at least half an hour. If you compare me with her it just shows you have no idea what you're talking about!"

Papa was taken aback by her vehemence. He loved Mama and hated to see her distressed.

"I only meant," he said, "that for an intelligent person like you there must be ways of simplifying . . ."

"Then you'd better ask Madame Fernand!" shouted Mama. "All I ever learned to do was play the piano!" – and she walked out of the room and slammed the door.

The following day when Anna came home from school, she met Papa in the lift. He was carrying a large wooden box with a handle.

"What is it?" asked Anna and Papa said, "A present for Mama."

Anna was all agog to see what it was and could hardly wait for it to be opened, but Mama's face fell at the sight of it.

"Surely you haven't bought . . ." she began, as Papa lifted the lid, and Papa said proudly, "A sewing machine!"

It was not a bit like Madame Fernand's sewing machine, thought Anna. Madame Fernand's sewing machine was silver but this one was greyish black and a peculiar shape.

"Of course it's not new," said Papa, "and it may need to be cleaned. But you'll be able to mend the pillow-cases and socks with it, and make the children's clothes without asking Madame Fernand . . ."

"I don't know how to make clothes," said Mama, "and you can't mend socks with a sewing machine." She looked absolutely horrified.

"Well, whatever it is you do with a sewing machine," said Papa.

They all stared at the thing on the table. It did not look, thought, Anna, as if it would do anything.

"How much did it cost?" asked Mama.

"Don't worry about that," said Papa. "They paid me for that extra article I wrote for the *Daily Parisian* today."

At this Mama became quite frantic.

"But we need that money!" she cried. "Don't you remember? I have to pay the rent and the butcher, and Anna needs new shoes. We said we'd use the money from the article to pay for them!"

Papa looked distressed. Clearly he had not remembered about these things, but before Mama could say any more the bell rang and Anna opened the door to Madame Fernand. In the excitement over the sewing machine everyone had forgotten that she was due to drop in for tea.

"Look!" cried Mama and Papa, but in very different tones of voice, as Anna led her into the dining-room.

Madame Fernand looked at the machine incredulously.

"Where on earth did you get it?" she said. "It must be out of the Ark!"

"Is it so old?" said Papa.

Madame Fernand inspected the machine more closely.

"Did you buy it?" she asked, still sounding astonished.

"Certainly!" said Papa.

"But the needle-plate – it's broken," said Madame Fernand. "And the whole shaft is bent sideways – someone must have dropped it – so that it couldn't possibly work."

She noticed some raised marks on the side of the machine and rubbed at them with her handkerchief. Gradually some figures appeared from beneath the grime. They formed a date – 1896. Madame Fernand put her handkerchief back in her pocket.

"As an antique is may be interesting," she said firmly, "but as a sewing machine it's got to go back to the shop."

Papa still could not believe that his wonderful present was no use.

"Are you sure?" he asked.

"Quite sure," said Madame Fernand. "Take it

228

quickly and tell them to give you your money back."

"And then will I be able to have new shoes?" asked Anna. She knew it wasn't really the moment to ask about them, but her old ones were quite worn out, apart from pinching her toes, and she had been looking forward to a new pair for a long time.

"Of course, of course," said Mama impatiently, but Papa still hesitated.

"I hope they'll agree," he said. "The man who sold it to me did not seem very helpful."

"I'll come with you," said Madame Fernand. "I want to see this place where they sell antique sewing machines," and Anna went along too.

The shop did not sell sewing machines only as Anna had expected but all sorts of different things like old chairs and little rickety tables and cracked pictures. Some of these had been put out on the pavement and a small ill-dressed man was busy draping a balding tiger skin over a chest of drawers in the middle. When he saw Papa his eyes, which were strangely pale, half closed.

"Good afternoon," said Papa politely as always. "I bought this sewing machine earlier today but I'm afraid it doesn't work."

"Doesn't it?" said the man, but he did not seem very surprised.

"No," said Papa. "So I've brought it back."

The man said nothing.

"And I'd be glad if you would be so kind as to refund the money."

"Ah, no!" said the man. "I can't do that. A bargain's a bargain."

"But the machine does not work," said Papa.

"Look, sir," said the man, momentarily abandoning the tiger skin. "You came in here and bought a sewing machine. Now you've changed your mind and you want your money back. Well, I don't do business that way. A bargain's a bargain, and that's all there is to it."

"I quite agree," said Papa, "that a bargain is a bargain. But the machine is broken."

"Where?" said the man.

Papa pointed vaguely.

The man dismissed it.

"Few little bits out of order," he said. "Cost you almost nothing to replace those. After all, you can't expect it to be perfect – not at the price you paid for it."

"No, I suppose not," said Papa, "but since it does not work at all, don't you think you should take it back?"

"No, I don't," said the man.

Papa seemed at a loss what to say next and Anna could see the money for her new shoes slipping away. She knew that Papa had been cheated but she also knew that he had meant it all for the best and that he was not the sort of person who could force the man to hand back the money.

She sighed – but she had reckoned without Madame Fernand.

"Now you listen to me!" she shouted so loudly that several passers-by turned round to look at her. "You've sold this man a wreck of a sewing machine while giving him to understand that it works. That's an offence against the law. I intend to inform the police immediately and I have no doubt they will also be most interested in all the other junk you sell here."

"Now, lady – please!" cried the man. His eyes were suddenly wide open.

"Don't tell me you came by this stuff honestly!" shouted Madame Fernand, giving the tiger skin a contemptuous tug. "There's nothing honest about your business! When the police have finished with you my husband, who is a journalist, will expose you in his paper . . ."

"Please, lady!" cried the man again, digging in his pocket. "Just a little misunderstanding!" And he hurriedly handed Papa some notes from a grubby wallet.

"Is that the right amount?" asked Madame Fernand sternly.

"It appears to be," said Papa.

"Then we'll go," she said.

They had only walked a few steps when the man came running after them.

What was it now? thought Anna nervously.

The man pointed apologetically.

"Excuse me, sir, but would you mind?" he said.

Papa looked down and discovered that he was still carrying the sewing machine in his hand. He put it down quickly. "I am terribly sorry," he said. "I am afraid I was a little confused."

"Of course, sir. Very natural, sir," said the man with no conviction whatever.

When Anna looked back a moment later he was gloomily arranging the sewing machine on top of the tiger skin.

They accompanied Madame Fernand to her Metro station.

"Now let's have no more nonsense about sewing machines," she said before she left them. "You know you can borrow mine any time you like. And tell your mother," she added to Anna, "that I'll drop in tomorrow and give her a hand with the mending."

She looked at Papa with a kind of admiration.

"You two," she said. "You must be the two most impractical people in the world!"

Anna and Papa walked home together. It was cold, but the sky was a bright, clear blue, and though there was no sign yet of spring there was a feeling that it was not too far away. At school that morning Anna had got seven out of ten for her dictation – only three mistakes. The money for her new shoes was safe in Papa's pocket. She was very happy.

Chapter Twenty-One

Omama arrived at Great-Aunt Sarah's just before Easter and came to see Mama and the children the following afternoon. With the help of the concierge (whose leg was now better) Mama had cleaned and tidied the flat so that it looked as nice as possible, but nothing could disguise the fact that it was very small and sparsely furnished.

"Can't you find anywhere bigger?" asked Omama while they were all having tea on the red oilcloth in the dining-room.

"A bigger flat would cost more," said Mama, helping Omama to some home-made apple flan. "We can barely afford this."

"But surely your husband . . .?" Omama seemed quite surprised.

"It's the Depression, Mother," said Mama. "Surely you've read about it! With so many French writers out of work no French paper is going to engage a German to write for them, and the *Daily Parisian* can't afford to pay very much."

"Yes, but even so . . ." Omama looked round the little room, rather rudely, thought Anna, for after all it wasn't as bad as all that – and at that very moment Max, tilting his chair as usual, collapsed on the floor with a plateful of apple flan in his lap. ". . . This is no way for children to grow up," Omama finished her sentence, exactly as though Max had crystallized the thought for her.

Anna and Max burst into uncontrollable laughter, but Mama said, "Nonsense, Mother!" quite sharply and told Max to go and get himself cleaned up. "As a matter of fact the children are doing extremely well," she told Omama and added when Max was safely out of the room, "Max is working for the first time in his life."

"And I'm going to take the *certificat d'études*!" said Anna. This was her big news. Madame Socrate had decided, since her work had improved so much, that there was now no reason why she shouldn't take the examination in the summer with the rest of the class.

"The *certificat d'études*?" said Omama. "Isn't that some kind of elementary school examination?"

"It's for French twelve-year-old children," said Mama, "and Anna's teacher thinks it remarkable that she should have caught up so quickly."

But Omama shook her head.

"It all seems very strange to me," she said and looked sadly at Mama. "So very different from the way you were brought up."

She had bought presents for everyone and during the rest of her stay in Paris, as in Switzerland, she arranged several outings for Mama and the children which they enjoyed and would never normally have been able to afford. But she did not really understand their new life.

"This is no way for children to grow up" became a sort of catch-phrase in the family.

"This is no way for children to grow up!" Max would say reproachfully to Mama when she had forgotten to make his sandwiches for school, and Anna would shake her head and say, "This is no way for children to grow up!" when the concierge caught Max sliding down the banisters.

After one of Omama's visits Papa, who usually managed to avoid meeting her, asked Mama, "How was your mother?" and Anna heard Mama reply, "Kind and utterly unimaginative as usual."

When it was time for Omama to go back to the South of France she embraced Mama and the children fondly.

"Remember now," she told Mama, "if ever

you're in difficulties you can send the children to me."

Anna caught Max's eye and mouthed, "This is no way for children to grow up!" and though it seemed mean in the face of all Omama's kindness they both had to make terrible grimaces to stop themselves from bursting into giggles.

After the Easter holidays Anna could hardly wait to go back to school. She loved it all since she had learned to speak French. Suddenly the work seemed quite easy and she was beginning to enjoy writing stories and compositions in French. It was not a bit like writing in German – you could make the words do quite different things – and she found it curiously exciting.

Even homework was no longer such a burden. The large lumps of French, history and geography which had to be learned by heart were the hardest part, but Anna and Max had discovered a way of mastering even this. If they studied the relevant passage last thing before going to sleep they found they always knew it in the morning. By the afternoon it began to fade and by the following day it was completely forgotten – but it stuck in their memories just as long as they needed it.

One evening Papa came into their bedroom when they were hearing each others' lessons. Anna's was about Napoleon and Papa looked amazed as she reeled it off. It began "Napoleon was born in Corsica" and then followed a long list of dates and battles until the final "he died in 1821."

"What an extraordinary way to learn about Napoleon," said Papa. "Is that all you know about him?"

"But it's everything!" said Anna, rather hurt, especially as she had not made a single mistake.

Papa laughed. "No, it's not everything," he said, and settling down on her bed he began to talk about Napoleon. He told the children about Napoleon's childhood in Corsica with his many brothers and sisters, about his brilliance at school and how he became an officer at fifteen and commander of the entire French army at the age of twenty-six; how he made his brothers and sisters kings and queens of the countries he conquered but could never impress his mother, an Italian peasant woman.

"*C'est bien pourvu que ça dure*," she would say disapprovingly at the news of every new triumph, which meant, "It's good as long as it lasts".

Then he told them how her forebodings came true, how half the French army was destroyed in the disastrous campaign against Russia, and finally of Napoleon's lonely death on the tiny island of St Helena.

Anna and Max listened entranced.

"It's just like a film," said Max.

"Yes," said Papa thoughtfully. "Yes, it is."

It was nice, thought Anna, that Papa had more time to talk to them these days. This was because owing to the Depression the *Daily Parisian* had been reduced in size and could no longer print so many of his articles. But Mama and Papa did not think it was a good thing at all and Mama, in particular, was always worrying about money.

"We can't go on like this!" Anna once heard her say to Papa. "I always knew we should have gone to England in the first place."

But Papa only shrugged his shoulders and said, "It'll sort itself out."

Soon after this Papa became very busy again and Anna could hear him typing till late at night in his room, so she assumed that it had indeed "sorted itself out" and stopped thinking about it. She was, in any case, much too interested in school to pay much attention to what was happening at home. The *certificat d'études* loomed ever larger and closer and she was determined to pass it. After only a year and nine months in France she thought this would be a very splendid thing.

At last the day arrived and early one hot morning in July Madame Socrate led her class through the streets to a neighbouring school. They were to take the exam supervised by strange teachers so as to make it quite fair. It had all to be got through in one day, so there was not much time for each of the many subjects they were to be examined in. There was French, arithmetic, history, geography, singing, sewing, art and gym.

Arithmetic came first – an hour's paper in which Anna thought she acquitted herself quite well, then French dictation, then a ten-minute break.

"How did you get on?" Anna asked Colette.

"All right," said Colette.

So far it had not been too bad.

After break they were given two papers of questions on history and geography, each lasting half an hour, and then – disaster!

"As we are a little short of time," announced the teacher in charge, "it has been decided that this year, instead of examining candidates in both sewing and art, and adding the marks together as in previous years, you will be examined in sewing only and that this will count as a whole subject."

Sewing was what Anna was worst at. She could never remember the names of the different stitches and, perhaps because Mama was so bad at it, she thought the whole business was an awful waste of time. Even Madame Socrate had never been able to persuade her to become interested in it. She had cut out an apron for her to hem, but Anna had been so slow at getting on with it that by the time it was finished she had grown too tall to wear it.

The teacher's pronouncement therefore plunged her into deep gloom which was confirmed when she was given a square of material, a needle and thread and some incomprehensible instructions. For half an hour she guessed wildly, tore her thread and picked frantically at knots which seemed to appear from nowhere, and finally handed in a piece of sewing so ragged and crumpled that even the teacher collecting it looked startled at the sight of it.

Lunch in the school playground with Colette was a glum affair.

"If you fail one subject, do you automatically fail the whole exam?" Anna asked as they sat eating their sandwiches on a bench in the shade.

"I'm afraid so," said Colette, "unless you get distinctions in another subject – then that makes up for it."

Anna ran through the exams she had already taken in her mind. Except for sewing she had done well in them all – but not well enough to have got distinctions. Her chances of passing seemed very slender.

However, she cheered up a little when she saw the subjects set for French composition in the afternoon. There were three to choose from and one of them was "A journey". Anna decided to describe what she imagined Papa's journey must have been like when he travelled from Berlin to Prague with a high temperature, not knowing whether or not he would be stopped at the frontier. There was a whole hour allowed for it and as she wrote Papa's journey became more and more vivid to her. She felt she knew exactly what it must have been like, what Papa's thoughts must have been and how, owing to the temperature, he would keep getting confused between what he was thinking and what was actually happening. By the time Papa had arrived in Prague she had written nearly five pages, and she just had time to check them through for punctuation and spelling before they were collected. She thought it was one of the best compositions she had ever written, and if only it had not been for the beastly sewing she would be sure now of having passed.

The only exams still to come were singing and gym. The singing tests were held separately for each child but as time was getting short they were very brief.

"Sing the *Marseillaise*," commanded the teacher but stopped Anna after the first few bars. "Good – that will do," she said and then cried, "Next!"

There were only ten minutes for gym.

"Quickly! Quickly!" cried the teacher as she herded the children into the playground and told them to spread out. There was another teacher to help her, and together they arranged the children in four long lines a metre or two apart.

"Attention!" cried one of the teachers. "Everyone stand on your right leg with your left leg raised off the ground in front of you!"

Everyone did, except Colette who stood on her left leg by mistake and had surreptitiously to change over. Anna stood dead straight, her arms held out to balance herself and her left leg raised as high as she could. Out of the corner of her eye she could see some of the others, and nobody's leg was as high off the ground as her own. The two teachers walked between the lines of children, some of whom were now beginning to wobble and collapse, and made notes on a piece of paper. When they came to Anna they stopped.

"Very good!" said one of them.

"Really excellent," said the other. "Don't you think . . ."

"Oh, definitely!" said the first teacher, and made a mark on the piece of paper.

"That's it! You can go home now!" they called when they got to the end of the line, and Colette rushed up to Anna and embraced her.

"You've done it! You've done it!" she cried. "You've got distinctions in gym, so now it won't matter if you've failed in sewing!"

"Do you really think so?" said Anna, but she felt pretty sure of it herself.

She walked home through the hot streets glowing with happiness and could hardly wait to tell Mama all about it.

"You mean to say that because you were so good at standing on one leg it won't matter that you can't sew?" said Mama. "What an extraordinary exam!"

"I know," said Anna, "but I suppose it's things like French and arithmetic that are really important and I think I did quite well in those."

Mama had made some cold lemon squash and they sat drinking it together in the dining-room while Anna rattled on. "We should have the results in a few days' time – it can't be much more because it's nearly the end of term. Wouldn't it be grand if I'd really passed – after less than two years in France!"

Mama agreed that it would indeed be grand, when the door bell rang and Max appeared looking pale and excited.

"Mama," he said almost before he had got through the door. "You've got to come to the prize-giving on Saturday. If you've got anything else on you've got to cancel it. It's very important!"

Mama looked very pleased.

"Have you won the Latin prize then?" she asked.

But Max shook his head.

"No," he said, and the rest of the sentence seemed somehow to stick in his throat. "I've won . . ." he said, and finally brought out, "I've won the *prix d'excellence*! That means they think I'm the best student in the class."

Of course there was delight and praise from everyone. Even Papa was interrupted in his typing to hear the great news, and Anna thought it was just as wonderful as everyone else. But she could not help wishing that it had not come just at this very moment. She had worked so hard and thought so long about passing the *certificat d'études*. After this, even if she did pass, how could anyone possibly be impressed? Especially since her success would be partly due to her talent for standing on one leg?

When the results were announced it was not nearly as exciting as she had expected. She had passed, so had Colette and so had most of the class. Madame Socrate handed each successful candidate an envelope containing a certificate with her name on it. But when Anna opened hers she found something more. Attached to the certificate were two ten franc notes and a letter from the Mayor of Paris.

"What does it mean?" she asked Madame Socrate.

Madame Socrate's wrinkled face broke into a delighted smile.

"The Mayor of Paris has decided to award prizes for the twenty best French compositions written by children taking the *certificat d'études*,"

244

she explained. "It seems that you have been awarded one of them."

When Anna told Papa he was just as pleased as he had been about Max's *prix d'excellence*.

"It's your first professional fee as a writer," he said. "It's really remarkable to have earned it in a language not your own."

Chapter Twenty-Two

The summer holidays arrived and Anna suddenly realized that no one had said anything about going away. It was very hot. You could feel the heat of the pavement through the soles of your shoes and the sun seemed to soak deep into the streets and the houses, so that they did not cool even at night. The Fernands had left for the seaside right after the end of term, and as July turned into August Paris gradually emptied. The paper shop at the corner was the first to put up a sign saying "Closed until September" but several others soon followed. Even the owner of the shop where Papa had bought the sewing machine had put up his shutters and gone away.

It was difficult to know what to do during the

long hot days. The flat was stifling, and even in the shady square where Anna and Max usually played the heat was too great for them to do anything very interesting. They would throw a ball about or play with their spinning tops for a while, but they soon became tired and sank on to a seat to dream of swimming and cold drinks.

"Wouldn't it be lovely," said Anna, "if we were sitting by the edge of Lake Zurich and could just jump in!"

Max pulled at his shirt where it had stuck to his skin.

"It's not likely to happen," he said. "We've hardly enough money to pay the rent, let alone go away."

"I know," said Anna. But it sounded so gloomy that she added, "Unless someone buys Papa's film script."

Papa's film script had been inspired by his conversation with the children about Napoleon. It was not about Napoleon himself but about his mother – how she had brought up her children without any money, how all their lives were changed by Napoleon's success and how at last she outlived him, an old blind lady, long after his final defeat. It was the first film script Papa had ever written and he had been working on it when Anna imagined that things had "sorted themselves out" with the *Daily Parisian*. Since the paper was now in greater difficulties than ever she hoped that the film would make Papa's fortune instead – but up to now there had been little sign of it.

Two French film companies to whom Papa had shown it had returned it with depressing speed. Finally Papa had sent it to a Hungarian film director in England, and this seemed an even less likely bet since it was not known for certain whether the Hungarian could read German. Also, thought Anna, why should the English, who had been Napoleon's greatest enemies, be more eager to make a film about him than the French? But at least the script had not yet come back, so there was still hope.

"I don't really think anyone's going to buy that film, do you?" said Max. "And I don't know what Papa and Mama are going to do for money."

"Oh, something will turn up," said Anna, but secretly she was a little frightened. Suppose nothing turned up. What then?

Mama was more irritable than they had ever known her. Quite small things seemed to upset her, like the time when Anna had broken her hairslide.

"Why couldn't you have been more careful?" Mama had stormed, and when Anna pointed out that the hairslide only cost thirty centimes, Mama had shouted, "Thirty centimes is thirty centimes!" and had insisted on trying to glue the hairslide together again before buying a new one.

Once she had said, out of the blue, "How would you children like to stay with Omama for a while?"

Max had answered, "Not at all!" and they had all laughed, but afterwards it did not seem so funny.

At night in the dark, hot bedroom Anna worried what would happen if Papa's financial situation did not improve. Would she and Max really be sent away?

Halfway through August a letter arrived from England. It was signed by the Hungarian film director's secretary. She said that the Hungarian film director thanked Papa for the script and that he looked forward to reading anything written by so distinguished an author, but that he felt he must warn Papa of the general lack of interest in films about Napoleon at present.

Mama, who had got quite excited at the sight of the English stamp, was deeply disappointed.

"He's had it nearly a month and he hasn't even read it yet!" she cried. "If only we were in England! Then we could do something about it!"

"I can't think what," said Papa – but lately "if only we were in England" had become Mama's constant cry. It was not only because of the nice English governess she had had as a child, but she kept hearing of other refugees who had settled in England and found interesting work. She hated the French papers for not asking Papa to write for them and she hated the French film companies for rejecting his film, and most of all she hated being always so short of money that even the purchase of small necessities like a new tube of toothpaste became a major worry.

About two weeks after the letter from England, things came to a head. It began when something went wrong with Mama's bed. She was trying to make it after breakfast, and when she had packed the sheets and pillows away and was about to turn it back into a sofa, it suddenly stuck. The padded seat-cum-mattress which was supposed to slide over the bedding refused to move. She called Max to help her and they both pushed, but it was no use. The seat stuck obstinately out into the room while Mama and Max mopped their faces, for it was already very hot. "Oh, why does something always have to go wrong!" cried Mama and then added, "The concierge will have to fix it. Anna, run and ask her to come up."

This was not a very attractive task. Recently, in order to save money, Mama had terminated the arrangement by which the concierge came up each day to help with the cleaning, and now the concierge was always very bad-tempered. But fortunately Anna met her just outside the door.

"I've brought up the mail," said the concierge – it was only a circular – "and I've come for the rent."

"Good morning, Madame," said Papa politely as always, meeting the concierge in the hall, and, "Could you have a look at this bed?" asked Mama as the concierge followed Anna into the room.

The concierge gave the bed a perfunctory push.

"I expect the children have been messing about with it," she said and then repeated, "I've come for the rent."

The children haven't been near it," said Mama crossly, "and what's all this about the rent? It's not due till tomorrow."

"Today," said the concierge.

"But it's not the first of September."

In reply the concierge pointed silently to the date on a newspaper she was carrying in her hand.

"Oh, very well," said Mama and called to Papa, "It's the rent."

"I didn't realize it was due today," said Papa. "I'm afraid I shall have to give it to you tomorrow," whereupon a peculiarly unpleasant expression came over the concierge's face.

Mama looked worriedly at Papa.

"But I don't understand," she said quickly in German. "Didn't you go to the *Daily Parisian* yesterday?"

"Of course," said Papa, "but they asked me to wait until this morning."

Recently the *Daily Parisian* had been in such difficulties that the editor sometimes found it hard to pay Papa even for the few articles that he was able to publish, and just now he owed him for three of them.

"I don't know what you're talking about to each other," the concierge interrupted rudely, "but the rent is due today. Not tomorrow but today."

Both Mama and Papa were surprised by her tone.

"You'll get your rent," said Mama, the colour rising in her face. "Now will you please fix this ramshackle contraption so that I shall have somewhere to sleep tonight!"

"Hardly worth my while, is it?" said the concierge, making no move to do so. "I mean – people who can't even pay the rent on time . . .!"

Papa looked very angry.

"I will not have you talk to my wife in that tone!" he said, but the concierge was unimpressed.

"Giving yourself airs," she said, "with nothing to show for it!"

At this Mama lost her temper.

"Will you please fix this bed!" she shouted. "And if you can't fix it, get out!"

"Ha!" said the concierge. "Hitler knew what he was doing when he got rid of people like you!"

"Get out!" shouted Papa and pushed the concierge towards the front door.

As she went through Anna heard her say, "The

government should have had more sense than to let you into our country!"

When they went back to Mama she was standing motionless, staring at the bed. There was an expression on her face which Anna had never seen, and as Papa came in she shouted, "We can't go on like this!" and gave the bed a tremendous kick. It must have dislodged something, for all at once the padded seat shot forward across the frame and closed with a bang. At this everyone laughed except Mama, who suddenly became very calm.

"It's Thursday," she said in a abnormally quiet voice, "so there'll be a children's matinée at the cinema." She searched in her purse and handed Max some money. "You two go."

"Are you sure?" said Max. The children's matinées were a franc each and for some time now Mama had said they were much too expensive.

"Yes, yes," said Mama. "Go quickly or you'll be late for the beginning."

There was something that did not feel right about it, but it was too big a treat to miss. So Anna and Max went to the cinema and watched three cartoons, a newsreel and a film about deep-sea fishing. When they returned they found everything normal. Lunch was on the table and Mama and Papa were standing very close together by the window, talking.

"You'll be glad to hear," said Papa when the children came in, "that the monstrous concierge has been paid her rent. I extracted my dues from the *Daily Parisian*."

"But we must have a talk," said Mama.

They waited while she dished out the food.

"We can't go on like this," said Mama. "You can see that for yourselves. It's impossible for Papa to earn a decent living in this country. So Papa and I think the only thing is to go to England, to see if we can start a new life there."

"When would we go?" asked Anna.

"Only Papa and I would go to start with," said Mama. "You and Max would go to stay with Omama and Opapa until we get things sorted out."

Max looked depressed but nodded. Clearly he had been expecting this.

"But supposing it took you quite a long time to get things sorted out," said Anna. "We wouldn't see you."

"It just wouldn't have to take us too long," said Mama.

"But Omama . . ." said Anna. "I know she's very kind, but . . ." She couldn't very well say that Omama did not like Papa, so she asked Papa instead, "What do you think?"

Papa's face had the tired look that Anna hated, but he said quite firmly, "You'll be properly looked after there. And you'll go to school – your

254

education won't be interrupted." He smiled. "You're both doing so well."

"It's the only thing to do," said Mama.

Something hard and unhappy rose inside Anna.

"Is it all settled, then?" she asked. "Don't you even want to know what we think?"

"Of course we do," said Mama, "but the way things are, we haven't much choice."

"Tell us what you think," said Papa.

Anna stared at the red oilcloth in front of her.

"It's just that I think we should stay together," she said. "I don't really mind where or how. I don't mind things being difficult, like not having any money, and I didn't mind about that silly concierge this morning – just as long as we're all four together."

"But Anna," said Mama, "lots of children leave their parents for a while. Lots of English children go to boarding schools."

"I know," said Anna, "but it's different if you haven't got a home. If you haven't got a home you've got to be with your people." She looked at her parents' stricken faces and burst out. "I know! I know we have no choice and I'm only making it more difficult. But I've never minded being a refugee before. In fact I've loved it. I think the last two years, when we've been refugees, have been much better than if we'd stayed in Germany. But if you send us away now I'm so

terribly frightened . . . I'm so terribly frightened
. . ."

"Of what?" asked Papa.

"That I might really feel like one!" said Anna and burst into tears.

Chapter Twenty-Three

Afterwards Anna was very ashamed of her outburst. After all, she had really known all the time
that Mama and Papa had no choice but to send
her and Max away. All she had done was to make
everyone feel worse about something that had to
happen anyway. Why couldn't she have kept
quiet? She worried about it in bed and when she
woke up early the next morning she felt she must
do something. She still had some of her prize
money left – she would go out and buy croissants
for everybody's breakfast.

There was a little breeze blowing for the first
time in weeks and when she came back from
the baker's with the hot croissants in a bag
she suddenly felt much happier. It would all

work out somehow – everything would be all right.

A man was talking to the concierge in a strong German accent and as she passed Anna heard him asking for Papa.

"I'll take you up," she said, disregarding the concierge, and the concierge, in offended silence, handed her a letter. Anna looked down at it and saw with a sudden quickening of the pulse that it had an English stamp. All the way up in the lift she could think of nothing but what might be inside the letter, and she only remembered Papa's visitor when he spoke to her.

"You must be Anna," he said and she nodded.

He was a shabby-looking man with a sad voice.

"Papa!" cried Anna as they entered the flat. "I've bought some croissants for breakfast and there's a letter and someone to see you!"

"Someone here? Now?" said Papa as he emerged from his room, tying his tie.

He drew the visitor into the dining-room and Anna followed with the letter in her hand.

"How do you do, Herr . . .?"

"Rosenfeld," said the man with a little bow. "I used to be an actor in Berlin but you don't know me. Only small parts, you understand." He smiled, showing irregular yellow teeth and added with apparent irrelevance, "I have a nephew in the confectionery business."

"Papa . . ." said Anna, holding out the letter, but Papa said, "Later!"

Herr Rosenfeld seemed to find it difficult to say what he had come for. His sad eyes kept roaming round the dining-room while he considered one opening after another and dismissed each one. At last he put his hand in his pocket and pulled out a small parcel wrapped in brown paper.

"I have brought you this," he said and handed it to Papa. Papa unwrapped it. It was a watch – an old silver watch – and there was something familiar about it.

"Julius!" cried Papa.

Herr Rosenfeld nodded sadly. "I am the bearer of bad news."

Onkel Julius was dead.

While Mama gave Herr Rosenfeld some coffee and he absent-mindedly nibbled one of Anna's croissants he told them how Onkel Julius had died. He had been dismissed from his post as curator of the Berlin Natural History Museum nearly a year ago.

"Surely you knew," said Herr Rosenfeld. "He had a Jewish grandmother."

Onkel Julius had not been able to work as a naturalist after this but had found a job sweeping up in a factory. He had moved from his flat into a cheap room, and this was where he had made friends with Herr Rosenfeld who had the room

259

next door. In spite of his difficulties Onkel Julius had been quite cheerful at this stage.

"He just . . . accepted things, didn't he?" said Herr Rosenfeld. "I was planning even then to come to Paris and join my nephew, and I said to him, "You come too – there's room for us both in the confectionery trade!" But he wouldn't. He seemed to think that the situation in Germany was bound to change."

Papa nodded, remembering Onkel Julius in Switzerland.

Herr Rosenfeld and Onkel Julius had had many conversations together and Onkel Julius had talked a great deal about Papa and his family. Once or twice Herr Rosenfeld had accompanied him to the Zoo where he now spent all his Sundays. Though Onkel Julius had so little money he always managed to bring some peanuts for the monkeys and scraps for the other animals, and Herr Rosenfeld had been amazed to see how they rushed to the bars of their cages as soon as he appeared.

"It wasn't just the food," he said. "It was more like a sort of gentleness in him that they recognized."

Again Papa nodded . . .

During the autumn Onkel Julius had even dropped into the Zoo after work in the evenings. His whole life now centred round the animals.

There was a monkey that let him stroke it through the bars of its cage . . .

And then, just before Christmas, the blow had fallen. Onkel Julius had received an official letter revoking his pass to the Zoo. No reason was given. The fact that he had a Jewish grandmother was enough.

After this Onkel Julius had changed. He could not sleep and did not eat properly. He no longer talked to Herr Rosenfeld but spent the Sundays in his room, staring at the sparrows on the rooftop opposite. At last, late one night in spring, he had knocked on Herr Rosenfeld's door and begged him, when he went to Paris, to take something to Papa. Herr Rosenfeld had explained that he would not be going for some time yet, but Onkel Julius had said, "Never mind, I'll give it to you now," and Herr Rosenfeld had accepted a small parcel to calm him. Next morning Onkel Julius had been found dead, an empty bottle of sleeping tablets beside him.

Herr Rosenfeld had not been able to leave Germany till several months later, but had at once come to see Papa and to deliver the parcel.

"There's a note as well," he said.

The handwriting was as meticulous as ever.

It said simply, "Goodbye. I wish you well," and was signed "Julius".

* * *

For quite a long time after Herr Rosenfeld had left Anna forgot about the other letter from England which she was still holding in her hand, but at last she remembered and gave it to Papa. He opened it, read it silently and passed it to Mama.

"They want to buy your film script!" cried Mama and then, as though she could hardly believe it, "A thousand pounds . . .!"

"Does that mean we don't have to go and stay with Omama?" Max asked quickly.

"Of course!" said Mama. "There's no need now for you to go away. We can all go to England together!"

"Oh Papa!" cried Anna. "Papa, isn't it wonderful!"

"Yes," said Papa. "I'm glad we shall all be together."

"To think that they're going to film your script!" Mama's hand was on his shoulder. Then she noticed the frayed collar under her fingers. "You'll need a new jacket," she said.

"Let's tell the concierge and give her notice!" said Max.

"No – wait!" cried Mama. "But if we're going to London, we ought to let your schools know. And we must find out about hotels. And it'll be colder there – you'll need some woollies . . ."

Suddenly there seemed to be a thousand things to talk about.

But Papa, who had made it all happen, did not want to talk about any of them. While Mama and the children chattered and made plans he sat quite still and let the words flow round him. Onkel Julius's watch was in his hand and he was stroking it, very gently, with one finger.

Chapter Twenty-Four

It seemed strange to be leaving again for yet
another country.

"Just when we'd learned to speak French properly," said Max.

There was no time to say goodbye to Madame
Socrate because she was still on holiday. Anna
had to leave a note for her at the school. But she
went with Mama to pay a farewell visit to Great-
Aunt Sarah who wished them luck in their new
life in England and was delighted to hear about
Papa's film.

"At last someone is paying that good man some
money," she said. "They should have done it long
ago already."

The Fernands returned from the seaside just in

time for the two families to spend a final evening together. Papa took everyone out to dinner to celebrate and they promised each other to meet again soon.

"We'll come back to France often," said Papa. He had a new jacket and the tired look had quite disappeared from his face.

"And you must visit us in London," said Mama.

"We'll come to see the film," said Madame Fernand.

The packing did not take long. There seemed to be less to pack each time they moved – so many things had been used up and thrown away – and one grey morning less than two weeks after the letter had come from England, they were ready to leave.

Mama and Anna stood in the little dining-room for the last time, waiting for the taxi to take them to the station. Cleared of the litter of small objects in everyday use which had made it familiar, the room looked bare and cheap.

"I don't know how we lived here for two years," said Mama.

Anna rubbed her hand over the red oilcloth on the table.

"I liked it," she said.

Then the taxi came. Papa and Max piled the luggage into the lift and then Papa shut the door of the flat behind them.

When the train drew out of the station Anna leaned out of the window with Papa and watched Paris slowly slip away.

"We'll come back," said Papa.

"I know," said Anna. She remembered how she had felt when they had gone back to the Gasthof Zwirn for the holidays and added, "But it won't be the same – we won't belong. Do you think we'll ever really belong anywhere?"

"I suppose not," said Papa. "Not the way people belong who have lived in one place all their lives. But we'll belong a little in lots of places, and I think that may be just as good."

The equinoctial gales were early that year and when the train reached Dieppe about lunch-time the sea looked wild and dark under the grey sky. They had chosen the slow crossing from Dieppe to Newhaven because it was cheaper, in spite of Papa's new-found wealth.

"We don't know how long the money will have to last us," said Mama.

As soon as the boat emerged from Dieppe harbour it began to pitch and roll and Anna's excitement at her first sea voyage quickly evaporated. She, Max and Mama watched each others' faces turn paler and greener until they had to go below and lie down. Only Papa was unaffected. It took six hours to cross the Channel instead of the customary four because of the bad weather, and long before they landed Anna felt that she did not care what England was like, just as long as they got there. When they finally arrived it was too dark to see anything. The boat train had left long ago and a kind but incomprehensible porter put them on a slow train to London instead.

As it started hesitantly on its way a spatter of raindrops appeared on the window.

"English weather," said Papa who was very cheerful because he had not been seasick.

Anna sat huddled in her corner of the compartment, watching the anonymous dark landscape rush past. You could not really see what any of it was like. After a while she got tired of looking at it and stole a glance, instead, at two men opposite her. They were English. In the rack above their heads were two black melon-shaped hats such as she had rarely seen before and they were sitting up very straight, reading newspapers. Although they had got on to the train together they did not speak to each other. The English seemed to be very quiet people.

The train slowed down and stopped, for the umpteenth time, at a small ill-lit station.

"Where are we?" asked Mama.

Anna spelled out the name of an illuminated sign.

"Bovril," she said.

"It can't be," said Max. "The last place we stopped at was called Bovril."

Mama, still pale from the crossing, looked for herself.

"It's an advertisement," she said. "Bovril is some kind of English food. I think they eat it with stewed fruit."

The train continued to crawl through the darkness and Anna became drowsy. There was something familiar about the situation – her tiredness, the sound of the train wheels, and the rain spattering on the windows. It had all happened before, some time long ago. Before she could remember when, she fell asleep.

When she awoke the train was going faster and there were lights flashing past the windows. She looked out and saw wet roads and street lamps and little houses which all looked alike.

"We're coming into London," said Mama.

The roads grew wider and the buildings bigger and more varied, and suddenly the sound of the wheels changed and they were on a bridge over a wide river.

"The Thames!" cried Papa.

It was lined with lights on both sides and Anna could see some cars and a red bus crawling along beneath them. Then they were across, the river was left behind, and as though a box had been clapped over the train, the brightness of a station with platforms and porters and crowds of people suddenly appeared all round them. They had arrived.

Anna climbed off the train and stood on the chilly platform while they waited for Mama's Cousin Otto who was to meet them. All round them the English were greeting each other, smiling and talking.

"Can you understand what they're saying?" asked Anna.

"Not a word," said Max.

"A few months and we'll be able to," said Anna.

Papa had got hold of a porter, but Cousin Otto was nowhere to be seen, so Mama and Papa went to look for him while the children stayed with the luggage. It was cold. Anna sat down on a suitcase and the porter smiled at her.

"*Français?*" he asked.

Anna shook her head.

"*Deutsch?*"

She nodded.

"Ah, *Deutsch*," said the porter. He was a tubby little man with a red face. "Ittla?" he added.

Anna and Max looked at each other. They did not know what he meant.

"Ittla! Ittla!" said the porter. He placed one finger under his nose like a moustache and raised the other hand in the Nazi salute. "Ittla?" he said.

"Oh, Hitler!" cried Max.

Anna said, "Do they have Nazis here?"

"I hope not," said Max.

They both shook their heads vehemently and made disapproving faces.

"No!" they said. "No Hitler!"

The porter seemed pleased.

"Ittla . . ." he began. He looked round to see if anyone was watching him and then spat forcefully on the platform. "Ittla," he said. That was what he thought of him.

They all smiled and the porter was just about to do another imitation of Hitler with his hair pulled down over his forehead, when Mama appeared from one side and Papa and Cousin Otto from the other.

"Welcome to England!" cried Cousin Otto, embracing Mama. Then, as Mama gave a little shiver, he added reprovingly, "In this country you should always wear woollen underclothes."

Anna remembered him from Berlin as a rather dapper man, but now he looked shabby in a crumpled coat. They followed him to the exit in a slow procession. There were people all round them. It was so damp that steam seemed to be rising from the ground and Anna's nostrils were filled with the smell of rubber from the mackintoshes which nearly all the English were wearing. At the end of the platform there was a slight hold-up, but nobody pushed or jostled as was usual in France and Germany – everyone just waited their turn. Through the misty air a fruit stall shone bright with oranges, apples and yellow bananas and there was a shop window entirely filled with sweets and chocolates. The English must be very rich to be able to buy such things. They passed an English policeman with a tall helmet and another one in a wet cape.

Outside the station the rain was coming down like a shining curtain and beyond it Anna could dimly see some kind of open square. Again the feeling came over her that this had all happened before. She had stood in the rain outside a station and it had been cold . . .

"Wait here and I'll get a taxi," said Cousin Otto, and this, too, was familiar.

Suddenly her tiredness and the bad crossing and the cold all combined. There was a great emptiness in her head and the rain seemed to be all about her and the past and the present became confused, so that for a moment she could not think where she was.

"All right?" said Papa, grasping her arm as she swayed a little, and Cousin Otto said in a concerned voice, "It must be quite difficult to spend one's childhood moving from country to country."

At the words something cleared in Anna's mind.

"Difficult childhood . . ." she thought. The past and the present slid apart. She remembered the long, weary journey from Berlin with Mama, how it had rained, and how she had read Gunther's book and wished for a difficult childhood so that she might one day become famous. Had her wish then come true? Could her life since she had left Germany really be described as a difficult childhood?

She thought of the flat in Paris and the Gasthof Zwirn. No, it was absurd. Some things had been difficult, but it had always been interesting and often funny – and she and Max and Mama and Papa had nearly always been together. As long as they were together she could never have a difficult childhood. She sighed a little as she abandoned her hopes.

"What a pity," she thought. "I'll never be famous at this rate!"

She moved closer to Papa and put her hand in his pocket for warmth.

Then Cousin Otto came back with the taxi.

"Quickly!" he cried. "He won't wait!"

They all ran. Papa and Cousin Otto shifted the luggage. The taxi driver threw it into the taxi. Mama slipped in the wet and almost fell, but Cousin Otto saved her.

"The English all wear rubber soles," he cried, pushing in the last suitcase.

Then they all piled into the taxi. Cousin Otto gave the address of the hotel. Anna pressed her face against the window, and the taxi started.

THE OTHER
WAY ROUND

Part One

1

Anna was standing in her room at the top of the Bartholomews' London house. She had finally remembered to stitch up the hem of her skirt which had been hanging down and she was wearing new lisle stockings – not black ones from Woolworth's but the more expensive beige kind from Marks and Spencer's. Her sweater, which she had knitted herself, almost matched her skirt, and her pretty shoes, inherited from one of the Bartholomews' daughters, were newly polished. She tilted the mirror on the dressing-table to catch her reflection, hoping to be impressed.

It was disappointing, as usual. The room outdid her. It was clear that she did not belong in it. Against the quilted, silky bedspread, the elegant wallpaper, the beautiful, gleaming furniture, she looked neat but dull. A small person dressed in brown. Like a servant, she thought, or an orphan. The room needed someone careless, richer, more smiling.

She sat on the chintzy stool and stared at her face with growing irritation. Dark hair, green eyes, an over-serious expression. Why couldn't she at least have been blonde? Everyone knew that blonde hair was better. All the film stars were blonde, from Shirley Temple to Marlene Dietrich. Her eyebrows were wrong, too. They should have been thin arcs, as though drawn with a pencil. Instead they were thick and almost straight. And as for her legs . . . Anna did not like even to think of her legs, for they were shortish, and to have short legs seemed to her not so much of a misfortune as a lapse of taste.

She leaned forward and her reflection came to meet her. At least I look intelligent, she thought. She frowned and pursed her lips, trying to increase the impression. Clever, they had called it at the Metcalfe Boarding School for Girls. That clever little refugee girl. She had not realised at first that it was derogatory. Nobody much had liked her at Miss Metcalfe's. At least I've finished with all that, she thought.

She picked up her handbag – cracked brown leather, an old one of Mama's brought from Berlin – extracted a powder compact and began carefully to powder her nose. No lipstick, yet. You didn't wear lipstick at fifteen unless you were fast.

I need never have gone to Miss Metcalfe's, she thought, if only we'd had a home. It was living in a hotel that had caused all the trouble – that, and having no money. Because when Mama and Papa could no longer pay for her hotel room (even though the hotel was so cheap) she had become like a parcel, to be tossed about, handed from one person to another, without knowing who would be holding her next. The only reason she had gone to Miss Metcalfe's was that Miss Metcalfe had offered to take her for nothing. The reason she was now living at the Bartholomews' (though the Bartholomews were, of course, old friends and much nicer than Miss Metcalfe) was that here, too, it did not cost anything.

She sighed. Which hair ribbon, she wondered. For once she had two to choose from – brown or green?

She decided on green, slipped it over her head and then back over her hair, and looked at herself. It's the best I can do, she thought.

A clock somewhere struck ten – time she left. Mama and Papa were expecting her. She picked up her coat and checked her handbag. Keys, torch, identity card, purse. Her purse felt curiously light and she opened it. It was empty. The fourpence for her fare must have fallen out into the bag. She turned the bag upside down. Keys, torch, identity card, powder compact, two pencils, a bus ticket, the paper wrapping off a chocolate biscuit and some crumbs. There was no money. But it must be there, she thought. She'd had it. She was sure she'd had it the previous night. Feverishly, she searched through the pockets of her coat. It wasn't there either. Oh damn! she thought. Just when I thought I was all right. Oh damn and damn and damn!

She swept the contents back into the bag, took her coat and went out of the room. What am I going to do? she thought, they'll be waiting for me and I haven't got my fare.

The landing was dark – the maids must have forgotten to draw back the blackout curtains. Could she borrow from the maids? No, she thought, I can't. Hoping that, somehow, a miracle would happen, she started down the thickly-carpeted stairs.

In the hall, as she passed what had been the school-room but was now a kind of sitting-room, a friendly American voice called out, "Is that you, Anna? Come in a minute – I haven't seen you for days."

Mrs Bartholomew.

Could she ask her?

She opened the door and found Mrs Bartholomew drinking coffee in her dressing-gown. She was sitting at the old school-room table and in front of her on the ink-stained surface were a tray and an untidy pile of old children's books.

"You're up early on a Sunday," said Mrs Bartholomew. "Are you off to see your parents?"

Anna thought of answering, "Yes, but I'm afraid I haven't . . ." or "Could you possibly lend me . . . ?" Instead, she stood just inside the door and said, "Yes."

"I bet they'll be glad to see you." Mrs Bartholomew waved what appeared to be Hans Andersen. "I've been sitting here missing the girls. Judy used to love this book – three, four years ago. Jinny too. It was such fun, wasn't it, when you all did lessons together!"

Anna reluctantly dragged her mind away from her problem.

"Yes," she said. It had been fun.

"This war really is crazy," said Mrs Bartholomew. "Here we all sent our children out of London, thinking that Hitler was going to bomb it out of existence, and a half-year later still nothing at all has happened. Personally, I'm tired of it. I want them back here with me. Jinny says there's a chance the whole school may move back into town – wouldn't that be nice?"

"Yes," said Anna.

"They'd enjoy having you live in the house with them." Mrs Bartholomew seemed suddenly to notice how Anna was hovering half-in and half-out of the room.

"Well, come in, dear!" she cried. "Have some coffee and tell me – how is everything? How's the great Polytechnic art course?"

"I really should go," said Anna, but Mrs Bartholomew insisted, and she found herself sitting at the schoolroom table with a cup in her hand. Through the window she could see grey clouds and branches waving in the wind. It looked cold. Why couldn't she have asked for her fare money when she had the chance?

"So what have you been doing? Tell me," said Mrs Bartholomew.

What had she been doing?

"Well, of course it's only a junior art course." It was difficult to bring her mind to bear on it. "We do bits of everything. Last week we all drew each other. I liked doing that."

The teacher had looked at Anna's drawing and had told her that she had real talent. She warmed at the memory.

"But of course it's not very practical – financially, I mean," she added. The teacher was probably just being nice.

"Now listen!" cried Mrs Bartholomew. "You don't have to worry about finance at your age. Not while you're in this house. I know it's difficult for your parents being in a strange country and everything, but we love having you and you can stay just as long as you like. So you just concentrate on your education. I'm sure you'll do very, very well, and you must write and tell the girls all about it because they'd love to hear."

"Yes," said Anna. "Thank you."

Mrs Bartholomew looked at her. "Are you all right?" she asked.

"Yes," said Anna. "Yes, of course. But I think I should go."

Mrs Bartholomew walked with her into the hall and watched her put on her coat.

"Wait a minute!" she cried, diving into a cupboard, to emerge a moment later with something thick and grey. "You'd better wear Jinny's scarf."

She made Anna wind it round her neck and then kissed her on the cheek.

"There!" she said. "Are you sure you've got everything you need? Nothing you want?"

Now, surely, was the moment to ask. It would be so simple, and she knew Mrs Bartholomew wouldn't mind. But standing there in Judy's shoes and Jinny's scarf and looking at Mrs Bartholomew's kind face she found it suddenly impossible. She shook her head and smiled. Mrs Bartholomew smiled back and closed the door.

Damn! thought Anna as she started to trudge up Holland Park Avenue. Now she would have to walk all the way to Bloomsbury because she didn't have fourpence for the tube.

It was a cold, bright day, and at first she tried to think of it as an adventure.

"I really like exercise," she said experimentally to Miss Metcalfe in her mind, "as long as it isn't lacrosse." But, as usual, she could not extract a satisfactory reply, so she abandoned the conversation.

A few people were still in bed as it was Sunday and you could see their blackout curtains drawn above the shuttered shops. Only the paper shop at Notting Hill Gate was open, with Sunday papers displayed on racks outside and printed posters saying "Latest War News" but, as usual, nothing had happened. The pawnbroker next to the tube station still had the sign which had so much puzzled Anna when she had first come to London and couldn't speak English properly. It said "Turn Your Old Gold Into Cash", but a little piece had fallen off the G in Gold, turning it into Cold. Anna remembered how every day when she had passed it on her way to do lessons with Jinny and Judy she had wondered what it meant and whether, if she went into the shop and sneezed, they would give her some money.

Of course nowadays no one talking to Anna would guess that she hadn't spoken English from birth, and she had lost the American accent she had originally picked up from the Bartholomews. She hadn't been meant just to learn English from them – they had also been meant to learn some of her native German and the French she had acquired in Paris after escaping from Hitler. But it hadn't worked out like that. She and Jinny and Judy had become friends and spoken English, and Mrs Bartholomew hadn't minded.

There was a sharp wind blowing across Kensington Gardens. It rattled the signs pointing to air-raid shelters which no one had ever used and the few crocuses still growing between newly-dug trenches looked frozen. Anna pushed her hands deep into the pockets of her old grey coat. Really, she thought, it was ridiculous for her to be walking like this. She was cold, and she would be late, and Mama would wonder where she'd got to. It was ridiculous being so short of money that the loss of fourpence threw everything out of gear. And how could anyone be so stupidly shy as not to be able to borrow fourpence when they needed it? And how had she managed to lose the money, anyway – she was sure she'd had it the previous day, a silver threepenny bit and two halfpennies, she could see them now. I'm sick of it, she thought, I'm sick of being so ineffectual – and Miss Metcalfe's tall figure rose unbidden before her, cocked a sarcastic eyebrow and said, "Poor Anna!"

Oxford Street was deserted, the windows of the big stores covered in criss-crossings of brown paper to stop them splintering in case of air raids, but Lyons Corner House was open and filled with soldiers queuing for cups of tea. At Oxford Circus the sun came out and Anna felt more cheerful. After all, the reason for her predicament was not only that she was shy. Papa would understand why she couldn't borrow money from Mrs Bartholomew, not even such a small sum. Her feet were tired, but she was two thirds of the way home and perhaps she was really doing something rather splendid.

"Once," said a grown-up Anna negligently to an immensely aged Miss Metcalfe, "Once I walked all the way from Holland Park to Bloomsbury rather than borrow fourpence," and the aged Miss Metcalfe was suitably impressed.

At Tottenham Court Road a newsvendor had spread an array of Sunday papers along the pavement. She read the headlines ("Tea Ration Soon?" "Bring Back The Evacuees!" and "English Dog Lovers Exposed") before she noticed the date. It was the fourth of March 1940, exactly seven years since she had left Berlin to become a refugee. Somehow this seemed significant.

Here she was, penniless but coping triumphantly, on the anniversary of the day her wanderings had begun. Nothing could get her down. Perhaps one day when she was rich and famous everyone would look back . . .

"Of course I remember Anna," said the aged Miss Metcalfe to the interviewer from Pathe Newsreel, "She was so bold and resourceful – we all admired her tremendously."

She trudged up High Holborn. As she turned down Southampton Row, not very far now from the hotel, she noticed a faint clinking in the hem of her coat. Surely it couldn't be . . . ? Suspiciously, she felt around in her pocket. Yes, there was a hole. With a sinking feeling of anticlimax she inserted two fingers and, by lifting up the hem of her coat with the other hand, managed to extract two halfpennies and a threepenny piece which were lying in a little heap at the bottom of the lining. For a moment she stood quite still, looking at it. Then she thought, "Typical!" so vehemently that she found she had said it out loud, to the astonishment of a passing couple. But what could be more typical than her performance that morning? All that embarrassment with Mrs Bartholomew, all that worrying about whether or not she had done the right thing, all that walking and her aching legs, and in the end it had just been a huge waste of time. No one else behaved like this. She was tired of it. She would have to change. Everything would have to change.

With the money clutched in her hand she strode across to the other side of the road where a woman was selling daffodils outside a tea-shop.

"How much?" she asked.

They were threepence a bunch.

"I'll have one," she said.

It was a ridiculous piece of extravagance – and the daffodils weren't worth it, either, she thought, seeing them droop over her hand – but at least it was something. She would give them to Mama and Papa. She would say, "It's seven years today since we left Germany and I've brought you some flowers." And perhaps the flowers would bring them luck, perhaps Papa would be asked to write something or someone would send him some money and perhaps everything would become quite different, and it would all be just because she'd saved her fare money and bought some daffodils. And even if nothing happened at all, at least Mama and Papa would be pleased and it would cheer them up.

As she pushed open the swing-doors of the Hotel Continental the old porter who had been drowsing behind his desk greeted her in German.

"Your mother has been in quite a state," he said, "wondering where you'd got to."

Anna surveyed the lounge. Scattered among the tables and sitting in shabby leatherette chairs were the usual German, Czech and Polish refugees who had made the hotel their home while hoping for something better – but not Mama.

"I'll go up to her room," she said, but before she could start a voice called, "Anna!" and Mama burst in from the direction of the public telephone. Her face was pink with excitement and her blue eyes tense.

"Where have you been?" she cried in German. "I've

just been talking to Mrs Bartholomew. We thought something had happened! And Max is here – he can only stay a little while and he wanted specially to see you."

"Max?" said Anna. "I didn't know he was in London."

"One of his Cambridge friends gave him a lift." Mama's face relaxed as always when she spoke of her remarkable son. "He came here first and then he's meeting some other friends and then they're all going back together. English friends, of course," she added for her own pleasure and for the edification of any Germans, Czechs or Poles who might be listening.

As they hurried upstairs Mama noticed the daffodils in Anna's hand. "What are those?" she asked.

"I bought them," said Anna.

"Bought them?" cried Mama, but was interrupted in her astonishment by a middle-aged Pole who emerged from a door marked W.C.

"The wanderer has returned," said the Pole in satisfied tones as he observed Anna. "I told you, Madame, that she had probably just been delayed," and he disappeared into his room on the other side of the corridor.

Anna blushed. "I'm not as late as all that," she said, but Mama hurried her on.

Papa's room was on the top floor and as they went in Anna almost fell over Max who was sitting on the end of the bed just inside the door. He said, "Hi, sister!" in English like someone in a film and gave her a brotherly kiss. Then he added in German, "I was just leaving. I'm glad I didn't miss you."

Anna said, "It took me ages to get here," and squeezed round the table which held Papa's typewriter to embrace Papa. "Bonjour, Papa," she said, because Papa loved to speak French. He was looking tired but the expression in the intelligent, ironically smiling eyes was as usual. Papa always looked, thought Anna, as though he would be interested in whatever happened even though nowadays he clearly did not expect it to be anything good.

She held out the daffodils. "I got these," she said. "It's seven years today since we left Germany and I thought they might bring us all luck."

They were drooping more than ever but Papa took them from her and said, "They smell of spring." He filled his toothglass with water and Anna helped him put the flowers in. They immediately fell over the edge of the glass until their heads rested on the table.

"I'm afraid they've already overstrained themselves," said Papa and everyone laughed. Well, at least they had cheered him up. "Anyway," said Papa, "the four of us are together. After seven years of emigration perhaps one shouldn't ask for more luck than that."

"Oh yes one should!" said Mama.

Max grinned. "Seven years is probably as much as anyone actually needs." He turned to Papa. "What do you think is going to happen about the war? Do you think anything is going to happen at all?"

"When Hitler is ready," said Papa. "The problem is whether the British will be ready too."

It was the usual conversation and, as usual, Anna's mind edged away from it. She sat on the bed next to Max and rested her feet. She liked being in Papa's room. No matter where they had lived, in Switzerland, Paris or London, Papa's room had always looked the same. There had always been a table with the typewriter, now getting rather rickety, his books, the section of the wall where he pinned photographs, post cards, anything that interested him, all close together so that even the loudest wallpaper was defeated by their joint size; the portraits of his parents looking remote in Victorian settings, a Meerschaum pipe which he never smoked but liked the shape of, and one or two home-made contraptions which he fondly believed to be practical. At present he was going through a phase of cardboard boxes and had devised a mousetrap out of an upside-down lid propped up by a pencil with a piece of cheese at the base. As the mouse ate the cheese the lid would drop down over it and Papa would then somehow extract the mouse and give it its freedom in Russell Square. So far he had had little success.

"How is your mouse?" asked Anna.

"Still at liberty," said Papa. "I saw it last night. It has a very English face."

Max shifted restlessly on the bed beside her.

"No one is worrying about the war in Cambridge," he was saying to Mama. "I went to see the Recruiting Board the other day and they told me very firmly not to volunteer but to get my degree first."

"Because of your scholarship!" cried Mama proudly.

"No, Mama," said Max. "It's the same for all my friends. Everyone has been told to leave it for a couple of years. Perhaps by then Papa might be naturalised." After four years of public school and nearly two terms at Cambridge Max looked, sounded and felt English. It was maddening for him not to be legally English as well.

"If they make an exception for him," said Mama.

Anna looked at Papa and tried to imagine him as an Englishman. It was very difficult. Just the same she cried, "Well, they should! He's not just anyone – he's a famous writer!"

Papa glanced round the shabby room.

"Not very famous in England," he said.

There was a pause and then Max got up to go. He embraced Mama and Papa and made a face at Anna. "Walk to the tube with me," he said. "I've hardly seen you."

They went down the many stairs in silence and as usual the residents of the lounge glanced at Max admiringly as he and Anna walked through. He had always been handsome with his fair hair and blue eyes – not like me, thought Anna. It was nice being with him, but she wished she could have sat a little longer before setting out again.

As soon as they emerged from the hotel Max said in English, "Well, how are things?"

"All right," said Anna. Max was walking fast and her feet were aching. "Papa is depressed because he offered himself to the B.B.C. for broadcasting propaganda to Germany, and they won't have him."

"Why on earth not?"

"It seems he's too famous. The Germans all know that he's violently anti-Nazi, so they won't take any notice of anything he says. At least that's the theory."

Max shook his head. "I thought he looked old and

tired." He waited for her to catch him up before he asked, "And what about you?"

"Me? I don't know." Suddenly Anna didn't seem to be able to think of anything but her feet. "I suppose I'm all right," she said vaguely.

Max looked worried. "But you like your art course?" he asked. "You enjoy that?"

The feet receded slightly from Anna's consciousness.

"Yes," she said, "But it's all so hopeless, isn't it, when no one has any money? I mean, you read about artists leaving their homes to live in a garret, but if your family is living in a garret already . . . ! I thought perhaps I should get a job."

"You're not sixteen yet," said Max and added almost angrily, "I seem to have had all the luck."

"Don't be silly," said Anna. "A major scholarship to Cambridge isn't luck."

They had arrived at Russell Square tube station and one of the lifts was about to close its gates, ready to descend.

"Well –" said Anna, but Max hesitated.

"Listen," he cried, "Why don't you come up to Cambridge for a week-end?" And as Anna was about to demur, "I can manage the money. You could meet some of my friends and I could show you round a bit – it would be fun!" The lift gates creaked and he made a dash for it. "I'll write you the details," he cried as he and the lift sank from sight.

Anna walked slowly back to the hotel. Mama and Papa were waiting for her at one of the tables in the lounge and a faded German lady had joined them.

". . . the opera in Berlin," the German lady was saying to Papa. "You were in the third row of the stalls. I remember my husband pointing you out. I was so excited, and you wrote a marvellous piece about it next morning in the paper."

Papa was smiling politely.

"Lohengrin, I think," said the German lady. "Unless it was the Magic Flute or perhaps Aîda. Anyway, it was wonderful. Everything was wonderful in those days."

Then Papa saw Anna. "Excuse me," he said. He bowed to the German lady and he and Mama and Anna went into the dining-room for lunch.

"Who was that?" asked Anna.

"The wife of a German publisher," said Papa. "She got out but the Nazis killed her husband."

Mama said, "God knows what she lives on."

It was the usual Sunday lunch, served by a Swiss girl who was trying to learn English but was more likely to pick up a bit of Polish in this place, thought Anna. There were prunes for pudding and there was some difficulty afterwards about paying for Anna's meal. The Swiss waitress said she would put it on the bill, but Mama said no, it was not an extra item since she herself had missed dinner on the previous Tuesday when she wasn't feeling well. The waitress said she wasn't sure if it was all right to transfer meals from one person to another. Mama got excited and Papa looked unhappy and said, "Please don't make a scene." In the end the manageress had to be consulted and decided that it was all right this time but must not be regarded as a precedent. By this time a lot of the good had gone out of the day.

"Shall we sit down here or shall we go upstairs?" said Mama when they were back in the lounge – but the German lady was looming and Anna didn't want to talk about the opera in Berlin, so they went upstairs. Papa perched on the chair, and Anna and Mama sat on the bed.

"I mustn't forget to give you your fare money for next week," said Mama, opening her handbag.

Anna looked at her.

"Mama," she said, "I think I ought to get a job."

2

Anna and Mama were sitting in the waiting room of the Relief Organisation for German Jewish Refugees.

"If only they'll help us with the fees for this secretarial course," said Mama for at least the sixth time, "you'll always be able to earn your living."

Anna nodded.

All round the room other German refugees were sitting on hard chairs like Mama and herself, waiting to be interviewed. Some were talking in nervous, high-pitched voices. Some were reading newspapers – Anna counted one English, one French, two Swiss and one Yiddish. An elderly couple were eating buns out of a paper bag and a thin man was hunched up in a corner by himself, staring into space. Every so often the receptionist came in and called out a name and the owner of the name followed her out.

"You'll have something to build on," said Mama, "which I've never had, and you'll always be independent."

She had at first been taken aback by Anna's suggestion of getting a job but then had thrown herself into the search for some suitable training with her usual energy. She had been adamant that Anna must have training of some sort, but it was hard to decide what. A secretarial course was the obvious choice, but Anna's complete inability to learn shorthand had been one of her many failures at Miss Metcalfe's. "It's not so much that it's difficult but it's so boring!" she had cried, and

Miss Metcalfe had smiled pityingly as usual and had pointed out that arrogance never helped anyone.

Mama had quite understood about the shorthand and by dint of asking everyone she knew for advice had discovered a secretarial school where they taught a different system. It was not written down but tapped out on a little machine like a typewriter and had the further advantages of being quickly learned and easily adapted to other languages. The only trouble was that the full course cost twenty-five pounds.

"Mr and Mrs Zuckerman!" The receptionist had come in again, catching the elderly couple in the middle of their buns. They hastily stuffed the half-eaten remains back into the paper bag and followed her out.

"I think we're bound to get some help," said Mama. "We've never asked for anything before." She had not wanted to ask the Refugee Organisation even this time, and it was only the fear that Anna, like herself, might have to get a job without any qualifications that had persuaded her. Mama spent five and a half days a week in a basement office typing and filing letters, and she hated it.

"Mr Rubinstein! Mr and Mrs Berg!"

A woman opposite Mama shifted uneasily. "What a long time they keep you waiting!" she cried. "I don't think I can bear to sit here much longer, I really don't!"

Her husband frowned. "Now then, Bertha," he said. "It's better than queueing at the frontier." He turned to Anna and Mama. "My wife's a bit nervous. We had a bad time in Germany. We only just managed to get out before the war started."

"Oh, it was terrible!" wailed the woman. "The Nazis were shouting and threatening us all the time. There was one poor old man and he thought he'd got all his papers right, but they punched him and kicked him and wouldn't let him go. And then they shouted at us, 'You can go now, but we'll still get you in the end!'"

"Bertha . . ." said her husband.

"That's what they said," cried the woman. "They said, 'We're going to get you wherever you go because we're going to conquer the world!'"

The man patted her arm and smiled at Mama in embarrassment.

"When did you leave Germany?" he asked.

"In March 1933," said Mama. Among refugees, the earlier you had left the more important you were. To have left in 1933 was like having arrived in America on the Mayflower, and Mama could never resist telling people the exact month.

"Really," said the man, but his wife was unimpressed. She looked at Anna with her frightened eyes.

"You don't know what it's like," she said.

Anna closed her mind automatically. She never thought about what it was like in Germany.

"Miss Goldstein!"

The next person to be called was a woman in a worn fur coat, clutching a briefcase. Then came a bespectacled man whom Mama recognised as a minor violinist and then suddenly it was Anna's and Mama's turn. The receptionist said, "You want the students' section," and led them to a room where a grey-haired lady was waiting behind a desk. She was reading through the application form which Anna had filled in before making the appointment and looked like a headmistress, but nicer than Miss Metcalfe.

"How do you do," she said, waving them into two chairs. Then she turned to Anna and said, "So you want to be a secretary."

"Yes," said Anna.

The grey-haired lady glanced at her form. "You did extremely well in your School Certificate examinations," she said. "Didn't you want to stay on at school?"

"No," said Anna.

"And why was that?"

"I didn't like it," said Anna. "And almost no one stayed on after School Certificate." She hesitated. "They didn't teach us very much."

The lady consulted the form again. "The Lilian Metcalfe School For Girls," she said. "I know it. Snob rather than academic. What a pity." And having thus disposed of it, she applied herself to solving the problems of Anna's secretarial course. Had Anna tried it? How long would it take? And what sort of job did Anna have in mind? Buoyed up by the demolition of Miss Metcalfe, Anna answered fully and less shyly than usual, and after a surprisingly short time the lady said, "Well, that all seems very satisfactory."

For a moment Anna thought it was all over, but the lady said a little reluctantly to Mama, "Forgive me, but there are so many people needing help that I have to ask you a few questions as well. How long have you been in this country?"

"Since 1935," said Mama, "but we left Germany in March 1933 . . ."

Anna had heard it all explained so many times that she almost knew it by heart. Six months in Switzerland . . . two years in France . . . the Depression . . . the film script on the strength of which they had come to England . . . No, the film had never been made . . . No, it didn't seem to matter then that Papa didn't speak English because the script had been translated, but now of course . . . A writer without a language . . .

"Forgive me," said the lady again, "I do realise that your husband is a very distinguished man, but while you're in this difficulty, is there not anything more practical he could do, even for a little while?"

Papa, thought Anna, who couldn't bang a nail in straight, who couldn't boil an egg, who could do nothing but put words together, beautifully.

"My husband," said Mama, "is not a practical man. He is also a good deal older than I am." She had flushed a little and the lady said very quickly, "Of course, of course, do excuse me."

It was funny, thought Anna, that she should be so much more impressed by Papa's age which no one meeting him would particularly notice, than by his impracticality, which stuck out a mile. Once in Paris Papa had spent nearly all the money they had on a sewing machine which didn't work. Anna remembered going with him to try and return it to the second-hand dealer who had landed him with it. They had had no money in Paris either, but somehow it hadn't mattered. She had felt as though she belonged there, not like a refugee.

Mama was telling the lady about her job.

"For a while I worked as social secretary," she said. "To Lady Parker – you may have heard of her. But then her husband died and she moved to the country. So now I'm helping sort out the papers belonging to his estate."

The lady looked embarrassed. "And – er – how much . . . ?"

Mama told her how much she earned.

"I have no qualifications, you see," she said. "I studied music as a girl. But it helps to pay the bills at the Hotel Continental."

Perhaps, thought Anna, she had felt different in Paris because Mama hadn't had to work, or because they had lived in a flat instead of a hotel – or perhaps it was simply that England didn't suit her. She didn't really know a lot of English people, of course, only the ones at Miss Metcalfe's. But certainly a lot of things had gone wrong for her soon after her arrival. For one thing she had grown much fatter, bulging in unexpected places, so that all her clothes suddenly looked hideous on her. Mama had said it was puppy fat and that she would lose it again, and in fact much of it had already melted away, but Anna still suspected England of being somehow to blame. After all, she had never been fat before.

The other girls at boarding-school had been fat too – Anna remembered great red thighs in the changing room and heavy figures lumbering over the frozen grass of the lacrosse field. But at least they hadn't been shy. Her shyness was the worst thing that had happened to Anna in England. It had come upon her soon after the puppy fat, quite unexpectedly, for she had always been easy with people. It had paralysed her, so that when the English girls had made fun of her for being bad at lacrosse and for speaking with a funny accent, she hadn't been able to answer. She had never had this trouble with Judy and Jinny, who were American.

"Well, Anna," said the grey-haired lady as though she had been listening to Anna's thoughts, "I hope you'll enjoy the secretarial course more than your time at Miss Metcalfe's."

Anna came back to earth. Was it all settled then?

"I'll speak to my committee tomorrow", said the lady, "but I'm quite sure that there will be no difficulty." And as Anna stammered her thanks she said, "Nonsense! I think you'll be a very good investment."

The sun had come out and it was quite warm while Anna and Mama walked back to the hotel.

"How much do you think I'll be able to earn?" asked Anna.

"I don't know," said Mama, "but with your languages you should get at least three pounds."

"Every week!" said Anna. It seemed an enormous sum.

Papa congratulated her, a little sadly.

"I must say, I'd never seen you as a secretary," he said and Anna quickly pushed aside the thought that she hadn't either.

"Papa," she cried, "They said I was a good investment!"

"There I agree with them," said Papa. He was wearing his best suit, or the one he considered least worn at present, ready to go out. "A meeting of the International Writers' Club," he explained. "Would you like to come? It's not much of a celebration, but there is to be a tea."

"I'd love to," said Anna. The Writers' Club was not very exciting, but now that her future was settled she felt restless. She walked quickly to the bus stop with Papa, trying not to think of the fact that soon her days would be filled with shorthand instead of drawing.

"The meeting is for the German section," said Papa who was its president. "But the tea" – he smiled at himself for explaining the treat – "will be genuine English."

When they arrived at the club's premises near Hyde Park Corner most of the other writers were already assembled – a collection of the usual intelligent refugee faces and the usual frayed refugee collars and cuffs. Several of them came to greet Papa at the door, were introduced to Anna and said how like him she was. This often happened and always cheered her up. Nobody, she thought, who looked so like Papa could be completely hopeless.

"Is she going to follow in your footsteps?" asked a small man with pebble lenses.

"I used to think so," said Papa, "But now I think she is more interested in drawing. At the moment" – he raised a hand regretfully – "she is planning to become a secretary."

The man with the pebble lenses raised both hands in regretful echo. "What can one do?" he said. "One has to live."

He and Papa went to sit on a small platform while Anna found a seat among the other writers. The theme of the meeting was "Germany" and a number of writers got up to speak. What a lot of them there were, thought Anna. No wonder there was no work for them.

The first one spoke about the rise of the Nazis and how it could have been avoided. Everyone except Anna was very interested in this and it provoked a whole succession of smaller speeches and arguments. "If only . . ." cried the writers. If only the Weimar Republic . . . the Social Democrats . . . the French in the Rhineland . . .

At last it came to an end and a sad man in a pullover rose to read out extracts from a diary smuggled out through Switzerland which had been kept by a Jewish writer still at liberty in Germany. Anna knew how such people lived, of course, but it was still horrifying to hear the details – the penury, the petty persecutions, the constant threat of the concentration camp. When he had finished the other writers sat in silence and gazed gratefully at the moulded ceiling, the large windows overlooking Hyde Park. At least they had got out in time.

There followed a completely uninteresting dissertation on the regional differences between Frankfurt and Munich, and then Papa stood up.

"Berlin," he said, and began to read.

When, at the age of eight or nine, Anna had first realised that Papa was a famous writer, she had begged him to let her see something he had written and he had finally given her a short piece that he thought she might understand. She could still remember her embarrassment after reading it. Why, she had thought in shame, why couldn't Papa write like everyone else? She herself was going through a phase at school of writing long, convoluted sentences full of grandiose phrases. She had imagined that Papa's writing would be the same, only even grander. But instead Papa's sentences had been quite short. He used ordinary words that everyone knew, but put them together in unexpected ways, so that you were startled by them. It was true that once you got over your surprise you saw exactly what he meant, but even so . . . Why, Anna thought, oh why couldn't he write like other people?

"A little too soon, I think," Papa had said afterwards and for years she had been shy of trying again.

Now Papa was reading something he must have typed quite recently on the rickety typewriter in his room. It was about Berlin. She recognised the streets, the woods nearby, there was even a bit about their house. That's just what it was like, thought Anna.

Then Papa had written about the people – neighbours, shopkeepers, the man who looked after the garden (Anna had almost forgotten him), the owl-eyed secretary who typed Papa's work. This bit was rather funny and the writers in the audience all laughed. But where were all these people now? asked Papa. Did the owl-eyed secretary raise her hand in the Hitler salute? Had the grocer joined the Storm Troopers – or had he been dragged off to a concentration camp? What had become of them after the Nazis had stolen their country? (Here Papa used a very rude word which made the writers gasp and then titter in relief.) We do not know, said Papa. Hitler has swallowed them up. And yet, if one went back perhaps it would all look just as it had looked before. The streets, the woods nearby, the house . . . He ended with the words with which he had begun. "Once I lived in Berlin."

There was a moment's silence and then the writers rose up as one writer and clapped and clapped. As Papa came down from the platform a small crowd formed round him, congratulating him and shaking his hand. Anna kept back but he found her near the door and asked "Did you like it?" She nodded, but before she could say any more they were swept into the room beyond where tea had been prepared. It was a lavish spread and while some writers made an effort not to appear too keen, others could not resist flinging themselves upon it. The tea had been provided by the main English section of the club and a sprinkling of English writers appeared along with it. While Anna ate an eclair and tried to tell Papa how much she had liked the piece about Berlin, one of them came up to talk to them.

"I heard the applause," he said to Papa. "What were you speaking about?"

Papa, as usual, did not understand, so Anna translated for him.

"Ach so!" said Papa and adjusted his face to speak English. "I talk-ed," he said, mispronouncing the mute *ed* at the end of the word as usual, "about Germany."

The Englishman was taken aback by the Shakespearian accent but recovered quickly.

"It must have been most exciting," he said. "I wish so much that I could have understood it."

When Anna got back to the Bartholomews', much later, she found a letter from Max inviting her to Cambridge for the week-end. Everything is happening at once, she thought. She forgot her shyness in telling Mrs Bartholomew all about the invitation, about Papa's reading at the club and about her new career.

"And when I've finished the course," she ended triumphantly, "I'll be able to earn three pounds a week!"

Like Papa, Mrs Bartholomew looked a little regretful.

"That's very good news," she said after a moment. "But you know, don't you, that you can live in this house as long as you like, so that if ever you should change your mind . . ."

Then she went off to find a coat of Jinny's for Anna to wear during her week-end with Max.

3

All the way to Cambridge in the train Anna wondered what it would be like. What would they do? What would Max's friends be like? Would she be expected to talk to them and if so, what on earth would she say? The weather had turned cold again and soon after the train had left London it began to drizzle. Anna sat staring out at the soggy fields and the cattle sheltering under dripping trees and almost wished she hadn't come. Supposing nobody liked her? And indeed, why should they like her? Nobody else did much, she thought morosely – at least not people of her own age. The girls at Miss Metcalfe's had not thought much of her. They had never elected her as a prefect, or as dormitory captain, or even as dining-room table monitor. For a brief time there had been talk of making her guinea-pig orderly, but even that had come to nothing. And Max's friends were boys. How did one talk to boys?

"Not a very nice day," said a voice, echoing her thoughts. It belonged to a tweedy woman in the seat opposite. Anna agreed that it wasn't and the woman smiled. She was wearing a hat and expensive, sensible shoes like the mothers at Miss Metcalfe's on Parents' Day.

"Going up to Cambridge for the week-end?" said the woman. Anna said, "Yes," and the woman went at once into a description of the social delights of what she called the "varsity". Her three brothers had been there years ago, and two of her cousins, and they had all invited her for week-ends – a gel could have such fun. Theatre parties! cried the tweedy woman, and May balls, and picnics at Grantchester, and everywhere you went so many, many delightful young men!

Anna's heart sank farther at this account but she comforted herself with the thought that there could hardly be May balls in March and that Max would surely have warned her if he had planned any grand goings-on.

"And where do you come from, my dear?" asked the tweedy woman, having exhausted her reminiscences.

Normally when people asked her where she came from Anna said, "London," but this time for some inexplicable reason she found herself saying, "Berlin," and immediately regretted it.

The woman had stopped in her tracks.

"Berlin?" she cried. "But you're English!"

"No," said Anna, feeling like Mama at the Refugee Relief Organisation. "My father is an anti Nazi German writer. We left Germany in 1933."

The tweedy woman tried to work it out. "Anti-Nazi," she said. "That means you're against Hitler."

Anna nodded.

"I should never have thought it," said the tweedy woman. "You haven't got a trace of an accent. I could have sworn that you were just a nice, ordinary English gel."

This was a compliment and Anna smiled dutifully, but the woman was suddenly struck by another thought.

"What about the war?" she cried. "You're in enemy country!"

Damn, thought Anna, why did I ever start this?

She tried to explain as patiently as she could. "We're against Germany," she said. "We want the English to win."

"Against your own country?" said the woman.

"We don't feel that it is our country any more," began Anna, but the tweedy woman had become offended with the whole conversation.

"I could have sworn you were English," she said reproachfully and buried herself in a copy of *Country Life*.

Anna stared out at the grey landscape rolling past the spattered window. It was ridiculous, but she felt put out. Why couldn't she just have said she came from London as usual? Max would never have made such a mistake. This whole expedition is going to be disaster, she thought.

When the train finally drew into the station at Cambridge her worst suspicions seemed to be confirmed. She stood on the platform with an icy wind blowing straight down it, and Max was nowhere to be seen. But then he appeared from behind a corner, breathless and with his gown flying behind him.

"Sorry," he said. "I had a lecture." He looked at the scarlet coat which Mrs Bartholomew had lent her. "That's very dashing," he said. "Judy's or Jinny's?"

"Jinny's," said Anna and felt better.

He picked up her case and hustled her out of the station.

"I hope you've brought a thick woollen nightie as well," he said. "Your lodgings are somewhat cool."

They turned out to have no heating at all – a vast, icy cave of a room – but it was not far from his own and the landlady promised to put a hot-water bottle in her bed at night. While Anna was tidying herself she tried to imagine the tweedy woman spending a night there and decided that her Cambridge week-ends must have been very different. Max paid for the room – bed and breakfast cost ten shillings – and then they set off to walk through the town.

By now the rain had stopped, but there were still patches of water everywhere. The sky above the rooftops was wet and grey with shambling clouds which thinned occasionally to shimmer in half-hearted sunlight. They crossed the marketplace, picking their way between shoppers and dripping tarpaulins, and then they were suddenly engulfed by a crowd of under-graduates. The High Street was filled with them. They were splashing through the puddles on their bicycles and pushing along the pavement in noisy groups. There were black gowns everywhere, and long striped scarves, and everyone seemed to be talking, or shouting greetings to friends across the road. Several of them waved to Max, who seemed to be very much at home among them, and Anna thought what fun it must be to belong here.

Every so often, between greetings, he pointed out a landmark through the turmoil – a building, an ancient bit of wall, a cloistered passage where, centuries ago, someone had walked, a seat where someone else had written a poem. The stone of which they were made was the same colour as the sky and looked as though it had been there forever.

In the doorway of a tea-shop Max was accosted by two gowned figures.

"Discovered at last!" cried one. "And with a strange woman!"

"A strange scarlet woman," said the other, pointing to Anna's coat.

"Don't be an idiot," said Max. "This is my sister Anna. And these are George and Bill who are having lunch with us."

Anna remembered hearing about George who had been to school with Max. He was a good foot taller than herself, so that she would have had to throw back her head to see what he looked like. Bill's face was more within range and looked pleasant and ordinary. They pushed their way through the crowded shop to a table in the corner. As they sat down George's face sank into view and turned out to be cheerful, with an engaging look of permanent astonishment.

"Are you really his sister?" he asked. "I mean, if you had to be somebody's sister, surely you could have found someone better than old Max here?"

"With his lecherous ways –"

"And his boots so stout –"

"And his eyes which swivel round about –"

"And the horrible way his ears stick out!" George finished triumphantly.

Anna stared at them in confusion. Had they just made that up? Or was it some kind of English verse that everyone except her knew?

George was leaning towards her.

312

"Surely, Anna – I trust I may call you Anna – surely you could have found someone more suitable?"

She would have to say something. "I think –" she began, but what did she think? At last she brought out, "I think Max is very nice." She was blushing as usual.

"Loyal," said George.

"And comely," said Bill. "Wouldn't you say comely, George?"

"Definitely comely," said George.

They were off again and she found that all that was required of her was to laugh, which was easy. They ate baked beans on toast followed by doughnuts and cups of strong tea. Bill tried to wheedle an extra spoonful of sugar out of the waitress, but she refused.

"Don't you know that there's a war on?" she said, and Bill pretended to be amazed and cried, "No one told me – how ghastly!" and made so much noise that she gave him some sugar just to stop him.

"You young gentlemen are so insinuating," she said, snatching the sugar bowl away and, as an afterthought, "I don't know what the Government would say."

The idea of the Government worrying about Bill's extra teaspoonful of sugar was so remarkable that George, Bill and Max all needed another doughnut to get over it.

Anna watched them admiringly. How witty they were, she thought, and how handsome, and how English – and how strange to see Max virtually undistinguishable from the other two.

"Actually it's funny," said George. "That business of 'Don't you know that there's a war on'.

It doesn't really seem as though there were, does it?"

"No," said Max. "I don't know what I thought it would be like if there was a war, but you'd imagine something more – well, urgent."

Bill nodded. "When you think about the last one. All those people being killed."

There was a pause.

Anna took a deep breath and decided to contribute to the conversation. "When I was small," she said, "I was always very glad that I was a girl."

They stared at her. Max frowned slightly. She'd made a mess of it as usual.

"Because of wars," she explained. "Because girls couldn't be sent into the trenches."

"Oh yes, I see," said George. They seemed to expect something more, so she gabbled on.

"But later my mother told me that there'd never be another war. Only by then I'd got used to the idea – of being glad that I was a girl, I mean. So I suppose it was really a good thing. Because," she added with a degree of idiocy that astonished even herself, "I *am* a girl."

There was silence until, mercifully, Bill laughed.

"And a jolly good thing too!" he said.

Never again, thought Anna. Never again will I say anything to anybody, ever.

But George nodded just as though she had said something sensible. "My mother was the same. She was always telling us that there'd never be another war. She was quite upset when this one happened." His normal look of astonishment had intensified and some sugar from the doughnut had become stuck round his mouth, so that he looked suddenly very young.

"But I suppose if someone carries on like Hitler in the end there's nothing you can do but fight him."

"Fight him to the death!" Bill narrowed his eyes. "My God, Carruthers, there's a machine gun nest on that hill!"

George raised his chin. "I'll go alone, Sir." His voice trembled with emotion. "But if I don't come back . . ."

"Yes, yes, Carruthers?"

"Tell them it was – for England." George stared bravely into the distance. Then he said in his ordinary voice, "Well, I mean, it's so silly, isn't it?"

They finished their doughnuts thinking how silly it was. Then Bill said, "I must fly."

"Literally?" asked Max.

"Literally," said Bill. He belonged to the University Air Squadron and they practised every Saturday afternoon.

George struggled to extract his long legs from under the table. "Flicks tonight?" he said.

"Sure." Bill waved in a way that might or might not include herself, thought Anna. "See you then." And he loped off into the street.

They waited while George wrapped a scarf round his long neck. "Actually," he said, "I suppose it must feel even funnier to you – the war, I mean." He looked at Max reflectively. "I always forget that you weren't born here. It never occurs to anyone, you see," he explained to Anna. "I'm sure Bill thinks he's British to the backbone."

"Sometimes I almost forget myself," said Max so lightly that only Anna guessed how much it meant to him.

They walked back to the digs which Max and George shared. The landlady had lit a fire in their little sitting-room and Max at once sat down by it with a pile of books and papers to write an essay on some aspect of Roman Law. George disappeared with the intention of taking a bath and could be heard in the next room discussing with the landlady the chances of the water becoming hot enough in time for him to profit from it before he had to go out again.

"Max," said Anna, "I'm sorry – I know I'm not good with people."

Max looked up from his work. "Nonsense," he said. "You're all right."

"But I say such stupid things. I don't mean to but I do – because I'm nervous I suppose."

"Well, so is everyone else. You should have seen George and Bill before you came. They don't know many girls. I'm the only one who does."

Anna looked at him admiringly. "The trouble is," she said, "I'm not like you." In a burst of confidence she added, "Sometimes I wonder if I really belong in this country."

"Of course you do!" Max looked shocked. "You belong just as much as I do. The only difference is that you went to a lousy school and it put you off."

"Do you really think so?"

"I know it," said Max.

It was an encouraging thought. Max seemed about

to go back to his books, so she said quickly, "There's another thing."

"What?" said Max.

"Well," said Anna, "don't you ever feel that we're unlucky?"

"Unlucky? You mean about being refugees?"

"No, I mean for the countries we live in." He looked puzzled, so she said, "Well, look what's happened to Germany. And in France we'd hardly been there a year before they had a Depression. And as for England – you remember how solid it all seemed when we came, and now there's a war, and rationing . . ."

"But that's not our fault!" cried Max.

Anna shook her head glumly. "Sometimes," she said, "I feel like the Wandering Jew."

"You don't look like the Wandering Jew. He had long whiskers. Anyway, as far as I remember he wasn't considered to bring bad luck."

"No," said Anna. "But I don't suppose anyone was very pleased to see him."

Max stared at her for a moment and then burst out laughing. "You're potty," he said affectionately. "Absolutely potty. And now I must do some work."

He went back to his books and Anna watched him. The room was quiet except for the crackling of the fire. How marvellous to live like this, she thought. For a moment she tried to imagine herself at University. Not, of course, that they'd ever give her a scholarship like Max. But anyway, what would she do? Study law like Max, or English like George, or engineering like Bill? No – the only thing she really liked was drawing, and that was no use.

"By the way," said Max telepathically, "what's all this you wrote to me about a secretarial course?"

She said, "I'm starting next week."

He considered it, looking already, she thought, like a lawyer weighing up a tricky question in Court. Finally he said, "Well, I suppose it's the right thing to do at the moment. But not for good. Not for you. Not in the long run." Then a thought occurred to him. He leafed impatiently through one of his books, found what he wanted and started again to write.

Anna walked back to her digs, brushed her hair and changed into the only other dress she had. It was her old school dress made of grey corduroy and when she had worn it at Miss Metcalfe's on Sundays she had thought it hideous. But Mama had found an old lace collar at the bottom of one of the trunks they had brought away from Berlin and with that, now that Anna had lost most of her puppy fat, it looked quite elegant. She returned to find Max putting away his papers and George surveying the high tea which the landlady had spread out in front of the fire. George's bath had not been a success. Fearing that if he delayed too long he would not be able to have one at all, he had plunged in when the water was barely luke-warm and had sat in it, getting progressively colder, unable to face climbing out into the even colder air of the bathroom. However, at least it had now been dealt with and the problem of washing himself would not arise for another week, he told Anna with satisfaction. "Which prompts me to remark," he added, "that you look remarkably clean and wholesome. Is that the latest fashion?"

318

She explained that it was what she had worn at school on Sundays.

"Really?" said George. "How extraordinary. My sister always wears a sort of a brown sack."

From this they got to talking about George's sister's school where they had to curtsey to the headmistress every time they met her and which sounded not much better than Miss Metcalfe's, and then about schools in general. Perhaps Max was right, thought Anna. Perhaps George was just as nervous of her as she was of him, and with this thought she began to relax a little. She was in the middle of telling him about a remarkable ceremony at Miss Metcalfe's when a guinea-pig monitor had been stripped of her rank, when it was time to leave for the cinema.

They picked their way through the icy blackout to see a thriller in the company of Bill and a girl with frizzy hair whom Max, to Anna's surprise, appeared to admire. Her name was Hope and she looked at least three years older than Max, but when he whispered, "Don't you think she's attractive?" Anna did not like to say "no". The film was very bad and the audience, which consisted largely of undergraduates, took a noisy interest in it. There were boos for the villain and ironical cheers for the heroine who was trying to ward him off, and cries of "Come on Clarence!" whenever the lumbering hero appeared in pursuit. In the end the villain threatened to throw the heroine to a poorly looking crocodile which, the audience pointed out, was clearly in need of feeding, and when she was rescued in the nick of time the remaining dialogue was drowned in cries of "Shame!" and "R.S.P.C.A.!" Anna thought it all wonderfully funny and glowed through the rest of the evening which they spent eating more doughnuts in a café. At last George and Max said goodnight to her at the door of her lodgings and she felt her way through the darkened house to her room and her freezing bed where she clutched her hot-water bottle, thought in wonder about this extraordinary world her brother was part of, and fell asleep.

"Well, how do you like Cambridge?" asked Max the next afternoon. They were waiting for her train at the station and she did not in the least want to leave. They had spent part of the day punting on the river – the weather had been warmer – with Max and Hope arguing fitfully in a punt propelled by George while Anna was in another with Bill. George and Bill had tried to ram each other and in the end Bill had fallen in and had invited them back to sherry in his rooms while he changed his clothes. He lived in a college three hundred years old, and under the mellowing influence of the sherry George and Bill had both urged her to come back to Cambridge soon.

She looked earnestly at Max on the darkening platform. "I think it's marvellous," she said. "Absolutely marvellous."

Max nodded. "I'm glad you've seen it." She could see the happiness in his face in spite of the darkness. Suddenly he grinned. "And there's another thing," he said. "Don't tell Mama, but I think I'm going to get a First."

Then the train roared in, astonishingly filled with soldiers and sailors. She had to squeeze past a pile of kit-bags to get on, and by the time she had managed to pull the window down the train had started. She shouted, "Thank you, Max! Thanks for a marvellous week-end!" But there was a lot of noise and she was not sure whether he heard her. One of the sailors offered her part of his kit-bag and she sat on it all the way back to London. It was a long, weary journey – much slower than on the previous day. The light from the blue-painted bulb in the corridor was too dim to read by and every time the train stopped more soldiers got on, even though there hardly seemed room for them. Liverpool Street too was filled with troops and as Anna picked her way among them in the patchy half-light of the station she wondered where they could all be going. Then a newspaper poster caught her eye. It said "Hitler Invades Norway And Denmark!"

4

At first when Anna had learned the news of Hitler's attack on Scandinavia she had been very frightened. In her mind she had heard again the voice of the woman at the Relief Organisation talking about the Nazis. "They said, 'We'll get you wherever you go because we're going to conquer the world!'" But then nothing had happened and life seemed to go on much as usual. Some troops were sent to Norway – the Danes had given in without a fight – and there had been a battle at sea, but it was hard to tell who was winning. And after all, Scandinavia was a long way off.

She started her secretarial course and Judy and Jinny came home for the holidays. Papa was asked by the Ministry of Information to compose the text of some leaflets to be dropped over Germany – the first work he had had for months – and Max and George went on a walking tour and sent her a postcard from a Youth Hostel.

Her one overwhelming desire now was to learn shorthand as quickly as possible, so as to get a job and earn some money. Each day she went to the secretarial school in Tottenham Court Road and practised taking down dictation on the little machine provided. It was quite fun. Instead of pressing down the keys singly as on a typewriter you pressed them down like chords on a piano, and each time the machine printed a syllable in ordinary letters on a paper tape. It reproduced the sound of the syllable rather than the spelling so that "general situation" for instance became "jen-ral sit-you-ai-shn", but it was still quite easy to read, unlike the shorthand squiggles which had defeated her in the past.

Judy and Jinny were impressed with her new grown-up status, and she did not mind leaving them every morning to lounge about in the spring sunshine while she went off to practise her shorthand. There were one or two other refugees like herself at the school and the Belgian principal Madame Laroche said that with their knowledge of languages they were all bound to get good jobs. Anna, she said, was one of her best students, and she often sent for her to demonstrate the system to potential clients.

The week before Whitsun was warm and sunny and by Friday Anna was looking forward to the long week-end, as the secretarial school was closing at lunch time and Monday was a holiday as well. She was going to spend the afternoon with Mama and Papa, and Mama's cousin Otto was coming to see them. For once she was bored with practising and she was glad when, half way through the morning, Madame Laroche sent for her to demonstrate her shorthand to a middle-aged couple and their mousy daughter. They did not seem very promising customers, as the father kept saying how stupid it was to waste money on new-fangled methods and the daughter just looked frightened.

"Ah, and here is one of our students," cried Madame Laroche as Anna came in – or at least that was what Anna thought she had probably said. Madame Laroche talked with an impenetrably thick Belgian accent and was very hard to understand. She motioned Anna to a chair and took a book from a shelf. Anna looked round for the English assistant who normally dictated to her, but there was no sign of her.

"I will dictate to you myself," said Madame Laroche excitedly, or words to that effect. Clearly the father had stung her into determination to prove the excellence of her system at all costs. She opened the book and said, "Der doo glass terweens."

"What?" said Anna, startled.

"Der doo glass terweens."

"I'm sorry," said Anna, beginning to blush, "I didn't quite understand . . ."

"Der doo glass terweens, der doo glass terweens!" cried Madame Laroche impatiently and she tapped her finger on Anna's machine and shouted something that sounded like "Write!"

There was nothing for it but to take it down.

Anna typed "der doo glass ter-weens" carefully on the paper tape and hoped that the next bit might be easier to understand – but it wasn't. It was just as incomprehensible as the beginning and so was the next bit and so was the bit after that. Every so often Anna recognised a real word, but then the dictation dropped back again into gibberish. She sat there, red-faced and miserable, and took it all down. She wished it would stop, but she knew that when it did she would have to read it back, which would be worse.

It stopped.

And just as Anna was wondering how she could possibly survive the next few minutes she was struck by an idea. Perhaps the dictation really had no meaning. Perhaps Madame Laroche had dictated gibberish to her on purpose, to demonstrate that the system could record even sounds that did not make sense. She suddenly felt much happier and began quite confidently to read back what she had taken down.

"Der doo glass terweens," she read, carefully pronouncing it just as Madame Laroche had done, and went on from there.

But something was wrong. Why was the father puffing and choking with suppressed laughter? Why were the mother and even the mousy daughter tittering? Why had Madame Laroche's face gone pink with anger and why was she shouting at Anna and piling the book, the machine, the paper into her arms and pushing her out of the room? The door slammed behind her and Anna stood in the corridor, dumbfounded.

"What happened?" asked one of the English teachers, emerging from another room. She must have heard the noise.

Anna shook her head. "I don't know," she said.

The teacher took the book which was still open from the top of the machine. "Is this what she dictated to you?" she asked. "The Douglas twins?"

"No," said Anna. What Madame Laroche had dictated to her started with "der doo glass terweens". You could not possibly mistake "the Douglas twins" for "der doo glass terweens".

But you could, with Madame Laroche!

"Oh!" she cried. "They must have all thought . . ." She looked at the teacher. "What shall I do? They must have all thought I was making fun of her accent! D'you think I'd better explain?"

They could hear Madame Laroche shouting excitedly in her office.

"Not just now," said the teacher.

"But I've got to do something!"

There was the sound of chairs being pushed back in the office, overlaid by a burst of masculine laughter and an incomprehensible but clearly unfriendly remark from Madame Laroche.

"Come along," said the teacher firmly and propelled Anna along the corridor and into one of the classrooms. "Now you just get on with your work and put this little misunderstanding right out of your mind. I'm sure that by Tuesday it will all have been forgotten."

Anna sat down at an empty desk and began, automatically, to take down the dictation slowly read out by a senior student. But how could she forget all about it? she thought. It had been so unfair. Madame Laroche had no right to shout at her when she had always worked so well. No one in the school could understand her Belgian accent – she must know that. And as for thinking that Anna was making fun of her . . . I'll go and tell her! thought Anna. I'll tell her she can't treat me like this! Then she thought, suppose she doesn't believe me? Could one be expelled from secretarial school?

By the end of the morning she was in such a state of confusion that she could not make up her mind either to go home or to face Madame Laroche. She went to the cloakroom where she stared at her reflection in the mirror and alternated between framing grand phrases with which to justify herself and taking the teacher's advice and forgetting the whole thing. Eventually a cleaner came to lock up and she had to go.

When she emerged into the corridor she found that everyone else had left. Probably Madame Laroche had gone home too, she thought, half-relieved – but now the whole weekend would be spoiled with worrying. Oh, damn! she thought – and then, as she passed Madame Laroche's office, she heard someone talking inside. Quickly, without giving herself time to think, she knocked and went in. She had expected to see one of the teachers, but Madame Laroche was alone. The voice came not from her but out of her radio.

"Madame Laroche," said Anna, "I just wanted to explain . . ." She had meant to sound fierce but found to her annoyance that she merely sounded apologetic. "About this morning . . ." she started again.

Madame Laroche looked at her blankly and then waved to her to go away.

"But I want to tell you!" cried Anna. "It wasn't at all as you thought!"

The radio had suddenly stopped and her voice sounded absurdly high in the silence.

Madame Laroche got up and came towards her and Anna saw to her horror that there were tears in her eyes.

"Mon enfant," said Madame Laroche quite clearly in French, "the Germans have invaded Belgium and Holland."

Anna stared at her.

"What will my people do?" asked Madame Laroche as though Anna would be able to tell her. Then she said again, "What will they do?"

Anna wanted to say something sympathetic but could think of nothing. "I'm sorry," she stammered. Guiltily, she realised that she was still fretting about the misunderstanding over the Douglas twins. But as Madame Laroche seemed to have forgotten all about it, it must be all right.

"Mon Dieu!" cried Madame Laroche. "Don't you understand what it means? How would you like to have the Germans here, in England?" And as Anna remained helplessly silent she shouted, "Well, don't just stand there! Go home, for heaven's sake! Go home to your parents!"

Anna went out of the office, through the building and out into the sunshine. The street looked just as usual. Even so, she began to run, dodging the other pedestrians on the pavement. When she was out of breath she walked as fast as she could, then she ran again until she reached the Hotel Continental. There she found Mama and Papa in the lounge with Cousin Otto and surrounded by excited Germans, Czechs and Poles. Cousin Otto's eyes were shining above his large Jewish nose and his hair hung untidily into his face. Everyone was talking and even the porter behind the desk was giving his views to anyone who would listen.

"They'll be smashed to pieces!" Cousin Otto was saying triumphantly. "It's just what the English have been waiting for. They'll go in there and smash the Germans to smithereens. The French will help, of course," he added as an afterthought. Cousin Otto had an infinite admiration for England. To be English to him was to be perfect, and he was quite upset when Papa disagreed with him.

"I don't trust Chamberlain," said Papa. "I don't believe the English are ready for battle."

"Aha!" cried Cousin Otto. "But you don't understand them. Just because a man like Chamberlain *appears* not to be doing anything doesn't mean that he's not organising it all secretly. That is the British understatement. No drama or fuss – and he's fooled the Germans completely."

"He seems also to have fooled the British Parliament," said Papa. "I understand they are trying to get rid of him at this very moment."

"Such a time to choose!" wailed an old Czech lady, astonishingly dressed in a tweed coat and flowery hat as though ready to flee from the Germans at a moment's notice.

Cousin Otto looked troubled. "Parliamentary procedure," he said, comforting himself with the Englishness of the phrase.

It was touching, thought Anna, that he should be so pro-English for he had, so far, not fared too well in his adopted country. In spite of two Physics degrees he had only succeeded in finding work in a shoe factory.

"What I want to know," cried the old lady, poking Cousin Otto in the chest with a bony finger, "is, who is minding the shop?"

"Perhaps we should go upstairs," said Mama.

The Hotel Continental did not provide lunch on weekdays and they usually filled in the gap between breakfast and dinner with a snack in Papa's room.

Cousin Otto accepted gratefully. "I'm dying for a cup of tea," he confessed as Mama went scurrying in and out with the kettle, cups and some buns she had

329

stored in her room next door. He sat on Papa's bed, drinking tea with milk like the English, and asked Anna if she had any messages for her brother, as he was leaving for Cambridge himself that afternoon in the hope of getting a job.

"What sort of a job?" Mama wanted to know.

Cousin Otto began to touch every bit of wood within reach. "Touch wood!" he cried. "In my own line. There is a professor of physics there – I was a student of his in Berlin – and he has asked me to come and see him."

"Oh, Otto, it would be wonderful," said Mama.

"Touch wood! Touch wood!" said Cousin Otto and touched the bits of wood all over again. It was difficult to remember, with his old-maidish ways, that he was barely thirty.

"Well, just give Max lots of love and ask him to write," said Mama.

"And wish him luck for his exams," said Anna.

"Oh, I forgot," cried Mama. "The exams must be quite soon. Tell him not to write – he'll be too busy."

Papa said, "Would you give Max a message from me?"

"Certainly," said Cousin Otto.

"Would you tell him –" Papa hesitated. Then he said, "I think that now the Germans have attacked, Max may want to volunteer for one of the fighting forces. And of course he must do whatever he thinks right. But would you ask him, please, to discuss it with the University authorities first, before he makes up his mind?"

"But he's only eighteen!" cried Mama.

"It's not too young," said Cousin Otto. He nodded at Papa. "I promise I'll tell him. And when I get back to London I'll ring you up and tell you how he is."

"That would be most kind," said Papa.

Cousin Otto stayed a little longer, chatting and drinking tea, and then it was time for him to catch his train. Soon afterwards Anna went back to the Bartholomews'. She had arranged to spend Saturday with Judy and Jinny. She had hardly seen them since their return from school and they had such a good time playing tennis and sunning themselves in the garden that they decided to spend Sunday the same way.

Most of the Sunday papers carried pictures of Winston Churchill, who had become Prime Minister instead of Chamberlain, and there were several eye-witness accounts of the German invasion of Holland. Huge numbers of Nazi parachutists had been dropped from aeroplanes, disguised as Dutch and British soldiers. To add to the confusion, Germans who had been living in Holland for years and whom no one suspected of being Nazis, had immediately rushed to their aid. The Dutch were fighting back and the French and the British were on their way to help them, but clearly the Germans had a strong foothold. There was a map of Holland with thick arrows breaking into it from Germany and an article headed "If Germany Captures Dutch And Belgian Coasts", but, said Jinny, the Sunday papers always exaggerated and it was no use minding them.

Monday was hotter and sunnier than ever and when Anna arrived at the Hotel Continental to spend the day with Mama and Papa it seemed a pity to waste such lovely weather indoors.

"Couldn't we go to the Zoo?" she asked on a sudden inspiration.

"Why not?" said Papa. He was feeling cheerful because Winston Churchill had been made Prime Minister – the only man who understood the situation, he said.

Mama was worried about how much it would cost, but then she too found the sunshine irresistible and they decided to be extravagant and go.

It was an extraordinary day. Anna had not been to the Zoo for years and she walked round in a daze, looking. The sand-coloured and orange tigers with their black stripes which seemed to have been poured over them, peacocks with unbelievable embroidered tails, monkeys with elegant beige fur and tragic eyes – it was as though she had never seen any of them before. And giraffes! she thought. How could anyone have invented giraffes!

She looked and looked, and all the time some other part of her mind was being careful not to think of the map in the Sunday papers and of the Nazi horror seeping out of Germany into other parts of Europe which had, until now, been safe.

They stayed until late afternoon and by then Anna's mind was so full of all she had seen that it no longer needed any effort to forget about the war. It was as though those long hours in the sun had changed something, as though everything were suddenly more hopeful. Mama and Papa, too, were more light-hearted. Papa had discovered a creature in the

Small Cat House which looked, he said, exactly like Goebbels, and all the way home in the bus he imagined it making speeches in German to the other small cats and inspecting them for signs of Jewishness. He kept Mama and Anna laughing and they arrived back at the Hotel Continental tired and relaxed, as though they had been away on a holiday.

The lounge was dark after the sunlit street and it took Anna a moment to focus on the porter who looked up from his desk as they came in.

"Someone rang you from Cambridge," he said, and she wondered why Max should telephone rather than write.

Papa lingered for a moment, glancing at a newspaper that someone had left lying on a table, and the porter observed him. "Nothing in there," he said. "But it's bad – I've heard the radio."

"What's happened?" said Papa.

The porter shrugged. He was a little discouraged man with a few hairs carefully arranged in stripes across his bald head. "The usual," he said. "It's all up in Holland. The Nazis are everywhere and the Dutch royal family have escaped to England."

"So quickly!" said Papa, and the feeling of having been away on holiday slipped away as though it had never been.

Just then the telephone rang. The porter answered it and said to Anna, "For you – from Cambridge."

She rushed to the telephone cabin and picked up the receiver.

"Max?" she said – but it was not Max, it was George.

"Look, something awkward has happened," he said. "I don't quite know how to put it, but Max – he's been arrested."

"Arrested?" What had he done? Anna thought of undergraduate pranks, getting drunk, knocking off policemen's helmets, but surely Max would never . . . Stupidly, she asked, "You mean by the police?"

"Yes," said George and added, "as an enemy alien."

"But they don't arrest people for being enemy aliens!" cried Anna. "And anyway he isn't one. We lost our German nationality years ago. He's just waiting to become naturalised British."

"I know, I know," said George. "We told them all that, but it made no difference. They said they were interning all male enemy aliens in Cambridge and his name was on the list."

"Interning?"

"Yes," said George. "In some kind of camp."

Anna suddenly felt quite empty, as though it were pointless even to go on talking.

"Are you still there?" said George anxiously and continued, "Listen, everyone here has made an awful fuss. Me, his tutor, the College – everyone. Bill got so wild at the police station that they threw him out. But we can't move them. It's a Government order. Bit of a panic, if you ask me, after what's been happening in Holland."

"Yes," said Anna because it seemed to be expected of her.

"Max was hoping – I don't know how much use it would be – that perhaps your parents could do something. Exams start in two weeks and he thought perhaps if they knew someone who could explain to the police . . . He's only taken his law books with him, almost no clothes."

"Yes," said Anna again.

"Anyway, I promised to let you know at once." George sounded suddenly depressed, as if it had in some way been his fault. "It's all a mess," he said. "I'll ring again if I hear anything."

Anna roused herself. "Of course," she said. "Thank you very much, George. And thank you for all you did. I'll tell my parents at once."

That would be almost the worst part of it.

5

Explaining to Mama and Papa about Max was just as bad as Anna had feared. Papa said almost nothing, as though Max's internment were only part of a huge catastrophe that he could see rolling towards them, towards England, perhaps towards the whole world, and that he was helpless to avert. Mama shouted and got excited and would not be calmed. Why hadn't Max explained to the police about Papa? she asked again and again. Why hadn't the College done anything? Why hadn't his friends? When Anna told her that indeed they all had, she simply shook her head disbelievingly and cried, "If only I'd been there! I would never have let them take Max away!"

The nine o'clock news brought an announcement that all male enemy aliens in southern and eastern coastal areas had been arrested and were to be sent to internment camps. ("If only Max had come to spend Whitsun in London!" cried Mama.) Anna had not realised that Cambridge was in a coastal area – it must be just on the edge. Presumably these were the parts of England most vulnerable to attack. The announcer went on to say that the government understood the hardship to innocent people that might result from its action, but that it was hoped to alleviate this in due course. This was cold comfort and the rest of the news was no more encouraging. At the end there was an interview with the Dutch royal family, who had escaped from the Nazis by the skin of their teeth, and a quote from Churchill's first speech as

Prime Minister. "I can offer you nothing," he told the House of Commons, "except blood and toil and tears and sweat."

The next day the Dutch army collapsed.

Anna heard the news at the Bartholomews' that evening.

"That's lousy!" said Jinny. "I'm sure now they'll get all worried again about air raids and they won't let our school come back to London!"

Judy agreed. "I don't think I could bear to go back to that place in the middle of nowhere."

"Well, you may not . . ." began Mr Bartholomew and suddenly looked at Anna and stopped.

"Pa!" cried Judy. "You mean we might go back to the States?"

"Oh, how do we know what's going to happen," said Mrs Bartholomew. "Your father's business is here and obviously we'd only leave if things became really serious, so let's not even talk about it." She turned to Anna and asked, "Did you hear from your mother today? Has she had any more news of Max?"

Anna shook her head. "We don't even know where he is," she said. "Mama range the police in Cambridge, but they're not allowed to tell us." The call had cost over two shillings and Mama had been full of hopes that she might be able to speak to Max, but the police would only say that Max was no longer in their charge and that he would, in any case, not be allowed to receive or send any messages.

"I'm so very sorry," said Mrs Bartholomew.

"His exams are quite soon," said Anna. She kept

thinking of the law books Max had packed instead of clothes.

"I believe they've even interned some of the professors," said Mr Bartholomew, and added, "Everything's in chaos."

The weather continued very hot and made everyone irritable. When Anna went round to the Hotel Continental on Wednesday after her secretarial course she found Papa depressed and Mama in a terrible state of nerves. They had been trying to contact anyone who might be able to help about Max, or at least advise them what action to take, but their acquaintances were few and no one seemed to know.

"There must be something we can do!" cried Mama and listed, yet again, her various forlorn hopes. If one wrote to the College, to the University, if George asked again at the police station . . . Her tense, unhappy voice went on and on and only stopped at the ringing of the porter's telephone. Then she sat with her hands clenched in her lap, willing him to tell her that it was for her, that it was news of Max. But the only call that came was from Otto's mother, to say that Otto, too, had been interned, and so had the professor of physics who had invited him to Cambridge.

"You see, it's the same for everyone – a national emergency," said Papa, but Mama would not listen.

She had had a wretched day at her office. Instead of sorting Lord Parker's innumerable bills and receipts, she had tried to telephone people she hardly knew about Max, all to no avail. In the end her boss had objected and she had had a row with him.

"As though it mattered about Lord Parker," she cried.

"He's dead, anyway. The only thing that matters is doing something about Max!"

Papa tried to reason with her, but she shouted, "No! I didn't care about anything else, but now it's too much!" She stared accusingly at an innocent Polish lady who happened to be sitting at the next table. "Wasn't it enough," she said, "for us to have lost everything in Germany? Wasn't it enough to have to rebuild our lives again and again?"

"Of course –" began Papa, but Mama swept him aside.

"We've been fighting Hitler for years," she shouted. "All the time when the English were still saying what a fine gentleman he was. And now that the penny's finally dropped," she finished in tears, "the only thing they can do is to intern Max!"

Papa offered her his handkerchief and she blew her nose. Anna watched her helplessly. The Polish lady got up to greet a man who had just come in and they began to talk in Polish. Anna caught the word Rotterdam and then some other Poles joined them and they all became excited.

At last one of them turned to Papa and said haltingly in English, "The Germans have bombed Rotterdam."

"It is thought," said another, "that ten thousand people were killed."

Anna tried to imagine it. She had never seen a dead person. How could one imagine ten thousand dead?

"Poor people," said Papa.

Did he mean the dead or the ones who were still alive?

The Polish lady sat down on a spare chair and said,

"It is just like Warsaw," and another Pole who had seen Warsaw after the Germans had bombed it tried to describe what it was like.

"Everything is gone," he said. "House is gone. Street is gone. You cannot find . . ." He spread his hands in a vain attempt to show all the things you could not find. "Only dead people," he said.

The Polish lady nodded. "I hide in a cellar," she remembered. "But then come the Nazis to seek for Jews . . ."

It was very warm in the lounge and Anna suddenly found it difficult to breathe.

"I feel a bit sick," she said, and was surprised by the smallness of her voice.

Mama at once came over to her and Papa and one of the Poles struggled to open a window. A rush of cool air came in from the yard at the back of the hotel and after a moment she felt better.

"There," said Papa. "You've got your colour back."

"You're worn out with the heat," said Mama.

One of the Poles got her a glass of water, and then Mama urged her to go home to the Bartholomews', to go to bed, get some rest. She nodded and went.

"I'll ring you if we hear anything about Max," Mama cried after her as she started down the street.

It was awful of her, but when she reached the corner of Russell Square, out of reach of Mama's voice, of everyone's voice, she felt a sense of relief.

By Friday Brussels had fallen and the Germans had broken through into France. A French general issued the order, "Conquer or Die!" but it made no difference –

the German army swept on across France as it had swept across Holland. Madame Laroche was too upset to come to the secretarial school and some of the students, especially the refugees, spent their time listening to the radio and running out to buy newspapers – but not Anna.

Curiously enough she was no longer worried about the German advance. She simply did not think about it. She thought a lot about Max, wherever he had been taken, desperately willing him to be all right, and every morning at the Bartholomews' she rushed to the letter box, hoping that at last he might have been able to write. But she did not think about what was happening in the war. There was nothing she could do about it. She did not read the papers and she did not listen when the news was on. She went to her secretarial school each day and worked at her shorthand. If she became good enough at it she would get a job and earn some money. That was why the Refugee Organisation had paid her fees and that was what she was going to do. And the more she thought about her shorthand the less time she would have to think about anything else.

When she returned to the house one afternoon, Mrs Bartholomew was waiting for her. Anna had stayed on at the school after hours to do some typing and she was late.

"My dear," said Mrs Bartholomew, "I must talk to you."

Mei dea-r, thought Anna, automatically moving her fingers into position on an imaginary keyboard, Ei mus-t tor-k tou you. Lately she had developed this habit of mentally taking down in shorthand everything she heard. It had improved her speed and saved her from having to make sense of what she did not want to hear.

Mrs Bartholomew led her into the drawing-room.

"We have been advised by the American Embassy to return at once to the States," she said.

Wea hav bean ad-veis-d bei the A-me-ri-can Em-ba-sea tou re-turn at wuns tou the Stai-ts, went Anna's fingers, but then something in Mrs Bartholomew's voice broke through her detachment.

"I'm so very sorry," cried Mrs Bartholomew, "but we shall have to give up this house."

Anna looked at her face, and her fingers stopped moving in her lap.

"What will you do?" asked Mrs Bartholomew.

It was nice of her, thought Anna, to be so upset about it. "I'll be all right," she said. "I'll go and stay with my parents."

"But will they be able to manage?" asked Mrs Bartholomew.

"Oh yes," said Anna airily. "And anyway, I'll probably get a job quite soon."

"Oh dear," said Mrs Bartholomew, "I hate doing this." Then she picked up the telephone to explain to Mama.

Mama always shouted when she was excited and Anna realised that of course she must have been hoping that the call would bring her news of Max. All the same, she wished that her sole reaction to Mrs Bartholomew's news had not been so loud and accusing.

"Does that mean," cried Mama, and her distorted voice came right out of the telephone to where Anna was sitting across the room, "that Anna won't be able to stay in your house any more?"

Anna knew as well as Mama that there was no money to pay for her to stay at the Hotel Continental, but what was the use of shouting at Mrs Bartholomew about it? There was nothing she could do. Mama should at least have wished her a safe journey, thought Anna, and her fingers tapped out in her lap, shea shoud at lea-st have wi-shd her a sai-f jur-nea.

The Bartholomews began to pack up their possessions and a growing pile of garments was put aside for Anna because Jinny and Judy would not need them in America. She carried them to the Hotel Continental with her own, a few at a time, on the tube, so as to save a taxi for the move. Mama had counted all their money – she had added what was left of Papa's earnings from the leaflets to the few pounds she had managed, somehow, to save from her meagre weekly wage, and she had worked out that there would be enough to pay Anna's bills at the hotel for three weeks. After that they would have to see. It was really no use looking farther ahead. In the meantime they did not spend a halfpenny that was not absolutely necessary and Anna hoped that the Bartholomews would not mind her staying at the house until the last moment.

"Well, of course we don't mind," Mrs Bartholomew reassured her. "We'd love you to be here just as long as you can."

All the same, as the preparations progressed and more and more familiar objects disappeared into packing cases, it began to feel rather strange. Judy and Jinny still played tennis and sat in the sun and chatted, but they were excited at the prospect of going to America and sometimes it was as though they had already gone. When the day for their departure arrived it was difficult to know what to say. They stood outside the house in Campden Hill Square and looked at each other.

"Promise you'll write," said Jinny.

"And don't let any bombs drop on you," said Judy.

Mr Bartholomew said, "We'll be seeing you . . ." and then looked confused and said, "Good luck!"

Mrs Bartholomew hugged Anna and murmured, "Take care of yourself," and then climbed quickly into the taxi, dabbing at her face with her handkerchief. Then the taxi drove off and Anna waved until it turned the corner. When it had completely disappeared she began to walk, slowly, towards the tube station.

The square was green and leafy and the chestnut tree at the bottom was covered with blossom. She remembered how, her first spring in England, Jinny had shown it to her and pointed out the "candles". "Candles?" Anna had said. "Candles are only on Christmas trees," and everyone had laughed. She could hear the plop of tennis balls from the courts where they had played only a few days before. When she reached the shop in Holland Park Avenue where they had always gone for sweets she stopped for a moment and looked in through the window. She was tempted to buy a chocolate bar as a sort of memento. But she would probably only eat it and then it would be a waste of money, so she didn't. A poster outside the tube station said "Germans Reach Calais".

It was May 26th, exactly a fortnight since Whitsun – the day Max should have started his exams.

6

At the Hotel Continental Anna was allotted a small room close to Mama's and Papa's on the top floor.

When they had first come to England and still had some money they had lived lower down where the rooms were larger and more expensive, but Anna liked this better. From her window she could see right across the rooftops with only the sky above, or down into the scrappy yard, four storeys below, where cats fought among the dust and the weeds. A church clock nearby chimed out the quarters and sparrows hopped and fluttered on the sooty tiles. She was so busy settling into her new surroundings that she almost did not notice Dunkirk.

In a way it was quite easy to miss, even if one read the papers, which Anna didn't, because no one said much about it until it was over. Dunkirk was a place in France on the Normandy coast, and at the end of May the retreating British army was trapped there by the Germans. Only the papers, trying to keep everyone cheerful, never quite said so in so many words. However, by fighting off the Germans and with the help of the Navy and the Air Force, nearly all the soldiers managed to escape back to England, and by the beginning of June the papers suddenly came out in triumphant headlines. "Bloody Marvellous!" said one, surprising Anna into reading it. She discovered that apart from the Navy thousands of ordinary people had crossed the Channel in tiny boats, again and again, to help take the soldiers off the beaches in the midst of battle. It was disappointing that what had sounded like a great victory was only an ingenious escape from defeat. But weren't the English amazing, she thought. She could not imagine the Germans doing a thing like that.

The Hotel Continental had become very crowded. In addition to the German, Czech and Polish refugees, there were now Dutchmen, Belgians, Norwegians and French. You never knew what language you were going to hear in the narrow corridors and on the stairs. The Swiss waitress who had come to London to learn English complained constantly, and after supper the lounge was like the tower of Babel.

The streets, too, were in turmoil. Every day there were long crocodiles of children with gas masks slung over their shoulders, each with a label attached somewhere to its person, trudging in the wake of grown-ups who were taking them to the railway stations, to be sent out of London, to the safety of the country.

Everyone was talking about the invasion of England, for now that Hitler was only the other side of the Channel he would surely want to cross it. To confuse the Germans when they came, names were being removed from street corners and Underground stations, and even buses lost their destination plates, so that the only way to find out where they were going was to ask the conductor.

One morning on her way to the secretarial school Anna discovered a rusty car with no wheels and two broken bedsteads dumped in the middle of the grass of Russell Square. First she thought it was some kind of joke, but then the porter at the Hotel Continental explained to her that it was to stop German parachutists from landing.

"Could they really land in Russell Square? There doesn't seem room," said Anna, startled.

"There's no knowing what they can't do," said the porter.

Parachutists were an inexhaustible source of speculation. There were endless stories of people who claimed actually to have seen some, disguised as British soldiers, as farm workers or most often as nuns, in which case, according to the stories, they always gave themselves away by their carelessness in wearing army boots under their habits.

Anna tried, as always, not to think about them, but sometimes in bed at night her guard slipped and then she saw them dropping down silently among the trees of Russell Square. They were never in disguise but in full uniform covered with black leather and swastikas which were clearly visible even though it was dark. They called whispered commands to each other, and then they set off down Bedford Terrace towards the Hotel Continental to look for Jews . . .

One morning after she had been kept awake a long time by her imaginings, she came down late to find a stranger sitting at the breakfast table with Mama and Papa. She looked more closely and discovered that it was George.

Mama was in a state of confusion between happiness and distress, and as soon as she saw Anna she jumped from her chair.

"Letters from Max!" she cried.

George waved an envelope. "I got one this morning, so I brought it round," he said. "But I see you've got your own. They must all have been posted at the same time."

"Max is all right," said Papa.

She began quickly to read.

There were four letters, all addressed to Mama and Papa. Max had written them at intervals of a week or so and their tone changed gradually from indignant surprise at being interned to a kind of despairing resignation. He had had a bad time, being pushed from one temporary camp to another, often without the simplest necessities. Now he had reached his permanent destination which was better organised, but he was not allowed to say where it was. ("On the Isle of Man!" said George impatiently. "Everyone knows that's where they've been put – why can't they be allowed to say so?") The camp was full of students and professors from Cambridge – so many that it might even be possible to continue with some of his studies. "So it's not too bad," wrote Max. But he clearly hated it. He hated being imprisoned and he hated being treated as an enemy, and most of all he hated being forced back into some kind of German identity which he had long discarded. If there was anything Mama and Papa could do . . .

"We must!" cried Mama. "We must think of something!"

"I'll do anything to help, of course," said George and got up to leave.

Papa got up too. "Are you going backwards to

Cambridge now?" he asked politely. His French was perfect, but he could never get his English right.

George did not smile.

"I'm no longer at Cambridge," he said. "I got tired of fiddling with bits of Chaucer while Rome burns, as it were." Then he said almost apologetically, "I've joined the army." He caught Anna's eye and added, "Ridiculous, isn't it? English Youth Fights Nazi Hordes. D'you think I'll be terribly, terribly brave?"

A few days later it was Anna's birthday.

"What would you like to do?" asked Mama.

Anna thought. She had already spent two full weeks at the Hotel Continental and did not see how they could afford to do anything, but Mama was looking at her expectantly, so she said, "Could we go to a film?" There was a cinema in Tottenham Court Road where you could get in at half-price before one o'clock. She added quickly, in case it was too expensive, "Or we could have a knickerbocker glory at Lyons."

Mama worked it out. The film would cost one shilling and three pence and the knickerbocker glory would be a shilling. She was looking in her purse, but suddenly she threw it down and cried, "I don't care! You're going to be sixteen and you're going to have a proper birthday even if we *are* broke. We'll do both."

"Are you sure?" said Anna.

"Yes," said Mama quite fiercely. "It's your birthday and it's going to be a nice day for you." Then she said, "God knows what will have happened to us all by next year."

Papa said he did not want to come. He must have

arranged it with Mama beforehand, thought Anna, for even in a fit of extravagance they could hardly have afforded cinema tickets and knickerbocker glories for three. So Anna and Mama went to see a film called *Mr Deeds Goes To Town*.

It was about a young millionaire who wanted to give away his money to the poor. ("I wish he'd give us some!" whispered Mama.) But some other mean millionaires wanted to stop him and tried to have him declared insane. In the end he was saved by a girl journalist who loved him, and all ended happily.

The leading part was played by a young actor called Gary Cooper, and both Anna and Mama thought it very good. Afterwards they went to Lyons and ate their knickerbocker glories very slowly, to make them last. They were a recent importation from America and consisted of layers of strawberry and vanilla ice-cream, interspersed with other layers of cream, strawberries and nuts, all served in a tall glass with a special long spoon. Anna had only eaten one once before, and knowing how much it cost, was a little nervous in case it wasn't quite as good as she remembered – but as soon as she tasted the first mouthful she was reassured.

While they ate they talked – about the film, about Anna's shorthand course and the money she would earn when she had finished. "Then we'll be able to go to the cinema every day," said Mama, "and buy knickerbocker glories for breakfast."

"And for lunch and for tea," said Anna. When she got to the bottom of her glass she scraped it out so assiduously with her spoon that the waitress asked if she would like another. This made both her and Mama laugh, and they strolled back contentedly to the Hotel Continental.

On the way they met Papa, who had been sunning himself on a bench in Russell Square.

"How was the film?" he asked.

"Marvellous," said Anna.

"And the other thing – the knickerbocker splendour or whatever it was?"

"Marvellous too," said Anna, and Papa seemed very pleased.

It was a pity that the news of the fall of Paris had to come through that evening. Everyone had been expecting it, of course, but Anna had been hoping against hope that the French would manage to hold out until the next day. If it didn't happen on her birthday it wouldn't be quite so bad. As it was, it seemed somehow as though it were her fault. She thought of the French family who had befriended them when she and Max and Mama and Papa had first gone to live in Paris after leaving Germany, of her teacher who had taught her to speak French, of the Arc de Triomphe and the Champs Elysées, which she had passed every day on her way to school, of the chestnut trees and the people drinking in cafés and the Prisunic and the Metro. Now the Nazis had taken possession of it all and France, like Germany, had become a black hole on the map, a place you could no longer think about.

She sat next to Papa in the lounge and tried not to cry because after all it was worse for the French. There was a middle-aged couple from Rouen staying in the hotel and they both wept when they heard the news.

351

Afterwards the husband said to Papa, "It is the end," and Papa could find no answer.

A little later he got up and went to the telephone, and when he came back he told Mama, "I've spoken to Sam and he'll see me tomorrow. And Louise said, could you and Anna come as well."

"Are you ill, Papa?" asked Anna.

Professor Sam Rosenberg was a doctor and though his wife Louise had been at school in Germany with Mama, and Anna could not remember a time when they had not known them, they did not usually see them without some reason.

"No, I'm not ill," said Papa. "It's just something I want to talk to him about."

The Rosenbergs lived in a vast flat in Harley Street with a porter and a lift and a brass plate on the door. When Anna rang the bell a maid let them in, deposited Papa in the waiting-room and led Anna and Mama along a passage filled with packing cases to Aunt Louise's boudoir.

This too was in a state of upheaval. There were dust covers over some of the pretty velvet chairs, an open packing case stood in a corner and a gilt mirror had been taken down and was leaning against the wall, half-smothered in wadding. In the midst of it all Aunt Louise was sitting in her silk dress and pearls and with her hair beautifully curled, looking distraught.

"My dear, it's all so awful!" she cried in German as soon as they came in. "We have to pack up everything – Sam has taken a house in the country, he says it will be safer there."

"Where in the country?" asked Mama, embracing her.

"Buckinghamshire, I think – or perhaps it's Berkshire – anyway, it's miles from anywhere, and he's going to close up this flat completely except for the consulting room and drive up to see his most important patients only." She drew a deep breath, looked at Anna and said, "How are you?"

"All right, thank you," said Anna indistinctly.

Aunt Louise with her delicate features and beautiful clothes always made her feel uncomfortable. Also it was Aunt Louise who, admittedly with the best intentions in the world, had persuaded Miss Metcalfe to take Anna into her school.

Aunt Louise smiled. "Still at the awkward age," she cried gaily to Mama. "Never mind, they all grow out of it. And how are those charming American friends of yours?"

Mama explained that the Bartholomews had gone back to America and that Anna was now living at the Hotel Continental.

"Oh dear, how difficult for you!" cried Aunt Louise, but it was not clear whether she meant the financial aspect or simply the fact that Mama had someone in the awkward age living with her.

"It's all such a rush," she wailed. "Sam says we've got to be out of London in two days, or he won't be responsible, with the French collapsing the way they have. And you can't get anyone to move the furniture – so many people have had the same idea. Do you know, I rang up eleven different firms before I found one which could do it?"

Mama made a sympathetic noise in her throat.

"And I'm sure they're going to break all the china, they're such galumphing great louts," said Aunt Louise. Then, quite unexpectedly, she flung her arms round Mama's shoulders to cry disarmingly, "And I know it's dreadful of me to fuss about it when people like you are staying behind in London and God only knows what's to happen to us all – but you know, my dear, that I was always a fool, ever since you were at the top of the class in Berlin and I at the bottom!"

"Nonsense," said Mama. "You were never a fool, and even at school you were always the prettiest, most elegant . . ."

"Oh yes I am," said Aunt Louise. "Sam has told me so many a time and he knows."

As though settling the matter once and for all, she rang a bell by her side and the maid appeared almost at once with a silver tea-pot on a tray and little sandwiches and cakes. Aunt Louise poured out delicately. "I looked out a few things for you while I was packing," she said. "I thought they might be useful." Then she cried, "Oh, she's forgotten the lemon again, I can't bear tea without lemon, she knows that perfectly well! Anna dear, could you possibly . . . ?"

Anna set off obediently in search of a lemon. The flat was large and rambling, with the dust-sheets everywhere making it more confusing, and she got lost several times before she found the kitchen. There she discovered half a lemon in the huge refrigerator and by the time she had ransacked all the drawers for a knife and cut the lemon into slices, which she was sure were much too thick, she feared Aunt Louise must have lost all interest in her tea.

She decided to try a different way back and after going down a passage and through a little ante-room found herself in the Professor's study. The blinds had been drawn against the sun, so that you could only guess at the medical books which lined the walls. Her feet sank into the deep carpet and it was almost spookily silent.

Suddenly she heard Papa's voice.

"How long does it take to act?" he asked, and Professor Rosenberg's voice answered, "Only a few seconds. I've got the same for myself and Louise."

Then she rounded a bookcase and discovered Papa and the Professor on the other side. Papa was putting something into his pocket and the Professor was saying, "Let's hope none of us will ever need it." Then he saw Anna and said, "Hullo – you're growing up. You'll be as tall as me soon!" This was a joke, for the Professor was short and round.

Anna smiled half-heartedly. She felt uneasy in this room, in the half-darkness, at finding Papa and the Professor so close together and talking about – what?

The Professor looked at her with his sad black eyes which were like a monkey's and said to Papa, "If things get bad in London send the girl to us. All right?" he added to Anna.

"All right," said Anna out of politeness, but she thought that even if things did get bad she would rather stay with Mama and Papa. Then she took the lemon to Aunt Louise and they all had some tea.

When it was time to leave Aunt Louise handed

Mama a parcel of clothes which she had packed up for her. (At the rate people were leaving London, thought Anna, she and Mama would soon have a vast wardrobe.) She hugged Mama several times and even the Professor embraced Papa and came down to the bus stop with them.

Back at the Hotel Continental Mama opened her parcel and found that it contained three dresses and an envelope. In the envelope was a note which said, "To help you through the next difficult weeks," and twenty pounds.

"Oh God!" cried Mama. "It's like a miracle! Anna, this will pay your hotel bills until you get a job!"

Anna thought Papa might say that they shouldn't accept the money or at least treat it as a loan, but he didn't. He just stood by the window as though he hadn't heard. It was very strange. He was staring out at the evening sky and fingering, fingering something in his pocket.

She felt suddenly very frightened.

"What is it?" she cried, although she really knew. "Papa! What did the Professor give you in his study?"

Papa tore his gaze away from the sky and looked at Mama, who stared back at him. At last he said slowly, "Something I had asked him to give me – for use in an emergency."

And Mama threw her arms round Anna as though never to let her go.

"Only in an emergency!" she cried. "Darling, darling, I promise you – only in an emergency!"

7

Three days later the French signed an armistice with the Germans and the only people left to fight Hitler were the English.

London was curiously empty. All the children had gone, and so had many of the old people. There were air-raid warnings almost every day. The first few times everyone rushed for shelter as soon as the sirens started. At the secretarial school they filed into the cellar of the building which was damp and smelled of mice. At the Hotel Continental they went into the basement which was also the kitchen and stood about awkwardly among the pots and pans. But nothing happened, no bombs fell, and after a while people began to ignore the warnings and just go on with whatever they had been doing.

Once Anna heard what sounded like a heavy piece of furniture being knocked over a long way off, and next day everyone said that a bomb had been dropped in Croydon, and once Anna and Papa saw two planes in a dog-fight right above the hotel. It was in the evening – the sky was pink and the planes were very high up so that you could hardly hear their engines or the rattle of their guns. They circled and dived and you could see little orange flashes and puffs of smoke as they fired at each other. But it didn't seem real. It looked like some beautiful, exciting display, and Papa and Anna craned out of the window, admiring it, until an air-raid warden shouted at them that there was shrapnel dropping all over Bedford Terrace and to get inside.

Every day, you wondered if the invasion would come. There were notices in the newspapers telling people what to do when it did. They were to stay in their homes – they must not panic and try to escape.

"Like in France," said the Frenchman from Rouen. "The people fled from the cities and blocked the roads, so that our armies could not get through. And then the Germans flew over them in their Stukas and machine-gunned them."

"Terrible," said Mama.

The Frenchman nodded. "The people were mad," he said. "They were so frightened. Do you know, after Holland we put our German residents into camps because we did not know – some of them might be collaborators. But of course most of them were Jews, enemies of Hitler. And when the Nazis were coming, these people cried and pleaded to be set free so that at least they could hide. But the guards were too frightened. They just locked the Jews into the camps and handed the keys over to the Nazis, to do with them what they would."

Then he saw Mama's face.

His wife said, "Madame's son has been interned," and he added quickly, "Of course such a thing could never happen in England."

After this Mama was more desperate than ever about Max. All the appeals which had been made on his behalf by friends, teachers, even important professors at Cambridge, had come to nothing. They simply were not answered. Gradually people grew to feel that it was hopeless and gave up. Anyway, they all had their own worries.

The only one still trying was the headmaster of Max's old school. He wanted Max to come back there to teach. "It's not much for a boy of his ability," he told Mama, "But it's better than being stuck in a camp," and he continued to bombard the authorities with demands for his release. But so far he had had no more luck than anyone else.

In the meantime, letters from Max arrived at irregular intervals, informative, matter of fact and sometimes funny, but always with the same underlying note of despair.

Cousin Otto had arrived at the camp and they were sharing a room. He was very upset at having been interned and Max was trying to cheer him up. Food was a bit short sometimes. Could Mama send some chocolate? One of the internees had committed suicide – a middle-aged Jew who had been in a German concentration camp before escaping to England. "He just couldn't face being in a camp again – any camp. It was nobody's fault, but we are all very depressed . . ." Cousin Otto was very low. The only thing that cheered him up was reading P. G. Wodehouse. "He reads late into the night as he can't sleep, and I don't get to sleep either because he will laugh out loud at the funny bits. I daren't say anything for fear of making him depressed again . . ." The authorities were sending shiploads of internees to the Commonwealth and quite a lot had chosen to go, rather than face indefinite internment in England. "But not me. I still think I belong in this country, even though they don't seem to agree with me at the moment. I know you're trying all you can to get me out, Mama, but if there is anything more you can do . . ."

The weather continued hot and dry.

"Best summer we've had for years," said the porter of the Hotel Continental. "No wonder Hitler wants to come here for his holidays."

There were battles now every day in the sky above England, and each night on the nine o'clock news the B.B.C. announced the results as though they were cricket scores. So many German planes shot down, so many British planes lost, eighteen for twelve, thirteen for eleven. The Germans always lost more planes than the British, but then they could afford to. They had so many more to start with.

Each night the porter switched on the old-fashioned radio in the lounge and the assembled refugees from countries already overrun by the Nazis stopped talking in their various languages and listened. If they could understand nothing else they could understand the figures, and they knew that they meant the difference between survival and the end of their world.

In August the fighting in the sky came to a head. No one knew how many British planes there were left, but everyone guessed that they must be nearly exhausted. The American press announced that according to reliable sources the invasion of England would take place within three days. It became more difficult to ignore the air-raid warnings, for you wondered each time whether the sirens had been set off yet again by a stray dog-fight in the vicinity of London or whether this time it was something quite different.

In bed at night Anna's wide-awake dreams grew worse. She no longer saw the Nazis dropping from the sky above Russell Square. Now they had already landed and England was occupied by them. She was alone, for when the Nazis had come battering on the doors of the Hotel Continental Mama and Papa had swallowed what the Professor had given Papa that day in the half darkness of his study, and now they were dead. She was stumbling through a vast grey landscape all by herself, searching for Max. But there were Nazis everywhere and she dared speak to no one. The landscape was huge and hostile and unfamiliar, and she knew that she would never find him . . .

In the daytime she applied herself more assiduously than ever to her shorthand, and she was glad when one of the Germans in the hotel asked her to do some typing for him, so that even her spare time would be accounted for. He was writing a book on the nature of humour and wanted one chapter typed out so that he could submit it to a publisher who, he was convinced, would wish at once to have it translated into English. It was a good moment, said the German, to publish a book about humour, for everyone was clearly much in need of it, and once he had explained exactly what it was everyone would be able to have it.

Anna thought the German was probably being over-optimistic, for the sample chapter struck her as very dull. Most of it was taken up with denunciations of various other authors who had thought they knew what the nature of humour was, but who had been quite wrong. She could not imagine people queueing up to read it. But she was going to be paid a full pound for the job and the manageress said she could use the office typewriter, so each day, as soon as she got back from secretarial school, she settled down to work in a corner of the lounge.

One evening she had just begun to type after supper when Mama cried in English, "Anna, we have a visitor."

She looked up and saw a thin man with untidy grey hair and a nice smile. It was Mr Chetwin, Max's headmaster.

"I'm afraid I have no news of Max," he said at once. "But I happened to be in town and I thought I'd just drop in to tell you that I haven't given up hope."

They all sat down together at one of the tables, and Mr Chetwin began to tell Mama and Papa to what government departments he had already written about Max and to what others he was still going to write, even though no one so far had replied. From this he got on to talking about Max himself.

"One of the best boys I ever had," he said, "though he would eat peppermints in prep – I remember having to beat him for that. But a brilliant footballer. He made the school team his first term, you know . . ."

Then he remembered Max's various successes at school – the scholarship after only two terms, so that there were no more fees to be paid, the major scholarship to Cambridge later – and Mama remembered all sorts of smaller successes that Mr Chetwin had forgotten, and Papa thanked him for all his kindness, and at the end of the conversation, even though nothing at all had changed, Anna noticed that Mama and Papa looked much happier than before.

By this time people were crowding into the lounge for the nine o'clock news and an elderly Pole excused himself and sat down at their table. He eyed Mr Chetwin respectfully.

"You are English?" he asked. Englishmen were rare in the Hotel Continental.

Mr Chetwin nodded, and the Pole said, "I am Pole. But I wish very, very much that England shall win this war."

There was a murmur of assent from other Poles and Czechs nearby and Mr Chetwin looked pleased and said, "Very good of you." Then all conversation was drowned by the deafening tones of Big Ben, for the porter had put the radio on too loud as usual.

A familiar voice said, "This is the B.B.C. Home Service. Here is the news, and this is Bruce Belfrage reading it."

The voice did not sound quite as usual and Anna thought, what's the matter with him? It had a breathlessness, a barely discernible wish to hurry, which had never been there before. She was listening so hard to the intonation of each word that she hardly took in the sense. Air battles over most of England . . . Heavy concentrations of bombers . . . An official communiqué from the Air Ministry . . . And then it came. The voice developed something like a tiny crack which completely robbed it of its detachment, stopped for a fraction of a second and then said slowly and clearly, "One hundred and eighty-two enemy aircraft shot down."

There was a gasp from the people in the lounge, followed by murmured questions and answered as those who did not understand much English asked what the news-reader had said, and the others checked with each other that they had heard aright. And then the elderly Pole was leaping up from his chair and shaking Mr Chetwin by the hand.

"It is success!" he cried. "You English show Hitler he not can win all the time! Your aeroplanes show him!" and the other Poles and Czechs crowded round, patting Mr Chetwin on the back, pumping his hand and congratulating him.

His grey hair became untidier than ever and he looked bemused but glad. "Very kind of you," he kept saying, "though it wasn't me, you know."

But they insisted on treating him as though he personally had been out there and shot down a whole lot of German bombers, and when at last he left to catch his train, one of them called after him triumphantly, "Now Hitler must think from something else!"

The trouble was, thought Anna a few days later, what would he think of? The fine weather had broken at last, heavy cloud had put an end to all air activity, and no one knew what would happen next.

Anna had finally got to the end of the chapter on the nature of humour and had collected her pound which she planned to spend on a pair of trousers –

a new fashion for women – and she and Mama were searching Oxford Street for a suitable pair.

In spite of the clouds it was still hot, and each of the big stores they went into seemed stickier and more airless than the last. The trousers on offer were all too expensive and it was not until just before closing time that they found a pair that would do. They were navy blue and made of some unidentifiable substance which Mama said would probably melt at the sound of an air-raid warning, but they were the right size and only cost nineteen shillings, elevenpence and three farthings, so they bought them – Anna triumphantly and Mama wearily.

Mama was depressed. She had had a letter that morning from Mr Chetwin full of kindness and concern for Max, but reporting no progress at all, and she was beginning to feel that this, her last hope, was going to fail like all the rest.

They had to queue a long time for a bus and when it finally came she sank into a seat and, instead of admiring Anna's trousers, picked up a newspaper which someone had left behind and began to read. The bus moved only slowly to save petrol and she had time to read the paper from cover to cover.

Suddenly she cried, "Look at this!"

Anna peered over her shoulder and wondered why a film review should have excited her so.

"Read it!" cried Mama.

It was a very sympathetic account of a film about the difficulties and disasters which beset an anti-Nazi family trying to escape from Germany. It was written not by a film critic but by a politician.

"You see?" cried Mama. "They can be sympathetic when the people are stuck in Germany, but what happens when they get to England? They put them in internment camps."

She hastily folded the paper and crammed it into her handbag.

"I'm going to write to this man," she said.

As soon as they got back she showed the article to Papa. At first Papa was not sure if they should write to the paper. He said, "We are guests in this country – one should not criticise one's host." But Mama got very excited and shouted that it was not a question of etiquette but of Max's whole life, and in the end they composed a letter between them.

They explained about Papa's long fight against Hitler and about Max's scholarships and about Mr Chetwin who wanted him to teach at his school. Then they gave a list of all the people at Cambridge who had protested about Max's internment, and ended up by asking whether this was not an absurd situation. Then they all walked down to Russell Square together and posted it.

The reply came two days later.

Anna had been awake half the night because there had been so many air-raid warnings, and for the first time a few bombs had fallen not in the distant suburbs but frighteningly near, in the middle of London. She was tired and depressed and eyed the letter warily, feeling that this was not the sort of day on which people received good news.

Mama, too, seemed almost afraid to open it, but

finally ripped at it so clumsily that a corner of the letter tore off with the envelope. Then she read it and burst into tears.

Papa took it from her and he and Anna read it together.

It was from the editor of the paper. He said that his paper had long protested against the government's policy which had caused some of the most brilliant and dedicated anti-Nazis to be put into internment camps. He had been much moved by Mama's and Papa's letter and had passed it on to the Home Secretary who had promised to look into Max's case himself, immediately.

"Does that mean they'll release him?" asked Anna.

"Yes," said Papa. "Yes, it does."

They sat in the cramped breakfast room and looked at each other. Suddenly everything was different. There had been bombs in the night, a new air-raid warning had already sounded, the headline in the morning paper said "Invasion Barges Massing In Channel Ports" – but none of it mattered because Max was going to be released.

At last Papa said slowly, "The English really are extraordinary. Here they are, threatened with invasion at any moment, and yet the Home Secretary can find time to right an injustice to an unknown boy who wasn't even born here."

Mama blew her nose.

"But of course," she said, "Max is a very remarkable boy!"

8

Max arrived home about a week later, unannounced, in the middle of an air raid. It was in the late afternoon. Mama was not yet back from work, Papa had walked to Russell Square to meet her, and Anna had just washed her hair in the bathroom at the end of the passage. She came back to her room with a towel wrapped round her head, and there he was standing in the corridor.

"Max!" she cried and was about to throw her arms round him, but then she stopped, in case he might not like it, in case it was too sudden.

"Hullo, little man," said Max. It was a nickname he had had for her since they were both quite small. "I'm glad to see you're keeping clean."

"Oh, Max," cried Anna, throwing her arms around him after all, "you haven't changed!"

"What did you think?" said Max. "That I'd be hard and embittered? Never smile again? I don't change." He followed her into her room. "But I learn from experience," he said. "And I'm going to make sure that nothing like the last four months ever happens to me again."

"How can you?" asked Anna.

Max moved some clothes off the only chair and sat down. "I'm going to teach for a year," he said. "Old Chetwin wants me to, and I owe it him after all he tried to do. Then I'm going into the Forces."

"But Max," said Anna, "do they take Germans in the British Forces?"

Max's mouth tightened. "We'll see," he said.

Then the door flew open and there was Mama, with Papa behind her.

"Max!" she cried, and at the same time there was a thud and a rumble and Max looked startled and said, "Was that a bomb?"

"Yes," said Anna apologetically, "but it was a long way off."

"Good God," said Max, and as Mama rushed to embrace him he added reproachfully, "Really, Mama – so this is what you've brought me back to!"

At supper they drank a bottle of wine that someone had given Papa months before and which he had kept specially. It did not taste quite right – perhaps, said Papa, the bottom of the clothes cupboard had not been the best place to store it – but they drank to Max, to Mr Chetwin and to the Home Secretary, and at the end of it all Anna felt pleasantly muzzy.

Mama could hardly take her eyes off Max. She heaped his plate with food and hung on his every word, but he did not talk much. Mostly he was worried about Otto who, he said, would be lost without him and who was thinking of going on a transport to Canada. "His professor is going," he said, "but what's he going to do in Canada? And anyway, the last transport that went got sunk by a U-boat."

The All Clear had sounded shortly after Max's arrival, but there was another air-raid warning a little while later and the sound of planes and distant bombs continued throughout the evening. After dark it got worse rather than better and Mama said, "I don't know what they're up to," quite crossly to Max, like a hostess whose arrangements for the evening had broken down.

"Is there anything to see?" asked Max. "I'll just take a look." And in spite of Mama's and Papa's warnings about shrapnel, he and Anna edged aside the heavy black-out material round the door and went out into the street.

It was not dark at all outside and the sky was bright pink, so that for a moment Anna thought stupidly that she had made a mistake about the time. Then there was a whistling, tearing sound and a crash as a bomb fell, not so very far away, and a man in a tin hat shouted at them "Get inside!"

"Where's the fire?" asked Max.

Of course, thought Anna, it must be a fire, that was why the sky was so bright.

The man backed against a wall as another bomb came down, but farther away. "In the docks," he said. "And Jerry's dropping everything and the kitchen sink into it. Now stop messing about and get in!" And he pushed them back into the hotel.

Max looked bemused. "Is it always like this?" he asked.

"No," said Anna. "This is the worst we've had." She thought of the pink sky and added, "It must be a very big fire."

By bed-time there was no sign of the raid abating and Frau Gruber, the manageress, said that anyone who wished could sleep in the lounge. She bustled about with rugs, and everyone helped to move the tables so as to make more room, and soon the lounge looked like a camp. There were people curled up with pillows

370

in the brown leatherette chairs and people stretched out on blankets on the floor. Some had changed into pyjamas and dressing-gowns, but others had kept on their ordinary clothes and covered themselves with their coats, in case a bomb dropped and they might suddenly have to rush out into the street. The author of the book on the nature of humour wore striped pyjamas, a tweed jacket and his hat.

When everyone was more or less settled, Frau Gruber appeared in her dressing-gown with cups and a jug of cocoa on a tray, as though they were having some kind of dormitory feast. At last the lights were put out, all except one small one in a corner, and Frau Gruber who had become astonishingly cheerful as a result of all this activity, said, "I hope you all have a very good night," which Anna thought funny in the circumstances.

She was lying on the floor with her head under one of the tables, next to Max – Mama and Papa were in two chairs the other side of the lounge – and as soon as the room darkened, the thumps and bangs outside became impossible to ignore. She could hear the sound of the planes, a quivering hum like having a mosquito in the room with you only many octaves lower, and every so often the thud of a bomb. The bombs were mostly some distance away, but even so the explosions were quite loud. Some people, she knew, could tell the difference between German planes and British ones, but they all sounded the same to her. They all sounded German.

All round her she could sense people moving and whispering – no one was finding it easy to go to sleep.

"Max?" she said very quietly.

He turned towards her, wide awake. "Are you all right?"

"Yes," she whispered. "Are you?"

He nodded.

Suddenly she remembered how, when she was quite small and frightened of thunderstorms, Max had kept her heart up by pretending that they were caused by God having indigestion.

"Do you remember . . ." she said, and Max said, "Yes, I was just thinking – God's indigestion. He's really got himself upset this time."

She laughed and then they both stopped talking to listen to the buzzing of a plane, as it seemed right above their heads.

"To think I could be peacefully in bed on the Isle of Man with Otto reading Wodehouse," said Max.

The sound of the plane grew fainter, then louder again – it must be circling, thought Anna – and finally faded away in the distance.

"Max," she said, "was it very bad in the camp?"

"No," said Max. "Not once we'd got settled. I mean, nobody was beastly or anything like that. The thing that got me was simply the fact of being there at all. I didn't belong there."

Anna wondered where she belonged. Here, in the hotel, among the other refugees? Probably as much as anywhere, she thought.

"You see," said Max, "I know it sounds arrogant to say so, but I know I belong in this country. I've known it ever since my first year at school – a feeling of everything being suddenly absolutely right. And it wasn't only me. Other people like George and Bill thought so too."

"Yes," said Anna.

"All I want," said Max, "is just to be allowed to do the same things as everyone else. Do you know, there were some people in the camp who thought they were lucky to be there because it was safe. Well, I'm not a particularly warlike person and God knows I don't want to be killed – but I'd a thousand times rather be in the Army with George or in the Air Force with Bill. I'm sick to death of always having to be different!"

There was a crash, closer than the rest, which shook the building and as Anna felt the floor move a little beneath her the word "bombardment" came into her mind. I'm in a bombardment, she thought. I'm lying on the floor of the Hotel Continental in my pink pyjamas in the middle of a bombardment.

"Max," she said, "are you frightened?"

"Not really," he said.

"Nor me."

"I suppose," said Max, "it's a relief just for once to have the same worries as everyone else!"

The raid lasted all through the night. Anna slept fitfully, lulled to sleep by the drone of the planes and startled awake again by distant thuds and crashes, until the All Clear went at half-past five in the morning and Frau Gruber, who seemed to see this new development in Hitler's air warfare as a personal challenge, appeared with cups of tea. She had pulled the blackout curtains aside and Anna saw, somehow to her surprise, that Bedford Terrace looked just as usual. The street was empty and the shabby houses stood silent under the pale sky, as though it had been a night like any other. While she watched, a door opened opposite and a woman dressed in trousers and a pyjama top appeared. She looked up searchingly at the sky, as Anna had done before. Then she yawned, stretched and went back inside to go back to bed or to start cooking breakfast.

Max was anxious to get off to his new job as soon as possible. He had managed with difficulty to get through to Euston Station on the telephone and had been told that due to enemy action there would be long delays on all lines. So Anna and Mama said good-bye to him as he packed his suitcase, with Papa sitting on the bed to keep him company, and went to work as usual.

It was a beautiful clear morning and as Anna walked through the back streets to Tottenham Court Road she was again amazed at how ordinary everything looked. Only there were more cars and taxis about than usual, often with luggage piled high on roof-racks – more people leaving London. While she was waiting to cross a road, a man just opening up his greengrocer's shop smiled at her and called out, "Noisy last night!" and she answered, "Yes," and smiled back.

She hurried past the back of the British Museum – this was the dullest part of her daily journey – and turned into a more interesting street with shops. There was some glass on the pavement in front of her – someone must have broken a window, she thought. And then she looked up and saw the rest of the street.

There was glass everywhere, doors hanging on their hinges, bits of rubble all over the road. And in the terrace opposite where there should have been a house there was a gap. The entire top floor had gone, and so had most of the front wall. They had subsided into a pile of bricks and stone which filled the road, and some men in overalls were shovelling them into the back of a lorry.

You could see right inside what remained of the house. It had had green wallpaper and the bathroom had been painted yellow. You could tell it was the bathroom because, even though most of the floor had gone, the part supporting the bath tub appeared to be suspended in space. Immediately above it was a hook with a flannel still hanging from it and a toothmug in the shape of Mickey Mouse.

"Horrible, isn't it?" said an old man next to Anna. "Lucky there was no one in it – she'd taken the kids to her sister's. I'd like to give that Hitler a piece of my mind!"

Then he went back to sweeping up the glass outside his shop.

Anna walked slowly down the street. The part closest to the bombed house had been cordoned off, in case any more of it fell down, and on one side of it a man and a woman were already nailing up sheets of cardboard in place of their broken windows. She was glad there had been nobody in the house when the bomb fell. One of the men shovelling rubble shouted to her to keep away and she turned down a side street.

There was only little damage here – broken windows and some dust and plaster underfoot – and as she picked her way among the fragments of glass scattered on the pavement she noticed how the sun sparkled on them. A little breeze blew the dust into swirls round her feet. Her legs were brown from the endless fine weather and she suddenly wanted to run and jump. How awful to feel like this, she thought, when there had been an air raid and people had been killed – but another part of her didn't care. The sky was blue and the sun was warm on her bare arms and there were sparrows hopping about in the gutter and cars hooting and people walking about and talking, and suddenly she could feel nothing but a huge happiness at still being alive. Those poor people who lost their house, she thought, but the thought had hardly time to emerge before it was swallowed up by her happiness.

She took a deep breath – the air smelled of brickdust and plaster – and then she ran to the end of the street and down Tottenham Court Road and all the way to the secretarial school.

9

After this there were air raids every night. The sirens went at dusk, to be followed a few minutes later by the drone of German bombers, and the All Clear did not go until first light. They were so regular you could almost set your watch by them.

"Mama," Anna would say, "can I go and buy some sweets for the air raid?"

Mama would say, "All right, but be quick – they'll be here in ten minutes." And Anna would run through the warm, darkening streets to the sweet shop next to the tube station for two ounces of toffees which the woman in the shop would weigh out hastily, with one eye on the clock, and then she would race back to the hotel, arriving together with the first wail of the sirens.

Each night she and Mama and Papa slept in the lounge. There was plenty of room, for a lot of people had left after the first big raid, and more went every day. It was unnerving just lying there in the dark and waiting for the Germans to drop their bombs. There seemed to be nothing at all to stop them. But after a few nights the din of the raids suddenly increased with a series of bangs, like a great drum being blown full of air and exploding, and Frau Gruber, who had become an expert overnight, at once identified this as anti-aircraft fire. It made sleep even more difficult than before, but even so, everyone rejoiced in it.

It was curious, thought Anna, how quickly one could get used to sleeping on the floor. It was really quite snug. There were plenty of blankets, and the heavy wooden shutters over the lounge windows not only muffled the noise but gave her a feeling of security. She never got enough sleep, but nor did anyone else, and this was another thing one got used to. Everywhere you went during the day there were people having little catnaps to catch up – in the parks, on the buses and tubes, in the corners of tea-shops. One girl even fell asleep over her short-hand machine at the secretarial school. When they talked to each other they would yawn hugely in the middle of a sentence and go straight on with what they were saying without even bothering to apologise.

During the third week of the raids a bomb fell in Russell Square, making a crater in the soft earth and breaking most of the windows in Bedford Terrace. Anna was asleep at the time and fortunately for her the blast sucked everything out into the street, so that the glass and the shutters (which had not been so safe after all) landed on the pavement instead of on the people in the lounge.

She leapt up from the floor, hardly awake and unable to understand what had happened. There was a curtain fluttering round her face and she could see straight into the street where an air-raid warden was blowing his whistle. All round her people were stumbling in the darkness and asking what had happened and above it all came Mama's voice shouting, "Anna! Are you all right?"

She shouted back, "Yes!" and then Frau Gruber arrived with a torch.

Afterwards she found to her surprise that she was trembling.

After this no one slept in the lounge any more. The man from the Council who came to board up the gaps where the windows had been told Frau Gruber that it was not safe and that it would be better, in future, to use the basement.

Anna boasted a little at the secretarial school about her escape, but no one was very impressed. By now most of the people still remaining in London had a bomb story of some sort. If they hadn't lost any windows they had just failed, by some remarkable coincidence, to be in some building which had received a direct hit. Madame Laroche had returned from a public shelter at dawn to find that a landmine had somehow got through her roof without exploding and was now dangling from its parachute at the top of the staircase, ready to go off at the slightest tremor. This had so unnerved her, on top of the worry about her family in Belgium, that her doctor had ordered her to rest in the country.

The school hardly missed her. It had almost run down, anyway. There were scarcely a dozen students left and it had become impossible to take down dictation and read it back, for the special paper for the machines had come from Belgium and there was no more to be had. So the students practised by moving their fingers on empty keyboards while the one remaining teacher read out light novels to them. It was perfectly logical, but sometimes, as Anna listened to yet another chapter of Dorothy Sayers or Agatha

Christie after walking through the broken streets, it occurred to her that this was a strange way of spending what might be the last days of her life.

At night everyone now slept in the basement. Its stone floor was cold and hard, so if you wanted to be at all comfortable you had to drag the mattress down from your bed. But it always seemed like the last straw, after a largely sleepless night, to have to drag it all the way up again when the All Clear went at dawn.

The cellar they slept in had been a storage room and Anna hated it. To reach it you had to go down a narrow flight of stone steps from the dining room to the kitchen and then down a few further steps beyond it. It was little more than six feet high and both damp and stuffy. Once you were installed on your mattress listening to the air raid outside and staring up at the low ceiling it was easy to imagine everything collapsing above you, and Anna had an unreasonable wish, even when no bombs had fallen nearby, to keep checking that the stairs to the dining room were still there.

Sometimes when she could not bear it any longer she would whisper to Mama, "I'm going to the lavatory," and in spite of the grumbles of the other sleepers she would pick her way across them and go up into the deserted main part of the hotel. She would climb up the four flights to her room and stay there, with the sound of the bombs and the guns, until she felt ready to brave the basement again.

One night when she entered her room she was startled to see a figure outlined against the window which, by some freak of the blast, had remained unbroken.

"Who is it?" she cried.

Then it turned and she recognised Papa.

"Look," he said, and she joined him in the darkness.

The night outside was brilliant. The sky was red, reflecting the fires on the ground, and in it hung clusters of orange flares which lit up everything for miles around. They looked like gigantic Christmas decorations floating slowly, slowly down through the night air, and though Anna knew that they were there to help the Germans aim their bombs she was filled with admiration at the sight. It was so bright that she could see the church clock (which had long been stopped) and a place on the rooftop opposite where some of the tiles had been ripped off by blast. In the distance yellow flashes like lightning were followed by muffled bangs – the anti-aircraft guns in Hyde Park.

Suddenly a searchlight swept across the sky. It was joined by another and another, crossing and re-crossing each other, and then a great orange flash blotted out everything else. A bomb or a plane exploding in mid-air – Anna did not know which – but the accompanying crash sent her and Papa scuttling away from the window.

When it was over they looked out again at the illuminated night. The orange flares had been joined by some pink ones and they were drifting slowly down together.

"It may be the end of the civilised world," said Papa, "but it is certainly very beautiful."

As the days grew shorter the air raids grew longer. By mid-October the All Clear did not sound until half-past six in the morning and it was hardly worth trying to get to sleep afterwards.

"If only this fine weather would stop!" cried Mama, for when the weather was bad enough the bombers did not come and they had the incredible, marvellous experience of sleeping all night in their beds. But one bright day followed another, and though it was exhilarating, each morning, to go out in the crisp autumn air and find that one was still alive, each night the bombers came back and with them the closeness and the fear in the basement.

One night the sirens sounded earlier than usual, while everyone was still having supper. They were followed almost immediately by the drone of planes and a succession of crashes as bombs fell not far away.

One of the Poles stopped with a forkful of shepherd's pie half-way to his mouth.

"Bang-bang!" he said. "It is not nice when people are eating." He was a large middle-aged man with an unpronounceable name and everyone called him the Woodpigeon because of his passion for imitating a pair of scraggy birds which haunted the yard behind the hotel.

"They're going for the stations again," said Frau Gruber.

"Oh surely not!" cried the German lady whose husband had been killed by the Nazis. "They went for the stations yesterday."

The Hotel Continental lay half-way between Euston and St Pancras and when the Germans tried to bomb the stations it always meant a bad night.

"But not did they hit them," said the Woodpigeon, and then everyone froze as a tearing, whistling sound was followed by an explosion which rocked the room.

A glass slid off one of the tables and broke on the floor.

"That was quite close," said Mama.

Frau Gruber started in a matter of fact way to collect the dishes.

"It's prunes and custard for pudding," she said, "but I think we'd better leave it and go to the shelter."

While Anna went to fetch her mattress from her room there was another crash and the whole building – walls, floors, ceiling – moved perceptibly around her. She grabbed the mattress quickly and rushed down the stairs with it bumping behind her. For once she was glad to get down into the basement – at least it didn't move.

Frau Gruber had hung up a blanket in the middle of the storage room, so that the men could sleep on one side and the women on the other. Anna pushed her mattress into an empty space and found herself next to the German lady whose husband had been killed by the Nazis. Mama was somewhere behind her. Before she had time even to lie down there was another shattering crash and Frau Gruber, who had been tinkering with the prunes and custard in the kitchen, abandoned them and made for the storage room.

"Oh dear," said the German lady, "I do hope it's not going to be one of those awful nights."

This was followed by an even louder crash and then a third, fortunately farther away.

"It's all right," said Anna. "He's passed us."

The Germans always dropped sticks of six or more bombs in a row. As long as the explosions were coming towards you it was terrifying, but once they had moved past you knew that you were safe.

"Thank God!" said the German lady, but Anna could already hear the drone of another plane.

"They're coming in on a different flight-path," said Frau Gruber. Mama added, "Straight overhead," and then the next lot of bombs began to fall. They listened to them screaming down from the sky. One . . . two . . . three . . . four very close – five and six, thank goodness, receding. Then there was another plane and another – it can't go on like this, thought Anna, but it did.

Next to her the German lady was lying with her eyes shut and her hands clenched on her chest, and on the other side of the blanket she could hear the Woodpigeon muttering, "Why you not hit the station and go home? You stupid, silly Germans, why you not can hit it?"

At last, after what seemed an eternity, there was a lull. The last bomb dropped by one plane was not followed immediately by the sound of another plane approaching.

It was quiet.

For a few moments everyone waited and when nothing happened they began to move and relax. Anna looked at her watch. It was still only ten o'clock.

"That was the worst we've had," said Mama.

Papa lifted a corner of the blanket and looked through. "Are you all right?" he asked, and Anna nodded. Curiously enough she did not feel her usual urge to see if the stairs were still there. How silly, she thought – if they really collapsed one would hear it.

"Well, we may as well try and get some sleep," said Frau Gruber and at the same moment there was a distant thud and the light went out.

"They've hit a cable," said Frau Gruber, snapping on her torch.

"The kind Germans have switched off for us the light," said the Woodpigeon, and everyone laughed.

"Well, I won't waste the battery," said Frau Gruber and the cellar was plunged into darkness.

Anna closed her eyes so as not to see it. She had been frightened of the dark when she was small and still was. It was quiet except for some bumps in the distance. There was nothing to see, nothing to hear, and she drifted off into sleep.

Suddenly everything seemed to explode. The cellar shook around her and before she could collect herself in the darkness another bomb came screaming down, the loudest she had ever heard, it burst with a huge roaring reverberation that was almost too loud to hear and something came down on top of her and covered her, she could not see or breathe, it was what she had always dreaded . . .

And then she moved and found that it was only the blanket which had fallen on her, and the white faces of Papa and the Woodpigeon appeared with a click of Frau Gruber's torch.

"Are you all right?" said Papa.

She said, "Yes," and lay where she was without moving, still filled with the terror of it. Next to her the German lady was crying.

Mama began to say something but stopped because

there was another plane above them and the bombs came tearing down again.

"I'll just take a look," said Frau Gruber after the last one, and the cellar leapt and darkened as she moved with her torch into the kitchen.

"All right," she said. "We're still standing."

Anna lay quite still.

"I mustn't panic," she thought. But she wished the German lady would stop crying as the cellar shook with another explosion.

At the rate they're bombing us, she thought, we're bound to be hit.

A wave of terror swept over her, but she managed to contain it. If she could just get used to the idea, she thought. If she could manage to keep calm when it happened. Because they always came to dig you out, and if you didn't panic you didn't use up so much oxygen, and then you could last until they came.

Mama leaned over to her in the darkness. "Would you like to come next to me?" she said.

"I'm all right here," said Anna.

Mama could not help her.

Another plane came over and another stick of bombs tore down.

If I think about it now, thought Anna, if I imagine it, then when it happens, when I'm trapped in a little hole with tons of rubble on top of me . . .

Again the terror surged over her.

She tried to fight it down. I mustn't fight and scrabble to get out, she thought, I must keep quite still. There may not be much room, much air . . .

Suddenly she could almost feel the tight, black

cavity shutting her in and it was so frightful that she leapt into a sitting position as though she had been stung, to make sure it hadn't happened. She was panting for breath and Mama said, "Anna?" again.

"I'm all right," she said.

The German lady was moaning and beyond her two Czech voices were murmuring some kind of prayer.

I have to get used to it, she thought, I must! But before she had even finished the thought such terror engulfed her that she almost cried out. It was no good. She couldn't do it. She lay with clenched teeth and clenched hands, waiting for it to subside.

Perhaps it won't be so bad when it happens, she thought. Perhaps it's worse thinking about it. But she knew that it wasn't.

The planes kept coming and the bombs kept bursting while the German lady wept beside her. Once Mama shouted at the German lady to control herself and at some time during the night Papa moved his mattress over to Mama so that they were all near each other, but it made no difference.

She lay alone in the dark, trying to shut out the terrible picture of herself screaming mutely in a black hole.

At last she became so exhausted that a kind of calm came over her. I've got used to it, she thought, but she knew that she hadn't. And when at last the shuddering crashes stopped and a little light filtered into the cellar with the sound of the All Clear, she thought, well, after all, it wasn't so bad. But she knew that this, too, was untrue.

When they inspected the damage they found that the few remaining windows had gone. The top of the church tower which Anna had been able to see from her room had collapsed and there was a ragged hole in the roof of the church. And on the other side of Bedford Terrace, only a few yards along, where there should have been a house, there was only a heap of rubble in which nobody and nothing could have survived.

"Direct hit," said the porter.

"Who lived there?" asked Anna.

She was standing in the cold morning air in her trousers and an old sweater. The wind blew through her clothes and she had wrapped a handkerchief round her hand where she had cut herself on a piece of broken window glass.

"Refugees from Malta," said the porter. "But they always went to the public shelter."

Anna remembered them – frail, dark-skinned people in clothes far too thin for an English autumn. As soon as the air-raid warning sounded they would pour out of the house with a curious twittering sound and hurry fearfully down the street.

"All of them?" she asked. "Did all of them go to the public shelter?"

"Nearly all of them," said the porter.

Then a large blue car swept round the corner from Russell Square, negotiated some rubble in the road and stopped inexplicably outside the hotel. The driver opened the door and a little round man climbed out. It was Professor Rosenberg.

"I heard it was bad last night," he said. "Are you all right?"

Anna nodded and he swept her ahead of him into the lounge where Mama and Papa were drinking some tea which Frau Gruber had made.

"I think the girl should get out of all this for a bit," he said. "I'm driving back to the country this evening. I'll pick her up and take her with me."

Anna demurred. "I'm all right," she said, but tears kept coming into her eyes for no reason and Mama and Papa both wanted her to go.

In the end Mama decided it by shouting, "I can't stand another night like the last with you here – I wouldn't mind if I knew you were safe!" and Papa said, "Please go!" So Mama helped her to pack, and about five o'clock she drove off in the back of the Professor's great car.

She leaned out of the window, waving frantically until the car had turned the corner. All the way to the country she carried with her the picture of Mama and Papa waving back as they stood among the rubble of the shattered street.

10

It was night when they arrived. Already as the car had zig-zagged out of London, detouring round blocked streets and unexploded bombs, dusk had begun to fall, and the Professor had urged the driver to hurry so as to get clear of the city before the bombers came. Anna climbed out into the country darkness, sensed rather than saw great bushy trees surrounding a large house and caught a whiff of acorns and autumn leaves before the Professor propelled her through the front door. While she was still getting adjusted to the brightness of the hall a gong sounded somewhere in the depths of the house. The Professor said, "Go and find your Aunt Louise," and disappeared upstairs.

Anna wondered where Aunt Louise could be and, for lack of a better idea, decided to follow the sound of the gong. She went through a large drawing-room furnished with soft chairs, sofas and elaborately shaded lamps, into an equally large dining-room where the long lace-covered table was laid for about a dozen people. There she found another door covered in green baize and had just decided to open it when the gonging stopped and Aunt Louise, dressed in a long velvet gown, burst into the dining-room with the stick still in her hand.

"There will be no dinner . . ." she cried.

Then she saw Anna and threw her arms round her, accidentally hitting her with the padded end of the stick.

"My dear!" she cried, "Are you all right? I told Sam to bring you. Are your parents all right?"

"We're all all right," said Anna.

"Thank God," cried Aunt Louise. "We heard that last night was terrible. Oh, it must be so awful in London – though here, too, there are problems. The dinner . . ." She drew Anna through the green baize door. "Come," she cried, "You can help me!"

In the narrow corridor beyond they met two maids in frilly aprons.

"Now Lotte! Inge!" said Aunt Louise. "Surely you must see reason!" But they looked at her sulkily and the one called Inge sniffed. "What's said can't be unsaid," she remarked, and the one called Lotte added, "That goes for me too."

"Oh really," wailed Aunt Louise. "Who would have thought, just because of some kippers!"

They passed the kitchen with five or six saucepans steaming on the range.

"Look at it!" cried Aunt Louise, "It will all spoil," and she almost ran to a room beyond. "Fraulein Pimke!" she shouted and tried to open the door, but it was locked and Anna could hear someone weeping noisily inside. "Fraulein Pimke!" Aunt Louise cried again, rattling the door handle. "Listen to me! I never said anything against your cooking."

There were some unintelligible sounds from within.

"Yes I know," cried Aunt Louise. "I know you cooked for the Kaiser. And for all the highest in the land. And I wouldn't dream of criticising, only how was I to know that the maids wouldn't eat kippers? And then, when the butter ration . . . Fraulein Pimke, please come out!"

There was a shuffling sound followed at length by

391

a click. The door opened a crack and an ancient, tear-stained face peered out.

". . . never had my food refused before," it quavered. "And then to be shouted at on top of it . . . eighty-two years old and still trying to do my best . . ." The corners of the mouth turned down and more tears ran down the wrinkled cheeks.

"Now Fraulein Pimke," said Aunt Louise, cunningly inserting an arm through the crack and drawing her through the door (very much, thought Anna, like extracting a snail from its shell). "What would the Kaiser say to see you weeping like this?"

Fraulein Pimke, deprived of the shelter of her room, blinked and looked confused, and Aunt Louise weighed in quickly while she had the chance.

"I didn't mean to shout at you," she said. "It's just that I was taken aback. When I found that the butter ration had gone on the kippers. And then, when the maids gave notice . . . Fraulein Pimke, you're the only one I can rely on!"

Fraulein Pimke, slightly mollified, blinked at Anna. "Who's this?" she said.

Aunt Louise saw her chance and took it.

"A bomb victim!" she cried. "A little victim of the London blitz!" She caught sight of the handkerchief round Anna's hand and pointed to it dramatically. "Wounded!" she cried. "Surely, Fraulein Pimke, you cannot let this child go without her dinner!"

By this time she had somehow manoeuvred the group towards the kitchen door, and Fraulein Pimke went in like a lamb.

"Thank you, thank you!" cried Aunt Louise. "I

knew I could count on you – the Professor will be so pleased!"

Then she led Anna back into the drawing-room which was now filled with people in evening dress. Anna's lack of sleep was catching up with her and after the terrors of the previous night everything was beginning to feel like a dream. She was introduced to various people, most of whom seemed to be related to the Professor, but it was difficult to remember who they all were.

There was a little cross-looking woman who was the Professor's sister and two boys younger than Anna who might or might not be her sons. But what was a man dressed in a silk suit and turban doing there, and was he really a maharajah as someone seemed to have said? She was uncomfortably conscious of her trousers and old sweater, but a red-haired woman in a black dress kindly told her that she looked very nice and even appealed to her husband for confirmation, and he said something about the battlefront and asked her what it was like being in the blitz.

It turned out that no one in the house had spent a night in London since the beginning of the air raids, and they asked her endless questions as though she were some strange creature from another world. The maharajah, if he was one, kept saying, terrible, terrible, and how did people survive, which was silly, thought Anna, for what else could you do if you had no choice, and an old lady with an ear-trumpet said, "Tell me, my dear, is it true that there is a great deal of noise?"

Dinner, served sulkily by Inge and Lotte, was

unbelievably good and with her stomach delight-
fully full Anna almost fell asleep during the ritual
listening to the nine o'clock news which followed
it.

The Professor put a proper bandage on her cut
hand, which everyone insisted on referring to as a
wound, and by this time the dreamlike quality of
the evening had so far taken over that she was not
in the least surprised when Fraulein Pimke appeared
in dressing-gown, slippers and hairnet to kiss everyone
good night. "Was the dinner good?" she whispered to
each guest, and even the maharajah said, "Yes," and
let her kiss his hand.

Anna was almost staggering on her feet when at last
Aunt Louise took her to her room. It was clean and
pretty with new sheets on the bed. Outside the window
there were trees and a great calm sky. No bombs, no
planes, no noise. Mama and Papa . . . she thought as
her head sank into the pillows, but she was so tired
and the bed was so soft that she could not finish the
thought and fell asleep.

It was bright daylight when she woke up. For a
moment she looked in astonishment at the white walls
and flowery curtains. Then she stretched out again in
the bed with a marvellous sense of well-being. She felt
as though she had just recovered from a severe illness –
it must be having slept all night without interruption,
she thought. When she looked at her watch she found
that it was nearly noon.

She got up quickly, putting on her skirt instead of
her trousers (but it had been difficult to wash anything

in London and it did not look much better) and went downstairs. The drawing-room was empty except for the old lady with the ear-trumpet. When she saw Anna she smiled and shouted, "A great deal of noise, eh?"

"Yes, but not here," Anna shouted back.

Outside the French windows she could see grey clouds moving across the sky. With luck Mama and Papa would have had a fairly quiet night. She was not hungry and anyway it was too late for breakfast, so she went outside.

The wind was strong but not cold and whirls of leaves skimmed across the terrace in front of her. At the end of the terrace was what had been a lawn, but now the damp grass coiled round her calves and even her knees as she walked through it. It was a very large lawn, and somewhere about the middle she stopped for a moment with the wind blowing round her face and the grass swaying below her. It was like being at sea and, perhaps because she had had no breakfast, she felt almost giddy with the motion.

Beyond her the grass sloped down towards a row of trees and when she reached them she discovered a stream running beneath them. She squatted down to look at it, and just as she did so the sun came out and the water, which had been mud-coloured, turned a bright greeny blue. A small fish appeared, hardly moving above the sandy bottom and very clear in the sudden light. She could see every shiny scale fitting round the plump body, the round, astonished eyes, the shape of the delicate tail and fins. As it stood among the currents it looked sometimes green and sometimes silver and its spade-shaped mouth stretched and shrank as it opened and closed. She sat staring at it, almost feeling it with her eyes, but she must have moved, for it suddenly darted away, and a moment later the sun went in and the stream turned brown and dull again.

Some leaves floated down from the trees above her and after a moment she got up and walked back towards the house. She could still see the fish in her mind. If one could paint that, she thought. The wind blew through her hair and through the grass and, suddenly intoxicated, she thought, and giraffes and tigers and trees and people and all the beauty of the world!

She found most of the house-guests assembled in the drawing-room and they all asked her if she was feeling better, except for the old lady with the ear-trumpet who was too busy peering through the dining-room door to see if lunch was ready yet. Aunt Louise, worn out with the domestic dramas of the previous night, was resting in her room, and the maharajah was nowhere to be seen.

The Professor was talking about the old days in Berlin.

"Grandmother's birthday," he said. "Do you remember how all the children used to come?"

His sister nodded. "She used to give them all presents," she said.

"Thank God she didn't live to see how it all ended," said the Professor.

Then the door opened and the maharajah appeared, rather to Anna's relief, for she half-thought she might have dreamed him. He was still wearing his turban but an ordinary dark suit, and everyone at once tried to speak English for his sake. Only the old lady with the ear-trumpet suddenly said loudly in German, "She used to serve the best gefilte fish in Prussia."

Anna wondered whether the maids who had given notice would be serving lunch, but to her surprise they were both in the dining-room, all smiles and attention. (She discovered later that Aunt Louise had simply raised their wages.) She sat next to the maharajah who asked her again about the air raids and told her that he had been so frightened by the first one that it had made him ill, and that the Professor had brought him out to stay in the country until he could get a passage back to India.

"You are my benefactor," he said to the Professor, pressing his hand.

"And of all of us in this house," said the red-haired lady, and the Professor looked pleased, but in a worried way, and said a little later that it was awful how food prices had risen since the war.

Anna asked where the two boys were, and the Professor's sister told her that they went to a grammar school in the nearby town but were not learning anything because all the good teachers had been called up.

"Nonsense, you fuss too much," said the red-haired lady, which made the Professor's sister very angry, and within minutes, to Anna's surprise, everyone had been drawn into a fierce quarrel. Only the maharajah contented himself with saying, "Education is the finest jewel in a young man's crown," with which no one could disagree, and the old lady asked Anna to pass the gravy and quietly ate everything in sight.

On the whole it was a relief when lunch was over and most of the house-guests announced that they were going to their rooms to rest. From what? wondered Anna. It had begun to drizzle and she did not feel like going out again, so she wrote a note to Mama and washed some of her clothes in a laundry room she discovered beyond the kitchen.

When she returned to the drawing-room it was still only half-past three and there was no one in it except the old lady who had fallen asleep in her chair with her mouth open. There was a magazine on a table and Anna leafed through it, but it was all about horses and in the end she just sat. The old lady emitted a faint snore. There was a bit of fluff on her dress quite close to her mouth and every time she breathed it moved very slightly. For a while Anna watched it in the hope that something might happen – the old lady might swallow it, or sneeze, or something – but nothing did.

The room grew slowly darker. The old lady snored and the bit of fluff moved with her breath, and Anna was beginning to feel that she had been there for ever when there was a sudden flurry of activity.

First Lotte came in with the tea trolley. The old lady who must have smelled the tea in her sleep immediately woke up. Aunt Louise, followed by the other house-guests, appeared in her long velvet gown and drew the curtains and switched on the lamps, and then the two boys burst in from school. Their mother at once began to cross-question them. Had they learned anything? What about their homework? Perhaps Anna could help them with it? But they brushed her aside with a quick look of dislike at Anna, and turned on the radio very loud.

Aunt Louise clapped her hands over her delicate ears. "Must we have that frightful din?" she cried.

One of the boys shouted, "I want to hear Forces' Favourites!"

Their mother, suddenly changing sides, said, "Surely the children can have *some* pleasure!" and at once everyone became involved in another argument which continued long after the boys had crept out to listen to their programme in the kitchen. Aunt Louise said they were spoiled. Their mother said that Aunt Louise, having no children of her own, knew nothing about it. The red-haired lady said that there was a terrible atmosphere in the house – you couldn't breathe – and the old lady made a long speech which no one could understand, but which seemed to accuse some unspecified person of interfering with her sugar ration.

Anna could not think what to do, so she went over to the window and peered out into the dusk. The sun had not quite set and she could see that the sky was still overcast. If it was like this in London it shouldn't be too bad. She thought of Mama and Papa getting ready for the night. They would be wondering whether to spend it in the cellar or to risk sleeping in their beds.

Behind her, a voice cried, "And it was just the same last week over the wellington boots!" and suddenly she wondered what on earth she was doing in this house, at this time, among these people.

11

All the days at the Professor's house, Anna discovered, were much like the first one. There were long periods of boredom which she filled as best she could with walks and attempts to draw, interspersed with violent rows. Except for the Professor none of the house-guests had anything to do except to wait for the next meal, the news, the end of the blitz, and as only the two boys ever seemed to leave the house they all got on each others' nerves.

It was extraordinary, thought Anna, what little things could start an argument – for instance the business over God Save The King. This cropped up almost every time the radio was on and seemed quite insoluble.

It began one evening when Aunt Louise leapt to her feet and stood to attention while God Save The King was being played after the news. Afterwards she told all the people who had remained seated that they were guilty of rudeness and ingratitude to the country that was giving them shelter. The Professor's sister said her sons had reliably informed her that no Englishman would ever dream of standing up for God Save The King in his own home, and as usual there was a row and everyone took sides.

Anna tried to avoid the whole issue by arranging not to be in the drawing-room after the news when God Save The King was most likely to be played, but the situation was made more complicated by the fact that Aunt Louise was tone-deaf. She was never quite sure whether any rousing tune she heard was really God Save The King or not, and once tried to make everyone stand up for Rule Britannia, and twice for Land Of Hope And Glory.

Then there was the great mystery of the sugar ration. This was started, needless to say, by the old lady who had been complaining for some time that her sugar ration was being tampered with, but no one took any notice until she gave a triumphant cry one morning at breakfast and said that she had proof.

To avoid arguments, the sugar rations, like the butter and margarine rations, were carefully weighed out once a week into separate little dishes, each marked with the owner's name, and the dishes were put out by Lotte on the breakfast table for people either to eke out day by day or devour all at once in one greedy feast. The old lady had cunningly marked the level of her sugar with pencil on the side of the dish, and now here it was, a good quarter of an inch lower. Roused to suspicion, the others marked their sugar also and, lo and behold, next day both the Professor's sister and the red-haired lady's husband had lost some, though everyone else's remained untouched.

The ensuing row was bitterer than any Anna had yet witnessed. The red-haired lady accused the two boys, the Professor's sister cried, "Are you suggesting that they'd steal from their own mother?" which, Anna thought, showed a strange attitude, and Aunt Louise insisted that the Professor must interrogate the servants, as a result of which Lotte and Inge gave notice again.

The mystery was eventually cleared up. Fraulein Pimke, in the course of providing sweet puddings for dinner, had helped herself to the nearest dishes at hand. But so many unforgivable things had been said that almost no one was on speaking terms with anyone else for two days. The maharajah, as the only member of the household to remain aloof from the battle, found it very depressing. He and Anna walked glumly round the park under the dripping trees and Anna listened while he talked wistfully about India, until the cold autumn air drove them back into the house.

It was after the row about the sugar that Anna decided to return to London. She put it as tactfully as she could to Aunt Louise.

"Mama needs me," she said, though Mama hadn't actually said so.

Even so, Aunt Louise was quite distressed. She did not want Anna to go back into the air raids and also she thought it might upset Fraulein Pimke who had become used to seeing her about the house. And what about the maids, she said. If they really left she would need all the help she could get. But characteristically, just as Anna was beginning to feel rather cross, she flung her arms about her, crying, "I'm a fool, don't take any notice of me," and insisted on giving her a pound for the journey.

The Professor was not driving up to London that week, so Anna went by train, which took four and a half hours instead of the scheduled fifty minutes. She had deliberately not told Mama that she was coming because Mama and Papa had both urged her in their letters to stay in the country as long as possible, and she did not want to give them the chance to argue with her.

As the train drew into London she could see gaps in almost every street where bombs had fallen, and there were no windows left in any of the houses backing on to the railway line. Paddington Station had lost all the grimy glass in its roof and it was strange to be able to see sky and clouds beyond the blackened girders. Some sparrows were fluttering in and out among them, swooping down every so often to the platforms in search of crumbs.

The streets were empty – it was early afternoon and everyone was at work – and from her bus crawling along the Euston Road Anna noticed that weeds had begun to grow on some of the bomb-sites, which made them look as though they had been there for years. Altogether the city looked scarred but undramatic, as though it had become used to being bombed.

In Bedford Terrace almost half the houses had been boarded up and abandoned, but the Hotel Continental did not seem to have suffered any further damage and some of the windows had even been repaired. She found Papa in his room – Mama was still at her office – in the middle of typing something on his shaky typewriter.

"Why didn't you stay in the country?" he cried, but since she was there and there was nothing he could do about it, he was clearly delighted to see her. Mama's reaction, an hour or two later, was much the same. Neither of them seemed altogether surprised. Of course, thought Anna, they knew the Rosenbergs a good deal better than she did.

There were fewer people than ever in the hotel. The German lady, Mama told her, had not been able to stop crying after that very bad night in the cellar, and in the end a doctor had sent her to a charitable institution in the country where she would be looked after until her nerves recovered. The porter, too, had left, to stay with his brother in Leicester, and so had many of the staff and guests. The ones who remained looked grey-faced and weary, even though Mama and Papa insisted that since the changeable autumn weather they were getting quite a lot of sleep.

Supper was almost a family affair. The Woodpigeon made a little speech to welcome Anna back. "Though you are a foolish girl," he said, "for not staying in the beautiful countrysides with the sheeps and the grasses."

"Really, Mr Woodpigeon," said Frau Gruber who could pronounce his name no more than anyone else, "your English is getting worse each day."

The air-raid warning did not sound until sometime after dark and Mama waved it aside contemptuously. "They won't come tonight," she said. "There's too much cloud."

"I don't see how you can be so sure," said Papa, but everyone else seemed ready to accept Mama as an expert, and it was decided not to sleep in the cellar.

Anna found that she had been given a room on the first floor, next to Mama. ("No point in sleeping under the roof when the whole hotel is empty," said Frau Gruber.) She had been worried that she might get very frightened again during the night, but her rest in the country must have done her good, for the few bumps which woke her did not trouble her at all, and even the following night which had to be spent in the cellar was not too bad.

When she returned to the secretarial school she found that it had acquired a new air of purposeful activity. Madame Laroche, thinner and more excitable than ever, had taken over the reins again and her incomprehensible Belgian accents could be heard in every classroom. There was paper for the machines again – someone had unearthed an English source of supply – and there were even some new students.

No one talked about air raids any more. They had become part of everyday life and were no longer interesting. Instead, all the talk was about jobs. There was a sudden demand for shorthand typists since London had come to terms with the bombing, and Madame Laroche had pinned up a list of vacant positions on a notice board in the corridor.

"How soon do you think I could get a job?" Anna asked her, and to her delight she replied something that sounded like "get back into practice" followed by "a few weeks". In fact Anna's shorthand came back to her very quickly and one morning about ten days after her return she said proudly to Mama, "I'm going to ring up about a job from school today. So if anyone asks me to go for an interview I may be home late." She felt very grand saying this, and as soon as the first lesson was over she made for the school telephone with a copy of Madame Laroche's list and a shilling's worth of pennies.

The best jobs were at the War Office. A girl Anna knew had just been taken on there at three pounds ten shillings a week, and she only spoke mediocre French. So what wouldn't they pay someone like herself, thought Anna, with perfect French and German? And indeed, when she rang up and explained her qualifications the voice at the other end sounded enthusiastic.

"Absolutely splendid," it cried in a military sort of way. "Can you come round at o-eleven hundred hours for an interview?"

"Yes," said Anna, and one part of her was still trying to work out what on earth was meant by o-eleven hundred hours while another part was announcing to Mama that she had a job at four pounds or even four pounds ten a week, when the voice said as an afterthought, "I take it that you're British-born?"

"No," said Anna, "I was born in Germany, but my father . . ."

"Sorry," said the voice, several degrees cooler. "Only British-born applicants can be considered."

"But we're anti-Nazi!" cried Anna, "We've been anti-Nazis long before anyone else!"

"Sorry," said the voice. "Regulations – nothing I can do." And it rang off.

How idiotic, thought Anna. She was so disappointed that it took her some time before she could rouse herself to ring up the Ministry of Information, which was her second choice, but the reply she received was the same. No one could be considered unless they were British-born.

Surely, she thought with a sinking feeling in her stomach, everyone can't have that rule, but it appeared that they did. There were six large organisations on

406

Madame Laroche's list, all appealing for secretaries, and none would even grant her an interview. After the last one had refused her she stood for a moment by the telephone, completely at a loss. Then she went to see Madame Laroche.

"Madame," she said, "you told me that I would get a job at the end of this course, but none of the people on your list will even see me because I'm not British."

Madame Laroche's reply was difficult to follow as usual. The regulations about British nationality were new — or perhaps they were not new, but Madame Laroche had hoped that by now they might have been waived. Whatever it was, the one thing to emerge clearly was that it was hopeless for Anna to go on trying.

"But Madame," said Anna, "I must have a job. That was my one reason for coming here. You told me that I would get a job, and I told my mother this morning . . ." She stopped, for what she had told Mama was really nothing to do with it, but even so she had the greatest difficulty in keeping her composure.

"Well, there's nothing I can do about it now," said Madame Laroche unhelpfully in French, whereupon Anna, to her surprise, heard herself say, "But you'll have to!"

"*Comment?*" said Madame Laroche, looking at her with dislike.

Anna started back at her.

Madame Laroche mumbled something under her breath and began to rummage among the papers on her desk. Finally she extracted one and muttered something about a cross, red colonel.

"Won't he object to my nationality?" asked Anna, but Madame Laroche thrust the piece of paper into her hand and cried, "Go! Go! Ring up at once!"

Back at the telephone Anna looked at the paper. It said The Hon. Mrs Hammond, Colonel of the British Red Cross Society, and gave an address off the Vauxhall Bridge Road. She borrowed two more pennies and dialled the number. The voice that answered was gruff and brisk, but it did not ask whether she was British-born and suggested that she should come for an interview that afternoon.

She spent the rest of the day in fidgety anticipation. She wondered whether to ring Mama and let her know that she was going for an interview but decided not to, in case nothing came of it. At lunch she could not face her usual meal of a bun and a cup of tea at Lyons and wandered about the streets instead, eyeing her reflection in the few remaining shop windows and worrying whether she looked sufficiently like a secretary. At last, when the time arrived, she got there far too early and had to walk up and down the Vauxhall Bridge Road for the best part of half an hour.

It was not a very attractive neighbourhood. There was a brewery at one end and the sour smell of hops pervaded the entire district. Trams shrieked and clattered along the middle of the road. All the shops had been boarded up and abandoned.

Mrs Hammond's office turned out to be a little apart from all this, in a bomb-damaged hospital overlooking a large square, and after the noise of the main road it seemed very quiet when Anna finally rang her bell. She was admitted by a woman in an overall who led her through a vast, dark place which must have been one of the wards, through a smaller brightly-lit room where half a dozen elderly women were rattling away on sewing machines and to a tiny office where the Hon. Mrs Hammond was sitting stoutly behind a desk surrounded by skeins of wool. Her grey hair was covered with fluff and the wool seemed to have climbed all over her, hanging from her chair and her blue uniformed lap and lying in coils on the floor.

"Damn these things!" she cried as Anna came in. "I've lost count of them again. Are you any good at arithmetic?"

Anna said she thought so and Mrs Hammond said, "Jolly good. And what else can you do?" causing Anna to list her accomplishments from her School Certificate results to her ability to take down shorthand in three languages. As she went nervously through them Mrs Hammond's face fell.

"It won't do!" she cried. "You'd hate it – you'd be bored stiff!"

"I don't see why," said Anna, but Mrs Hammond shook her head.

"Languages," she cried. "Got no use for them here. You want somewhere like the War Office. Crazy for girls like you – French, German, Hindustani – all that."

"I've tried the War Office," said Anna, "but they won't have me."

Mrs Hammond absent-mindedly tried to unfasten a loop of wool which had wound itself round a button on her tunic. "Why?" she said. "What's wrong with you?"

Anna took a deep breath. "I'm not English," she said.

"Ha! Irish!" cried Mrs Hammond and added reproachfully, "You've got green eyes."

"No," said Anna, "German."

"German?"

"German-Jewish. My father is an anti-Nazi writer. We left Germany in 1933 . . ." She was suddenly sick of explaining, having to justify herself. "My father's name was on the first black list published by the Nazis," she said quite loudly. "After we'd escaped from Germany they offered a reward for his capture, dead or alive. I'm hardly likely, therefore, to sabotage the British war effort. But it's extraordinary how difficult it is to convince anyone of this."

There was a pause. Then Mrs Hammond said, "How old are you?"

"Sixteen," said Anna.

"I see," said Mrs Hammond. She stood up, scattering wool in all directions like a dog shaking water out of its fur. "Well now," she said. "Why don't we have a look at what the job consists of?"

She led Anna to some shelves stacked with bulky packets up to the ceiling.

"Wool," she said.

Then she pointed to a filing cabinet and flicked open a drawer full of record cards.

"Little women," she said, and as Anna looked puzzled, "They knit. All over the country."

"I see," said Anna.

"Send the wool to the little women. Little women knit it up into sweaters, socks, Balaclava helmets, what have you. Send them back to us. We send them to chaps in the Forces who need them. That's all."

"I see," said Anna again.

"Not very difficult, you see," said Mrs Hammond. "No need for languages – unless of course we sent some to the Free French. Never heard of them being short of woollies, though." She gestured towards the room with the sewing machines. "Then there's the old ladies out there. Bit more responsibility."

"What do they do?" asked Anna.

"Make pyjamas, bandages, all that, for hospitals. They live roundabout and come in. All voluntary, you understand. Have to give them Bovril in the morning and tea and biscuits in the afternoon."

Anna nodded.

"Fact is," said Mrs Hammond, "it's all jolly useful. Found out from my own son in the Air Force – never got any woollies, always cold. And I do need someone to help. Think you could do it?"

"I think so," said Anna. It was not exactly what she had hoped for, but she liked Mrs Hammond and it was a job. "How . . ." she stammered, "I mean, how much . . . ?"

Mrs Hammond smote her forehead. "Most important part of the business!" she cried. "I was going to pay three pounds, but reckon you could get more with all those languages. Say three pounds ten a week – that suit you?"

"Oh yes!" cried Anna. "That would be fine."

"Start on Monday, then," said Mrs Hammond and added, as she ushered her out, "Look forward to seeing you."

Anna rode triumphantly down the Vauxhall Bridge Road on one of the clattering trams. It was getting dusk and by the time she had walked to Hyde Park Corner the stairs leading down to the tube were crowded with people seeking shelter for the night. Quite a few had already spread out their bedding on the platform, and you had to be careful where you stepped. At Holborn there were people sitting on bunks against the walls as well as on the floor and a woman in green uniform was selling cups of tea from a trolley. At one end a knot of people had gathered round a man with a mouth organ to sing Roll Out The Barrel and an old man in a peaked cap called out, "Good night, lovely!" as she passed.

The sirens sounded just as she turned into Bedford Terrace and she raced them to the door of the Hotel Continental, through the lounge and up the stairs, to burst breathlessly into Mama's room. There was a droning sound, announcing the approach of the bombers.

"Mama!" she cried as the first bomb burst, some distance away, "Mama! I've got a job!"

12

Anna almost did not start her job on the following Monday after all, because something happened.

It was on the Friday. Max had come on one of his rare visits and was staying the night, and though there had not been very much to eat for supper – food rationing was getting stricter – they had sat over it a long time with Max talking about his life as a schoolmaster which he quite enjoyed, and Anna talking about her job.

"The lady is called the Hon. Mrs Hammond," she said proudly. "She must be related to some kind of a lord. And she's paying me three pounds ten a week!"

Mama nodded. "For the first time we can look ahead a little."

Her face was pinker and more relaxed than Anna had seen it for some time. It was partly because Max was there, but also because the November mists had finally arrived and they had been able to sleep in their beds two nights running. Tonight, too, the sky was heavy with clouds and Max who was not used to London had been much impressed with Mama's careless dismissal of the air-raid warning.

By the time they went to bed it was quite late and Anna fell asleep almost immediately.

She dreamed about the Hon. Mrs Hammond, whose office had inexplicably become entirely filled with wool which Anna and Mrs Hammond were trying to disentangle. Anna had got hold of an end and was trying to see where it led and Mrs Hammond was saying, "You have to follow the sound," and then Anna noticed that the wool was giving out a curious humming like a swarm of mosquitoes or an aeroplane. She pulled gently at the piece in her hand and the humming turned at once into a violent screeching.

"I'm sorry, I didn't mean . . ." she began, but the screeching grew louder and louder and came closer and closer and then it drew her right inside itself and she and Mrs Hammond were flying through the air and there was a shattering crash and she found herself on the floor in a corner of her room at the Hotel Continental.

All round her were fragments of glass from the shattered window – that's the third lot of windows gone, she thought – and the floor was grey with plaster from the ceiling. I mustn't cut myself this time, she thought, and felt carefully for her shoes, so as to be able to walk through the broken glass to the door. As she put them on, her hands were shaking – but that's just shock she thought. There hadn't really been time to be frightened.

The landing was a mess with a lamp hanging from its socket and plaster all over the floor, and Max and Mama appeared on it almost immediately.

Max was furious. "You said," he shouted at Mama, "that the Germans wouldn't come tonight!"

"Well, they didn't!" cried Mama. "Only just that one!"

"For God's sake!" Max shouted, pointing to the confusion about them. "Look what he's done!"

"Well, how was I to know," cried Mama, "that the

one German plane over London tonight would drop a bomb straight on us? I can't be responsible for every madman who takes to the air in the middle of a fog! It's easy for you to criticise . . ."

"For God's sake," said Max again. "We might all have been killed!" – and at this the same realisation hit all three of them.

"Papa!" cried Anna and rushed along the passage to his room.

The door was jammed, but there was a scuffling sound inside and after a moment the door was wrenched open and Papa appeared. He was black with dust and there was plaster all over his hair and his pyjamas, but he was all right. Behind him, Anna could see that most of his ceiling had collapsed and that it was only the presence of the heavy wardrobe which had prevented it from crashing down on his bed.

"Are you hurt?" cried Mama, close behind her.

"No," said Papa, and then they all stood and looked at the wreckage that had been his room.

Papa shook his head sadly. "To think," he said, "that I'd just tidied up my desk!"

Miraculously no one was hurt except for cuts and bruises, but the whole hotel was in chaos. There were ceilings down everywhere, the heating no longer worked, and downstairs in the lounge the wind blew through gaps where doorposts and window frames no longer fitted into the walls. The bomb had fallen on the adjoining house, fortunately empty, and fortunately it had been a very small bomb. ("You see!" cried Mama, still smarting from Max's criticism, "I told

415

you it wasn't a proper one!") But the damage looked to be beyond repair.

The experts from the Council who came round later thought so too.

"No use trying to fit this place up again," they told Frau Gruber. "For one thing it wouldn't be safe. You'd best find somewhere else," and Frau Gruber nodded, sensibly, as though it were the most ordinary thing in the world, and you had to look quite closely to notice the twitching of a muscle near her mouth as she said, "It was my livelihood, you know."

"You'll get compensation," said the man from the Council. "Best thing would be if you could find another house."

"Otherwise we all shall be without a roof on our head," said the Woodpigeon sadly, and the rest of the guests looked hopefully towards Frau Gruber as though she were capable of producing one out of a hat.

It was curious, thought Anna – ever since the beginning of the blitz everyone had known that this might happen, but now that it had no one knew what to do. How did one find a new home in a bomb-shattered city?

In the middle of it all Aunt Louise rang up. She was in London for the day and wanted Mama to have lunch with her. When Mama explained what had happened she cried at once, "My dear, you must buy the maharajah's place!"

Mama said rather tartly that Frau Gruber was looking for a house in London, not a palace in India, but Aunt Louise took no notice.

416

"I believe," she said, "that it's in Putney," and announced that since the maharajah was with her she would bring him round at once.

"Really," said Papa when Mama told him, "couldn't you have stopped her?"

He and Max had been moving his belongings out of the wrecked room into another that was less badly damaged. The hotel had grown very cold and no one had had any sleep since the bomb had fallen. The prospect of having to cope with Aunt Louise on top of everything else seemed too much to be borne.

"You know what Louise is like," said Mama, and went off to warn Frau Gruber.

When they arrived, the maharajah in his turban and Aunt Louise in a beautiful black fur coat, they looked like visitors from another world, but Frau Gruber received them with no sign of astonishment. Perhaps she felt, since the bomb, that anything could happen.

"You are the first maharajah I have met," she said in matter of fact tones and led him off to what remained of her office.

"Really, Louise," said Mama in the freezing lounge, "this is a mad idea of yours. She could never afford the sort of money he'd want."

"Oh dear, do you think so?" cried Aunt Louise. "And I thought it would be such a help. He really wants to sell the house, you know, because he's going back to India at last. And he is," she added, "only quite a *small* maharajah, so it might not be so expensive."

Then she went on to urge all of them and especially Anna to come down to the country for a rest, but Anna explained about her job and Mama said wearily that they must first find a new home, as it was clearly impossible to stay on in the hotel for more than a few days.

"Just when Anna had got settled," she said. "Why does something always have to go wrong!"

Aunt Louise patted her hand and said, "Don't worry," and just then Frau Gruber and the maharajah came back into the lounge smiling.

"Well," said the maharajah, tucking his hand under Frau Gruber's arm, "shall we go and have a look at the place?"

"What did I tell you?" cried Aunt Louise, and added quickly, "First we must have lunch."

They ate at a restaurant which Aunt Louise knew and even had a bottle of wine which made everyone feel more cheerful – in fact Frau Gruber became quite merry – and the maharajah paid the bill. Afterwards Max had to go back to his school, but the rest of them went to see the house in Aunt Louise's car.

Anna was surprised to see how far away it was. They seemed to drive past endless rows of little houses all looking the same, until they crossed the Thames to reach a narrow road lined with shops.

The maharajah pointed fondly. "Putney High Street," he said.

It was a dark afternoon, even though it was nowhere near sunset, and the shops were lit up, which gave the street an almost peace-time look. Anna caught a whiff of frying as they drove past a chip shop, there was a Woolworth's and a Marks and Spencer's and people everywhere were doing their weekend shopping. There was far less bomb damage than in the centre of

London, and as the car left the high street and drove up a hill flanked by large houses and gardens it began to smell almost like the country.

The maharajah's house was in a tree-lined side street – very big and spacious with about a dozen bedrooms and surrounded by a neglected garden. For a single person it must have been enormous, but for a hotel or a guest house Anna supposed it would be quite modest. It was empty except for the curtains on the windows and a few forgotten objects – a tall brass vase, a carved stool and, astonishingly, a flight of plaster ducks carefully pinned above a mantelpiece.

They walked slowly from room to room in the fading light and the maharajah explained the workings of the electricity, the blackout arrangements, the hot-water boiler, and every so often Frau Gruber would query something and they would go back and look at it all over again.

"I must say, it all seems very convenient," she said several times, and then the maharajah would cry, "Wait till you see the kitchen!" – or the scullery, or the second bathroom. All the downstairs rooms were dominated by the wild garden which lay outside the French windows, and when Frau Gruber said, for the third time, "I just want to have another look at the kitchen range," Papa and Anna left the rest of them to it and went out into the wintry dampness.

Mist was hanging like a sheet in the trees and there were fallen leaves everywhere. They clung to Anna's feet as she followed Papa along a path which led them to a wooden bench at the edge of what had once been a lawn. Papa wiped the seat with his handkerchief and they sat down.

"It's a big garden," said Anna and Papa nodded.

The mist was drifting across the long grass and the bushes, making everything beyond them uncertain, so that it seemed as though there were no end to it. Anna felt suddenly unreal.

"To think . . ." she said.

"What?" said Papa.

There was a clump of leaves stuck to one of her shoes and she removed it carefully with the other before she answered, "Last night must have been about the closest we've been to getting killed."

"Yes," said Papa. "If that German airman had dropped his bomb a fraction of a second earlier or later – we wouldn't be sitting in this garden."

It was strange, thought Anna. The garden would still be there in the mist, but she would not know about it.

"It's difficult to imagine," she said, "everything going on without one."

Papa nodded. "But it does," he said. "If we were dead, people would still have breakfast and ride on buses and there would still be birds and trees and children going to school and misty gardens like this one. It's a kind of comfort."

"But one would miss it so," said Anna.

Papa looked at her fondly. "You wouldn't exist."

"I know," said Anna. "But I can't imagine it. I can't imagine being so dead that I wouldn't be able to think about it all – the way it looks and smells and feels – and missing it all quite terribly."

They sat in silence and Anna watched a leaf drift slowly, slowly down from a tree until it settled among the others in the grass.

"For quite a long time last summer," she said, "I didn't think we'd live even till now. Did you?"

"No," said Papa.

"I didn't see how we could. And it seemed so awful to die before one had even had time to find out what one could do – before one had really had time to try. But now . . ."

"Now it's November," said Papa, "and the invasion hasn't happened." He put his hand over hers. "Now," he said, "I think there's a chance."

Then the gravel crunched behind them and Mama appeared through the mist.

"There you are!" she cried. "Louise wants to leave, so as to get out of town before dark. But the maharajah is coming back tomorrow to fix the final details with Frau Gruber. She's going to take the house. Don't you think it's a nice place?"

Anna got up from the seat and Papa followed her.

"We've been appreciating it," he said.

There seemed to be less room in the car on the way back. Anna sat squeezed between Papa and the driver, and it was hot and stuffy. Behind her the maharajah and Frau Gruber were talking about the house, with Mama and Aunt Louise chipping in. As the car crawled through the dusky suburbs the street names mingled with scraps of conversation into a hypnotic mixture which almost sent her to sleep. Walham Crescent . . . St Anne's Villas . . . Parsons Green Road . . . ". . .

such a very useful sink," said Frau Gruber, and Mama replied, ". . . and in the summer, the garden . . ."

There was a spatter of rain on the windscreen. She rested her head on Papa's shoulder, and the grey road and the grey houses sped past.

Everything is going to be different, she thought. I'm going to have a job, and we'll live in a house in Putney, and we'll have enough money to pay the bills, and perhaps we'll all survive the war and I shall grow up, and then . . .

But it was too difficult to imagine what would happen then, and probably rather unlucky, too, she thought, with the next air raid not far away, and as the strain of the previous night caught up with her she fell asleep.

Part Two

13

Compared with the summer, the winter was almost cosy. For one thing, the air raids abated. There were several nights in December when the sirens did not sound at all, and when the Germans did come over bombs rarely fell on Putney. As a result you could sleep in your bed every night, and though some nights were noisier than others, the desperate tiredness that had been part of everyday life gradually receded.

The house in Putney was friendlier than the Hotel Continental and it seemed a great luxury to have a garden.

"In the summer we'll get some deck-chairs," said Frau Gruber, but even in the winter the Woodpigeon and the other Poles, Czechs and Germans walked admiringly among the dead leaves and on the over-grown lawn.

The only thing Anna did not like was that she had to share a room with Mama. There were almost no single rooms in the house, and she could see that Papa, who was home all day, needed a place of his own to write in – but she still hated never being alone. However, there was nothing to be done about it, so she tried not to think about it more than she could help.

Most of the time her mind was on her job. It was not difficult, but she was nervous about it to begin with. Her first day had been an agony – not only because she was afraid of making some disastrous mistake, but because she had discovered two days before that she had caught lice in the tube. This was not uncommon – there was an epidemic of lice among the shelterers and it was only too easy to pick them up. But just before starting a new job!

Mama had rushed to get her some evil-smelling brown liquid from the chemist and she had spent the week-end trying to wash the lice out of her hair in the bombed hotel. At the end her hair had seemed to be clear, but just the same she had been haunted, the whole of her first day as a secretary, by the possibility that one louse – just one – might have escaped, and that it would emerge from her hair and walk across her ear or her neck just as the Hon. Mrs Hammond was looking at her. She was so worried about this that she kept rushing to the lavatory to examine her hair in the mirror, until one of the old ladies on the sewing machines asked her quite kindly if she had a tummy upset. Fortunately the Hon. Mrs Hammond put down her nervousness to the fact that she had so recently been bombed, and once Anna was convinced that all the lice had really been exterminated she was able to concentrate on the job and do it quite well.

There was not really much to it. First thing in the morning she would go through the post, unpack whatever woollies had arrived and send off more wool to the knitters. Then she would put out the half-made pyjamas and bandages for the old ladies who came in about ten, and the sewing machines would begin to hum.

She had to be careful about allocating the work, for the old ladies were quick to take offence. Different ones came on different days, but the most regular were Miss Clinton-Brown who was tall and religious, little Miss Potter who talked only about her budgie, and Mrs Riley who said she was a retired actress but had really been in music hall and who wore a frightful fringed shawl and smelled, causing the more genteel ladies to avert their noses.

They were always trying to persuade Mrs Hammond to get rid of her, but she was too good a worker.

"Bit niffy, I agree," said Mrs Hammond, "but chaps in hospital won't mind that. Pyjamas get washed before they wear them, anyway."

Mrs Hammond's arrival about eleven was the high point of the morning. As soon as they heard her taxi draw up the old ladies began to twitter and to preen themselves, and as she walked into the sewing-room their heads would be bent over their work and the machines would be racing along at twice their normal speed.

"Morning, ladies!" she would cry, and this was Anna's cue to pour the boiling water on the Bovril and hand it round. Mrs Hammond's mug went in her office, but to the ladies' delight she often carried it back into the sewing-room and chatted with them while she drank it. She lived at Claridge's Hotel during the week – at week-ends she went back to her estate in the country – and met all sorts of famous people and her careless mention of their names turned the old ladies quite dizzy with excitement.

"Met Queen Wilhelmina last night," she would say. "Poor old thing – quite dotty." Or, "Heard Mr Churchill speak at a dinner – marvellous man, but no taller than I am, you know," and the ladies would repeat the information to each other, rolling it round their tongues and enjoying the dottiness of the Dutch queen and the small stature of Mr Churchill for the rest of the week.

After the Bovril she would call Anna into her office and dictate letters to her until lunch time, and Anna would spend the afternoon typing them. The letters were mostly to high-ranking officers in the Forces, all of whom Mrs Hammond appeared to have known since childhood, and who wanted her to send them woollies for the men in their command. She nearly always managed to give them what they wanted.

Once or twice there was a note to her son Dickie who was in the Air Force, trying to become a navigator and finding it very difficult.

"Poor fellow's got enough to do working out sums without deciphering my scrawl," she would say, and dictate a brief, affectionate message of encouragement, to be accompanied by a small gift like a pair of Air Force blue socks or gloves.

Once he came to the office and Mrs Hammond introduced him to Anna – a stocky, open-faced boy of about nineteen, with a stammer. He was taking an exam the next day and was worried about it.

"You'll pass all right," cried Mrs Hammond. "You always do, in the end!" and he grinned at her ruefully. "T-trouble is," he said, "I have t-to work t-twice as hard as everyone else."

Mrs Hammond slapped his back affectionately. "Poor old chap!" she shouted. "No head for scholarship – but jolly good with animals, I can tell you. No one better than Dickie," she explained to Anna, "with a sick cow!"

At the end of every week Anna collected her wages and paid Frau Gruber two pounds five shillings for her room. Fifteen shillings went on fares, lunches and necessities like toothpaste and shoe repairs, five shillings to Madame Laroche to pay for the shorthand machine which had not been included in the tuition fees, and the remaining five shillings she saved. By May, she calculated, she would have paid Madame Laroche back and she would be able to save ten shillings a week. It seemed to her a wonderfully lavish income.

Mrs Hammond was kind to her in an amused sort of way. Sometimes she asked Anna if she was all right, if she liked the new boarding-house in Putney, if Papa had any work. But she insisted on keeping her German background a secret, especially from the old ladies.

"Old biddies wouldn't understand," she said. "Probably suspect you of sabotaging the Balaclava helmets."

Once, when Max was in London during the Easter holidays she took them both to a film.

Afterwards he said, "I like your Mrs Hammond. But don't you ever get bored?"

He had had to wait for Anna at the office and had watched her typing letters and parcelling up wool.

She looked at him without comprehension. "No," she said. She was wearing a new green sweater, bought with her own money. She had nearly paid back the money for the shorthand machine, and that morning Mrs Hammond had introduced her to a visiting Colonel as "my young assistant – practically runs this place single-handed." What could be boring about that?

As the weather grew warmer the fear of invasion also grew again – until one day in June, soon after Anna's seventeenth birthday, when there was an announcement on the radio which staggered everyone. The Germans had attacked Russia.

"But I thought the Russians and the Germans were allies!" cried Anna.

Papa raised one eyebrow. "So did the Russians," he said.

It was clear that if the Germans had opened up a new Russian front they could not at the same time invade England, and there was great rejoicing in the office. The Bovril session was extended to nearly an hour while Mrs Hammond quoted a general who had told her that the Germans could not last a month against Stalin. Miss Clinton-Brown thanked God; Miss Potter said she had taught her budgie to say, "Down with Stalin," and was worried whether this might now be misunderstood; and Mrs Riley rose suddenly from her chair, grabbed a pole used for putting up the blackout and demonstrated how she had posed as Britannia at the Old Bedford Music Hall in 1918.

After this Anna and Mrs Hammond retired to her office, but they had scarcely got through half a dozen letters when they were again interrupted. This time it was Dickie, on unexpected leave, wearing a brand-new officer's uniform.

"P-passed all my exams, Ma," he said. "Second

from the b-bottom, but I p-passed. F-fully f-fledged navigating Officer Hammond!"

At this Mrs Hammond was so delighted that she gave up all thoughts of further work and invited Anna to join them for lunch.

"We'll go home," she said, which meant Claridge's.

Anna had only been there once before, to deliver some letters which Mrs Hammond had forgotten at the office, and then she had only got as far as the hall porter. Now she was swept along in Mrs Hammond's wake, across the heavily carpeted foyer, through the swing doors and into the pillared dining-room, where they were met by the head waiter ("Good morning, Mrs Hammond, good morning, Mr Richard") and escorted to their table. All round them were people in uniform, mostly very grand ones, talking, eating and drinking, and the hum of their conversation filled the room.

"Drinkies!" cried Mrs Hammond, and a glass of what Anna decided must be gin appeared in front of her. She did not like it much, but she drank it, and then the waiter brought the food and as she worked her way through a large piece of chicken she began to feel very happy. There was no need for her to say anything, for Mrs Hammond and Dickie were talking about the estate and about a dog of Dickie's in particular ("Are you sure," he was asking, "that W-Wilson has w-wormed him?"), so she looked around the room and was the first to notice a thin man in Air Force uniform bearing down on them. There was a great deal of gold braid about him and as soon as Dickie saw him he leapt from his chair and saluted. The man nodded and smiled briefly, but his attention was on Mrs Hammond.

"Boots!" he cried, and she answered delightedly, "Jack! How lovely! Come and sit down!"

She introduced him to Dickie and Anna as an Air Chief Marshal of whom even Anna had heard, and ordered another round of gin, and then the Air Chief Marshal ordered a third, to celebrate the news about Russia.

"Best thing that's happened in the war," he said, "since we beat the bastards off last September," and plunged into a long conversation with Mrs Hammond about the effects of this new development.

Anna's feeling of happiness had increased with each gin, until now it was like a vast smile in which she was entirely enveloped, but Dickie was looking at her and she felt she ought to say something.

"I'm so sorry your dog isn't well," she brought out at last, a little indistinctly, and immediately found a wave of pity sweep over her for the poor animal which perhaps hadn't been wormed when it needed to be.

Dickie looked at her gratefully. "B-bit of a worry," he admitted, and started to tell her about the dog's lack of appetite, the state of its coat (why does it have a coat? thought Anna, until she remembered that he must mean its fur), and his lack of confidence in Wilson's judgment. Then there were the horses, too, and the cows. It was difficult, nowadays, to find chaps who looked after them properly. He sat there in his new officer's tunic, fretting about it all, and Anna listened and nodded and thought how nice he was and how nice to have lunch at Claridge's with an

Air Chief Marshal, and how nice that the Germans had attacked the Russians and would not now be invading England.

And when the Air Chief Marshal, on leaving, congratulated Dickie on his attractive girl friend, that was nice too, and rather funny, but an even funnier thing happened after he had gone.

"Ma," said Dickie reproachfully, "That m-man is in charge of a third of the Air F-force. Why does he call you Boots?" And Mrs Hammond answered in an astonished voice, "Always has done. Ever since we went to dancing classes together when we were five and I used to trample all over his feet."

At this Anna laughed so much that she found it difficult to stop and Mrs Hammond said, "Good God – we've made the poor child tight!"

She gave her some black coffee and then she drove her to Bond Street tube station, where she told her to take the afternoon off.

"My apologies to your Mama," she said. "But what with the Russian front and Dickie getting his commission . . ."

The rest of the sentence seemed somehow to have escaped her, and Anna suddenly noticed that Mrs Hammond's speech, too, was less precise than usual.

"Anyway," cried Mrs Hammond, retreating a little unsteadily into the car, "it was a damned good party!"

Anna still thought the story about the Air Chief Marshal quite funny even after the effects of the gin had worn off, and she told Max about it the next time she saw him. By this time it was July and Max was in deep gloom. The summer term was nearly over and he did not want to embark on a second year's teaching, but all his enquiries about getting into the Forces had brought only discouraging replies.

The Army and the Navy had firm rules forbidding the acceptance of foreign nationals. The Air Force, being a younger Service, had no such rule but didn't accept them anyway. Max had more or less given up hope, but when he heard the Air Chief Marshal's name he pricked up his ears.

"If I could talk to him –" he said. "Do you think Mrs Hammond would give me an introduction?"

"Well, I could ask her," said Anna doubtfully, but in fact Mrs Hammond did much more.

On the following Monday, after Anna had explained the situation to her, she rang the Air Chief Marshal in her presence, cutting through secretaries, adjutants and personal assistants as a ship cuts through the waves.

"Jack," she said. "Got a rather special young man I want you to meet. Can you have lunch?" Then, in answer to a question from the other end of the telephone, "I should think very bright indeed." This was followed by some chat about the war, a reference to Dickie who had just been posted to his first operational squadron, and a joke about the dancing class, until the conversation ended with a laugh and an inexplicable shout of "Tally-ho!"

"Well, that's settled," said Mrs Hammond. "Max and I are having lunch with Jack."

The appointment had been fixed for a day nearly a

fortnight away and Max was very nervous about it. He decided to learn as much as possible about aeroplanes in the meantime, and his pupils were set endless essays to write in class while he studied the characteristics of everything from Tiger Moths to Messerschmitts, and a book about the theory of flight for good measure.

Papa encouraged him in this. "Such an Air Chief Marshal," he said, "will expect you to be well informed." But Mama refused even to consider that there might be any difficulty.

"Of course the Air Chief Marshal will make an exception for you," she said, to Max's rage.

"But you don't know that!" he cried. "And if he doesn't, I don't know what I'll do!"

Anna just kept her fingers crossed. She knew that if Max didn't get into the Air Force he would feel it was the end of the world.

A few days before Max's appointment she was unpacking some woollies in the office. One of them was an Air Force sweater and she was holding it up, wondering whether Max would soon be wearing one like it, when Mrs Riley came in with a face wrapped in gloom.

"Terrible news," she said.

"About what?" said Anna. There had been nothing special on the radio.

Mrs Riley waved a tragic hand. "Poor lady," she said. "Poor, poor Mrs Hammond. And there she was yesterday, as happy as a sandboy."

Mrs Riley was always making dramas out of nothing, so Anna said irritably, "What's happened to her?" not expecting to hear anything that mattered."

She was shattered when Mrs Riley replied, "Her son has been killed in his aeroplane."

Dickie, she thought, with his nice, not-too-bright face and his worries about the cows and the horses. It hadn't even been an operational flight, just a practice one. The plane had stalled and crashed, and all the crew had died. Mr Hammond had brought the news later the previous afternoon – Anna had already left to post some parcels – and then he had taken Mrs Hammond home.

"Their only child," said Miss Clinton-Brown, who had arrived just after Mrs Riley.

Anna tried to think of something to say, but there was nothing. What could you say about the death of this decent, simple person?

"He was the glory of his squadron," said Mrs Riley, striking an attitude. But that was just what he hadn't been and for some reason it made it worse.

There was nothing to do but to carry on as usual. The old ladies hardly spoke while they raced their machines up and down the seams, as though a larger turn-out of pyjamas would somehow make up to Mrs Hammond for her loss. Anna decided to tidy up the stock of knitting wool and it was not until half-way through the morning that she remembered about Max. What would happen about that now?

When no news came from Mrs Hammond except a message through her chauffeur asking everyone to keep going in her absence, she decided to ring Max at the end of the day.

"I don't think she'll want to keep the appointment," she said, and could feel Max's depression like a miasma leaking down the telephone. "And I think that's a very good thing!" she cried, with a sudden vivid memory of Dickie smiling and talking about his dog only such a short time ago.

Max said blankly, "If you speak to Mrs Hammond please tell her how sorry I am. But if I don't hear from you I'll come anyway, just in case."

The next few days in the office were full of gloom. The Bovril sessions were the worst times. The old ladies would sit sipping their hot drinks in silence and return to their work as soon as possible. Only once little Miss Potter paused while handing Anna her empty mug. "Why should it have been him?" she asked, and added with no sense of anti-climax, "He always used to ask me about my budgie."

There was no news of Mrs Hammond, and on the day of Max's appointment Anna felt more and more depressed at the thought that he was coming all the way from the country to no purpose. He was due to arrive at twelve, and a little before this she waited for him in the disused ward, so that they would not have to talk in the sewing-room.

"No news?" he said at once, and she shook her head, taking in his shining shoes and carefully brushed suit.

"I didn't really think there would be." He looked suddenly somehow crumpled. "Poor woman," he said and added apologetically, "It's just that I knew this was my only chance."

They stood in the half-darkness, wondering what to do next. They'd better have some lunch, thought Anna, as soon as the old ladies had gone – perhaps she could hurry them up.

"I'll just go into the sewing-room," she began, when she heard a car door slam.

They looked at each other.

"Do you suppose . . . ?" said Max.

There were footsteps outside – not like Mrs Hammond's, thought Anna, these were slower and more slurred – but a moment later the door opened and there she was. She blinked a little at seeing them unexpectedly in this dim place, but otherwise she seemed just as usual with not a hair out of place and her face carefully made up. Only her eyes were different and her voice, when she spoke, was hoarse, as though she were having to force it to work.

She shook her head as they stumbled into some attempt at condolences.

"It's all right," she said. "I know."

For a moment her glance rested on Max as though she were trying, through him, to recreate poor Dickie who might even have stood in the same spot only a week or two before. Then she said, "I can't face the old ladies. We may as well go."

She started towards the door with Max following, but stopped before she reached it.

"Max," she said in her strange, hoarse voice, "you know you don't have to do this. Are you sure it's really what you want?"

Max nodded and she stared at him with something almost like contempt. "Like a bloody lamb to the slaughter!" she shouted. Then she shook her head and told him to take no notice.

"Come along," she said. "We'll go and see Jack."

14

Two weeks later Max was accepted by the Air Force.

Mama said, "I told you so," and he was sent to a training camp in the Midlands where conditions were rough and he spent most of his time marching and drilling, but when he came home on leave in his uniform he looked happier than he had done for a long time.

The very first time he had a day in London he came to the office to thank Mrs Hammond, but she was not there. Since Dickie's death she had come in less and less, and Anna found herself almost running the place on her own. It was not difficult, but it was dull. She had not realised how much her interest had depended on Mrs Hammond's presence, and the old ladies missed her even more than Anna did.

They looked at Anna glumly when she poured out the Bovril, as though it were hardly worth drinking without Mrs Hammond to tell them about Mr Churchill and Queen Wilhelmina, and quarrelled a good deal among themselves. Miss Clinton-Brown had been put in charge of cutting out pyjamas (which had previously been supervised by Mrs Hammond) and endlessly thanked God for having made her the sort of person others could rely on, while Miss Potter and Mrs Riley sat together and said nasty things about her under cover of the hum of their sewing machines.

There were fewer letters to type and Anna spent much of her time checking through the card index and keeping the peace. Sometimes when she could think of nothing else to do she made drawings of the old ladies on a pad under her desk. Some of them came out quite well, but she always felt guilty afterwards because after all that was not what she was getting paid for.

Winter came early and almost at once it got quite cold. Anna first noticed it while she was waiting at the bus stop in the mornings. Her coat suddenly seemed too thin to keep out the wind and when she got to the office she had to thaw out her feet over the gas fire. On Sundays when the weather was fine she would walk across Putney Heath with Mama and Papa. The grass crunched frostily under their feet, the pond at Wimbledon Parkside was frozen even though it was barely November, and the ducks stood gloomily about on the ice.

Sometimes, if they were feeling rich, they would stop at the Telegraph Inn and Papa would have a beer while Anna and Mama drank cider, before returning to the hotel for lunch. They tended to delay until the last possible minute, for once you were back, there was nothing much to do.

After lunch everyone sat in the lounge, now filled with the tables and leatherette chairs which Frau Gruber had brought from the Hotel Continental, because it was the only room with heating. It had an open fire and in the maharajah's day, when you could get as much coal as you liked, there must have been a great blaze which would have warmed every corner. But now, with fuel hard to come by, it never seemed to get quite as warm as one would have liked.

It was not very exciting sitting in the lukewarm room with nothing to do except wait for supper, but people occupied themselves as best they could. They read, the two Czech ladies knitted endless scarves, and for a while the Woodpigeon tried to teach Anna Polish. He had a book which she tried to read, but one day when he was feeling depressed he took it from her in the middle of a sentence.

"What is the good?" he said. "None of us will ever see Poland again."

Everyone knew that no matter whether the Germans or the Russians won the war, neither would ever give Poland back her independence.

Sometimes a couple called Poznanski organised group discussions about it. They never reached any conclusions, but just talking about Poland seemed to cheer them up. Anna quite enjoyed these, for the Poznanskis handed out paper and pencils in case anyone should wish to make notes, and instead of listening she would surreptitiously draw the other people.

Once she made a funny drawing of the two Czech ladies knitting in unison. She carried it with her to the dining-room when the gong went for supper and Mama picked it up while they were waiting for the trayloads of mince and cabbage to reach them.

"Look," she said, and showed it to Papa.

Papa looked at it carefully. "This is very good," he said at last. "Like an early Daumier. You ought to draw far more."

"She ought to have lessons," said Mama in a worried voice.

"But Mama," said Anna, "I've got my job."

"Well, perhaps in the evenings or at week-ends," said Mama. "If only we had some money . . ."

It would be nice, thought Anna, to have something to do in the evenings, for they were very dull. She and Mama had already read their way through half the books in the public library and the only other distraction was bridge, which Anna disliked. She was glad, therefore, when Mama announced that they had been invited to spend an evening with Mama's Aunt Dainty.

Aunt Dainty was Cousin Otto's mother, and the invitation was to celebrate Otto's return from Canada where he had been first interned, then released and finally sent home for some special purpose which Aunt Dainty was vague about.

"Are you coming, Papa?" said Anna.

But Papa had finally persuaded the B.B.C. to broadcast one of his pieces to Germany and was busy writing a second one in the hope that they would take this, too – so Mama and Anna went on their own.

As their bus crawled through the blackout towards Golders Green, Anna asked, "Why is she called Aunt Dainty?"

"It was a nickname when she was a child," said Mama. "Somehow it stuck, even though it hardly suits her now." Then she said, "She's had a bad time. Her husband was in a concentration camp. They got him out before the war, but he's never been the same."

It was difficult finding the address – a basement in a long street of houses which all looked the same – but as soon as Mama pressed the bell the door was flung open by one of the largest and plainest women Anna had ever seen. She was wrapped in a long black skirt almost down to the ground and there were various sweaters, cardigans and shawls on top of it.

"Ach hallo – come in!" she cried in German, revealing a mouthful of irregular teeth, but the eyes half buried in the heavy face were friendly and warm and she embraced Mama enthusiastically.

"Hello, Dainty," said Mama. "How lovely to see you."

Aunt Dainty swept them down some steps and into a large room which must have been a cellar but had been so draped with curtains and hangings of every kind that it had acquired a certain grandeur.

"Sit down, sit down," she cried, waving them towards a sofa piled high with cushions, and added, "Goodness, Anna, you're so grown up – you look just like your father."

"Do I?" said Anna, pleased, and while she warmed her hands over the oil stove which heated the room, Mama and Aunt Dainty embarked on the usual conversation of how many years was it, and don't you remember that time at Lyons in Oxford Street, and oh no perhaps she was at school then but I'm sure you must have seen her – until Otto came in.

He looked better dressed than Anna had ever seen him and Aunt Dainty at once put her arm round his shoulder as though she had not yet got used to having him home.

"He's leaving again quite soon," she said. "Back to Canada."

"Canada?" cried Mama. "But he's only just left there."

"I came home to see some people and get some things

cleared up – papers and so forth," said Otto. "Then I'm going back to Canada to do a job of research. Touch wood," he added, just to be on the safe side.

"To and fro across the Atlantic like a pendulum," wailed Aunt Dainty. "And with German U-boats everywhere waiting to catch him."

She pronounced them ooh-boats, which made them sound as though they had their mouths open ready to swallow him up.

"What sort of research?" asked Mama who had been good at physics at school. "Anything interesting?"

Otto nodded. "Rather hush-hush, I'm afraid," he said. "You remember the Cambridge professor who was interned with me – he's in it too, with a few other men. It could be quite important."

"But do you know," cried Aunt Dainty, "when he came home his father didn't recognise him. I talked to him. I said, 'Victor, this is your son – don't you remember?' But we're not sure if he realises even now."

"I'm sorry," said Mama. "How is Victor?"

Aunt Dainty sighed. "Not good," she said. "In bed most of the time." Then she cried, "The soup – we must eat!" and rushed out of the room.

Otto pulled some chairs round a table which was laid in a corner and then helped his mother carry in the food. There were hunks of brown bread and soup with dumplings.

"Knoedel!" cried Mama, munching one. "You always were a wonderful cook, Dainty!"

"Well, I've always liked it," said Aunt Dainty. "Even in Germany when we had a cook and six

442

maids. But I've learned something new now – how do you like my curtains?"

"Dainty!" cried Mama. "You didn't make them!"

Aunt Dainty nodded. "And the cushions on the sofa, and this skirt, and a whole lot of bits and pieces for the lodgers."

"She saved the money for a sewing machine out of the rent," said Otto. "She had to let the rooms upstairs when I was interned – with Father the way he was. And now," he said fondly, "she's turning the place into a palace."

"Ach Otto – a palace!" said Aunt Dainty, and for someone so large she looked quite girlish.

Mama, who could hardly sew on a button, couldn't get over it. "But how did you do it?" she cried. "Who showed you?"

"Evening classes," said Aunt Dainty, "at the London County Council. They cost practically nothing – you should try them."

While she was talking she had cleared away the soup dishes and brought in an apple tart. She cut a piece for Otto to take to his father and doled out the rest.

"Do you think Victor would like me to go in and see him?" asked Mama, but Aunt Dainty shook her head.

"It would be no use, dear," she said. "He wouldn't know who you were."

After supper they moved back to the oil stove and Otto talked about Canada. He had had a bad time on the way there, locked in the overcrowded hold of a boat, but it had not shaken his faith in the English.

"It wasn't their fault," he said. "They had to lock

us up. For all they knew we might have been Nazis. Most of the English Tommies were very decent."

The Canadians, too, had been very decent, though not quite as decent, he implied, as the English, and he was particularly pleased that his new job was an English venture. "But I'll get paid in Canadian dollars," he said, "and I'll be able to send some home."

Mama questioned him again about his work, but he would only smile and say that it was very small.

"And Otto so clumsy with his fingers!" cried Aunt Dainty, "Just like his cousin Bonzo."

"Whatever happened to him?" asked Mama, and they quickly slid into the kind of conversation which Anna had heard at every meeting of grown-ups since she had left Berlin at the age of nine. It was an endless listing of relatives, friends and acquaintances who had been part of the old life in Germany and who were now strewn all over the world. Some had done well for themselves, some had been caught by the Nazis, and most of them were struggling to survive.

Anna had either never known or forgotten nearly all these people, and the conversation meant little to her. Her eyes wandered round the room, from Aunt Dainty's curtains past Otto's books piled high on a shelf to the table with its bright cover and to the door beyond it.

It was half-open and she suddenly realised that there was someone standing outside, staring in. This was so unexpected that it frightened her and she glanced quickly at Aunt Dainty, but she was pouring coffee and Mama and Otto were both facing the other way.

The figure at the door was old and quite bald and

there was a curious lopsided look about the head which had a scar running down one side. It was dressed in a kind of shift and as Anna looked at it, it moved one hand in a vague gesture of silence or farewell. Like a ghost, thought Anna, but the eyes that stared back at her were human. Then it tugged its shift closer about its body and a moment later it was gone. It could not even have been wearing shoes, thought Anna, for there had been no sound.

"Black or white?" said Aunt Dainty.

"White, please," said Anna, and as Aunt Dainty handed her the cup she heard the front door close.

Aunt Dainty started. "Excuse me," she said and hurried out of the room. She was back almost at once, looking distraught.

"Otto!" she cried. "It's your father. Quickly!"

Otto leapt up from the sofa and rushed for the front door while Aunt Dainty stood helplessly among the coffee cups.

"He runs away," she said. "He keeps doing it. Once he got right to the end of the street – in his nightshirt. Luckily a neighbour saw him and brought him back."

"What makes him do it?" said Mama.

Aunt Dainty tried to speak in a matter-of-fact voice.

"Well, you know," she said, "when he first came out of the concentration camp it was happening all the time. We couldn't make him understand that he was no longer there, and I suppose he had some idea of escaping. Then it got better, but lately –" she looked at Mama unhappily. "Well, the brain was damaged, you see, and as people get older these things get worse."

There were muffled voices outside and Aunt Dainty said, "Otto has found him."

The voices sorted themselves into Otto's, trying to soothe, and a kind of thin crying.

"Oh dear," said Aunt Dainty. She looked anxiously at Anna. "Now you mustn't let this upset you." Suddenly she began to talk very fast. "You see, when he gets like this he doesn't know any of us, especially Otto because he hasn't seen him for so long. He thinks he's still in the concentration camp, you see, and he thinks we're . . . God knows who he thinks we are, and poor Otto gets very distressed."

The front door slammed and Anna could hear them on the stairs, Otto talking and the old man's voice faintly pleading. There was a bump at the bottom of the stairs – someone must have slipped – and then Otto appeared at the open door with his arms round his father, trying to guide him back to his bedroom, but the old man broke away and tottered towards Mama who involuntarily stepped back.

"Let me go!" he cried in his thin voice. "Let me go! Please, for God's sake, let me go!"

Otto and Aunt Dainty looked at each other.

"Did he get far?" she asked, and he shook his head.

"Only two doors away."

The old man had found some apple tart on the table and began absently to eat it.

"Father –" said Otto.

"My dear, it's no use," said Aunt Dainty, but Otto

ignored her. He moved a few steps towards his father – carefully, so as not to frighten him.

"Father," he said, "it's me – Otto."

The old man went on eating.

"You're no longer in the concentration camp," said Otto.

"We got you out – don't you remember? You're safe now, in England. You're home."

His father turned his face towards him. The cake was still in his hand and his nightshirt had somehow got caught round one of his bare ankles. He stared at Otto intensely with his old man's eyes. Then he screamed.

"Ring the doctor," said Aunt Dainty.

"Father –" said Otto again, but it was no use.

Aunt Dainty went quickly over to the old man and took him by the shoulders. He tried to struggle, but he was no match for her, and she led him back to bed while Otto went to the telephone. Anna saw his face as he passed her and it looked as though he were dead.

She and Mama did not speak at all until Aunt Dainty came back into the room. "I'm sorry," she said. "I wish it hadn't happened while you were here."

Mama put her arms round her large shoulders. "My dear Dainty," she cried, "I didn't know!"

"It's all right," said Aunt Dainty. "I'm used to it now – as far as one ever gets used . . ." Suddenly tears were running down her face. "It's Otto," she cried. "I can't bear to see him. He's always been so fond of his father. I remember when he was small he used to talk about him all the time." She looked towards the bedroom where the old man was battering feebly on the door.

"How can people do such things?" she asked. "How can they do them?"

When they were sitting on the bus on the long ride home Anna asked, "How did they get Uncle Victor out of the concentration camp?"

"It was a kind of ransom," said Mama. "Dainty sold all her possessions – she was quite rich – and gave the money to the Nazis. And Otto was already in England. He talked to someone at the Home Office and got them to agree that Victor could come here – otherwise the Nazis would never have let him go."

"That's why he always says the English are wonderful," said Anna.

She wondered what it would feel like to be Otto. Supposing it had been Papa in the concentration camp . . . It did not bear even thinking about. She was glad that at least Otto had his job. She could imagine him in Canada, throwing himself into the work with no thought of anything else, to blot out what had been done to his father, to help the wonderful English win their war. Whatever research Otto was given to do, she thought he would do it extremely well.

"Mama," she said, "what's very small in physics?"

Mama was cold and tired. "Oh, you must know," she said. "Molecules – atoms – things like that."

Atoms, thought Anna – what a pity. It did not sound as though Otto's research would be very important.

A few days later Otto came to say good-bye. His father was better, he said. The doctor had prescribed some new sedatives and he now slept most of the time.

"Keep an eye on my mother," he asked Mama, who promised to do so.

Just before he left he handed her a leaflet. "My mother asked me to give it to you," he said, a little embarrassed. "She thought you might be interested – it's all about her evening classes."

Anna glanced through it after he had gone. It was extraordinary what you could learn for a modest fee – anything from book-keeping through Ancient Greek to upholstery. Suddenly she noticed something.

"Look, Mama," she said. "There are even classes in drawing."

"So there are," said Mama.

Unbelievingly they checked the fee. Eight shillings and sixpence a term.

"We'll ring up first thing in the morning," said Mama.

15

They spent Christmas in the country with the Rosenbergs. The Professor's sister and her two boys had gone to stay with another relative in Manchester, where the schooling was better, and the atmosphere was much more peaceful than when Anna had been there before. Everyone was happy because the Americans had finally come into the war, and the Professor even said it might all be over by the end of 1942.

Aunt Louise had decorated a Christmas tree which filled a corner of the dining-room, and on Christmas Day Max managed to come for lunch by dint of hitching lifts both ways. He was learning to fly and had almost completed his training as a pilot. As usual, he had emerged top of all the exams and had already been recommended for a commission.

Anna told him that she was going to drawing lessons after the holidays.

"A life class," she said, "at a proper art school."

"Good show," said Max because that was what people said in the Air Force, but Aunt Louise flew into a flutter of amazement.

"A life class!" she cried. "Oh dear! You'll meet all sorts of people there!"

It was impossible to tell whether she considered the prospect dangerous or attractive, but she clearly thought it fraught with excitement. As a result Anna was a little disappointed when, a week or two later, she went to her first evening class at the Holborn School of Art.

She was directed to a large, bare room with a wooden platform and a screen at one end. A few people were sitting about, some with drawing boards propped up in front of them, some reading newspapers. Nearly all of them had kept their coats on, for the room was very cold.

Just after she had come in a little woman with a shopping bag arrived and hurried behind the screen. There was a thump as she put the bag down and a potato rolled out from under the screen, but she retrieved it quickly and emerged a moment later in a pink dressing-gown.

"Christ, it's freezing," she said, switched on an electric fire aimed at the platform and crouched in front of it.

By this time Anna had helped herself to some drawing paper from a stack marked one penny a sheet and pinned it to one of the boards which seemed to be for general use. She got out her pencil and rubber and sat astride one of the wooden forms provided, propping up her board against the easel-shaped front like the other students. She was ready to learn to draw, but nothing happened. On one side of her an elderly woman was knitting a sock and on the other a youth of sixteen or so was finishing a sandwich.

At last the door opened again and a man in a duffel coat appeared.

"Late again, John!" sang out the youth next to Anna in a strong Welsh accent.

The man looked across the room with absent-minded blue eyes before his attention focused.

"Don't be cheeky, William," he said. "And you'd

better do me a good drawing today, or I'll tell your father what I really think of you!"

The Welsh boy laughed and said, "Yes sir," with mock respect, while the man threw off his duffel and went to confer with the model.

Anna heard him say something about a standing pose, but the model shook her head.

"Not tonight, Mr Cotmore," she cried. "My feet aren't up to it."

She had taken off the pink dressing-gown and was standing there with no clothes on at all and with the electric fire casting a red glow on her rather tubby stomach.

Anna had been a little nervous of this moment. She had wondered what it would feel like to be in a roomful of people all looking at someone naked. But everyone else took it so much for granted that after a minute or two it seemed quite normal.

"I've been queueing an hour for fish," said the model and indeed, even without her clothes, it was only too easy to imagine her with a shopping bag in her hand.

"A sitting pose, then," said the man called Cotmore and covered a chair on the platform with what looked like an old curtain for the model to sit on. When he had arranged her to his satisfaction he said, "We'll keep this pose for the whole evening." There was a rustle of newspapers being put down; the woman with the sock reluctantly rolled up her wool, and everyone began to draw.

Anna looked at the model and at her blank sheet of paper and wondered where to start. She had never spent more than a few minutes drawing anyone, and now she would have two and a half hours. How could one possibly fill in the time? She glanced at a girl in front of her who seemed to be covering her entire paper with pencil strokes. Of course, she thought – if you made the drawing bigger it was bound to take longer and you could put in more detail. She grasped her pencil and began.

After an hour she had worked down from the model's head to her middle. There was something not quite right about the shoulders, but she was pleased with the way she had drawn each of the many curls in the model's hair and was just about to start on the hands which were folded on one side of the stomach, when the man called Cotmore said, "Rest!"

The model stretched, stood up and wrapped herself in her dressing-gown and all the students put down their pencils. How annoying, thought Anna – just when she was getting into her stride.

A murmur of conversation went up from the class, newspapers were unfolded, and the woman next to her went back to her knitting. Anna found that in spite of having kept her coat on, her feet and hands were frozen.

"Chilly tonight," said a man with a muffler and offered her a toffee out of a paper bag.

The model came down from her throne and walked slowly from one drawing-board to the next, inspecting the different versions of herself all round the room.

"Have we done you justice?" called Mr Cotmore. He was surrounded by a small group of students, the

Welsh boy among them, and they were all chatting and laughing.

The model shook her head. "They've all made me look fat," she said, and went glumly back to her chair.

When Anna returned to her drawing at the end of the rest it did not seem quite as good as before. The shoulders were definitely wrong: the trouble, she realised, was that she had drawn the right shoulder higher than the left, whereas the way the model was sitting it was the other way round. How could she not have seen this before? But it was too late to change it, so she concentrated on the hands.

They were folded together in a complicated way, with the fingers interlaced, and as she tried to copy all the joints and knuckles and fingernails she became increasingly confused. Also she could not help noticing that as a result of the mistake over the shoulders, one arm had come out longer than the other. She was staring at it all, wondering what to do, when a voice behind her said, "May I?"

It was Mr Cotmore.

He motioned to her to get up and sat down in her place.

"Don't draw it all in bits," he said, and began a drawing of his own at the side of the paper.

Anna watched him, and at first she could not think what he was drawing. There were straight lines like scaffolding in different directions, then a round shape which turned out to be the model's head and then, gradually, the rest of her appeared among the scaffolding, supported by the straight lines which indicated,

Anna now realised, the angle of the shoulders, the hips, the hands in relation to the arms. It was all finished in a few minutes and although there were no details – no curls and no fingernails – it looked far more like the model than Anna's drawing.

"See?" said Mr Cotmore, as he stood up and walked away.

Anna was left staring at his work. Well, of course it was easier to do it small, she thought. And she wasn't sure that putting in all those guide lines wasn't a kind of cheating. All the same . . .

She could hardly bear to look at her own drawing after his. It wambled all over the paper with its funny shoulders and its one long arm and one short arm and its fingers like sausages. She wanted to crumple it up and throw it away but had just decided that this would attract too much attention, when she became aware of the Welsh boy looking down at it.

"Not bad," he said.

For a moment her heart leapt. Perhaps after all . . . ?

"One of Cotmore's best," said the boy. "He's in form tonight." He must have sensed her disappointment, for he added, "Your first attempt?"

Anna nodded.

"Yes, well –" The Welsh boy averted his eyes from her drawing and searched for a kindly comment. "It's often difficult to start with," he said.

When Anna got home Mama was waiting to hear how it had all gone. "I think it's very good," she cried when she saw the drawing, "for someone who's never done anything like that before!"

Papa was more interested in Mr Cotmore's version. "John Cotmore," he said. "I've read something about him recently. An exhibition, I think – very well reviewed."

"Really?" said Mama. "He must be good then."

"Oh yes," said Papa, "he's quite distinguished."

They were sitting on the beds in the room which Anna and Mama shared, and Mama was trying to re-heat the supper Anna had missed earlier in the dining-room. She had lit the gas-ring which Frau Gruber had provided in each of the bedrooms and was stirring up some unidentifiable meat, boiled potatoes and turnips in a saucepan she had bought from Woolworth's.

"It's a bit burned," she said. "I don't know – perhaps next time it might be better to eat it cold."

Anna said nothing.

It was nearly ten o'clock and she was tired. Her appalling drawing lay on the floor beside her. Next time? she thought. There did not seem much point.

However, by the following week she was anxious to try again. Surely, she thought, she was bound to do better this time.

It turned out that the model was the same, but this time Mr Cotmore had persuaded her into a standing pose. Divested of her pink dressing-gown, she leaned with one hand on the back of the chair to steady herself and stared gloomily at her feet.

Anna, remembering the lesson of the previous week, at once attacked her paper with scaffolding lines in every direction. She tried not to be distracted by details, and the upper part of her drawing came out better than before, but all her newfound skill deserted her when she reached the legs and feet.

She could not make her drawing stand. The feet were at the bottom, but the figure appeared to float or hang on the paper with no weight and nothing to support it. Again and again she rubbed out and re-drew, but it was no use until, towards the end of the evening, Mr Cotmore came round to her. He sat down without a word and drew a foot at the side of her paper. It was facing straight forward like the model's, but instead of drawing a line round it, as Anna had tried to do, he built it up section by section from the foreshortened toes at the front, through the arch of the foot, to the heel at the back, each piece fitting solidly behind the other, until there on the paper was a sturdy foot standing firmly on an invisible floor.

"See?" he said.

"Yes," said Anna and he smiled slightly.

He must be about forty, she thought, with intelligent eyes and a curious wide mouth.

"Difficult things, feet," he said, and walked away.

After this Anna went to art school every Tuesday night. She became obsessed with learning to draw. If she could just do one drawing, she thought, that looked as she wanted it to – but each time she mastered one difficulty she seemed to become aware of two or three more whose existence she had not even suspected. Sometimes Mr Cotmore helped her, but often she spent the whole evening struggling alone.

"You're getting better, though," said the Welsh boy. His name was Ward but everyone called him Welsh

William. "Remember the first drawing you did? It was bloody awful."

"Were your drawings awful when you first started?" asked Anna.

Welsh William shook his head. "I've always found it easy – perhaps too easy. John Cotmore says I'm facile."

Anna sighed as she looked at the beautiful fluid drawing which he had produced apparently without effort.

"I wish I was," she said. Her own work was black with being redrawn and almost in holes with being rubbed out.

Sometimes, as she travelled home on the half-empty tube after the class had finished, she despaired at her lack of talent. But the following week she would be back with a new pencil and another sheet of paper, thinking, "Perhaps this time . . ."

She came home from the classes looking so peaky that Mama worried about her.

"It can't be good for you, sitting for hours in the cold like that," she said, for there was a fuel shortage and often the art school was entirely without heating, but Anna said impatiently, "I'm all right – I keep my coat on."

There was heavy snow in February and again in March. Everyone was depressed because Singapore had fallen to the Japanese, and the German army, far from succumbing to the Russians, seemed about to enter Moscow. At the office Mrs Hammond caught 'flu and did not come in for nearly three weeks, so the old ladies were steeped in even deeper gloom. Miss Clinton-Brown no longer thanked God for letting her cut out the pyjamas, but instead had formed a new alliance with Miss Potter against Mrs Riley who upset them all with her Japanese atrocity stories.

She knew an amazing number and always told them with all possible drama. Leaning on the table with one hand, she would peer over her Bovril with narrowed eyes to impersonate a Japanese commander of unspeakable cruelty, and then open them wide for the noble, well-spoken replies from his English captives who were, however, invariably doomed. Miss Potter always became very distressed by these dramatics and once had to go home in the middle of a pyjama jacket to see, she said confusedly, if her budgie was safe.

When Mrs Hammond recovered from her bout of 'flu she told Mrs Riley very firmly to stop repeating such ill-founded rumours about the fate of British prisoners. Mrs Riley sulked for two days and Miss Clinton-Brown thanked God that there were still some sensible people left in the world who were not afraid to speak their mind. It would all have been quite funny, thought Anna, if one hadn't suspected that most of Mrs Riley's stories were probably true.

Going to art school after all this was a relief. Anna had discovered that there was another life class on Thursdays which, for an extra three shillings and sixpence, she was entitled to attend, so she now went twice a week. All the classes had shrunk, for the intense cold kept the knitters and the newspaper-readers away, and Mr Cotmore had more time to teach those students who remained. He corrected most of their drawings every night and during the rest period he would sit in a corner of the life-room with a favoured few and talk. Anna watched them from a distance. They always seemed to have a good time, arguing and laughing, and she thought how splendid it must be to belong to that inner circle. But she was too shy to go anywhere near them, and after school they always left very quickly in a bunch.

One night she was packing up her things at the end of the class. She had worked with a kind of despair all evening and had managed at last to produce a drawing that bore some faint resemblance to what she had in mind. In the struggle a lot of pencil had got on her hands and somehow from her hands on to her face.

Welsh William looked at her with interest.

"Did you get any of it on the paper?" he asked.

"Certainly," she said, and showed him.

He was quite impressed. "Very forceful," he said. "We may make something of you yet. Why don't you wash your face and come and have a coffee?"

She scrubbed her face at the sink and they walked a few doors down the road to a café. As they opened the door there were welcoming cries from inside. She blinked in the sudden light and saw Mr Cotmore and his regular crowd of students looking back at her. They were sitting at two tables pushed together, with coffee cups in front of them, and occupied most of the narrow room.

"It's the little girl who gets pencil all over herself," cried one of them, a small man of about Mr Cotmore's age.

"But to good purpose," said Mr Cotmore before she had time to blush. "It's Anna, isn't it?"

She nodded, and they made room for her and Welsh William at the tables. Some coffee appeared before her and, half-excited and half-apprehensive, she buried herself in the cup, so that no one else should ask her any questions. Gradually the conversation resumed around her.

"You're wrong about Cezanne, John," said the small man and John Cotmore rounded on him with "Nonsense, Harry, you're just trying to start something!"

Two girls at the other side of the table laughed, but Harry had evidently been trying to do just that, for soon everyone was disagreeing about the French Impressionists, the Italian Primitives, Giotto, Matisse, Mark Gertler, Samuel Palmer – who on earth were they all? thought Anna, listening in silence for fear of revealing her ignorance. On one side of her Harry was waving his arms in argument, on the other Welsh William was absently drawing something on the edge of a newspaper. A pale man with a pale tie whispered intensely about form and content, one of the girls ordered a portion of chips and passed them round, everyone drank more coffee, and John Cotmore with his warm deep voice somehow kept the whole thing going. He spoke only little, but whenever he did everyone else stopped to listen.

Once he addressed her directly. "What do *you* think?" he asked. They had been talking about styles in drawing, some students extolling the sensitive line of someone Anna had never heard of and others defending another painter with a more chunky approach.

She stared at him, horrified.

"I don't know," she stammered. "I just want to draw it the way it looks. But I find it very difficult."

What a stupid answer, she thought, but he said seriously, "That's not a bad start," and she noticed that the others looked at her with new respect.

Later, when everyone else was talking, she plucked up courage to ask him something that had worried her for weeks.

"If someone was going to be any good at drawing," she said, "surely they wouldn't find it so difficult?"

"I don't think that follows," he said. "It might just mean that they had high standards. In your case," he added, smiling a little, "I would say that the situation looks very promising."

Very promising, she thought, and while he was drawn back into the general conversation she turned his answer over and over, inspecting it for alternate meanings. But there were none. He must really mean that her work was very promising. It was unbelievable, and she sat hugging the thought to herself until it was time to go home.

They sorted out how many coffees had been drunk by whom and then stood for a moment in the cold outside the café.

"See you on Thursday, Anna," said Welsh William, and several other voices echoed, "See you on Thursday." They sounded strangely disembodied in the dark. Good night, Harry. Good night, Doreen. Then the sound of footsteps as unidentifiable figures melted into the blackout.

Anna buttoned up her coat against the wind when

a voice, deeper than the rest, called out, "Good night, Anna!"

"Good-night . . . John!" she called back after a moment's hesitation, and as the happiness welled up inside her she broke away from the group into the invisible street beyond.

John Cotmore had said good night to her. And her work was very promising. The pavement rang under her feet and the darkness shone all about her, like something that she could almost touch. She was surprised to find Holborn tube station looking just as usual.

Something tremendous, she felt, had happened in her life.

16

When Anna arrived at the office a few weeks later she found Mrs Hammond already there. It was embarrassing because Anna was late as usual – there seemed no point in hurrying to work when there was so little to do – but luckily Mrs Hammond had not noticed. She was standing in the disused hospital ward, examining dusty shelves and cupboards, and as soon as she saw Anna she said, "Got a new job for you."

"What?" asked Anna.

Mrs Hammond was looking more positive than she had done since Dickie's death.

"Sad job, really," she said. "But jolly useful. Officers' clothing." And as Anna looked puzzled, she suddenly said, "Dead men's shoes! Can't call it that, of course – upset people. But that's what it comes to. Pass on uniforms – all sorts of clothes – from chaps who've been killed to chaps who are still alive and need them."

Anna noticed for the first time that on a dust-sheet in a corner of the ward was a pile of garments. There were suits, shirts, ties, bits of Air Force uniform. A used kitbag had P/O Richard Hammond stencilled on it in large white letters. Mrs Hammond followed her glance.

"Silly to hang on to them," she said, "when there are other boys who'd be glad of them." Then she said, "After all, he wasn't the only one."

It turned out that she had a partner in this new

enterprise – a Mrs James who had lost both her sons, one in the Army in the African desert and the other in the Air Force over Germany. Anna met her briefly later that day, a gaunt, elderly woman with huge tragic eyes and an almost inaudible voice.

She had brought with her a little pug-faced man of great energy who proceeded at once to turn the empty ward into a storeroom for the clothing they hoped to receive. He cleaned and hammered and moved furniture and by the end of the week it was ready, with a little office for Mrs James in one corner.

This consisted only of a table and chair behind two screens, and there was no heating in the whole freezing place except one bar of an electric fire directed at her feet, but she did not seem to notice. She just sat there, staring into space, as though it was as good a place to be as any other.

Mrs Hammond had kept her office next to the sewing-room but spent a good deal of time running in and out to see how everything was getting on. It was she who composed the advertisement in *The Times*, appealing for clothes to the wives and parents of the young men who had been killed. Anna typed it out and by the following week the clothes began to come in.

They varied from single, pathetic garments to whole trunkfuls and they all had to be acknowledged and sorted. It was strangely distressing work. Some trunks, arriving directly from Service stations, seemed to contain nearly all the dead men's possessions, and there were golf-clubs, paperbacks and writing-cases which no one knew what to do with. Once when Anna was pulling an R.A.F. tunic out of a suitcase a ping-pong ball flew out with it and bounced all over the floor of the empty ward. For some reason this upset her more than anything else.

At the same time the old ladies still needed attention – more than before, for they were jealous of Mrs Hammond's new interest – and the wool still had to be sent out to the knitters, and suddenly Anna found that she was very busy. She no longer arrived late in the mornings and barely had time for lunch. Sometimes when she finished at six o'clock she wondered if she wasn't too tired to go on to art school, but she always went in the end.

In the meantime Mrs Hammond had informed all the generals, admirals and air marshals she knew of her new scheme to help servicemen, and at last, less than three weeks after its inception, the first young man arrived to be kitted out. He was a naval lieutenant who had lost all his possessions when his ship had been sunk by a U-boat, and Mrs Hammond and Mrs James vied with each other to give him everything he wanted.

Mrs Hammond had been all a-bustle since the new scheme had started, so it was not surprising to see her turning over stacks of clothes to find trousers exactly the right length or a cap with the correct insignia. But it was astonishing, thought Anna, to see the change in Mrs James. For the first time her huge eyes stopped staring into the distance, and as she questioned the young man, gently and sensibly, about his needs, it was as though he were providing some kind of vitamin of which she had been deprived. She smiled and talked and even made a little joke, until Mrs Hammond led him away to try on some shoes, when she relapsed into inactivity like a wind-up toy that had run down.

After this there was a steady stream of young men in need and an equally steady supply of clothes from the relatives of other young men who had been killed in action. Anna sometimes wondered how it would feel to wear these garments, but the young men seemed to look on them in purely practical terms. Since rationing had been introduced the previous summer every kind of clothing was hard to come by, and it did not do to be too sensitive.

They were surprisingly cheerful on the whole and sometimes, intoxicated by the money they had saved, they asked Anna out for the evening. They took her to films and theatres and to West End restaurants, and it was fun to dress up in Judy's and Jinny's more elegant cast-offs for these grand places, just as though she were really the nice English girl they took her for. Afterwards they usually wanted to kiss her, and this, too, was exciting. I must really be quite attractive, she thought in wonder, but she did not find any one of them more interesting than the rest and she never went out with them on her art school nights.

"Why not?" cried Mama. "It's much better for you than those old evening classes!"

Anna shook her head. "It's an awful waste of time, really," she said in the special knowing-her-own-mind voice she had recently acquired. "And, honestly Mama, they seem so *young*!"

"I hear you're living in a social whirl," said Max.

"Well, it looks as though the war is going to go on for ever, so you may as well enjoy it."

He was depressed again, for although he had come out top of his course and was now a Pilot Officer, the Air Force had decided that he could fly neither bombers nor fighters.

"Just because of my background," he said. "They're afraid that if I was shot down and the Germans found out about me they wouldn't treat me as a prisoner of war. So I've got to be a flying instructor."

"Surely that's important too," said Papa, but Max was too annoyed to listen.

"You don't understand," he said. "Nearly everybody else is going to fly on operations. It's the same old thing – I'm always stuck with something different."

At this Mama, normally so sympathetic to his longing for equality, blew her top.

"For God's sake, are you determined to be killed?" she shouted, and added incongruously, "As though we hadn't got enough to worry about!"

"There's no need to get excited," said Max, "especially as I've got no choice."

Mama had been increasingly nervous of late, and a few days later Anna discovered why. It was when she came home from work. Nowadays she did not have many evenings at home, and she had planned this one exactly. First she was going to paint over the cracks in her shoes with some brown dye she had bought in her lunch-hour. Then, if there was any hot water, she would wash her hair, and after supper she would mend her two remaining pairs of stockings, so as to have some to wear the following day.

As she passed Papa's room she heard voices and went in. Mama was half-sitting, half-lying on the bed and Papa was holding her hand. Her blue eyes were swimming, her mouth was dragged down at the corners, and her whole face was soaked with tears.

"What's happened?" cried Anna, but Papa shook his head.

"It's all right," he said. "Nothing terrible. Mama has lost her job."

Mama at once leapt into a sitting position.

"What do you mean, nothing terrible," she cried. "How are we going to live?"

"We'll manage somehow," said Papa, and gradually Anna found out what had happened. It was not that Mama had been sacked, but that the job had simply come to an end.

"Of course I hated it anyway," cried Mama through her tears. "It was never meant to be more than a stop-gap after Lord Parker died."

Anna remembered once going to see Mama when she was still Lady Parker's social secretary. Mama had sat in a pretty, white-painted room with a fire, and a footman had brought her tea and biscuits, returning with an extra cup for Anna. Mama had never seemed to have much to do except answer the telephone and send out invitations, and in the evenings she and Anna had marvelled at the way Lady Parker lived.

"Her stockings cost a guinea a pair," Mama had told her. "And they can only be worn once because they are so fine."

Since Lord Parker's death Mama had worked in a basement entirely filled with his papers – such stacks and stacks of them that it had not occurred to her until recently that the task of sorting them could ever come to an end.

"What shall I do?" she cried. "I have to get a job somehow!"

"Perhaps you'll find something more interesting," said Anna.

Mama brightened.

"Yes," she said, "I suppose I might, now that so many people have been called up. And since you've been self-supporting I've been able to save a little, so we can last a while – I could pick and choose a bit." But then despair overcame her again. "Oh God!" she cried, "I'm so sick of always having to start again!" She looked at Papa who was still holding her hand. "How much easier it would be," she said, "if the B.B.C. would only use some of your stuff and broadcast it to Germany."

Papa's face tightened. He had not been able to sell anything to the B.B.C. since that first piece, and though he sat at his table and wrote each day, he was earning almost no money at all.

"I'll ring them again," he said, but they all knew that it would be no use.

The week-end after Mama had gone to her office for the last time she was quite cheerful. It was summer weather and everyone was sitting in the garden. The Woodpigeon had cut the grass with an ancient lawnmower he had discovered in a shed and the Czech ladies both wore triangles of stiff white paper over their noses to protect them from sunburn.

Mama was sitting in a deckchair with a pile of

newspapers beside her. She was checking through the "situations vacant" columns and writing letters of application for any that seemed possible. Every time she had finished one she would say, "Do you think that's all right?" and show it to Anna and Papa. The jobs were all secretarial, and as Anna and Papa read through them, Mama would say, "I didn't mention that I can't do shorthand because once they gave me the job I'm sure I could manage," or "I know it says British-born, but I thought if they just saw me . . ."

She looked so determined, sitting there in the sunshine with her blue eyes frowning at the paper while she attacked it with her pen, that it was easy to imagine her talking anyone into giving her any job she wanted.

However, by the following Thursday she had only had one request for an interview. This turned out to be with a little man in the City who said that actually they were looking for someone younger – just a girl, really – and sent Mama home in deep depression.

She wrote another batch of letters and waited for replies, but nothing happened. The weather continued lovely and hot, so she sat in the garden and wrote more letters and read books from the library. After all, she said, she had earned a holiday.

When the weather changed and the garden became chilly Mama cleared out her wardrobe. She walked down to Putney High Street with Papa to spend the shilling and sixpence they had allocated for their joint lunch and then they ate it together in his room. In the evening she played bridge with the Woodpigeon and the Poznanskis and, on special occasions, with

Miss Thwaites, a new arrival in the hotel. In fact Miss Thwaites did not play very well, but since she was English – not just half-English or naturalised English or English by marriage, but real, genuine born-and-bred English – she was the most soughtafter person there. She was a withered-looking spinster with a grey pudding-bowl hair-cut who worked in the local bank, and she accepted the respect accorded to her as her due.

It was not until Mama had been out of work for four weeks that she became really frightened. She calculated that in that time she had had only four replies to her letters, and two interviews, and when she checked her savings she found that, as always, they were dwindling faster than she had expected. She began to haunt the telephone and hang about the hall, waiting for the postman. When Anna came home in the evenings she would say, tight-lipped, "I still haven't heard anything," before Anna had even had time to ask, and at night she tossed and turned in her bed, unable to sleep.

"What are we going to do?" she cried one Sunday when the three of them were sitting in Papa's room after lunch. Papa had been reading them a poem he had written the previous day. It was addressed to his sister who was now somewhere in Palestine, and in it he remembered their childhood together in Silesia and wondered if they would ever meet again except perhaps in Paradise. If there were such a place, thought Papa, it would probably look rather like the woods and meadows among which they had grown up. It was a beautiful poem.

When Mama asked him what they were to do he looked at her, full of affection and confidence.

"You'll think of something," he said.

Mama who had been nervously clutching a newspaper suddenly flung it on the floor.

"But I don't want to have to think of something!" she cried. "Why should it always be me? Why can't you think of something for a change?"

Papa, one hand still holding the poem, seemed to be considering deeply and for a moment Anna thought he was going to come up with the solution to the whole thing. Then he put his other hand over Mama's.

"But you're so much better at it than I am," he said.

At this Mama burst into tears and Anna said, "I'm sure I could manage five shillings a week, or even seven-and-sixpence," but Mama shouted, "It wouldn't be enough!" Then she blew her nose and said, "I'll try and talk to Louise."

"Louise?" said Papa and made a face, but then he caught sight of Mama's expression and said, "very well, then, Louise."

Aunt Louise willingly gave Mama fifteen pounds to help eke out her savings.

"I'm sorry it isn't more," she said, "but I don't like to ask Sam at the moment."

The Professor had become anxious about money since his sister had unexpectedly returned to him with her two boys. He spent each meal-time watching expensive food disappear down the throats of his many impecunious relatives.

"And he worries," said Aunt Louise, "what is to become of us all."

"Anna insisted on contributing her five shillings a week and Max sent a cheque for ten pounds from his R.A.F. pay, so they were safe for a while at least. But Mama's anxiety continued. It was difficult to be in her company, for as she sat with her hands clenched in her lap and her blue eyes staring the tension was like a physical presence in the room and nothing could alleviate it.

"Do you really think so?" she would cry when Anna suggested that some particular application for a job looked hopeful and, five minutes later, again, "Do you really think they'll give me that job?"

The only thing that took her mind off her worries was playing bridge in the evenings. Then her fierce concentration would switch to the cards and as she argued about Culbertson, overtricks and bungled grand-slams the anxiety about her job receded.

Anna occasionally got dragged into these games – Papa couldn't tell a club from a spade – but only if there was no one else at all, for she was so bored by them that she cast a blight on the other players. She would sit there, making mistakes and drawing all over her score-pad, to escape gratefully at the end, irrespective of whether she had won or lost. She felt sorry for Mama and wished to help her, but she also found it a strain sharing one small bedroom with her and so was guiltily relieved whenever there was a reason for her to stay out late.

One morning just as Anna was leaving for work Mama caught her at the door.

"Miss Thwaites wants to play bridge tonight," she said. "The Woodpigeon is free, but we need a fourth."

"I can't," said Anna. "I've got my evening class."

Mama had slept badly and the morning post had failed, yet again, to produce the job she was hoping for.

"Oh, come on," she said. "It won't matter if you miss it just once."

"But I don't want to miss it," said Anna. "Can't the Poznanskis play?"

Mama said that they couldn't, and Anna could see the tension rising in her, like a kettle coming to the boil. She said, "Look, I'm sorry, Mama, but I really don't want to miss my evening class. I'm sure you'll find someone else."

She edged nervously towards the bedroom door, but before she could reach it Mama exploded.

"Surely," Mama cried, "you could do this one little thing for me! I don't ask you much! God knows if one of your boy friends asked you out you'd give up your evening class quick enough!"

"That's not true!" cried Anna. She had always refused invitations on art school nights. But Mama was now in full flood.

"It's my one pleasure in life," she cried. "The only thing that takes my mind off the endless worrying about money. And it's not as though anyone else in this family ever worried about how we're going to live. You just go off to your nice little job each morning and Papa sits in his room writing poems, and I am left with everything – everything!"

"Mama . . ." said Anna, but Mama cut straight through her.

"Who went and asked Louise for money?" she cried. "Did you? Did Papa? No, as always, it was left to me. Do you suppose I enjoyed that? And who arranged for you to learn shorthand-typing and found a way of paying your fees? And who got Max out of the internment camp? It wasn't you or Papa. Don't you think that in the circumstances you could give up one evening – just one single evening – to make my life a little easier?"

Anna looked at Mama's desperate scarlet face and had a curious, panicky sensation of being sucked into it. She backed away, feeling pale and cold.

"I'm sorry, Mama," she said, "but I must go to my evening class."

Mama glared at her.

"After all," cried Anna, "it's only a game of bridge!"

"And you, I suppose," yelled Mama, "are going to produce a masterpiece!"

Anna made for the door.

"If I did," she heard herself yell back, "you wouldn't even know that it was one!"

Then she escaped, trembling, into the corridor.

She worried about it all day at the office. She thought of ringing Mama up, but there always seemed to be someone near the telephone and, anyway, she wouldn't have known what to say. At six o'clock she still had not made up her mind whether to go home or to the art school. She decided to leave it to chance. If a tram passed her before she reached Victoria she would go

476

home – otherwise not. The tram came almost at once, but she ignored it and took the bus to Holborn, arriving just in time for the class.

And why shouldn't I? she thought. After all, it wasn't as though she'd been out a lot lately. Two of the young men who most frequently invited her had been posted away from London, so she'd had almost no social life at all. I was absolutely right, she thought, but it did not help, for she could not concentrate on her work and produced a drawing so poor that she crumpled it up and threw it away. At the end of the class she did not go to the café but made straight for the tube. If I get home quickly, she thought, there might still be time for a game or two of bridge.

Suddenly, on the train, she had a vision of Mama crying on the bed after she had lost her job. How could I? she thought, and was overwhelmed by pity and guilt. As she hurried down the street she thought of Mama in Paris, Mama helping her buy her first pair of slacks, Mama taking her out on her sixteenth birthday.

"Mama!" she cried as she burst into the lounge – and there was Mama playing bridge with Miss Thwaites against the Woodpigeon and Mrs Poznanski.

"You're early," said Mama, and Miss Thwaites added, "Mrs Poznanski found she didn't have to go out after all."

"But Mama . . ." cried Anna.

Then rage filled her and she turned on her heel and walked out of the room.

"I couldn't help it," she said later to Papa. "I've got a right to my own life. I can't just throw it all up to play bridge whenever Mama wants me to."

"No, of course not," said Papa. He was looking tired, and Anna realised that the day could not have been easy for him either.

"Mama is having a difficult time," he said after a moment. "I wish we could all live very differently from the way we do. I wish I could be more help."

There was a pile of closely-written sheets on his desk and Anna asked, "What are you writing?"

"Something about us – a kind of diary. I've been working on it for a long time." He shook his head at Anna's look of hope. "No," he said, "I don't think anyone would buy it."

He had some bread left over from lunch and as Anna couldn't face her cold supper he made her some toast. He suspended a slice of bread from a large paper clip and Anna watched as he held it over the gas fire at the end of a stick from the garden.

"It's so difficult," she said, "sharing a room."

Papa looked worried. "I wish I could . . ."

"No," she said. "I know you need yours to write in."

Outside on the landing a door slammed and there were voices and footsteps on the stairs. The bridge game must have broken up.

Suddenly Papa said, "Be nice to her. Be very, very nice to her. She is your mother and it's quite true what she says – life is not easy for her."

"I am," said Anna. "I always have been."

As she got up to leave him he said, "Try to forget all about today."

But she could not quite forget and nor, she suspected, could Mama. There was a carefulness between them which had not been there before. One side of Anna was saddened by this, but another secret, steely side, whose existence she had never even suspected, half-welcomed it for the increased privacy it brought her. All because I wanted to go to art school that one night, she thought. How complicated life became if there was something you really wanted to do.

The following week at the café she said to John Cotmore, "Do you think art, if one takes it seriously, is bad for personal relationships?"

She had never used so many abstractions before in one sentence, and his mouth twitched as he looked at her.

"Well," he said at last, "I think it probably makes them more difficult."

She nodded and then blushed, overcome by embarrassment. She had just remembered what someone had told her – that he did not get on with his wife.

17

In the autumn the National Gallery put on an exhibition of French Impressionist paintings. It was a great event, for all valuable pictures had been hidden away since the beginning of the war to save them from being bombed. But there had been only few air raids on London recently – the Luftwaffe must have been too busy fighting in Russia – and so it was considered worth taking a chance to show them again.

Anna had never seen them. There was a book about them in the library, but it had only black and white reproductions and you could not really tell from them what the paintings were like. So, on the first Sunday after the opening of the exhibition, she went along to look at it.

It was a brilliant cold day and she was feeling happy because it was the week-end, and because she had done two good drawings during the week, and because Mama had at last got a job – not a very good job, but after the worry of the past few months it was a relief for her to have got anything at all. As she crossed Trafalgar Square the stone lions cast hard shadows on the pavement and there were more people than usual milling round Nelson's column in the sharp air. The fountains had not worked since the beginning of the war, but as she passed between them a cluster of pigeons took off at her feet and she watched the spatter of their wings turn dark as they rose up into the shining sky. Suddenly she felt a great surge of joy, as though she were flying up with them. Something marvellous is going to happen, she thought – but what?

The National Gallery was crowded and she had a struggle to make her way up the steps and into one of the main rooms. This, too, was full of people, so that at first she could only see parts of the paintings between bobbing heads. She knew at once that she liked them. They looked like the square outside, brilliant with light and a kind of joyful promise.

They were hung in no particular order and as she walked from room to room she was bewildered by the profusion. She did not know what to look at first, since it was all unfamiliar, and stared at landscapes, figures and interiors indiscriminately between the shifting bodies of the crowd. When she got to the end she went round again and this time some things leapt out at her – a mass of green water lilies in a green pond, a woman in a garden, a miraculously drawn dancer tying her shoe.

But when she went round a third time she had already changed. The water lilies which had so dazzled her before now seemed less remarkable, and she was fascinated, instead, by some bathers painted entirely in tiny spots of brilliant colour. She looked and looked and finally, when she could see no more, she fought her way to the office near the main door in the hope of buying some postcard reproductions which she could look at at home, but the gallery was about to close and there were none left. She must have been looking at the pictures for nearly three hours, she thought in surprise.

As she emerged onto the steps above Trafalgar

Square, now purple in the dusk, she stopped for a moment. Suddenly she did not want the bother of catching buses and tubes and of sitting through supper at home. She stood and stared across the darkening square, feeling vaguely afloat.

A voice behind her said, "Hullo," and she turned to see John Cotmore in his old duffel coat.

"Well," he said, joining her at the balustrade, "and what did you think of the Impressionists?"

"I loved them," she said.

He smiled. "First time you've seen them?"

She nodded.

"First time I saw them was twenty years ago," he said. "In Paris. I was quite a dashing young man then."

She could not think what to answer. Finally she said, "I used to live in Paris. I went to school there."

"What, finishing school?" he asked, and she laughed.

"No, the école communale – elementary school."

There was a sudden exodus from the gallery and people streamed past them down the steps, hemming them in.

"I'm a German refugee," she said, and immediately wondered why on earth she had said it. But he seemed interested and not too surprised, so she went on to explain about Max and Mama and Papa and their life together since they had left Berlin.

"I don't usually tell people about it," she said at last.

This did surprise him. "Why not?" he asked.

"Well – " It seemed obvious to her. "People think it's odd."

482

He frowned. "I don't think it's odd."

Perhaps it isn't, she thought, as the darkness closed round them and the last footsteps clattered past. It was suddenly cold, but he seemed in no hurry to leave.

"You mustn't go round pretending you're something you aren't," he said. "Where you come from is part of you, just like your talent for drawing."

She smiled, hearing only the word "talent".

"So no more of this pretence." He took her arm. "Come on, I'm going to walk you to the tube."

They made their way along the narrow pavements of a side street, and as they reached the Embankment she was again filled with the happiness that she had felt earlier that afternoon. But this time, instead of being shapeless, it seemed to contain the paintings she had seen and the fact that she was walking through the dusk with John Cotmore, as well as a huge and mysterious sense of expectancy.

The feeling was so strong that she smiled involuntarily, and he said, "What's funny?" looking put out.

He had been talking, but she had hardly listened. Something about living alone, cooking his own supper. Had his wife moved out, then?

Hurriedly, she said, "I'm sorry, nothing's funny, it's just . . ." She hesitated because it seemed so idiotic.

"I've been feeling terribly happy all day," she brought out at last.

"Oh!" He nodded. "I suppose at your age . . . How old are you, anyway?"

"Eighteen," she said.

"Really," he said to her annoyance. "You seem much younger."

They had arrived at the tube station and stood together for a moment before she bought her ticket. Then, as she stepped into the lift, he called after her, "See you on Tuesday!"

"See you on Tuesday!" she called back, and the happiness welled up again inside her and lasted all the way home to Putney.

The cold, sunny weather persisted, and so did Anna's happiness. She felt almost painfully aware of all the sounds, shapes and colours around her and wanted to draw everything in sight. She drew on the tube and in her lunch-hour and when she got home in the evenings. She filled one notebook after another with drawings of people strap-hanging, sitting, eating and talking, and when she was not drawing she thought about it.

She loved everything. She felt as though she had been asleep for years and had just woken up. In the mornings when she took the bus down Putney Hill to the tube station she stood outside on the platform, so as not to miss a moment of the view as the bus crossed the river in the early light. She spent hours looking at a book about the French Impressionists which John Cotmore had lent her, and some of the reproductions so delighted her that it was almost as though she could feel them with her eyes. When there was music on the radio in the lounge it seemed to her unbearably beautiful, and the sight of the dead men's clothes at work made her unbearably sad. (But even this was curiously agreeable.) She joined the local firewatchers, which meant turning out at night whenever there was an air-raid warning, and stood endlessly in the dark, admiring the dim shapes of the suburban landscape in the starlight.

One night she was on duty with Mr Cuddeford, who was the leader of the group. There had been a few bombs, but nothing close, and some anti-aircraft fire from the guns on Putney Heath. No incendiaries, which was what Anna and Mr Cuddeford were watching for. It was very cold and the All Clear was a long time coming, and Mr Cuddeford began to talk about his experiences in the previous world war.

He had been in the trenches where there had been a lot of suffering and Mr Cuddeford, especially, had suffered with his legs. Other men had been wounded and others yet had had trench feet, but Mr Cuddeford had varicose veins. In case Anna did not know what varicose veins were, he explained them to her, and exactly how they felt, and what the doctor had thought about them.

Like everything else during the past weeks, Mr Cuddeford's varicose veins were very vivid to Anna, and as he proceeded with his description she found herself feeling slightly sick. How silly, she thought, but the feeling grew alarmingly until suddenly, when Mr Cuddeford said, "So the doctor told me, 'We'll have to cut those out,'" she was overwhelmed by a stifling wave of nausea.

She mumbled, "I'm sorry, but I'm feeling rather ill," and then, amazingly, the sky shifted sideways and the ground lurched up towards her and she was lying in some wet leaves and Mr Cuddeford was blowing his whistle.

"I'm all right," she said, but he told her to lie still

and almost at once the boots of another firewatcher appeared on the ground beside her.

"Passed out," said Mr Cuddeford with a certain satisfaction. "I reckon it's the cold."

"No, really —" said Anna, but suddenly they had a stretcher and were loading her on to it.

"Heave-ho," said Mr Cuddeford, they lifted her up and the stretcher began to move through the darkness. Trees and clouds passed erratically above her and for a while she watched them with pleasure, but as they approached the hotel she suddenly realised what her arrival would look like to Mama and Papa.

"Honestly," she said, "I can walk now."

But the firewatchers had seen no action for months, and there was no stopping them. They carried her through the front door and Mama, who must have seen them from the window, came rushing down the stairs in her dressing-gown.

"Anna!" she shouted so loudly that various doors opened and the Woodpigeon appeared behind her, followed by the two Czech ladies and the Poznanskis.

"Where is she hurted?" cried the Woodpigeon.

"Yes, where?" cried Mama, and Mr Poznanski, amazingly wearing a hairnet, suddenly called from the top of the stairs, "I will a doctor fetch."

"No!" shouted Anna, and Mr Cuddeford at last let her off the stretcher so that she could prove to everyone that she was all right.

"It was only Mr Cuddeford's varicose veins," she explained when her rescuers had left, and it seemed ridiculous even to herself.

Once Mama had got over her fright she thought the

whole incident very funny, but she said, "You never used to be so easily upset."

It was true, thought Anna, and wondered at the change in herself.

The evening classes were the focal point of her world. She now went to three a week and John Cotmore not only helped her with her life drawings but took an interest in the sketches she made out of school.

"These are very good," he once told her after looking at a series of drawings she had made of workmen shifting rubble on a bomb-site, and she felt as though she had suddenly grown wings.

It was disturbing and yet exciting to be absorbed in something of which Mama and Papa knew so little. Neither of them had ever had the slightest wish to draw. Once, while John Cotmore was talking at the café, Anna suddenly understood about abstract painting, which had always been a bit of a joke at home, and her feeling of elation was followed by a twist of something like regret.

How far away I am moving from them, she thought, and Mama must have sensed it too, for although she admired Anna's sketches she became increasingly irritated with the evening classes.

"Always that old art school," she would say. "Surely you don't have to go *again*!" And she would ask Anna about the people she met there and what on earth they found to talk about all that time.

Sometimes Anna tried to explain and Mama would listen, her blue eyes bright with concentration, while Anna expounded some thought she had about drawing.

"Oh yes, I understand that, it's quite simple," Mama would say at the end, and expound it all back to Anna to prove that she had indeed understood.

But Anna always felt that somehow during the explanation some essential ingredient had escaped, so that not only had Mama not *quite* understood, but the thought itself had somehow shrunk in the process and had been returned to her poorer and more meagre than before.

Talking to Papa was more satisfying. There was an initial difficulty to overcome in that she did not know the words for what she wanted to say in German, and Papa did not know them in English. She had to speak in each language in turn, with a bit of French thrown in for good measure, until her meaning came across – more, she sometimes felt, by telepathy than anything else. But then Papa understood completely.

"It's very interesting that you should think this," he would say, and talk about some comparable aspect of writing, or ask her what she thought of some painter she hadn't mentioned.

Both he and Mama were curious about John Cotmore and the students with whom she spent so much of her time.

"What sort of people are they?" asked Papa, and Mama said, "what sort of homes do they come from?"

"I suppose they come from all sorts of homes," said Anna. "Some of them have cockney accents. Harry, I think, is quite grand. I like them because they all draw."

"This John Cotmore," said Mama. "What sort of age is he?"

(Why did she have to call him *this* John Cotmore?)

"I don't know," said Anna. "Quite old – about forty." Later she said hypocritically, "It's a pity you can't meet them all," knowing full well that there was little opportunity for Mama to do so.

However, next time Max was home on leave he suggested coming to the café one day after school. Probably it was Mama's idea, thought Anna, but she did not mind – she had wanted him to come anyway.

At first it was difficult. Max sat there among the cracked coffee cups with his open smile and his uniform, looking like an advertisement for the R.A.F., while the pale young man and Harry discussed the influence of Cubism and the girls gazed at Max admiringly but dumbly. But then Barbara arrived. She was a recent addition to the group – a big blonde girl in her late twenties with a pleasant, placid face. She settled herself next to Max and asked such intelligent questions about the Air Force that he was delighted. Then she said, "We all have great hopes for your sister, you know," which was an exaggeration but made Anna blush with pleasure.

"Isn't that so, John?" asked Barbara, and added to Max, "John here thinks she's absolutely bursting with talent."

John Cotmore agreed that he did think Anna very promising, and Anna sat between them feeling pleased but foolish, exactly, she thought, as she had done when Mama came to talk to the teacher at the end of her first term at primary school.

Max must have felt something of the same sort, for he assumed an elderly air while phrases like "full-time art course" and "help from the Council" fell between them, and only became himself again when the pale young man asked him if flying wasn't very dangerous and Barbara offered him some chips.

"I like your friends," he told Anna later. "Especially that girl Barbara. And John Cotmore seems to think that you can draw."

They were travelling down the escalator to the tube and she glowed inwardly while he considered the evening.

"Do they all know about your background?" he asked. Harry had made a glancing reference to Germany.

"Yes, well, I told John Cotmore first," she said eagerly. "And he said it was wrong to pretend to be someone one wasn't. He said that people who mattered would accept me anyway, so there was no need."

"He's quite a chap," said Max.

"Yes, isn't he!" cried Anna. "Isn't he!"

Max laughed. "I take it you want me to reassure Mama about him. Don't worry, I'll tell her everything she wants to hear."

They had reached the bottom of the escalator and were walking down the steps towards the platform. Anna took his arm. "Did you really like him?" she asked.

"Yes," said Max. "Yes, I did." Then he said, "he's divorced or something, isn't he?"

18

There were air raids again in the spring. People called them "scalded cat" raids because the planes came in low, dropped their bombs and escaped again at top speed. They were not bad raids, but tiresome. Anna had to turn out with the local firewatchers every time the air-raid warning sounded. She still had chilblains left over from the winter and it was agony cramming her feet back into her shoes after the warmth of the bed had made them itch and swell.

However, one night when she was keeping watch with Mr Cuddeford he said to her, "I hear you're artistic."

Anna admitted that she was, and Mr Cuddeford looked pleased and told her that his aunt had just died. At first it was unclear how this could affect Anna, but then it transpired that the aunt had been artistic too – extremely artistic, said Mr Cuddeford – and had left a lot of equipment which no one knew what to do with.

"If there's anything there that you'd like, you're welcome to it," he told Anna, and so, the following week-end, Anna went to look at it.

The equipment was nearly all Victorian, for the aunt who had lived to the age of ninety-three had acquired most of it in her girlhood. There were two easels, several palettes and a clutter of canvases, all enormously heavy and solid. Anna was intoxicated at the sight of it. John Cotmore had been encouraging her for some time to try painting in oils, and here was nearly everything she would need for it.

"I think I could use it all," she said, "if you can spare it."

Mr Cuddeford was only too pleased to be rid of it and even lent her a wheelbarrow in which to carry the things home.

The problem now was where to put them. Anna's and Mama's joint bedroom could not possibly accommodate them.

"Perhaps I could use the garage," said Anna. This was a separate building in the garden at present filled with the old lawnmower and other paraphernalia.

"But you couldn't drag your easel up to the house every time you wanted to paint," said Mama. "And anyway, where would you set it up? You couldn't use oil paints in the lounge."

Then Frau Gruber had an idea. Above the garage was a small room where, in the maharajah's day, the chauffeur must have slept. It was dusty and unheated but empty, and there was even a basin with a tap in one corner.

"No one ever uses this," she said. "You could have it as a studio."

Anna was delighted. She moved in her equipment, wiping at the dust half-heartedly, for it did not bother her, and took a hard look round. All she needed now was some form of heating and some paints and brushes. She dealt with the heating by buying a second-hand paraffin stove, but after this her money was exhausted. It was difficult, nowadays, to save anything out of her wages, for prices had gone up and her wages hadn't.

"Max," she said next time she saw him, "could you lend me eight shillings and ninepence?"

"What for?" he asked, and she explained.

He pulled a ten shilling note from his pocket and handed it to her.

"A gift," he said, "not a loan," and when she thanked him he sighed and said, "I've always wanted to be a patron of the arts."

They were sitting in the buffet at Paddington, waiting for his train to take him back to his R.A.F. station. Nowadays he made frequent trips to London, often calling only briefly on Mama and Papa, and always seemed abstracted. She watched him nervously crumbling a bright yellow object described as a bun on his plate.

"Are you all right?" she said. "Why do you keep getting leave to come to London? Are you up to something?"

"Of course not," he said quickly. "I come to London to see you and Sally and Prue and Clarissa and Peggy . . ."

He had a host of girl friends, but she did not believe that was the reason.

"All right," he said at last, "but don't tell anyone. I'm trying to get on ops."

"You mean you're going to fly on operations?"

Max nodded. "Only I've had half a dozen interviews so far without getting anywhere, so there seemed no point in talking about it."

"It would be an awful risk, wouldn't it?" said Anna.

Max shrugged his shoulders. "No worse than what I'm doing now."

"But Max!" she cried. It seemed madness to her.

"Listen," he said, "I've been an instructor long enough. I'm bored, and when I'm bored I get careless. The other night –" He stopped.

"What?" said Anna.

"Well, I suppose I nearly killed myself. And my pupil." He suddenly noticed the bun in his fingers and dropped it on the plate in disgust. "It was a stupid mistake – something to do with the navigation. I thought I was approaching Manchester . . . Anyway, I almost flew into a Welsh mountain."

"What did you do?" asked Anna.

He grinned. "Turned left," he said. "Very quickly." Seeing her face, he added, "don't worry – I've been very careful ever since. And don't tell Mama."

Anna bought the brushes and paints the next day in her lunch-hour. In the evening at art school she asked John Cotmore's advice on how to use them. He told her how to set out the paints on her palette, how to thin them down when necessary and how to clean her brushes. By the week-end she felt she was ready to start painting.

She had decided, since her first painting might not be very good (though one could never tell), that she would not waste her only unused canvas on it. John Cotmore had explained to her that she could paint over a used canvas and she had chosen one that was not too big. It must have been one of Mr Cuddeford's aunt's last efforts, she thought, for it was only half-finished. It showed a worried-looking stag peering out of a bush, and there had evidently been some intention of having a whole lot more stags leaping about in the background, but either Mr Cuddeford's aunt had become discouraged or old age had gripped her – at any rate this part of the painting was barely sketched in.

Anna picked up a stick of charcoal and, ignoring the stag's reproachful eye, began to map out her design. She planned to paint a group of shelterers. Since the recent air raids many of them had returned to the tube with their bundles and blankets, and the painting was to show not only what they looked like but how they felt. It was to be very sombre and moving. She quickly sketched out the shapes of three women, two sitting and one lying on a bunk above them, so that they just filled the canvas. Then she squeezed some colours on to her palette, and then she stopped.

Were you supposed to thin the colours with turps or linseed oil? She was pretty sure John Cotmore had said turps, but suddenly felt it would be nice to talk to him before actually starting to paint. She flew up to the public telephone, looked up his number in the book, dialled and found herself almost choked with nerves when he replied.

"Hullo?" he said. He sounded half-asleep.

"It's Anna," she said, and he immediately woke up.

"Well, hullo," he said. "What can I do for you?"

"I'm just going to start to paint." She seemed to have less than her usual amount of breath, so she added as briefly as possible, "Is it turps or linseed oil that you should use as a thinner?"

"Turps," he said. "Linseed oil would make it sticky."

There was a pause and then he said, "Is that all you wanted to know?"

"Yes," she said, and then, to make the conversation last longer, "I thought you'd said turps, but I wasn't sure."

"Oh yes, definitely turps."

There was another pause and then he said, "Well, nice to hear your voice."

"And yours," she said with infinite daring.

"Is it?" He laughed. "Well, good luck with the painting."

After this she could think of nothing more to say and had to ring off.

She walked back through the garden and it was quite a long time before she could compose herself enough to start work.

She spent most of the day covering up the stag. It was impossible to see her composition properly as long as he was staring out of the middle of it, and in her hurry to get rid of him she quickly painted in the main shapes as best she could. The following morning she concentrated on improving them, and it was not until the afternoon that she began to have doubts. By this time she had painted everything except the bunk, which would be tedious, but the picture still did not look right. I'll leave it, she thought. I'll look at it again next week-end when I'm fresh.

"How's the painting?" John Cotmore asked her at art school the following week. It was the first time he had ever sought her out to speak to her alone.

"I'm not sure," she said.

496

The following Saturday she was shocked when she saw it again. Now that the paint had dried not only did the colours look unpleasant, but the whole thing had gone flat. Also, due to some chemical process, the stag's eye had reappeared and glowed faintly through one of the shelterers' faces.

Well, at least I know what's wrong with it, she thought. There's no light on it. She painted out the stag's eye and spent the rest of the week-end changing the colours and putting on dabs of light in various places. It was difficult because, as she gradually realised, she was not at all sure where the light would come. At the end the painting looked different but not much better – a speckled effect rather than a flat one – and she was very depressed.

"I'm having a lot of trouble with my painting," she told John Cotmore. "Could I show it to you sometime?"

"Of course," he said. Then he added casually, "It's difficult to talk properly here. Why don't you bring it round to my house? Come and have tea on Saturday."

She was at once thrown into confusion.

Girls didn't go alone to men's houses . . . did they? On the other hand, why not? She looked at him, carelessly perched on one of the stools in the art-room. He seemed quite unconcerned, as though he had suggested something very ordinary.

"All right," she said with a curious sense of excitement, and he wrote down the address for her on a piece of paper. Then he added the telephone number. "In case you change your mind," he said.

In case she changed her mind? Did that mean it wasn't so ordinary after all? Oh, she thought, I wish we'd always stayed in one country, then Mama would have been able to tell me what people do and what they don't do, and I'd know!

She worried about it for the rest of the week. She played with the idea of asking Mama's advice, of ringing up at the last moment and saying no, but all the time she knew with mounting excitement that she would go, that she would not tell Mama, and while part of her mind was still inventing excuses for calling the whole thing off another had already decided what she would wear. On Saturday she told Mama, as she had always known she would, that she was meeting a girl friend from art school, and went.

John Cotmore lived in a quiet road in Hampstead. It was the first warm day of the year and as Anna walked up slowly from the tube station she passed flowering trees, people working in their gardens and open windows everywhere. She was early and had time to make several detours before stopping outside his door. A notice above the bell said Out of Order and after a moment she used the knocker. Nothing happened and panic seized her at the thought that he might have forgotten and gone out – to be replaced by relief and a different kind of panic as the door opened and he appeared.

"Hullo," he said. He was wearing a blue sweater which she had never seen and was holding a spoon in one hand.

"Just getting the tea ready," he said.

She waved her painting, wrapped in brown paper, like a passport and followed him into the house.

It was bright and empty and specks of dust danced in the light of his large untidy living room.

"Sit down," he said, and she sat in a chair with the painting beside her.

Through the door at the end of the room she could see his studio and there were stacks of drawings everywhere.

"I'm working for another exhibition," he said. "These are some of the ones I've done recently."

"Oh!" she said and stood up again to look at them.

They were mostly figures and a few landscapes in pen and wash, all drawn with his usual perceptive precision. It was embarrassing to go through them while he watched, but she really admired them and so found various suitable things to say. There was one in particular, a wash drawing of trees and a wide expanse of sky, which had such a feeling of wetness and spring that she forgot all her careful phrases and cried instead, "It's lovely!"

He was looking at it critically over her shoulder.

"You think I should put it in?"

"Oh yes," she cried. "You must – it's beautiful."

He was standing quite close to her and for a moment she felt his hand on her arm.

"You're very sweet," he said. Then he said, "Must put the kettle on," and disappeared, leaving her alone and slightly light-headed.

She could hear him clattering in the kitchen nearby – he must have found more to do than just the kettle – and after a while she began to look through another stack of drawings on the sofa. These seemed to be mostly unfinished or discarded sketches, but there was one different from the rest. It showed a man working some kind of a machine. The man looked very strong and every bit of the machine, down to the tiniest screw, was carefully drawn and shaded. She was looking at it in surprise when she heard his voice behind her.

"That's not mine," he said. "That's my wife's."

He sounded put out, and she dropped it as though it were red-hot.

"I wondered why it was so different," she said quickly, and to her relief he smiled.

"Yes, amazing – all those nuts and bolts." He replaced the drawing and threw some others on top. "But a lot of precision there. She's very keen on social significance, whereas I –" He gestured towards his own work and Anna nodded sympathetically. It must be awful for a man of his sensitivity to be tied to someone so fond of nuts and bolts.

"It's easier since we live apart," he said. "We each go our own way – quite a friendly arrangement."

She did not know what to answer, and he added, "You probably don't know about such things at your age, but people make mistakes and marriages break up. It's no use blaming anyone."

She nodded again, touched by his generosity.

"Well then," he said, "let's have some tea."

The kitchen was even untidier than the living-room, but he had cleared a space among the clutter of jugs and saucepans and unwashed crockery for a tray laid ready for two. She helped him carry it into the living-room, suddenly less bright, for the sun had moved round a corner, and he lit the gas-fire and moved two chairs up close to it. She watched him as he poured the tea into two cups of different shape and then they sat together in the pale glow of the fire.

"I've been working flat out," he said, and began to tell her about his work, about his frame-maker and the difficulty of finding the right kind of paper in war-time.

Gradually the room grew warmer. She noticed how his sweater wrinkled at the elbows, how his stubby fingers fitted round his cup. A great contentment filled her. His voice droned pleasantly on and she had long ceased to listen to the words when it suddenly stopped.

"What?" she said. She had a feeling that there had been a question.

"What about your painting?" he said.

"My painting!"

She jumped up guiltily to fetch it.

It looked worse than ever as it emerged from its wrapping and there was no mistaking his expression when he saw it.

"It's awful," she said. "I know it's awful, but I thought you could help me with it."

He stared at it in silence. Then he pointed to a misty shape which had appeared in the centre and asked, "What's that?"

"A stag," she said.

"A stag?" he asked, startled.

Suddenly she was filled with rage and shame at having spoiled the afternoon with her awful picture.

"Yes," she cried. "A bloody great stag that was

underneath and keeps coming through, and I don't know how anyone can manage these impossible paints, and I think the only thing is for me to give it all up!"

She glared at him, daring him to laugh, and he put his arm round her shoulders.

"Come on," he said. "It's not as bad as all that. There's nothing wrong with what you were trying to do. Only you've got a lot to learn."

She said nothing.

He dropped the painting onto a chair but left his arm where it was.

"As a matter of fact," he said, "I've been offered another evening's teaching. I thought we might make it a painting class rather than a drawing class – what do you think?"

It flashed across her mind that if there was to be a painting class she could have shown him the picture at school instead of coming to his house, but she pushed the thought aside.

"It would be marvellous," she said faintly.

His face was very close to hers.

"I just wanted to know," he murmured, "what you thought."

And then, as she had always known he would, he put his other arm round her and kissed her gently, slowly and lovingly on the lips.

I'm being kissed! she thought and was horrified to find herself looking past him at the mirror above the fireplace to see what it looked like. Her hands were clasped behind his neck and she hurriedly unclasped them and put them on his shoulders. But at the same time something she had never felt stirred inside her and the happiness which had filled her for so long rose to a climax. This is it, she thought. This was what it was all about. This was the marvellous thing she had always known was going to happen.

After a long time he let her go.

"I'm sorry," he said. "I didn't mean to do that."

She found herself sitting down without quite knowing how she had got there.

"It's all right," she said. She thought of adding, "I don't mind," but it seemed inadequate.

He sat close to her in the other chair and for a long time there was nothing but the room and the fire and her own overwhelming happiness.

"I must talk to you very seriously," he said at last.

She looked at him.

"No, I mean it," he said. "You're very young."

"Eighteen," she said. For some reason she could not stop smiling.

"Eighteen," he nodded. "And you're quite happy. Aren't you?"

"Oh yes," she said. "Of course."

"Well – how shall I put this – I wouldn't want to disturb you."

Why did he have to do all this talking? She would have been quite content just to sit. And what did he mean, disturb her? If only I was English, she thought, I would know what he meant.

"Disturb me?" she said.

"If I made love to you now . . ." He waited. "It would disturb you, wouldn't it?"

But it wouldn't disturb her if he kissed her again, or held her hand. What did he mean, made love to her?

To cover her confusion, she said carelessly, "Not necessarily."

"It wouldn't disturb you if I made love to you?" He seemed very surprised.

An English girl would know, she thought desperately, she would know exactly. Why couldn't she have grown up in one country like everyone else?

He was waiting for her answer, and at last she shrugged her shoulders. "Well," she said in as wordly a voice as she could manage, "it didn't disturb me just now!"

He suddenly sat back in his chair.

"Would you like some more tea?" he asked after a moment.

"No."

But he poured a cup for himself and drank it slowly. Then he stood up and took her hand.

"Come along," he said. "I'm going to send you home."

"Now?"

"Now."

Before she could recover from her surprise, he had fetched her coat and put it on her as though she were a child. Then he handed her her painting, back in its paper bag.

"There," he said. "You'll just get home before the blackout."

"But I don't mind . . ." she said, as he propelled her gently out of the room, ". . . about the blackout . . ."

They had reached the front door and the rest of the words went out of her head as he kissed her again.

"You do understand," he murmured. "It's just that I don't want to disturb you."

She nodded, moved by the warmth of his voice. He seemed to expect something more, so she said, "Thank you."

All the way home on the tube she thought how wonderful he was. For he must have meant . . . But he loved her too much, he respected her too much. To take advantage of me! she thought, and the phrase seemed to her deliciously funny. Slowly she went over the afternoon look by look, word by word, gesture by gesture. He loves me! she thought incredulously. John Cotmore loves me! She felt that it must show on her somehow, that she must look different. She stared at her reflection, racing dimly down the tunnels in the window beside her, and was surprised to find it looking as usual. He loves me, she thought again, I am sitting here on the Bakerloo line and he loves me.

Then she thought, I must never forget this moment. Because even if nothing good ever happens to me again, it will have been worth living just to feel as I do now.

19

It was a poor summer, but Anna hardly noticed. She thought only of John Cotmore and of learning to paint. The painting classes had been introduced on Fridays, so she saw him four evenings a week. At school and even at the café afterwards he treated her just like everyone else – well, of course he had to do that, she thought. But when they found themselves alone in a corridor or walking to the tube he would kiss her as he had kissed her at his studio, dispelling any doubts she might have had about his feelings for her. Afterwards he always reproached himself for his weakness which showed, thought Anna, what a marvellous person he was and made her admire him more than ever. She lived in a daze of happiness from Mondays to Fridays (with a little dip on Wednesdays when there was no evening class) and somehow fought her way through the arid desert of the week-ends until Monday was once more in sight.

I'm in love, she thought. She had often wondered whether this would ever happen to her and it was satisfying that it had. If people only knew, she thought as she parcelled up wool and listed bits of uniform. If I suddenly said to them, I'm in love with my drawing teacher! Then she thought, how corny – Victorian girls were always falling in love with their drawing teachers. But how witty of her to realise that it was corny. And yet, how strange that knowing it was corny made not a bit of difference to the way she felt! She hugged the whole range of complicated new feelings to herself, posting navy wool to helpless old ladies who had particularly stipulated only Air Force blue, and tried a different track. I'm in love, she thought daringly, with a married man!

Fortunately her new emotions did not affect her work at the art school. On the contrary, she seemed to have developed an added perceptiveness and her drawings and even her newly-acquired skills in painting improved almost visibly from week to week.

"You seem to have struck a very happy patch," said Welsh William, and she smiled secretly at the aptness of the phrase.

Even the war was going better at last. The British army had at last won the battle of North Africa, and in August the Russians began to push the Germans back towards their own frontiers. Quite a lot of people thought it might all be over in another year.

Only at home things were worse rather than better. Frau Gruber, who had always tried not to charge too much, had finally had to raise the price for board and lodging by five shillings a week. Anna could just manage this out of her wages, but for Mama and Papa it made solvency suddenly impossible.

In despair Mama asked her new boss for a rise. He was a refugee dress manufacturer with a modest workroom at the back of Oxford Circus. His English was poor and Mama not only typed his letters but corrected them. However, the business brought in very little profit and when she spoke to him about the money he spread his arms wide and said, "I'm sorry, my dear, but more I cannot!"

At first she consoled herself by laughing with Anna at this strange phraseology, but they both knew it was disaster. It meant that, yet again, every new tube of toothpaste, every shoe repair, would cause a major crisis and that, however much she scraped and saved, she would not be able to pay the bills at the end of the week.

"Do you think perhaps Max . . . ?" said Anna, but Mama shouted, "No!"

Max had finally succeeded in getting transferred to operational flying and Mama was worried sick about him. He had persuaded Coastal Command to accept him, arguing that, even though R.A.F. rules forbade him to fly over enemy territory, there was nothing to stop him flying over the sea. So far he was still in training, but soon he would be risking his life three, four, five times a week.

"No," said Mama, "I'm not asking Max for money."

In the end Aunt Louise came to the rescue as usual. She gave Mama twenty pounds, and as the weekly deficit was only a matter of shillings, this would last for many months.

"She really is a good friend," said Mama. She thought it specially touching that Aunt Louise had asked, quite diffidently, whether in return Papa would mind just looking at something the Professor had written. "It would mean so much to him," she said, "to have the views of a great writer."

Papa sighed and said he could not imagine the Professor writing anything, unless it were a medical book.

"Heaven preserve us if it's poetry!" he said, and

Mama said nervously, "Whatever it is, you've got to be nice about it!"

It turned out that the Professor was writing neither poems nor medical books but his memoirs. He was dictating them to his secretary in the country and so far they had produced two chapters between them.

"What are they like?" Anna asked Papa.

Papa shrugged his shoulders.

"He can't write," he said, "but some of it is quite interesting. I didn't know, for instance, that the Minister of Justice under the Weimar republic had stomach ulcers."

Even this did not sound very interesting to Anna.

"What will you do?" she asked.

He pulled a face. "I suppose I'll have to go and talk to him about it."

The Professor was filled with encouragement even by Papa's careful comments. He listened only absently to Papa's advice on keeping sentences short and adjectives to a minimum.

"Wait till you see the next two chapters!" he cried. "About my social life!" Many of his patients in Berlin had been famous and he had gone to all their parties.

"I'm afraid he's going to write a lot of rubbish," said Papa when he got back, but Mama said, "Well, where's the harm in your just looking at it for him?"

The next two chapters must have taken the Professor longer to write, for no more typescript arrived for Papa for some time.

Anna went to the office and to her evening classes and dreamed about John Cotmore. She found it difficult to take an interest in her secretarial work, and once she caused a crisis in the sewing-room when she absent-mindedly put the cutting-out material in front of Miss Potter's place instead of Miss Clinton-Brown's. Miss Potter cut out three pairs of pyjama trousers before she could be stopped, with a total of six right legs and no left ones. When Mrs Riley pointed out her mistake she wept and had to go home to her budgie, and Miss Clinton-Brown was so outraged that she had to appeal to God for patience, with little success.

There was not much to do on the Officers' Clothing side. Fewer ships were being sunk, and the sailors who had often needed to be completely re-equipped only rarely came now. In fact, there seemed hardly enough young men to occupy both Mrs Hammond and Mrs James, and rather than embarrass them with their joint attentions they came to a tacit agreement to take it in turns to help them. This meant that both had more time on their hands. Mrs Hammond used it to dictate more letters or to chat with the old ladies in the sewing-room, but Mrs James seemed simply to shrink. She sat in her makeshift office, staring at the piles of dead men's clothing with her huge, empty eyes, and sometimes did not even notice Anna when she came in with a message or a cup of tea.

"I'm worried about her," said Mrs Hammond, but as soon as a young man in need appeared Mrs James came back to life.

One day Anna was taking down some notes in Mrs Hammond's office. Mrs Hammond had just finished supplying a Flight Lieutenant who had lost his possessions in an air raid. He had been particularly grateful and Mrs Hammond wanted to write to his commanding officer, to offer help to anyone else who might need it. However, she had hardly begun to dictate the letter when the door opened and Mrs James appeared. She looked more grey and gaunt than ever and, ignoring Anna, she looked straight at Mrs Hammond.

"I don't want to make a fuss," she said, "but it was my turn to look after that young man."

"But you looked after the Pilot Officer this morning," said Mrs Hammond, surprised.

Mrs James just stood there, staring at her with her great eyes, and Mrs Hammond motioned to Anna to go back into the sewing-room. As she went out Mrs James spoke again.

"The Pilot Officer only wanted a cap. He didn't count."

The old ladies had stopped machining at Mrs James's appearance.

"She strode past those pyjamas just like Lady Macbeth," declared Mrs Riley.

"Looking ever so poorly," said Miss Potter, and Miss Clinton-Brown murmured, "Such an odd way to behave."

They all strained their ears for sounds from the office but there was nothing to be heard above a low mumble of voices. Anna had just decided to put on the kettle for tea when one of the voices rose to a higher pitch.

"It's not fair!" cried Mrs James. "I can't work with someone who isn't fair!"

The door suddenly opened and Mrs James ran out.

"Especially as the whole thing was my idea in the first place!" she shouted and made for the storage room with Mrs Hammond in pursuit. Mrs Hammond tried to close the door behind her but missed, and Anna could see Mrs James stop short at the sight of the uniforms and begin to finger them in the semi-darkness.

"I have to explain to you," she said in a voice which was both reasonable and somehow alarming, "that far more young men have now died than remain alive. That's why we have all these clothes which nobody wants."

Mrs Hammond said something like "no" or "nonsense", but Mrs James swept her aside.

"And since there are so few young men left," she said in the same queer voice, "they have to be allocated very fairly. And the only fair way is for me to look after twice as many as you."

Mrs Hammond had been making vaguely soothing noises, but this last sentence so astonished her that she cried, "For heaven's sake, why?"

Mrs James turned and Anna caught a glimpse of her face which looked quite mad.

"Well, it's obvious, isn't it?" she said. "After all you only lost one son, but I lost two."

As Mrs Hammond stared at her, she added matter of factly, "I knew you wouldn't understand. There is no point in our continuing together."

Afterwards Mrs Hammond told Anna that Mrs James was suffering from strain and that she hoped to sort things out with her when she was feeling calmer. But Mrs James never re-appeared in the office. A few days later the pug-faced man arrived with a letter explaining that in future Mrs James would run the Officers' Clothing scheme by herself on different premises.

Since it had, indeed, been her idea, there was nothing anyone could do. He loaded up all the uniforms, shoes, handkerchiefs and shirts, the paperbacks and the odd golf-clubs and the writing cases which no one had known what to do with, and drove away, leaving Mrs Hammond alone in the empty store-room.

Many weeks later she heard that Mrs James had become too ill to work and that her scheme had been taken over by a charitable organisation.

"What made her suddenly break down after all this time?" wondered Anna.

"Four years of war," said Mrs Hammond. "And the news being better."

When Anna looked at her without understanding she said impatiently, "The thought of peace – when there's no longer any point."

Without the Officers' Clothing scheme, the place was very quiet. For a while Mrs Hammond continued to come in every day, as though to prove that it didn't matter, but there really was not much for her to do and gradually she stayed away once, twice and finally three or four times a week. The days grew long and dull again, and Anna found them hard to get through.

Only nine o'clock, she would think when she arrived in the morning. How could she break up those endless, pointless hours which stretched before her until she could go to her art class? Her lunch hour was the only bright spot and she could hardly wait for the old ladies to pack up their work and go, so as to get out of the place herself.

When the weather was wet she sat in the Lyons tea-shop, drawing everyone in sight, but when it was dry she would eat very quickly and then wander about the streets. She discovered some stables at the back of the Army and Navy stores where the mules that pulled the war-time delivery carts were quartered and spent several weeks trying to draw their gloomy, strangely proportioned faces. Once she saw some girls in Air Force uniform struggling with a barrage balloon in Vincent Square and drew them too. Sometimes she found nothing, or the drawings did not come out as she wanted, and then she returned to her typewriter guilty and depressed, and the afternoons seemed longer than ever.

Wednesdays were her worst days because there was not even an art class at the end of them and she only survived them by making small purchases – a pencil with a pre-war coat of yellow paint from a secret store she had discovered in a shop in Victoria Street, an ounce of unrationed sherbet powder to eat surreptitiously during the afternoon, a packet of saccharine for John Cotmore who liked his tea very sweet and found saccharine hard to get. Just having this in her pocket made her feel better since it was proof that she would be seeing him again soon.

One Wednesday when she came home she met Aunt Louise on the doorstep. She was saying good-bye to Mama and Papa and seemed in high spirits.

"I am sure," she was saying, "that we shall all be very happy with this arrangement."

Then she saw Anna who was wearing her old school coat over an ancient skirt and sweater because Wednesday was such an awful day that it wasn't worth wearing anything better.

"Well, hullo," she said, and her eyebrows rose at the sight of the dreadful clothes. Then she turned back to Mama. "It may help Anna as well," she said.

"What arrangement?" asked Anna after Aunt Louise had climbed into her big blue car and driven away.

"Louise has asked me to revise Sam's memoirs," said Papa.

"They want to give us another twenty pounds," said Mama.

Anna looked from one to the other.

"Are you going to do it?" she asked.

Papa said carefully, "I said I'd look at them."

At supper that evening Papa was very quiet. To while away the time between the main course – turnip pie – and the pudding, Mama was trying to do *The Times* crossword. Miss Thwaites had introduced her to this, and not only was Mama very good at it but it also made her feel very English. She read out clues, announced triumphant solutions and every so often asked for advice, which Anna gave her, until she noticed how isolated this made Papa.

"How are the Professor's memoirs?" she asked in German.

He raised his eyes to heaven. "Unbelievable," he said.

Mama at once came out of her crossword.

"But you're going to revise them!" she cried.

At that moment the waitress arrived with the pudding and Papa said, "Let's discuss it upstairs."

Afterwards, in his room, he leafed through the Professor's latest efforts.

"It's incredibly bad," he said. "Listen to this: "He had piercing eyes in a face framed by an ample grey beard." That's Hauptmann the playwright."

"Well, it's not so bad," said Mama.

"Wait!" cried Papa. "This is Marlene Dietrich." He turned a page and read, 'She had piercing eyes in a face framed by corn-coloured locks,' and again –" He waved Mama into silence – "'I was surprised by the piercing eyes in the face framed by a small moustache.' The last one is Einstein, and I can understand Sam being surprised. I should think Einstein would be surprised as well, seeing where his moustache had got to."

"Well, of course he's not used –" began Mama, but Anna interrupted her.

"Why does the Professor want you to revise this stuff?" she cried. "Surely he must know that no one would ever publish it!"

"You don't know anything about it," said Mama crossly. "One of his patients is a publisher and Louise says he's very interested. He's even suggested a translator."

"Gossip writing," said Papa. "It seems there's a market for it."

Anna suddenly remembered the piece Papa had read out at the International Writers' Club long ago, where each word had been exactly right, and how moved she had been and how everyone had clapped.

"I don't think you should have anything to do with

it!" she cried. "I think it's disgusting – someone who can write like you and this . . . this horrible rubbish. I think you should simply refuse!"

"Oh," cried Mama, "and what would you suggest I tell Louise? That we're grateful for all her help in the past, that no doubt we'll need it again, but that Papa refuses to do the one thing she's ever asked of us in return?"

"No, of course not!" cried Anna. "But there must be another way!"

"I'd be glad to hear what it is," said Mama.

Anna tried to think of one.

"Well, there must be something you can do," she said at last and added, to Mama's rage, "it's just a matter of using a little tact."

Mama exploded and it was some time before Papa could cut through the stream of angry words to say that it really wasn't Anna's problem and that it would be best if he and Mama discussed it alone.

Anna swept out and locked herself in the bathroom. For once the water was hot and she soaked herself in a huge bath, glaring defiantly at the line four inches from the bottom which denoted the maximum depth allowed in war-time. I don't care, she thought, but it did not make her feel any better.

Later in their joint bedroom Mama explained in a careful voice that she and Papa had agreed on a compromise. Papa would correct the Professor's worst excesses, but any further changes should be made by the publisher if and when the memoirs were translated into English.

"I see," said Anna in an equally careful voice, and

pretended almost at once to fall asleep. As she lay awake in the close, dark room she could hear Mama crying quietly a few feet away.

"Mama . . ." she said, overwhelmed by pity. But Mama did not hear and she found herself suddenly filled with an equally strong desire not to listen to the sounds from the other bed, not to be involved, to be somewhere else.

John, she thought. The previous evening at art school John Cotmore had shown her sketch book to Barbara. "Talented little thing, isn't she?" he had said, and later, when they were walking to the tube, he had kissed her secretly behind a pillar. She wished she could be with him now, that she could always be with him.

If I gave myself to him, she thought, and part of her felt full of love and daring while another giggled at the novelettishness of the phrase. But how did one set about it? She imagined herself saying something like "I am yours." But then? Suppose he looked embarrassed, or just not very keen? And even if he said exactly the right thing like "My darling," or "I love you," – how did one manage the rest? And where would they do it? she suddenly thought in alarm. She had never seen his bedroom, but if it was anything like the kitchen . . .

The sounds from the other bed had stopped. Mama must be asleep.

I'll make it up with her in the morning, thought Anna. And as she herself drifted off into sleep, she wished that Papa could suddenly earn a huge sum of money, that they didn't have to be grateful to the Rosenbergs, and that everything were quite, quite different.

518

20

"I think it's time you did something," John Cotmore said to Anna a few weeks later at art school. "I mean something more than drawing from the model or filling up sketch books." He was sitting on the edge of the model's throne with Welsh William and Barbara who nodded in agreement.

"What sort of thing?"

He gestured vaguely. "Something of your own. Illustrate a book – paint a wall – anything."

"A wall!" The idea at once appealed to her. But where would one find one?

"I did a mural in a school once," said Barbara. "It was great fun. All you need is some oil-bound distemper and a few large brushes."

"Not so many walls left, though," said Welsh William.

1944 had begun, ominously, with the heaviest air raids in years.

John Cotmore waved him aside. "All the more reason for painting them," he said.

The idea of the wall stuck in Anna's mind and she found herself examining any large vertical surface with a view to decorating it. She thought briefly about the disused ward where the officers' clothing had been stored, but dismissed it. It was dark and no one would ever see it – there would be no point.

There was nothing in the hotel either, but then, one day, she found just the right place. It was pouring with rain and, rather than get soaked walking to the Lyons tea-shop which was some distance away, she decided to have lunch in a café in Victoria Street. The tables were packed with steaming bodies and she ordered Russian steak (mince patriotically renamed from the Vienna steak of pre-war days) with a pleasant sense of extravagance.

While she was waiting for it to arrive she looked round and suddenly realised that the café was exactly what she had been looking for. It consisted of several rooms knocked into one and the result was an irregularly shaped space bounded by a great many walls at different angles. They were all painted pale cream and there was absolutely nothing on them except a few mirrors. Surreptitiously she counted them. Nine. Nine walls all crying out to be painted! She eyed them greedily all through the Russian steak and the eggless, sugarless trifle that followed it. I could really do something here, she thought.

She ate at the café again the following lunch-time, bankrupting herself for the rest of the week, and thought about it for several more days before she summoned up enough courage to do anything about it. Finally, one evening after she had finished work she walked past it twice, peered through the windows and at last went in.

"We're closed," said a stocky man who was scattering knives and forks over the empty tables.

"Oh, I haven't come for a meal," said Anna.

"What then?"

She produced the speech she had been rehearsing for three days. "I'm a painter," she said, "and I specialise in murals. I wondered if you'd like me to decorate your restaurant."

Before the stocky man could answer, a voice called out from the basement.

"Albert," it cried. "Who you talkin' to?"

"Little girl," Albert called back. "Wants to do some paintin'."

"What sort o' paintin'?" shouted the voice.

"Yeah, what sort o' paintin'?" said Albert.

"Decorations," said Anna as grandly as she could manage. "Pictures. On your walls."

"Pitchers," shouted Albert just as the owner of the voice emerged from the basement, saying, "I'eard."

It was a very large woman with a pale face and small, dark eyes like a hedgehog's, and she was carrying a trayful of glasses. She put the tray down on a table and looked from Anna to the walls and back again.

"What wouldyer paint on 'em then?" she asked.

Anna was prepared for this.

"I thought as it's called the Victoria restaurant," she said, "it might be nice to have some Victorian scenes. Men in top-hats, children playing with hoops – that sort of thing."

"Bit grand, init?" said Albert.

"Dunno – might brighten it up at that," said the large woman. "If it was done nice." She looked at Anna. "You don't seem like you was very old."

Anna by-passed this neatly. "Well, of course I'd let you see sketches," she said. "I'd do it all on paper first, so you could see what it would look like."

"Sketches," said the woman. "That'd be nice. Don't you think that'd be nice, Albert?"

Albert looked doubtful and Anna wanted to kill him. He searched his mind for objections and finally came up with, "What about me mirrors? I'm not takin' down none o' me mirrors."

"Young lady'd paint round 'em, wouldn't you, dear?" said the woman trustingly.

Anna had had no such intention.

"Well –" she said.

"He couldn't take 'em down," said the woman. "I mean, Albert paid good money for them mirrors, din you, Albert? He couldn't just waste 'em."

Nine walls, thought Anna. What did a few mirrors matter?

"All right," she said and added, to save her dignity, "I'll incorporate them in the design."

"That'd be nice," said the woman. "Wouldnit, Albert?"

Then they both stood looking at Anna in silence.

Was it settled? She decided to assume that it was.

"Good," she said as carelessly as she could. "I'll come and measure up the walls this time tomorrow."

No one objected.

"See you then," she said, and managed somehow to walk out of the place as though nothing special had happened.

"I'm going to decorate a restaurant!" she shouted triumphantly as soon as she saw John Cotmore, and he gave her a quantity of advice which ended with kissing her behind the paint cupboard.

It was not until she got home that she realised that she had completely forgotten to mention any payment for her work.

* * *

She spent the next three weeks making sketches. A book from the library gave her all the information she needed about Victorian dress, and she worked every week-end and often in the evenings, even giving up some of her life-classes so as to get the drawings done.

The mirrors were not nearly such a nuisance as she had expected. They were all different shapes and sizes, and she found that she could make them stand for some large object which she then surrounded with people. An upright mirror made the main body of a puppet theatre, with Punch and Judy painted at the top of it and children staring up from both sides. A long thin one, with a few reeds painted round about, suggested a lake. As she finished the design for each wall, she pinned it up in her room above the garage, and both Mama and Papa came to admire them.

At last she rolled them all up together and submitted them to her patrons, spreading them over half the tables in the café. They stared at them in silence. At last the woman said, "They're quite nice. Don't you think so, Albert?"

Albert looked gloomily at the drawings and at his pure cream walls.

"What's that, then?" he said, pointing to the puppet theatre.

"That's your mirror," said Anna. "I'm just going to paint these things round it."

Albert checked with the wall.

"Yeah," he said.

"It's the centre of the design," she explained.

Albert seemed pleased. "Yeah," he said. "It is, init?"

"I think it's ever so nice," said his wife, warming to it.

Albert made up his mind.

"Yeah," he said. "All right then. You can do the place up."

Anna had been wondering how to get round to the subject of money, but he forestalled her.

"How much was you thinkin' of askin'?" he said, and panicked her into coming out with the first sum she could think of.

"Fifteen pounds," she said and at once cursed herself for ruining everything with her excessive demands, but Albert remained calm.

"Yeah," he said. "All right."

After this Anna became frantically busy. The café closed for the week-end after lunch on Saturday, and she was there, waiting for the last customer to leave, from two o'clock onwards. Albert had provided a step-ladder, and she spent the first two week-ends drawing her designs all over the walls in chalk. There was no heating and spring was late, so she wore two pairs of socks and several sweaters which gradually became covered in chalk dust as she drew, climbed down to view her work from a distance and climbed back again to change it.

It was strange to spend so many hours alone, with her ideas gradually becoming visible around her, and by the end of the second Sunday she was almost giddy with it.

She had drawn in the last shape to her satisfaction and sat exhausted in the middle of the floor. The white outlines of the figures were everywhere, clustered round the puppet theatre, watching the ducks on the lake and moving round the room in a cheerful procession of parasoled ladies, gentlemen on penny-farthings and children with hoops and tops. Some appeared twice over as they were reflected in the mirrors on opposite walls, and the effect was strangely dreamlike.

It looks just as I hoped it would look, she thought, and a great joy welled up in her, but she quickly subdued it to stare at each wall severely in turn, trying to catch it out in some fault of composition or proportion.

She was so absorbed that she hardly noticed the sound of knocking until it became insistent, and she realised with a shock that there was someone at the door.

As long as it isn't Albert who's changed his mind, she thought, and went to open it, but it was not Albert – it was Max in his R.A.F. uniform, radiating warmth and energy.

"Well!" he said, looking round. "You seem to have found your *ambience*."

"What's an *ambience*?" she asked, and he grinned.

"What you've found."

She showed him round and he looked at all the walls and then at her sketches, full of enthusiasm and intelligence. But the parts he liked were not always the best and she was relieved to find that in this one thing, at least, her judgment was better than his.

"I didn't know you were coming up," she said at last. "Have you been home?"

He nodded. "I've got five days' leave. Finished my course."

That meant he would be posted to an operational squadron.

"Already," she said, as lightly as possible.

"Yes," he said, "and Mama and Papa both said 'already' in exactly the same always-keep-a-lamp-in-the-window voice as you. I'm only doing what thousands of others are doing."

"Oh, I know," said Anna.

"I'm going to live all my life in this country," said Max. "I have to take the same risks as everyone else."

"Everyone else," said Anna, "does not fly on operations."

Max was unmoved. "People like me do," he said.

She began to tidy up, rolling up her drawings and pushing tables and chairs back into place.

"How did you find Mama and Papa?" she asked.

He did not answer at once. Then he said, "They're not too good, are they?"

She shook her head. "Seeing them every day – one gets used to it."

Max pulled out one of the chairs she had just tidied away and sat on it.

"What worries me," he said, "is that I can't think of anything that would help even if one could arrange it. I mean, money would help, of course. But I still don't know how they'd live the rest of their lives."

"I've never thought beyond the money," said Anna.

There was a chalk mark at the side of the puppet theatre which bothered her and she wiped it off with her sleeve.

"Perhaps after the war . . ." she said vaguely.

"After the war," said Max, "if there's anything left in Germany to print books with, and if there are any people left who would want to read them, they'll probably re-publish Papa's works – in time. But he still wouldn't want to live there."

"No," said Anna. It would be impossible, after all that had happened. She had a vision of Mama and Papa floating in a kind of limbo. "It's funny," she said. "When I was small I always used to feel so safe with them. I remember I used to think that as long as I was with them I'd never feel like a refugee. Do you remember Mama in Paris? She was marvellous."

"Well, she still is," said Max. "She does everything, she keeps everything going – only the strain is making her difficult to live with." He looked round at the chalk figures promenading all over the walls. "I'm so glad about all this," he said, "and about the whole art school thing. You belong here now, just as I do. But Mama and Papa . . ."

She watched him make the face, half-smiling and half-regretful, which he always made when something was difficult, and suddenly remembered the countless times they had talked like this, sharing the worries of their disrupted childhood in four different countries.

"Oh, Max!" she cried, throwing her arms about him. "For God's sake take care of yourself!"

"There, there," he said, patting her back – gingerly, because of the chalk on her clothes. "Nothing is going to happen to me." And as she still clung to him, he added, "After all, if it did, Mama would never forgive me!"

It took Anna five more week-ends to finish painting her murals. On Barbara's advice, she used white distemper which she mixed with powder paints to get the colours she wanted. She stirred them up together in an ever-expanding collection of old tins and pots and it was a clammy, exhausting job – but she loved it. The murals continued to look as she had hoped, and as she finished the walls one after another and stood staring at them, covered in paint now as well as chalk dust, the same great joy welled up in her as on the day she had finished the drawings. Sometimes when she thought about them at home she imagined some frightful flaw which she had overlooked, and had to rush to the café early next day and peer through the windows to reassure herself. But they were always all right, and the customers as well as Albert and his wife seemed pleased.

Max got his posting and wrote after some time that he had now flown several operations and that nothing ever happened on them. "And we always get egg and bacon on our return," he said, "so it's a great improvement in every way."

No one was sure whether to believe this, but Mama could not bear to consider any other possibility and insisted that it must be true.

Finally, in May, Anna finished her murals. Albert paid her the fifteen pounds, and since she was now richer than ever before in her life, she decided to invite first Mama and Papa and then her friends from the art school to the café for a meal. Mama and Papa were both full of admiration and Anna sat happily between them in a new sweater, peering at her work through half-closed eyes and wondering only occasionally whether some hand might not have been better drawn or whether a figure on one wall might not have looked better on another.

"But it's so professional!" cried Mama, and Papa said, "It's delightful!"

She got a great kick out of the astonished way they looked at her, and out of paying the bill at the end.

But it was the art school outing that really mattered. Anna had hardly been to evening classes while she was working on her murals – there had not been time – but now she was excited at the prospect of seeing John Cotmore again. He'll have missed me, she thought. It seemed to her suddenly that the purpose of decorating the café had been solely to show it to him, and that when he had seen it and spent a whole evening with her something must change, that something extraordinary and quite unprecedented must happen between them. He'll realise that I'm grown-up, she thought, more of an equal, and then he'll . . . She was not sure herself what he would do. But there would be some sign, some way of committing himself, of showing her that from now on things between them would be quite different.

She was in a state of feverish expectancy by the time he arrived. Hiding behind the menu in a corner, she watched him stand for a moment inside the door and saw the sudden concentration in his face as he looked at her murals. He examined each wall in turn, walking slowly round and twice retracing his steps. At last he saw her and sat down beside her.

"Well," he said, "you *have* grown up!"

If she'd chosen the words for him she couldn't have done it better.

"I hoped you'd like it," she said, and then listened in happy confusion while he praised the composition, her drawing and the subtlety of the colours.

"I expected something good," he said, "but this is a surprise."

She could do nothing but sit and smile and watch him as he looked at her work again, and then from her work back to her.

"So this is what you were doing," he said, "instead of coming to art school!"

It was all happening just as she had hoped. She nodded and smiled and saw his eyes look back at her with a new seriousness . . . And then the others were upon them.

"It's enchanting!" cried Harry from the door. "Don't you think it's enchanting, John?"

He was followed by Welsh William who settled himself beside her. "I was afraid it would be ladies in crinolines," he said. "You know, standing about with no feet, the way they used to do on chocolate boxes. How can I eat my food, I asked myself, when it's been paid for by ladies in crinolines with no feet? But now –" he gestured respectfully towards the wall – "my conscience is clear."

"By Winterhalter out of Berthe Morrisot," said Barbara firmly, and Anna blushed with pleasure.

It seemed like the pleasantest evening she had ever spent. Even the food – dried egg omelette, Spam fritters, vegetable pie – seemed to her delicious. She basked in her friends' praises and listened to their news – Barbara had a new job and Welsh William had sold a drawing but was soon to be called up. She ordered food and ate it and glanced surreptitiously at her murals and watched John Cotmore's face, and all the time her excitement grew because she knew that something more was going to happen, that the best part of the evening was still to come.

At last all the food had been eaten and all the coffee had been drunk. Albert had presented her with the bill and she had paid it with a flourish, and they all stood outside the café in the early evening light.

"Well –" said John Cotmore.

Anna waited.

"Thank you for a lovely evening," he said. "And thank you for painting such good murals." He took her hand and suddenly turned to Harry. "I think one's allowed to kiss a favourite student, isn't one?" And before she had time to think he had kissed her formally on the cheek. "Congratulations," he said. "May you paint many more murals as successful as these."

Then he turned, called out something that could have been either "good night" or "goodbye", and walked away in the direction of Westminister, with Harry and Barbara following.

Anna could not believe that it had happened. She stood there with the smile still on her face, her hand still ready to take his arm, and the dust of Victoria blowing about her feet.

"Went off a bit sharpish, didn't he?" said Welsh William, and they both watched his figure rapidly diminish as it hared off down the street.

"Well," said Welsh William at last, "coming?"

She roused herself and, still in a daze, walked with him to the tube. He talked all the way, but she did not hear a word. She could think only of John Cotmore. What on earth had happened? Why had he kissed her like that and rushed away? And was it "good night" that he had called out or "goodbye"?

21

During the next few weeks Anna's mood varied between happiness and profound depression, and the war seemed to echo her state of mind.

In June the Second Front finally became a reality. This was the landing of British and American troops in the North of France, the first step in liberating the countries overrun by the Nazis four years before. To Anna, remembering the fearful summer of 1940, this was far more exciting than any victories in Africa or Russia, and once it became clear that the Allies were firmly established she began to think, with cautious amazement, that the end of the war might really be in sight.

However, hardly had everyone's spirits risen before they were dashed again by the arrival of the flying bombs. They were Hitler's new secret weapon – pilotless planes sent across the Channel with a large charge of explosive. When they ran out of fuel they fell to the ground and blew up everything in the vicinity. Most of them were primed to fall on London.

The first time Anna saw one neither she nor Mr Cuddeford could think what it was. They heard a puttering sound and saw a dark, rounded object with flames spurting from its tail move slowly across the sky. Suddenly it disappeared, the puttering had stopped, and a moment later there was a very loud explosion.

"It must have been a plane," said Anna, but Mr Cuddeford shook his head.

"None that I've ever seen," he said.

Next day, after an air-raid warning that lasted till dawn, the explanation was in all the papers.

At first only a few flying bombs came over and people laughed at them, telling each other how silly they looked bumbling along, and inventing funny names for them like buzz-bombs or doodle-bugs. But soon they began to arrive in large numbers both by day and by night. It was unnerving, as you went about your business, to listen to the sound of the engines which might cut out at any moment. You prayed for the buzz-bombs to keep going, but felt guilty while you did so because you knew they would only fall on someone else. And the fact that the war might soon be over made everyone wish, quite desperately, to stay alive.

People again began to leave London. The familiar crocodiles of children with labels reappeared at the railway stations, and every day there was new bomb damage among the old. Since the bombs came over all the time it was useless to go to a shelter, and those who remained in London simply dived into the nearest doorway or under the nearest piece of furniture when they heard a flying bomb cut out, as it seemed, immediately above their heads. Anna was constantly amazed by the agility of the old ladies. One moment they would be sitting at their machines, working away, and the next they would all be under the table, with only Miss Potter's primly overalled bottom sticking out at one side and Miss Clinton-Brown's size eight feet at the other. Mrs Riley, perhaps as a result of her early acrobatic training, always got the whole of herself tucked under.

Anna herself was not as frightened as she had been during the blitz and sometimes almost welcomed the drama of the flying bombs as a distraction from her other worries. John Cotmore had become inexplicably remote since the dinner at her restaurant and she felt as though the rug had been pulled from under her life. Then she thought about Max flying on operations, she did not know how many times a week, and it seemed to her, illogically, that by being in danger herself she must be diverting some of the danger which threatened him.

Mama was even more superstitious. She became meticulous in all her dealings, as though to satisfy some higher agency that might be watching her, and once Anna caught her, after years of only paying her bus fares when they were demanded of her, actually pressing the money into the conductress's hand. When she caught Anna's eye she said, "I don't think one should take any chances," and added defiantly, "with Max flying and everything!"

At the same time, strangely enough, Mama could not bear to admit that Max was in any danger and became furious with Papa for saying that he was.

"But they shoot at him!" said Papa, and Mama cried, "Not at him specially! And anyway, they'd never hit Max!"

The evening classes continued in spite of the flying bombs and Anna still lived from each one to the next, but they usually left her depressed and bewildered. Nothing was the same. She only spoke to John Cotmore when he formally discussed her work. Because of the bombs everyone hurried home immediately afterwards and there was only one occasion when they went to a café. This was when Welsh William was called up. He had come to show off his soldier's uniform and they plied him with talk and coffee as in the old days, but he looked forlorn and much too young to go to war, and on the whole everyone was relieved when the evening was over.

What had happened to everything? wondered Anna. Only a short time ago it had seemed so promising – the war nearly at an end, her work, and . . . and everything, she thought, unwilling to give even the vaguest shape to whatever she had expected from John Cotmore. And now it was like being back in the blitz and life seemed empty. When, at the end of July, the art school closed for the summer holidays, it seemed the end of an era.

She got a week's leave from Mrs Hammond and spent it in the country with the Rosenbergs. The Professor had abandoned his memoirs after the sixth chapter (so all that emotion had been for nothing, thought Anna) and was now deeply engrossed in growing vegetables for food. Aunt Louise carried on her usual running battle with the maids, and Anna spent much of her time painting a portrait of Fraulein Pimke in a corner of her kitchen. When she wasn't painting she helped with the vegetables and felt herself grow brown and healthy in the process.

Only at night was there nothing to do, and then she thought about John Cotmore. She re-lived her visit to his house, and the different times when he had put his arm round her, or kissed her, or said something affectionate. She even counted the number of times he had kissed her. There were eleven, not including the formal peck after dinner at her restaurant. You surely wouldn't kiss a person eleven times, she argued hopefully, unless you meant it? But what about his strange behaviour during the past weeks? That must be his conscience, she decided – because of his wife.

As she was dropping off to sleep she imagined the most unlikely situations in which he would be driven to declare his love for her. Sometimes it was when she had done a brilliant drawing in the life class. Sometimes he found her trapped under the rubble of a flying bomb explosion, in pain but terribly brave and of course quite unmarked. Other times it was she who saved him by her courage and cheerfulness when they were buried together under the wreckage of the art school. Part of her despised herself for these imaginings, but another part found them a great comfort.

On her return to London she found a message from Barbara suggesting a meeting, and snatched at the chance at least to talk about him. They ate a modest meal at Lyons Corner House while Anna held forth about his talents and his virtues, and Barbara nodded and agreed, with her pleasant, placid smile. This made Anna feel much better, and they met twice more, once to go to a film and once to a concert. But then Barbara became too busy for further meetings, and Anna was left more lonely than ever.

One day when she was sitting bored at her typewriter Harry rang up. He had been given a batch of tickets for a concert – Beethoven and Mozart, very

traditional, he said – and wondered if she'd like to
go.

"Bring a friend," he said. "I've asked everyone I can
think of and I've still got plenty of tickets left."

Everyone Harry could think of must include John
Cotmore, thought Anna, and her lethargy fell away
like an old skin.

"I'd love to come!" she cried, surprising him with
her enthusiasm, and at once made plans for what
she would wear, how she would look, and what she
would say.

"I'll be out tomorrow night," she announced to
Mama and Papa at supper. "I'm going to a concert."

"Who with?" asked Mama.

Anna frowned at Mama's curiosity. "No one special," she said. "Just some people from the art school.
There's a whole lot of tickets, but it's mostly Beethoven
and some of them think that's rather old-fashioned, so
not very many may turn up."

Frau Gruber came to clear away the plates.

"No appetite today?" she asked Papa who had
left most of his vegetable pie, and he smiled and
shook his head.

"Beethoven," he said, and Anna noticed that he
looked pale. "What are they playing?"

She told him – the Seventh Symphony and something else that she could not remember, and he nodded.

Mama began to say something about the food, but
Papa interrupted her.

"I should like," he said, "to come with you."

"To the concert?" cried Anna.

It was impossible.

538

"They're not proper seats," she said quickly. "Not like the ones you used to have in Berlin. These are right up in the gallery, just steps really, that you sit on – only students use them."

Papa nodded. "Nevertheless," he said, "I should like very much to come."

She stared at him, horrified.

"Do you really want to go?" asked Mama. "It does sound a bit spartan."

Anna waited hopefully, but Papa shook his head.

"The seats are unimportant," he said. "I should like to hear the music."

There was no answer to this.

After searching for one in vain, Anna mumbled some sort of agreement and spent the rest of the meal in deepest gloom. The first time in weeks that she might see John Cotmore, and she was going to be stuck with Papa! During her empty day at the office she had half-fantasised, half-formulated a plan to get him alone, perhaps even to ask him what was wrong, and then perhaps he would explain and he might say . . . But now Papa had made all that impossible.

She tried to believe, against all previous experience, that he might change his mind, but when she arrived at the theatre the following evening Papa was already there. He was looking at a poster in the foyer and in his shabby, foreign-looking coat he had a sad air which filled her with a mixture of love and irritation.

"Hullo," she said, but before she could say any more her heart leapt at the sight of John Cotmore hurrying past to the gallery entrance. So he had come!

She bustled Papa along to Harry who had the tickets,

and could hardly contain her impatience while Harry declared his delight at meeting Papa and Papa replied in his halting English. By the time they reached the gallery entrance John Cotmore had long disappeared. Papa embarked cheerfully on the long climb to the top, but it was a slow business and several student, from the art school passed them on the way. They'll all sit round John, thought Anna, for gallery seats were not numbered and you sat where you liked.

Sure enough, when she and Papa emerged from the stairs into the sloping space below the roof of the theatre, she discovered John Cotmore surrounded. A whiskered man whom she recognised as another art teacher was on one side of him, Barbara was on the other, and there were students all around. She stood looking at them glumly while Papa sniffed the air beside her.

"Marvellous!" he said. "The smell! It's years since I've been in a theatre, but it never changes."

He suddenly darted forward.

"Shall we sit here?" he said, indicating an empty space near the gangway. "Or perhaps," he added, "you would rather sit with your friends?"

Anna looked gloomily at the crowd round John Cotmore.

"This will do perfectly well," she said.

She heard only little of the concert.

It began with some over-symmetrical early Mozart which left her mind free for other thoughts. Perhaps I'll talk to him in the interval, she thought. But when the lights brightened John Cotmore did not move from his seat and the crowd of students remained. Only

Barbara came over to greet her and to be introduced to Papa. They had quite a long conversation and Anna felt better when Barbara said in her usual warm way, "Anna, I love your father – I do hope you'll let me meet him again."

Perhaps she would tell John Cotmore, and then he, too, would want to meet Papa – perhaps when the concert was over . . .

"Charming," said Papa, watching Barbara go, "Absolutely charming."

Seeing his clever, responsive face, Anna felt suddenly ashamed at having thought of him only in terms of usefulness. She moved closer to him on the hard seat.

All the same, she thought, why shouldn't she introduce him to John Cotmore? It would be a perfectly reasonable thing to do, and Papa would probably be pleased. She could seek him out after the concert . . .

The orchestra had finally reached Beethoven's Seventh Symphony and for a while she was swept along by the grandeur of the noise it made. Marvellous! she thought as it thundered through the funeral march in the slow movement. But the next movement was less compelling and gradually it lost her.

She would have to intercept John Cotmore before he left the gallery, she thought, otherwise he might have gone before she and Papa reached the bottom of the stairs. She would say, "John, I'd like you to meet my father." But she would have to be quick, so as to catch him before he passed them in the gangway. Instinctively, she moved in her seat, and as she did so she caught sight of Papa.

He was sitting quite still, his face a little raised and his hands folded over his coat. His eyes were half-closed, and then Anna saw that they were full of tears and that there were more tears running silently down his cheeks.

"Papa!" she said, all other thoughts stripped away.

He tried to speak but couldn't, shook his head to reassure her and finally whispered something about "the music".

Anxiously, she put her hand over his and sat close to him while the music roared about them, until at last it came to an end. All round them people clapped and stood up and put on their coats.

"Are you all right?" she whispered.

He nodded. "In a moment."

They stayed in their seats while the gallery began to empty.

"I'm sorry if I alarmed you," he said at last. "It's just –" He spread his hands. "I hadn't heard it for years."

He got to his feet and they moved out slowly in the wake of the others. Once in the fresh air he seemed to feel more himself. It was almost dark. As they picked their way through the crowd he looked back towards the shadowy theatre and murmured "Wonderful!" Out of the corner of her eye Anna could see John Cotmore with Harry and Barbara in a group, and for a moment she wondered – but it was no good. She took Papa's arm and they set off towards the tube. They were buying the tickets when he stopped in his tracks.

"Such emotion," he said, making her laugh, "and I've forgotten my hat!"

"I'll get it!"

She raced back to the theatre through the dusk, and at once the wild hope sprang up again inside her that she might yet meet John Cotmore, that the evening might yet turn out quite different.

The gallery entrance was closed and as she went round to the foyer she suddenly saw him. He was only a few feet away, a dim shape in a doorway, and his back was towards her. There was someone with him, so close as to be almost hidden behind him. They were clinging together and even before Anna heard them speak she knew who it must be.

"What shall we do now?" asked John Cotmore, and Barbara's voice answered him in the darkness, "Let's go home."

22

Anna never quite knew, afterwards, how she got home. Somehow she walked past the two shapes in the doorway, retrieved Papa's hat and rode home with him on the tube. The fact that he needed her was a help and at the sight of his face, still not quite re-set in its usual ironic composure, her own tumultuous feelings receded into some kind of proportion.

But Barbara! she thought. She could have understood if it had been his wife. How long had it been going on? Since the holidays? Or even last term? And did Barbara know about her? Had she and John Cotmore perhaps talked about her and laughed at her and her idiotic devotion to him? Showing him all her drawings, buying him saccharine in her lunch-hour . . . Each thought was more painful than the last and part of her wanted only to burst into tears and blurt it all out to Papa, while another knew that she couldn't possibly bear to talk about it.

"Are you quite well?" asked Papa. "You look pale."

She nodded. "How about you?"

He was sitting next to her in the tube, nervously massaging one hand with the other.

"I've got pins and needles," he said, and it was such an anti-climax after all her emotion that she laughed, and at the same time tears came into her eyes and she leaned against him and cried, "Oh Papa! Oh, dear Papa . . . !"

"There," he said, putting his arm round her shoulders, "I'm sorry I frightened you."

She shook her head. "It wasn't that."

For a moment she was afraid he would ask her what was the matter, but he only said, "There," again and then, very tenderly, "Whatever it was, it will pass."

The next day was dreadful. There was nothing to do at the office. Mrs Hammond didn't come in and even Miss Clinton-Brown and Miss Potter were away on holiday. Anna spent the morning alone with thoughts of John Cotmore while she pretended to busy herself with index cards and skeins of wool.

There's nothing left, she thought. Nothing I want to do, no one I want to see. She searched for phrases to comfort herself. Jilted? Abandoned? Crossed in love? They were corny, but they did not make her laugh. They could not keep out the humiliating memories of how she had smiled at him and hung on his lips, how she had been ready to take his arm that evening at the restaurant – and all the time he and Barbara . . . he and Barbara . . .

After lunch Mrs Riley arrived with a large scrap-book. "My life on the boards," she said. "I've brought it to show you."

There was nothing better to do, so Anna spent the afternoon with Mrs Riley by her side and Mrs Riley's miasma wafting over her. She looked at Mrs Riley in spangles in 1891, Mrs Riley in fishnet tights in 1902, Mrs Riley with a shepherd's crook and a stuffed sheep, Mrs Riley in bathing drawers. And all the time something inside her cried out for John Cotmore, for last night not to have happened, for everything to be as it had been before.

She got back late, for there was no more point in going home than in going anywhere else, and was completely unprepared for the desperate figure which rushed out to meet her.

"Anna!" cried Mama, all tears and clutching fingers. "Oh, Anna!"

"Dear God," said Anna, since the worst seemed determined to happen. "Is it Max?"

It was not Max. It was Papa.

Mama drew her into the house and then stopped and clutched her again in the hall.

"I found him when I came home," she said. "He was on the floor in his room. He'd been there for hours. His voice is all strange and there's something wrong with one of his hands."

They stared at each other.

"Sam is coming to see him – thank heavens he's in town." Mama let go of Anna's hand. "He'll know what to do."

"Can I go up to him?"

They went to his room together.

Papa was on the bed – Frau Gruber had helped Mama to lift him. His face looked heavy and half-asleep, but when he saw Anna his lips moved as though he were trying to smile.

"Papa!" she said.

The lips moved again. "I'm sor-ry . . ." His voice sounded thick and he could not find the words he wanted. One hand gestured helplessly while the other lay limp on the cover.

"Papa," said Anna again and sat on the edge of the bed. She put her hand over his unmoving one and smiled. She did not say anything, so that he wouldn't have to answer.

"Sam will be here soon," said Mama from the foot of the bed.

Papa seemed to nod and closed his eyes. After a while Mama made a sign to Anna and went out.

She stayed where she was and looked at him. Was he asleep? His eyes had remained closed and his face looked calm. The curly grey hair at the sides of his head (there had been none on top as long as Anna could remember) straggled a little on the pillow. She suddenly remembered how, when she was quite small in Berlin, she had played some form of Happy Families with Max. She had usually lost because she had sacrificed everything to getting hold of one particular card in the pack – the baker, who had a thin face and a balding head. "He looks so pretty," she had explained to Max, "just like Papa."

Now Papa was lying there with his shirt collar undone and breathing slowly. Of course he was quite old. Seventy-one? Seventy-two? Anna had always known this, but it had meant nothing. He had not seemed old. He was different from other people's fathers, but not because of his age – because of the sort of person he was. Suddenly, while she was looking at him, he opened his eyes and looked straight back at her.

"An-na," he said very slowly.

She tightened her hand over his and said, "Don't talk," but there was something he wanted to say.

"An-na," he said again and then, with great difficulty, "The con-cert . . ."

She nodded and smiled, and in spite of terrible obstacles his face moved, his lips stretched and he smiled back. "It was . . ." The word eluded him, but he pursued it and tracked it down.

"Beau-ti-ful!" said Papa triumphantly.

The Professor confirmed what Mama and Anna had already guessed. It was a stroke.

"How bad?" said Mama.

He shrugged his shoulders. "We'll know better in a few days."

Papa could not be left, so Mama stayed with him always, sleeping on a makeshift bed in his room. Anna relieved her for a few hours when she came home from work. Papa clearly knew exactly what was happening to him, but did not seem afraid. On the third day, when his speech had become easier, he suddenly said, "Strange."

"What?" said Anna.

Papa gestured towards himself, the bed, the shabby sickroom. "This," he said. He added, almost admiringly, "An amazing experience!"

When the Professor came to see him again he seemed pleased with his progress.

"We've been lucky this time," he told Mama. "He should recover quite quickly."

"Completely?"

He nodded.

"Thank God."

"But whatever possessed him?" said the Professor. "A man in his condition – to climb up to the gallery of a theatre?"

Mama was laughing with relief. "You know what he's like," she said. "And of course he didn't know – he had no idea –"

Something suddenly struck her.

"Did he?" she asked.

He looked at her with his sad black eyes.

"Three weeks ago," he said. "He came to me with all the classic symptoms. Headaches, pins and needles, very high blood pressure. I warned him then to be careful. And straightaway, what does he do? Drags himself up about a thousand steps to listen to Beethoven!"

Mama stared at him. "He knew," she said.

Anna remembered Papa during the Seventh Symphony.

"I suppose," she said, "that was why."

They were sitting in the garden. For once it was a warm evening. The Woodpigeon was mowing the lawn, the Poznanskis were arguing with each other in Polish, and Frau Gruber was shelling peas into a basin.

"You said earlier," said Mama, "'we've been lucky this time.'" What did you mean?"

"Just that," said the Professor.

"But – 'this time'?"

The Professor seemed put out. "My dear," he said, "your husband has had a stroke which could have been fatal. Instead, I think he'll make a complete recovery. So be grateful!"

"I am," said Mama, "but what did you mean?"

"For heaven's sake –" the Professor glanced uneasily at Anna – "you must know how these things are. Once there's been a stroke there may be another. Perhaps not for years, but your husband is not a young man. And next time –" He spread his hands. "Next time," he said sadly, "we may not be so lucky."

Papa recovered quite quickly. Even after a week, his

speech was back to normal. His hand still troubled him, but by the time Max came on leave he was up, and Max was surprised to find so few signs of his recent illness.

"He just looks a bit tired," he said.

But they all knew that from now on Papa was living on borrowed time.

Anna found it almost impossible to grasp.

"Don't worry," said Papa, glancing towards the ceiling. "The old rabbi up there is on my side."

Anna looked at him across the breakfast table, at the eyes now studying the newspaper, at the hands (one still a little clumsy) manipulating the knife and fork on the chipped plate, and tried to imagine that one day he would not be there. It seemed impossible.

She spent as much time with him as she could, always haunted by the thought that one day he would no longer exist. When she saw his spiky handwriting, so proliferous on his desk, in his room, everywhere they had ever lived, she thought that suddenly, one day, there would be no more of it. She even had the mad idea of asking him to write something, a whole lot, so that it would somehow not matter so much when he stopped.

She tried to paint his portrait. He sat for her patiently in the room above the garage, but it was no use. There was so much that she wanted to put in. Every time she had got anything down she wanted to scrap it and start again.

And all the time the best news of the war was coming in, like a film unrolling irrelevantly in the background. Paris was liberated, then most of France. Letters arrived from French friends who had, miraculously it seemed to Anna, survived the German occupation. If only Papa didn't have another stroke, if only Max didn't get killed, if only a buzz-bomb didn't fall on one . . .

One day Papa asked her, "Why don't you ever go to art school now?"

"Oh," she said. It all seemed so long ago. "I fell out with my drawing teacher."

"And that's all?"

"No." They were sitting in his room after supper – Mama was playing bridge. "I don't know," she said. "Perhaps he was all I was ever interested in, really. I don't seem to be able to draw any more. I don't even want to."

"A phase," he said.

She shook her head.

"Has the term started?"

She smiled at his vagueness. "About six weeks ago."

"Then you must go back. You can't give up your work just because you've had a tiff with someone."

"It wasn't just a tiff!" she cried, but he raised his hand.

"Please," he said. "I wish you to go back. Please go tomorrow."

She found the school much changed. The class had grown, and the whiskery man who had been with John Cotmore at the concert now shared the teaching with him. John and Barbara were openly devoted to each other and it was common knowledge among the students that she had moved into his house, and that it had taken her three days to clean up his kitchen.

"Where have you been?" he asked Anna, and she answered carefully, "My father has been ill."

She had drawn almost nothing for weeks, and waited tensely for the class to start. Perhaps at the sight of the model something inside her would revive. The model was fat and sat well back in the chair, with one hand on her knee. It was not a bad pose, but when Anna looked at it there seemed no reason why she should draw it. She felt quite dead. What am I doing here? she thought. How am I going to get through the evening?

In the end, rather than sit there doing nothing, she made some pencil marks that vaguely resembled what was before her, but there was no purpose in them and they bored even herself. When John Cotmore came round to see her she turned her drawing-board round to hide it, but he did not seem to notice.

"I'm glad you're back," he said. "I've been wanting to talk to you."

Her spirits rose violently. He was going to explain. Barbara was really his sister . . . his cousin . . . his aunt . . . !

"How would you like," said John Cotmore, "to have a scholarship?"

"A scholarship?" She was confused.

"Yes – full-time art school attendance for three years, no fees and a grant to live on."

She stared at him.

"How? When?"

"By showing your work to a selection committee, on your teacher's recommendation. With luck, beginning next September."

She could not think what to say.

"It won't arise until the spring," he said. "But the war looks like ending fairly soon and people are beginning to think about the peace. There are only going to be a few of these scholarships available, and I'd like to recommend you for one."

"But –" She still couldn't take it in. "I can't draw," she said.

"What do you mean?" He was becoming irritated with her lack of enthusiasm.

"Just that. I haven't done a decent drawing for months."

"Oh." He laughed briefly. "A bad patch. Happens to everyone."

"I doubt it."

"For heaven's sake," he cried. "You've thought of nothing but this for years – what's the matter?"

She looked round the room for guidance – at the model, the students bent over their work, Barbara frowning at a piece of charcoal. While she looked at her Barbara glanced up and caught her eye. The frown disappeared and she smiled. Anna smiled back uncertainly. Then Barbara nodded, with a sidelong glance at John Cotmore, and did the thumbs-up sign. What did she mean? Did she know what they were talking about? Then, suddenly, it hit her. Of course she and John Cotmore had discussed it. It was all arranged – a consolation prize. Poor little Anna, she'll be so upset, let's at least get her a scholarship.

She turned back to John Cotmore.

"I don't want it," she said.

"You don't want a scholarship?"

"Oh, leave me alone!" she said. "I don't know what I want!"

She continued to go to the classes, partly to please Papa, but nothing much came of them. Some of her drawings turned out better than others, but they all had a pedestrian quality which infinitely depressed her.

She dreaded the journey home on the tube, with nothing to think about except the failures of the evening, and carried a book with her wherever she went. As long as she was reading she couldn't think. It didn't seem to matter what she read – Tolstoy, Jack London, Agatha Christie – just as long as it was print. If she had finished a book, or forgotten it, she flew into a panic only to be assuaged by buying a newspaper. She wore her oldest clothes and forgot to wash her hair, because nothing mattered any more and there was no particular reason why she should exist.

And then, on top of everything else, Mama got 'flu. Anna found her red-faced and feverish one day when she came home, with Papa sitting on the edge of her bed. Mama had the huge thermometer from Paris tucked into her armpit, and they were having a ridiculous argument about Papa's work. Papa was saying that his prose was the best thing he had written, but Mama insisted that the poems were better.

"Ach, lyrical poems," said Papa. "They're easy."

"Nonsense!" cried Mama, causing the thermometer to quiver.

Papa shook his head. "The prose will last longer. After all, I wrote it. I ought to know."

"But you don't!" Mama half sat up in bed. "Just

because you find the poems so easy, you underrate them. No one else can write poems like you."

Papa got quite angry.

"I prefer the prose," he said. "If ever there's a chance of reprinting I should like it to be the prose rather than the poems. I shan't be here, so you'll have to see to it."

It was like a door closing.

Mama extracted the thermometer and found that it was 102.

"Oh, for heaven's sake," she cried. "Get off my bed, or you'll only catch it too!"

She was quite ill for a week.

It was bitterly cold, and there was a fuel shortage. To keep even a meagre fire in the lounge in the evenings, Frau Gruber and the Woodpigeon had to go each day to a distribution centre and collect some coal in a makeshift handcart. It was as they returned from one of these expeditions that Aunt Louise met them. She had come to commiserate with Mama, now sitting up in her dressing-gown, and she was horrified by the cold in the hotel.

"You've got to get out of here," she said. "You'll never get well in this icy place."

Mama demurred, but Aunt Louise would not be denied, and the following day she arrived in her car to wrap Mama in a large rug and carry her off to the country.

"Anna can look after her father, can't you, dear?" she said.

"There's nothing to do, anyway," said Anna ungraciously, and she and Papa waved from the freezing lounge as the car drove away.

"It's fearfully cold," said Papa the following week. "Do you really think you should drag all round Golders Green in this weather?"

"I'd better, I think," said Anna.

Aunt Dainty had rung up two days before to say that Victor, who had been getting steadily worse for months, had finally died. Since Mama was away, Anna had promised to go to the funeral.

"You hardly knew your great-uncle," said Papa. "I'm sure Aunt Dainty would understand."

"No, I'll go," said Anna.

It was not just that she felt sorry for Aunt Dainty, it was also the hope that — what? Something might happen to make her understand, she thought, to fight down the terrible vision of emptiness whenever she thought of the world without Papa.

"I'll come straight back," she promised, and saw him installed by his gas fire before she left.

She had put on her warmest clothes but even so, as she came out of the tube at Golders Green, the wind blew right through them. It was as though the weather, knowing that the war was coming to an end, was determined to do its worst while it could.

She had miscalculated the time it would take her to get there, and when she reached the cemetery the service had already begun. She could see it from the gate — a few shabby people standing forlornly in the cold. Aunt Dainty was wearing a large knitted black shawl and looked pale but composed. She saw Anna and nodded, and then Anna stood next to a woman with a feathery hat, wondering what to do.

Uncle Victor's coffin was already in the open grave – was he really in there? she wondered with a kind of horror – and a man with a book in his hand was making a speech over him, but the wind carried the words away and she could not understand them. She watched the mourners' frozen faces and tried not to stamp her frozen feet and thought of nothing. There was a buzzing sound in her ears, her hands were cold and she wondered whether it was disrespectful to keep them in her pockets, and then she realised that the buzzing sound had increased and that it was not only in her ears. The woman in the hat had heard it too, and her eyes met Anna's in embarrassment and alarm.

As the sound grew louder it became impossible not to look up and even the man making the speech glanced away from his book, to see the buzz-bomb puttering across the sky. It seemed to be coming directly towards them and Anna, calculating that there was no shelter she could possibly reach in time, decided to stay where she was. The other mourners must have come to the same conclusion, for nobody moved. Only the inaudible stream of words from the preacher gathered momentum. His mouth movements became faster, his arms gestured above the grave, there seemed to be some kind of quick blessing and at last he stopped.

As he did so, the puttering sound stopped also and the bomb tore down from the sky. For a split second Anna considered sheltering in the grave with the coffin but decided against it, everybody ducked or flung themselves on the ground, and then the bomb exploded – after all, some distance away.

There was a silence as the mourners picked themselves up and stared at each other, and then Aunt Dainty shook her fist at the sky.

"Even at his funeral!" she shouted. "Even at his funeral they couldn't leave him in peace!"

The reception afterwards in Aunt Dainty's basement almost had an air of celebration. It was warm by the paraffin stoves, and Aunt Dainty served hot chocolate sweetened with real sugar which Otto had sent from America.

"He's in the States now," she said proudly. "His work is so important that even President Roosevelt knows about it."

There were several hand-made rugs on the floor – rugmaking was Aunt Dainty's latest enthusiasm – and two women who turned out to be fellow evening-class students were inspecting them with interest. The rest of the mourners seemed to be either lodgers or neighbours and they sat on Aunt Dainty's home-made cushions, sipping chocolate and admiring the furnishings. Aunt Dainty bustled about with cups and seemed quite excited to have so many people to talk to at once. She introduced Anna to one of her lodgers, a little old man with bright eyes who threw up his hands when he heard who she was.

"But I know your father!" he cried. "I knew him in Berlin! Once we spent the most wonderful evening together."

"Really?" said Anna.

Next to her Aunt Dainty was telling someone about Otto.

"Even Einstein," she was saying. "Otto discusses things with him all the time."

"An unforgettable evening," said the old man. "I met him at a friend's – the poet Meyer in the Trompetenstrasse – do you remember?"

Anna shook her head. "I was quite small," she said.

The old man nodded regretfully.

"Your father had read a book I had written – he was quite complimentary about it. I remember it was a beautiful summer evening, and your father – he was supposed to go to a performance at the theatre and then to a party, something quite important, but suddenly, do you know what he said?"

"What?" said Anna.

"He said, "Let's take the steamer to the Pfaueninsel.' You must know the Pfaueninsel," said the old man anxiously. "An island in a lake near Berlin, with peacocks?"

Anna dimly remembered a school outing. Had that been the Pfaueninsel?

Aunt Dainty was saying, "And they've given him a house, and a car . . ."

The old man was waiting for her answer, so she nodded. He seemed relieved.

"Also a very good restaurant," he said with satisfaction. "So we went there, just your father and I and two others, and we ate, and we drank a very good wine, and we talked, and your father, he was so very amusing and witty. And when we came out we saw the peacocks asleep all together in the branches of a tall tree – your father had not known that they did this, he was very surprised. And then we took the steamer back to Berlin in the moonlight. Wonderful," said the old man. "Wonderful!"

Anna smiled. All she remembered of Berlin was the house and the garden and her school.

"It must have been lovely," she said.

The rug enthusiasts had seen their fill and prepared, reluctantly, to leave.

"Such a lovely party," said one, momentarily forgetting the occasion, and the other corrected her, "In the circumstances."

One of the neighbours said she must get back to her little boy and Anna, too, excused herself. As she put on her coat she thought that there had been, after all, no point in coming. She had felt nothing, learned nothing, received neither comfort nor enlightenment. Aunt Dainty saw her to the door.

"Give my love to your parents," she said.

It was the first time Anna had been alone with her and she suddenly realised that she had not offered her any condolences.

"I'm so sorry," she said awkwardly, "about Uncle Victor."

Aunt Dainty took her hand.

"Not to be sorry," she said in her warm, thick voice. "For me you can be sorry, because I loved him. But for him –" She shook her head above the large shoulders as though to ward something off. "For him, better it should have happened years ago."

Then she kissed her and Anna went out into the icy street.

Aunt Dainty was right, she thought as she hunched her shoulders against the wind. It would have been better for Uncle Victor if he had died before. There had been no point in those last years in England. She trudged along the frozen pavement and it struck her that this thought was even more depressing than the fact of his death. To have to go on living when you no longer wanted to, when it no longer made sense . . .

Like me, she thought, momentarily overwhelmed by self-pity, and was shocked by her own lack of courage. Rubbish, she thought, not like me at all. But like Papa? In her mind she saw him in his poky room with his typewriter that kept going wrong and his writings that no one wanted to publish, in a country whose language he did not speak. How did it feel to be Papa?

A few specks of snow were beginning to fall, dotting the walls, the bushes and the pavement with white.

Did Papa's life still make sense to him? When he remembered Berlin, did this shabby, frustrated existence among strangers still have any point? Or would he have preferred it if it had never happened? Would death, perhaps, come as a relief? She tried to find some comfort in the thought, but only felt worse. There's nothing, she thought, as the snow blew and whirled about her. Nothing . . .

She had to wait a long time for a train and by the time she got home she felt chilled to the bone. She went straight up to see Papa, but there was no reply to her knock and she found that he had nodded off in his chair. The gas fire was spluttering – it needed another shilling in the meter – and some of Papa's papers had fallen off the table. The room was cold and gloomy.

She stared at it dispassionately in the fading light. Why should anyone want to live here? Especially someone like Papa who had travelled and been acclaimed and whose life, until Hitler disrupted it, had been a series of choices between different kinds of fulfilment?

She must have moved inadvertently, for Papa woke up.

"Anna!" he said, and then, "How was it?"

"Awful," said Anna. "A buzz-bomb nearly fell on us and Aunt Dainty shouted at it."

"You look frozen," said Papa. He took a shilling from a tin box marked "shillings" and after a moment the gas flared yellow and the part of the room closest to it became a little warmer. "Would you like something to eat?"

She shook her head.

"Then come and get thawed."

He gave her a folded rug to sit on – there was only one chair – and she crouched at his feet by the fire. In spite of the shilling, it did not seem to give out much heat.

"I had a letter from Mama," said Papa. "She's quite recovered from her 'flu and she says she'll be home by the weekend." He looked at her anxiously. "I hope you're not catching it now."

"No," said Anna, though it was strange how the cold in her bones persisted.

She stared up at his face. What was he thinking? How could one ever tell how people really felt?

"Papa," she said, "do you ever regret – ?"

"What?" he asked.

She gestured vaguely at the room. "These last years. Here and at the Hotel Continental. I mean – after the way you used to live in Berlin?"

He looked at her attentively. "If you mean, would I rather have gone on living as before, well of course I would. There were so many more opportunities – so much to choose from. Also," he added simply, "I would have preferred to be more help to Mama, and to you and Max."

But that was not what she wanted to know.

"What I meant," she said, "is – did you ever feel . . . I mean, you must sometimes have wondered – if there was really any point . . . ?"

"In these last years?"

She nodded. Her head was throbbing and she had the strangest conviction that if Papa could reassure her she would get warm.

"Well, of course there was." Papa had got up from his chair and was looking at her in surprise.

"But it must have been so awful!" said Anna. "With losing your language, and never having any money, and Mama always so wretched, and all your work . . . all your work . . . !" She found to her horror that she was crying. A fat lot of good I am to him, she thought, and Papa bent down and touched her face.

"Your head is very hot," he said. "I'm sure you're not well."

"But I want to know!" she cried.

He searched among his things and produced the thermometer from a box marked "thermometer".

"In a moment," he said.

When she had tucked it under her arm he sat down again in the chair.

"The chief point about these last, admittedly wretched years," he said, "is that it is infinitely better to be alive than dead. Another is that if I had not lived through them I would never have known what it felt like."

"What it felt like?"

He nodded. "To be poor, even desperate, in a cold, foggy country where the natives, though friendly, gargle some kind of Anglo-Saxon dialect . . ."

She laughed uncertainly.

"I'm a writer," he said. "A writer has to know. Haven't you found that?"

"I'm not a writer," said Anna.

"You may be one day. But even an aspiring painter –" He hesitated, only for a moment. "There is a piece of me," he said carefully, "quite separate from the rest, like a little man sitting in my forehead. And whatever happens, he just watches. Even if it's something terrible. He notices how I feel, what I say, whether I want to shout, whether my hands are trembling – and he says, how interesting! How interesting to know that this is what it feels like."

"Yes," said Anna. She knew that she, too, had a little man like Papa's, but her head was spinning and she imagined him, confusedly, turning round and round.

"It's a great safeguard against despair," said Papa. He plucked the thermometer from under her arm and looked at it. "You've got 'flu," he said. "Go to bed."

She went along the freezing passage to her room and got between the cold sheets, but after a moment Papa appeared, awkwardly carrying a stone hot-water bottle.

"Is this all right?" he said, and she hugged it gratefully.

He lit the gas and drew the blackout curtains, and then he stood uncertainly at the foot of her bed.

"Are you sure you wouldn't like something to eat?" he said. "I've got some bread and fish-paste."

"No!" she said.

He insisted, slightly hurt, "You've got to keep your strength up," and the thought of keeping her strength up with fish-paste when the room was whirling round and her head was splitting seemed so funny that she laughed.

"Oh, Papa!" she cried.

"What?" he said, sitting on the edge of the bed.

"I love you very much."

"And I you." He took her hand and said, "The last years haven't been all unhappy, you know. You and Max have given us great joy. And I've always had Mama." There was a pause and then he said, "I have written about these years. A sort of diary. When you read it I hope you'll think, as I do, that it's the best thing I've done. And one day, perhaps, my works will be reprinted and this will be among them."

"In Germany?"

He nodded. "Mama will see to it."

He stroked her hot face.

"So you see, as long as I can think and write I am grateful to the old rabbi up there for every day that he keeps me on this extraordinary planet."

She felt better, but there was still something wrong. It was hiding from her, but it was there – a kind of horror, she imagined it crouching at the foot of the bed. It was to do with Uncle Victor and it was terribly important.

"Papa?" she said.

"What?"

She couldn't think. Think and write – he had said think and write. But Uncle Victor hadn't been able to think and write. He had just lain there – brain damage, Aunt Dainty had said, doesn't remember, better he should have died years ago. But didn't a stroke have the same effect – wouldn't Papa . . . ?

"Papa!" cried Anna, clutching his hand, "But if you couldn't think . . . ?"

His face was blurred as she tried to focus on it, but his voice was clear and calm.

"Then of course I should not want to go on living. Mama and I have talked about it."

"But how?" she cried. "How – how could you . . . ?"

She made a great effort and his face suddenly reassembled, so that she could see his eyes and the extraordinary, confident smile with which he spoke.

"Mama," he said, "will think of something."

24

The cold spell had ended by the time Mama came back from the country. Anna recovered from her 'flu in thin sunshine and the world suddenly looked more hopeful. The Professor announced that Papa's health had improved. His blood pressure was lower, and the effects of the stroke had almost disappeared.

"I told you," said Papa. "The old rabbi up there is on my side."

Gradually the war began to run down.

There were still buzz-bombs, so you could still get killed, but they were fewer. The news on the radio was always good, and for the first time since 1939 small glimmers of light were allowed in the streets at night. One day Max appeared to announce that his squadron was being disbanded.

"No more flying," he said quite regretfully, to Mama's rage. "I suppose it really will all be over quite soon."

As the armies advanced, pictures appeared in the papers and on newsreels of devastated German cities. Hamburg, Essen, Cologne – they were not places Anna had ever seen, and they meant nothing to her. Only once, when she heard on the news that the Grunewald had been set on fire, something stirred inside her.

The Grunewald was a wood near their old home. Long ago, when she and Max were small in the past which she never thought about, they had tobogganed there in the winter. Their sledges had made tracks in the snow and it had smelled of cold air and pine needles. In the summer they had played in the patchy light under the trees, their feet had sunk deep into the sand at the edge of the lake – and hadn't there once been a picnic . . . ? She couldn't remember.

But that was all before.

The Grunewald that was burned was not the one she had played in. It was a place where Jewish children were not allowed, where Nazis clicked heels and saluted and probably hid behind trees, ready to club people down. They had guns and fierce dogs and swastikas and if anyone got in their way they beat them up and set the dogs on them and sent them to concentration camps where they'd be starved and tortured and killed . . .

But that's nothing to do with me now, thought Anna. I belong here, in England.

When Max said to her, later, "Did you hear about the fire in the Grunewald?" she nodded and said, dead-pan, "It's just as well we left."

As the spring grew warmer, she started to draw again. It began one day in her lunch-hour. She was walking aimlessly through some little streets at the back of Vauxhall Bridge Road when she saw a child. He was the fourth she had seen since she had come out and she thought, the war really must be ending if the children are coming back! This one was about ten and was sitting on a heap of rubble, staring up at the sky with a pleased expression. I suppose he's glad to be home, thought Anna.

There was something about him – the way he was

clasping his skinny knees, the way his over-large sweater hung loosely on his shoulders, the way he squinnied up at the light – that was very expressive. Suddenly she had a great desire to draw him. She did not have a sketch-book with her, but found an old letter in her handbag. Feverishly, she started to draw on the back. She was so anxious to get the boy down on paper before he moved or stood up and walked away that she didn't have time to worry about how best to do it. She just thought, that goes like that and that goes like that, and there's light on his face and on his knees and a dark patch of shade under his chin . . . and suddenly there was the drawing, she'd done it and it looked just right!

She walked back to the office in a daze. It's come back, she thought. I can do it again! That evening at art school she made two good drawings and when she rode home on the tube, for the first time in months she chose not to read, but drew an old man asleep in his seat. That came out well, too.

Suddenly she couldn't stop. She bought a new sketch-book and filled it in a few days. At week-ends, in her room above the garage, she worked on a painting of shelterers. This time she planned it more carefully and it had at least something of the feeling she had wanted to put into it. She also painted a portrait of Mama. Mama posed for it, crouched over Anna's paraffin stove and looking, as always, both crushed and ebullient at once, and Papa said it was one of the best things Anna had done.

Finally she gathered all her work together in a portfolio and put it down in front of John Cotmore.

"You were talking about a scholarship," she said.

He looked pleased. "I hoped you'd do that," he said.

Anna glanced at the whiskery man, not far away. "Do you think he'd like to see my work as well?" She did not want the scholarship on John Cotmore's recommendation alone.

"All right," he said after a moment.

The whiskery man came over and he and John Cotmore looked through the portfolio together. John Cotmore said "Good" and "I like that" several times, but the whiskery man said nothing.

Damn, thought Anna, suddenly wanting nothing in the world so much as three years at art school, why couldn't I have left well alone?

John Cotmore had finished.

"Well," he said, "what do you think?"

The whiskery man ignored him. There were still two drawings which he hadn't seen and he looked at each one in turn, slowly and methodically. He was north-country and did not like to be hurried. At last he turned to Anna and she saw to her dismay that he looked quite annoyed.

"Don't act so daft, girl," he said. "You must know you've got enough here to get you anything you want."

After he had moved away, John Cotmore smiled at her.

"Well," he said, "that's that. Now the world lies before you."

She smiled back, carefully.

"You'll get your scholarship," he said, "and there'll

be peace and all the young men will be coming home."

She shrugged her shoulders. "Oh," she said, "the young men . . ."

"Who will be much better for you than I ever was. Except for your drawing."

She was packing her work back into the portfolio and one of the drawings caught her eye. It *was* good.

Suddenly, on an impulse, she said, "Thank you for teaching me to draw."

She could feel how pleased he was. The air all round them was filled with his pleasure.

"You always were my favourite student," he said and, almost absent-mindedly, he let his hand rest on her shoulder. She was conscious of a sudden warmth, a curious fluttering sensation (extraordinary! noted the little man in her forehead) and then Barbara was upon them. Her placid mouth was set in a firm line and she was carrying his brief-case and his duffel coat.

"Come on, John," she said. "We're having the rabbit."

He withdrew his hand quickly.

"It's been stewing for hours," she said. "And then you've got to look out those drawings for your exhibition."

He sighed and stood up.

"There, you see, Anna," he said, "all the world lies before you, while middle-aged people like us have to go home and eat rabbit."

"Speak for yourself," said Barbara. She peered at the drawings which Anna was putting away. "Are you going to try for that scholarship?"

Anna nodded.

"I should think so, too," said Barbara.

In April the British and American armies overran the first concentration camps, and the first horrifying descriptions appeared in the press and on the radio. Anna was astonished at the reaction. Why was everyone so surprised? She had known about concentration camps since she was nine years old. At least now the English will understand what it was like, she thought.

She watched the newsreels, repelled but not shocked. The gas-chambers, the piles of dead bodies, the pitiful, skeleton-like survivors – it was all terrible, she thought, terrible. But no more terrible than what she had tried for years not to imagine. As the appalling stories poured out, as the indignation burst forth all round her, she could think of only one thing – that at last it was over. At long, long last it had stopped.

Berlin fell at the beginning of May. Had there been fighting round their house, in their garden? She pushed the thought aside. It didn't matter. It's finished, she thought. I need never think about it again.

For a few days there were rumours and unconfirmed reports. Hitler was dead, he had been captured, he was holding out, he had surrendered – and then at last an official statement. The war in Europe was over.

On the day set aside for official rejoicing, Anna, Mama and Papa went to have lunch with the Rosenbergs. The flat in Harley Street was back in use, and Aunt Louise was already worrying about the peace.

"Whatever you do," she said to Mama, "don't tell Fraulein Pimke that the war is over!"

"Why not?" said Mama, surprised.

"Because she'll use up all the rations and we'll have nothing left to eat. She thinks that food will automatically become plentiful the moment the war stops."

"But surely –" began Mama.

Aunt Louise waved her down.

"After all, it doesn't really matter to her," she said. "And she's old and quite deaf and she doesn't speak a word of English, so she wouldn't hear from anyone else. In fact, if we're careful," – Aunt Louise suddenly became quite happy – "there's really no reason at all why she should ever find out about the peace!"

Max arrived in time for lunch, and the Professor proposed a toast.

"To us!" he said. "Who would have thought, five years ago, that we would outlive Adolf Hitler?"

"And to the English," said Papa. "They won the war."

Aunt Louise made everyone stand up to drink to the English and worried whether she wasn't supposed to fling her glass on to the floor afterwards ("Only we have so few left," she said) until Max reassured her.

"A wonderful wine," said Papa.

The Professor showed him the bottle.

"Johannisberger-Schloss," he said, "from the Rheingau. I've kept it specially for this."

They looked at each other.

"Perhaps one day . . ."

"Perhaps," said Papa.

Fraulein Pimke, though unaware of what was being celebrated, had cooked a delicious meal.

"Well, and what now?" asked Aunt Louise afterwards. "Will you be going back to Cambridge, Max?"

"When I'm demobilised," said Max. "I hope by next term."

"And then you'll become a lawyer," said the Professor. "Perhaps you'll become such a judge, with a wig like a poodle and a long coat with fur on. You could never have done that if it hadn't been for Hitler."

Max grinned. "I have a lot to thank him for."

"Anna has won a scholarship at her art school," said Papa, and she was warmed by the pride in his voice. "She too will be starting next term."

"Really?" said the Professor.

Anna looked at him. He was sitting with his back to the window, his arms folded across his chest. The colours of his face, his clothes and the chair he sat in glowed dark and rich in the shadows of the room. They made a curious, complicated shape against the rectangle of light behind him. I'd like to paint that, she thought as the conversation flowed round her, and began to work out how she would do it.

". . . isn't that true?" asked Max.

"What?" she said startled, and he laughed.

"I was explaining," he said, "that you're the only one of us to whom the emigration has made no difference. I mean, if Hitler had never happened you wouldn't have learned three languages and you might have avoided a certain amount of worry, but you'd have ended up exactly the same as you are now, wandering about with a vague expression on your face and looking for things

574

to draw. It really wouldn't matter whether you were in Germany or in France or in England."

"I suppose not," said Anna.

She thought of her scholarship, and John Cotmore, and Mrs Hammond with her old ladies, and a policeman who had once lent her a shilling, and fire-watching in Putney, and Trafalgar Square in the dusk, and the view of the river from the 93 bus.

"But I like it here," she said.

A little later, Max got up to go.

"Walk to the tube with me, Anna," he said.

Papa stood up too and embraced him.

"Good-bye, my son," he said. "May you be as successful in peace as you have been in war."

"And ring up as soon as you hear anything," said Mama. "About Cambridge and being demobilised. And don't forget to tell them about your scholarship."

Anna and Max rode down in the lift in silence. The commissionaire opened the door for them, and they could hear singing in the street outside. He glanced at Max's uniform.

"Quite a day," he said. "Young Englishmen like yourself have a right to be proud of themselves."

They grinned at each other.

The street was full of Union Jacks. A few girls in paper hats were dancing to the music of an accordion, and a soldier was sitting on the pavement with a bottle by his side. They picked their way among them.

"Well," said Max, as so many times before, "and how is everything?"

"All right," said Anna. "Papa seems quite well, doesn't he, and they're both very pleased about my scholarship. But Mama is going to lose her job again."

"Why?" asked Max.

"It seems her boss has promised it to his niece when she comes out of the Women's Land Army. Mama doesn't mind too much at the moment – she says it was just a stop-gap and she'd rather work for English people, anyway. But I don't know – once everyone comes out of the Forces it'll be even more difficult for her to find a job than before."

Max nodded. "It doesn't sound as though the peace would be much help to them."

They had reached Oxford Circus, but Max showed no sign of catching the tube and they walked on down Regent Street.

"Perhaps one day," said Anna, "Papa's works will be published again in Germany."

"It will be a long time," said Max.

"And I suppose now the war is over we'll all be naturalised."

They both smiled at the thought of Papa as an Englishman.

"Mama can't wait," said Anna. "She's going to drink tea with milk and love animals and go to cricket matches. There's no end to the things she's going to do."

Max laughed. "But it won't make any difference," he said.

"Won't it?"

He shook his head.

"You and I will be all right, but they'll never

belong. Not here." He made a face. "Not anywhere, I suppose."

The crowd had thickened and they stopped for a moment to let a man with a child on his shoulder pass them. Someone saluted Max and he had to salute back.

"You remember," he said, "what you used to say in Paris? That as long as you were with Mama and Papa you wouldn't feel like a refugee?"

She nodded.

"Well, now I suppose it's the other way round."

"How, the other way round?"

Max sighed. "Nowadays," he said, "I think that the only times *they* don't feel like refugees is when they're with us."

Anna stared at the scene around her – the flags, the noise, the relaxed, contented faces – and thought of Mama and Papa travelling back to Putney on the tube.

"We'll just have to do the best we can," she said.

At Piccadilly Circus Max left her, and she walked into the crowd. The square was swarming with people, they were all around her, old men, people in uniform, couples holding hands, women with children. Some danced or sang, some were drinking, but most of them, like herself, were just walking about. No processions, she thought. No waving of banners. A sailor had climbed to the top of a lamp-post. A small boy shouted, "Wheeee . . ." and then made a crunching noise like an explosion. "No," said the woman with him. "No more bombs."

As she reached the centre of the square, the sun

came out and everything suddenly leapt into colour. Water flashed in the fountain. An airman, his uniform changed from grey to blue, splashed some on a laughing girl in a pink dress. A bottle blazed momentarily, passed from hand to hand. Two women singing "Roll Out The Barrel" in printed blouses seemed to burst into flower. Pigeons wheeled. The sky shone.

At the foot of the fountain a soldier leaned, fast asleep. He was half-sitting, half-lying, his head supported by the stone. The sun lit up the top of his face, one hand clutched a kit-bag, the other trailed, open, on the pavement. The legs sprawled exhausted. There was something triumphant about the way he slept. If only he doesn't wake up, thought Anna.

She got out her sketch-book and began to draw.

A SMALL PERSON
FAR AWAY

For my husband

Saturday

The rug was exactly the right red – not too orange
and not too purple, but that lovely glowing shade
between the two which was so difficult to find. It
would look marvellous in the dining-room.

"I'd like it, please," said Anna. Clearly it was
her lucky day.

She glanced at her reflection in a glass-fronted
show-case full of table linen as the assistant led
her to his desk. Her green coat – not passed on to
her by friends but bought by herself – hung easily
from her shoulders. The printed silk scarf, the
well-cut dark hair and the reasonably confident
expression were all in keeping with the status
of the store around her. A well-heeled young
Englishwoman out shopping. Well, she thought,
nowadays I suppose that's what I am.

While she wrote out a cheque and the assistant copied her name and address for the rug's

delivery, she imagined telling Richard about it. It would make their flat almost complete. All that was needed now were little things like cushions and lampshades, and perhaps, if Richard finished his script soon, they would be able to choose those together.

She became aware of the assistant hesitating over her name on the cheque.

"Excuse me asking, madam," he said, "but is that any relation to the gentleman who writes for television?"

"My husband," she said and felt the usual fatuous, self-congratulatory grin spread over her face as she said it. Ridiculous, she thought. I should be used to it by now.

"Really?" The assistant's face was pink with pleasure. "I must tell the wife. We watch all his plays, you know. Wherever does he get his ideas from, madam? Do you help him at all with his writing?"

Anna laughed. "No," she said. "He helps me."

"Really? Do you write as well then?"

Why did I ever start on this? she thought. "I work in television," she said. "But mostly I just rewrite little bits of other people's plays. And if I get stuck, I ask my husband when I get home."

The assistant, after considering this, rightly dismissed it. "When that big serial of his was on last year," he said, "the wife and I stayed home for it every Saturday night. So did just about everyone else our way. It was so exciting – not like anything we'd ever seen."

Anna nodded and smiled. It had been Richard's first great success.

"We got married on the strength of that," she said.

She remembered the register office in Chelsea, next to the foot clinic. Richard's parents down from the north of England, Mama over from Berlin, their own friends from the BBC, cousin Otto passing out at the reception and saying it was the heat, but it had really been the champagne. And then the taxi coming and Richard and herself driving off and leaving them all behind.

"It was quite exciting for us too," she said.

When she walked out of the store into Tottenham Court Road, the world exploded into noise and light. A new building was going up next door and the sunshine trembled with the din of pneumatic drills. One of the workmen had taken off his shirt in spite of the October chill and winked at her as she passed. Behind him the last remains of a bombed building, scraps of wallpaper still adhering to the bricks and plaster, crumbled to a bulldozer. Soon there would be no bomb damage at all left visible in London. And about time too, she thought, eleven years after the war.

She crossed the road to get away from the noise. Here the shops were more or less unchanged – shabby and haphazard, selling things you could not imagine anyone wanting to buy. The Woolworth's, too, was much as she remembered it. She had come here with Mama when they had first arrived in England as refugees from Hitler, and Mama had bought herself a pair of silk stockings for a shilling. Later when Papa could no longer earn any money, Mama had been reduced to buying the stockings one at a time for sixpence, and even though they were supposed to be all the same colour, they had never quite matched.

"If only, just once, I could buy myself two stockings together," she had cried.

And now here was Anna buying expensive rugs, and Mama earning dollars back in Germany, as though none of the hardships had ever happened. Only Papa had not lived to see everything change.

For a moment she considered trying to find the boarding house somewhere nearby which had been her first English home, but decided against it. It had been bombed during the Blitz and would probably be unrecognizable anyway. Once she had tried to show Richard the other boarding house in Putney where they had moved after the bomb, but had found it replaced by three skimpy family dwellings with identical tree-less lawns and crazy-paving. The only thing that had been the same was the bench at the end of the street where Papa had sometimes sat in the sun with his pipe. He had eked out the tobacco with dried leaves and rose petals, and for lunch he had eaten bread toasted over the gas ring and spread with exactly one seventh of a jar of fish paste. If only he could have lived to see all this, thought Anna, as she passed a wine shop crammed with bottles – how he would have enjoyed it.

Oxford Street was bustling with Saturday shoppers. Should she walk through to Liberty's for a look at their lamps? But a number 73 bus stopped just as she was passing and she jumped on, climbed to the top deck and sat with the sun warming her face, visualizing the new rug in their tiny dining-room and planning what to wear to go out that evening, while the bus made its slow way through the traffic.

Outside Selfridges people were staring up at a brightly coloured plaster figure which was being hoisted into place above the main entrance. "Come and see Uncle Holly and his grotto of dwarfs," read posters in every window. Heavens, she thought, they're getting ready for Christmas already.

In Hyde Park, clearly making for Speakers' Corner, a small procession moved briskly under the thinning plane trees. Its members carried handmade placards with "Russians out of Hungary" on them, and one had mounted that morning's newspaper on a piece of cardboard. It showed a photograph of Russian tanks under the headline "Ring of Steel round Budapest". Most of them looked like students, but a few elderly people in dark old-fashioned clothes were probably Hungarian refugees. One of them, a man in a shabby coat with a pale, clever face reminded Anna of Papa.

At Knightsbridge the traffic thinned a little, and as the bus rolled past Kensington Gardens, she could see the leaves floating down from the trees on to the grass below, where groups of school children, urged on by their teachers, were playing football and rounders.

She got off at the bottom of Kensington Church Street and set off on her way home through the tree-lined residential streets at the foot of Camden Hill. Here there were almost no cars and few people. Cooking smells wafted across shrubby front gardens. A baby slept in its pram. Cats dozed on walls and pavements, and the falling leaves were everywhere. One drifted down quite close to her. She stretched up and caught it in mid-air. That means more luck, she thought, remembering a childhood superstition. For a moment she held it in her hand. Then she loosened her fingers and watched it spiral down to mingle with the others on the ground.

The block of flats where she and Richard lived was brand-new, and as soon as she could see it from the corner of the street, she automatically started to hurry. This always happened: she knew it was silly after being married for more than a year, but she still did it. She ran across the road, up the stone steps and along the red brick terrace so thick with leaves that she almost slipped. Outside the porter's flat below, the porter was talking to a boy on a bicycle. He waved when he saw her and called something that she did not catch, but she was in too much of a rush to stop. The lift was not there and, rather than wait for it, she ran up the two flights of stairs, opened the door with her key, and there was Richard.

He was sitting at his typewriter, much, as she had left him hours earlier. There was a neat stack of paper on the table before him and a collection of crumpled pages overflowing from the wastepaper basket on to the floor. Behind him in the tiny living-room she could see their new striped sofa, the little red chair she had bought the previous week, and the curtains made from material designed by herself in her art school days. The vivid colours set off his dark hair and pale, restless face as he frowned at the paper, typing furiously with two fingers.

Normally she would not have interrupted him, but she felt too happy to wait. She let him get to the end of a line. Then she said, "It's lovely out. I've been all over town. And I've found a rug for the dining-room."

"Really?" He came back slowly from whatever world he had been writing about.

"And the man in the shop had seen all your plays on the telly and practically asked me for my autograph when he found out I was married to you."

He smiled. "There's fame!"

"Are you right in the middle of something?"

She saw him glance at the page in his typewriter and resign himself to abandoning it for the present. "I suppose it's lunch time. Anyway, I've got quite a bit done." He stood up and stretched. "What's the rug like? Is it the right red?"

She was beginning to describe it to him when the door bell rang. ". . . exactly what we were looking for," she said, and opened the door to find the porter outside.

"Telegram," he said and handed it over. It was for her. She knew it must be good news, for it was that sort of a day, and opened it quickly. And then, for a moment, everything seemed to stop.

For some strange reason she could see Richard quite clearly with part of her mind, even though her eyes were on the print. She heard him say, "What is it?" and after what seemed like an enormous gap of time of which she could later remember nothing but which could not really have lasted more than a few seconds, she pushed it into his hand.

"I don't understand it," she said. "Mama is never ill."

He spread it on the table and she read it again, hoping that she had got it wrong the first time. "YOUR MOTHER SERIOUSLY ILL WITH PNEUMONIA STOP YOUR PRESENCE MAY BE NEEDED STOP PLEASE BOOK PROVISIONAL FLIGHT TOMORROW STOP WILL TELEPHONE NINE O'CLOCK TONIGHT." It was signed Konrad.

"All she's ever had is 'flu," said Anna. She felt that if she tried hard enough, she would be able to disprove the whole thing. She said, "I don't want to go to Berlin."

Then she found she was sitting down with Richard beside her. His face was troubled and she thought illogically that she shouldn't be distracting him in this way from his work. He tightened his arm round her shoulders.

"It's only a provisional booking," he said. "You may not need to go. By the time Konrad rings up, she may be better."

Of course, she thought, of course. She tried to remember what Konrad was like. During the years Mama had known him he had always seemed ultra-responsible. Probably he would act even on the off-chance of trouble. By tonight Mama might be sitting up in bed, her blue eyes outraged. For heaven's sake, Konrad, she would cry, why on earth did you cable the children?

"D'you suppose he's cabled Max as well?" she asked. Max was her brother, at present in Greece.

Richard shook his head. "Goodness knows." Then he said suddenly, "Would you like me to come with you?"

She was both touched and horrified. "Of course not. Not in the middle of your serial. Anyway, what could you do in Berlin?"

He made a face. "I wish I could speak German."

"It isn't that. But you know it would throw you completely to stop writing now. And Mama is my responsibility."

"I suppose so."

Eventually she rang Pan Am who were sympathetic when she explained the situation and said they would book her a seat. This seemed to make the whole thing more definite and she found herself suddenly close to tears.

"Come on," said Richard, "You need a drink." He poured her some of the whisky they normally kept for visitors and she gulped it down. "And food," he said. By the time they had made sandwiches and coffee and were sitting down to eat them in the little living-room, she felt better.

"But I still don't understand it," she said, clasping the hot mug for comfort. "Surely nowadays when people get pneumonia the doctors just fill them with penicillin? Unless the Germans haven't got it yet."

"They must have."

"Anyway, the Americans would have it, and they're the ones she works for. And how did she ever get pneumonia in the first place?"

Richard considered it. "Didn't she say something about sailing in her last letter? Perhaps if they'd had an accident – if she'd got very wet and cold and hadn't changed her clothes –"

"Konrad would make her."

For a moment they shared a vision of Konrad, solid and dependable, and Mama laughing and shouting, "It's only a bit of water." She always said a bit of water – it was one of the few mistakes she made in English. But perhaps she and Konrad spoke German together when they were alone. It astonished Anna that she had no idea whether they did or not.

"I'll see if I can find the letter," she said and

suddenly remembered something. "I don't believe I ever answered it."

"We haven't had it that long, have we?"

"I don't know."

The letter, when she uncovered it, turned out to be like most of Mama's – a fairly emphatic account of small successes in her work and social life. She had been chosen to go to Hanover for a few days in connection with her work, and she and Konrad had been invited to a Thanksgiving party by an American general. The only reference to sailing was that the weather was now too cold to do so, and that she and Konrad were playing a lot of bridge instead. It was exactly one month old.

"It doesn't matter, love," said Richard. "You'll be talking to Konrad tonight and if it's really serious you'll see your mother tomorrow."

"I know." But it still worried her. "I kept meaning to write," she said. "But with the flat and the new job –" Somehow she felt that a letter would have protected Mama from catching pneumonia.

"Well, no one can catch pneumonia from playing bridge," said Richard. "Not even your mother," and she laughed because it was true. Mama did everything to excess.

Suddenly, for no particular reason, she remembered Mama trying to buy her some boots when they had first come to England. Mama had walked her the whole length of Oxford Street from Tottenham Court Road to Marble Arch and they had gone into every shoe shop on the way. Anna had soon noticed that the various branches of Dolcis, Lilley and Skinner and Mansfield all had the same stock, but Mama had remained convinced that somehow, somewhere, there might be lurking a pair of boots just fractionally better or cheaper than any of the rest. When at last they bought some similar to the very first pair they had seen, Mama had said, "Well, at least we know that we haven't missed anything."

Mama could never bear to miss anything, real or imaginary, from a cheaper pair of boots to a day in the sun.

"She's a romantic," said Anna. "She always has been. I suppose Papa was too, but in a different way."

"What I've always found surprising is that she resented being a refugee so much more than he did," said Richard. "At least from what you've told me. After all, as a writer he really lost everything. Money, a great reputation and the language he wrote in." He looked troubled, as always when he talked about Papa. "I don't know how one could go on after that."

For a moment Anna saw Papa quite clearly in his shabby room, sitting at his rickety typewriter and smiling fondly, ironically, without a trace of self-pity. Reluctantly, she let the picture fade.

"It sounds odd," she said, "but in a way I think he found it interesting. And of course it was hard for Mama because she had to cope with the practical things."

When Papa could no longer earn any money, Mama had supported the family with a series of

594

secretarial jobs. Though she had learned neither shorthand nor typing, she had still managed, somehow, to reproduce approximately what had been dictated to her. She had survived, but she had hated it. At night, in the bedroom which she and Anna shared in the Putney boarding house, she had talked of all the things she had hoped to do in her life and now might never do. Sometimes when she set out for her boring work in the mornings, she was filled with such rage and despair that they made a kind of aura round her. Anna remembered that one of her employers, a man with slicked-down hair who dealt in third-rate clothing, had sacked her because, he said, just being in the same room with her made him feel exhausted. Mama had come home and cried and Anna had felt helpless and guilty, as though she ought to have been able to do something about it.

"It's such bad luck that this illness should have happened now," she said to Richard. "Just when everything is so much better for her at last."

She cleared away the lunch things while Richard picked at his script and then she looked out some clothes to pack, in case it should really be necessary for her to go to Berlin. For some reason the thought filled her with horror. Why? she thought. Why should I mind so much? She could not convince herself that Mama's illness was really dangerous, so it wasn't that. Rather it was a fear of going back. Back to Berlin? Back to Mama? Silly, she thought. It's not as though they could keep me there.

When she returned to the living-room, Richard was crumpling yet another page into the waste-paper basket.

"No good," he said. "Real life is too distracting." He looked at his watch. "What do you want to do till Konrad rings up?"

Something clicked in her memory. "Good heavens!" she cried. "We're supposed to go to the Dillons. I'd totally forgotten. I'd better ring him quickly."

"The Dillons? Oh," he said. "Drinks with the boss." He put out his hand as she reached for the telephone. "Don't cancel it. You'll have to tell him anyway if you go to Berlin."

James Dillon was head of the BBC Drama department and the invitation was to mark her promotion from editor to script writer.

"But we have to be here when Konrad rings."

"It's only a brisk walk. There's plenty of time. Come on," he said. "It'll be better than sitting here and brooding."

It was dark when they set out, and suddenly cold with a thin drizzle of rain. She pulled her coat tight about her and let Richard lead her through the network of quiet streets. Though Richard had met James Dillon's family before, she had never been to their house. Her promotion had been James Dillon's idea, but it was Richard who had originally encouraged her to write. When they had first met, he had read a short story she had written in between the paintings which she considered her real work. "This is good," he had said. "You must do more."

At first it had seemed like cheating, for though words came to her fairly easily ("Runs in the family," Richard had said), she had set her heart on being a painter. But no one seemed eager to buy her pictures, whereas she had no trouble at all in landing a minor job in television. By the time she and Richard were married, she was editing plays, and now here she was, officially a script writer. It had all happened so quickly that she still thought of it as his world rather than hers. "I hope I can really do this job," she said, and then, "What's James Dillon's wife like?"

"Nice," he said. "Don't worry."

They were reaching the end of a narrow side street and became aware of many voices and footsteps ahead of them. As they turned into the brightness of Notting Hill Gate, they found themselves suddenly surrounded by a great crowd. In spite of the rain which had begun to fall in earnest, a mass of people blocked the pavement, overflowing into the gutter, and were moving slowly but determinedly all in the same direction. In the road beyond, two policemen were trying to keep a space between the crowd and the passing cars. For a moment Anna and Richard were swept along with the rest.

"Who are they?" said Richard, and then they saw, swaying in the darkness above them, the pale handwritten placards.

"It must be Hungary again," said Anna. "I saw a procession in Hyde Park this morning."

At that moment the crowd slowed to a stop, and simultaneously a noisy party emerged from a pub nearby, causing a congestion. One of them, a large drunken looking woman, almost tripped and swore loudly.

"What the hell's this then?" she said, and another member of the group answered, "Bloody Hungary."

A placard bearer near Anna, an elderly man in dark clothes, mistook this exchange for interest in his cause and turned towards them. "The Russians kill our people," he explained with difficulty in a thick accent. "Many hundreds die each day. Please the English to help us . . ."

The woman stared incredulously. "Think we want another war?" she shouted. "I'm not having anyone drop bombs on my kids just for a lot of bloody foreigners!"

Just then the crowd began to move again and a gap opened between Anna and the kerb. "Come on," said Richard and pushed her through. They ran across Notting Hill Gate in the increasingly heavy rain, then zig-zagged through dark side streets on the other side until they were standing outside a tall terrace house and Richard was ringing the bell. She only had time to take in an overgrown front garden with what looked like a pram under a tarpaulin, when the door was opened by a slight, pretty woman with untidy fair hair.

"Richard!" she cried. "And you must be Anna.

I'm Elizabeth. How lovely – we've been longing to see you."

She led the way through the narrow hall, edging with practised ease round a large balding teddy and a scooter leaning against the wall.

"Did you get caught up in the procession?" she called back as they followed her up the narrow stairs. "They've been demonstrating outside the Russian embassy all day. Poor souls, much good may it do them."

She suddenly darted sideways into a kitchen festooned with washing, where a small boy was eating cornflakes with a guinea pig squatting next to his dish.

"James thinks no one is going to lift a finger to help them. He thinks it's Munich all over again," she said as Anna and Richard caught up with her and, almost in the same breath to the little boy, "Darling, you won't forget to put Patricia back in her cage, will you. Remember how upset you were when Daddy nearly trod on her."

In the momentary silence while she snatched some ice cubes from the refrigerator into a glass bowl, the sound of two recorders, each playing a different tune and interspersed with wild childish giggles, drifted down from somewhere above.

"I'm afraid the girls are not really musical," she said and added, "Of course no one wants a third world war."

As they followed her out of the kitchen, Anna saw that the guinea pig was now slurping up cornflakes, its front paws in the dish, and the small boy called after them, "It wasn't Patricia's fault. Daddy should have looked!"

In the L shaped drawing-room next door James Dillon was waiting for them, his Roman emperor's face incongruous above the old sweater he was wearing instead of his usual BBC pinstripes. He kissed Anna and put an arm round Richard's shoulders, and when they were all settled with drinks, raised his glass.

"To you," he said. "To Richard's new serial which I'm sure will be as good as his first and to Anna's new job."

This was the cue she had nervously been waiting for. She said quickly, "I'm afraid I may not be able to start straight away," and explained about Mama's illness. The Dillons were immediately full of sympathy. James told her not to worry and to take as much time off as she liked and Elizabeth said, how awful for her but nowadays with penicillin pneumonia wasn't nearly as serious as it used to be. Then she said, "But whatever is your mother doing in Berlin?"

James said, "It's where you came from, isn't it?" and Anna explained that Mama was translating documents for the American Occupation Force and that, yes, she and her family had lived in Berlin until they had had to flee from the Nazis when she was nine.

"I didn't see any horrors," she said quickly, alarmed by more sympathy in Elizabeth's eyes. "My parents got us out before any of it happened. In fact, my brother and I rather enjoyed it. We lived in Switzerland and in France before we came here and we really liked all the different schools and different languages. But of course it was very hard for my parents, especially my father being a writer."

"Terrible." James shook his head, and Elizabeth asked, "And where is your father now?"

"Oh," said Anna, "he died soon after the war." She felt suddenly dangerously exposed. Something was rising up inside her and she began to talk very fast so as to keep it under. "He died in Hamburg," she almost gabbled. "Actually it was very strange because he'd never been back to Germany since we left. But the British Control Commission asked him to write about the German theatre which was just starting up again. He'd been famous as a drama critic before Hitler, you see, and I think it was supposed to be good for German morale."

She paused, but the Dillons were both looking at her, absorbed in the story, and she had to continue.

"They flew him over – he'd never flown but he loved it. I don't think he knew quite what to expect when he got there, but when he stepped off the plane, there were reporters and photographers waiting for him. And then a great lunch with speeches, and a tour of the city. And when he walked into the theatre that evening the audience stood up and applauded. I suppose it was all too much for him. Anyway –" She glanced at Richard, suddenly horribly unsure if she could go on. "He had a stroke and died a few weeks later. My mother was with him, but we . . . my brother and I . . ."

Richard put his hand over hers and said, "I've always been so sorry that I never knew him. Or read him. It seems he's untranslatable," and the Dillons, after James had refilled her glass, tactfully embarked on a discussion of translations in general and that of a recent French play in particular.

She was grateful for Richard's hand and for not having to talk. She had not expected to be so upset. After all it had happened years ago. It was the thought of how it had happened, of course. She remembered Papa's coffin draped with the Union Jack. Common practice, they had said for a British subject dying abroad. It had seemed strange, for Papa had never managed to speak English properly and had been a British subject only for the last year of his life. Then the icy hall where the German musicians had played Beethoven's Seventh which Papa had loved so much, and the British soldiers who, together with Max and a local newspaperman, had helped to carry his coffin.

As Papa had planned.

If Mama died, it wouldn't be like that. Anyway, Mama couldn't die. She was too strong. Anna suddenly remembered with total clarity how Mama had looked when she and Max had arrived, stunned, in Hamburg.

"*Bitte etwas Tee.*" Tea in the hotel bedroom,

the only warm place in the devastated city. Mama saying, "There is something I must tell you about Papa."

As though anything else could possibly matter, Anna had thought, apart from the fact that Papa was dead. Then Mama talking about how Papa had failed to recover from the effects of the stroke. But they knew that already. Something about German doctors. How you could get anything for a packet of cigarettes. What?? Anna had thought. What??

"He was paralysed and in pain. He felt he could no longer think as clearly as he wished. I'd always promised to help him if that happened."

The sharp intake of breath from Max beside her. Mama's eyes shifting minutely towards him.

"So I did what he asked. I helped him."

She had said it in such matter of fact tones that even then Anna had not immediately understood.

"It was what he wanted." Mama had stared at them both, white faced and steely.

Max had said in a forlorn voice, "But we never said goodbye to him."

She could not remember what she herself had said. But she had known with complete certainty that what Mama had done was right.

She became aware of Richard looking at her. As usual, he knew what she was thinking. She sent him a reassuring look back and tried to listen to the conversation which seemed to have moved on from the French play to a discussion of its author.

James Dillon said something witty and everyone laughed. Elizabeth, relaxed in her chair, brushed a strand of hair out of her face. She thought, I am the only person in this room to whom such things have happened. I don't want to be. I want to belong here.

"Of course the French system of education . . ."

"What was it like being a child in Paris?"

She realized that Elizabeth was addressing her.

"In Paris? Oh –" She made an effort and began to talk about her school, the teacher called Madame Socrate who had helped her learn French, the friends she had made, outings to the country and to celebrate the 14th July. "I loved it," she said and found herself smiling.

"Of course you did." James Dillon had risen and she saw that he was wearing his Head of Drama expression which she knew from the BBC. "Now here's what we're going to do. If your mother needs you, you'll go and cope with whatever has to be done. And when you come back you'll do that adaptation we talked about. But I'd like you also to think about writing something of your own."

For the first time she was startled into total attention. "Of my own?"

"Why not? Needn't be very long, but all your own work." He raised his extravagant eyebrows. "Might be interesting."

It was so good to think about coming back from Berlin rather than going away that she tried to stifle her doubts about writing something original.

"All right," she said. "Though I'm not absolutely sure . . ."

"Think about it," said James.

She was saved from having to say anything more by the arrival of the small boy with the guinea pig clutched to his chest. After being introduced, he wandered over to his mother and allowed himself to be hugged. Then he whispered in her ear, was told not to whisper and said loudly, "Can Patricia have a crisp?"

"I didn't know she liked crisps," said Elizabeth.

"I don't know either." His small face furrowed as he searched for the right word. "It's an experiment," he said precisely.

He was given a potato crisp from a dish and they all watched while the guinea pig sniffed it in a corner of the floor and finally decided to crunch it up.

"She likes it," said the child, pleased.

"Go and get a saucer," said Elizabeth. "Then you and Patricia can have some crisps all to yourselves."

"All right." He scooped up the guinea pig. "Come on, Patricia," he said. "You're going to have . . ." He hesitated, but as he got to the door they heard him say happily, "A banquet."

In the quiet after he'd gone, Anna could hear the recorders, now both on the same tune, from the floor above.

"He's got quite a vocabulary," said Richard. "How old is he?"

"Six," said Elizabeth. Clearly he was the apple of their eye.

"Loves words," said James. "Been reading since he was four. Taken to writing stories now."

"Most of them about Patricia," giggled Elizabeth. "I bet you didn't know guinea pigs can pilot aeroplanes." She stopped as the child reappeared and helped him fill a saucer with crisps. Then she was struck by a thought. "I do find it absolutely extraordinary," she said to Anna, "that when you were his age you were speaking nothing but German. Can you still speak it?"

"A bit," said Anna. "I've forgotten a lot of it."

Elizabeth handed the child the saucer. "This lady has forgotten nearly all the words she knew when she was your age, can you imagine?" she said. "And she's learned a whole lot of new ones instead."

He stared at Anna in disbelief. Then he said, "I wouldn't."

"Wouldn't what?" asked his father.

"Forget." He saw everyone looking at him and took a deep breath. "I wouldn't forget the words I know. Even if – even if I learned a million trillion new words. I'd always remember."

"Well, it would only be if you went to a place where no one spoke English," said James. "And you're not going to do that, are you?"

"I'd still remember," said the child.

His father smiled. "Would you?"

"I'd remember Patricia." He pressed the guinea pig hard to his small chest. "And what's more," he said triumphantly, "I'd remember her in English!"

Everyone laughed. Richard got up and said they must leave, but before they could do so there was a noise on the landing and a girl of about nine appeared, lugging a large impassive baby in her arms.

"He wants his supper," she announced, and a slightly younger girl following behind her shouted, "And so do I!" They both dissolved into giggles and Anna found herself being introduced to them while at the same time saying her farewells to their parents. In the confusion the baby was dumped on the floor with the guinea pig until Elizabeth picked it up again and it began with great concentration to suck the end of her sleeve.

James saw Anna and Richard to the door. "Best of luck," he said through the children's shouted goodbyes. "And think about what I said."

Anna was left with the picture of Elizabeth standing at the top of the stairs and smiling with the baby in her arms.

"I told you she was nice," said Richard as they started on their walk back.

She nodded. The rain had stopped but it must have lasted some time, for the pavements were sodden.

"I wonder if I could really write something of my own," she said. "It'd be interesting to try. If I do have to go to Mama, I don't suppose I'd have to be away very long."

"Probably just a few days."

Notting Hill Gate was deserted. The demonstrators, no doubt discouraged by the downpour, had all gone home. A torn placard lying in a puddle was the only sign that they had ever been there.

"You know what I really hate about going to Berlin?" said Anna, picking her way round it. "I know it's stupid, but I'm frightened the Russians might suddenly close in and take it over and then I'd be trapped. They couldn't, could they?"

He shook his head. "It would mean war with America."

"I know. But it still frightens me."

"Were you very frightened when you escaped from Germany?"

"That's what so silly. I never realized till much later what it had been about. In fact, I remember making some idiotic remark at the frontier and Mama having to shut me up. Mama made it all seem quite normal." They trudged along among the puddles. "I wish at least I'd answered her letter," she said.

Once back in the flat, she became very practical. "We'd better make a list," she said, "Of all the things that have to be seen to, like the rug being delivered. And what are you going to eat while I'm away? I could cook something tonight for you to warm up."

She made the list and decided about the food, and by the time Konrad's call was due she felt ready to cope with anything he might say. Sitting by the telephone, she rehearsed the various things she wanted to ask him and waited. He came through punctually at nine o'clock. There was a jumble of German voices and then his, reassuringly calm.

"How is Mama?" she asked.

"Her condition is unchanged," he said and then in what was obviously a prepared speech, "I think it is right that you should come tomorrow. I think that one of her relatives should be here."

"Of course," she said. She told him the number of her flight and he said that he would meet it.

Richard, listening beside her, said, "What about Max? Has he told him?"

"Oh yes," she said. "What about Max?"

Konrad said that he had not yet cabled Max – that must mean that there was no immediate danger, thought Anna – but that he would do so if necessary in the morning. Then he said in his concerned refugee voice, "My dear, I hope you're not too upset by this. I'm sorry to have to break up the family. With luck it won't be for long."

She had forgotten that he always referred to Richard and herself as the family. It was friendly and comforting and she suddenly felt much better.

"That's all right," she said. "Richard sends his love." There was something more she wanted to ask him, but she had trouble remembering what it was. "Oh yes," she said. "How did Mama ever develop pneumonia in the first place?"

There was a silence, so that at first she thought he had not heard. Then his voice answered, and even through the distortion of long distance she could tell that it sounded quite different.

"I'm sorry," he said flatly. "But your mother took an overdose of sleeping pills."

Sunday

Anna's feet were so heavy that she could only walk very slowly. It was hot in the street and there was no one about. Suddenly Mama hurried past. She was wearing her blue hat with the veil, and she called to Anna, "I can't stop – I'm playing bridge with the Americans." Then she disappeared into a house which Anna had not even noticed. She felt sad to be left alone in the street like that, and the air was getting hotter and heavier all the time.

It shouldn't be so hot so early in the morning, she thought. She knew it was early because Max was still asleep. He had taken the front wall off his house to let out the heat, and she could see him sitting in his living-room with his eyes closed. Beside him his wife Wendy was blinking drowsily in a chair with the baby in her arms. She looked at Anna and moved her lips, but the air had become too thick to carry the sound and Anna could not hear her, so she walked away, along the hot, empty street, with the hot, empty day stretching before her.

How did I come to be so alone? she thought. Surely there must be someone to whom I belong? But she could think of no one. The heavy air pressed in on her, so that she could hardly breathe. She had to push it away with her hands. And yet there *was* someone, she thought, I'm sure there was. She tried to remember his name, but her mind was empty. She could think of nothing, neither his name nor his face nor even his voice.

I must remember, she thought. She knew that he existed, hidden in some tiny wrinkle of her brain, and that without him nothing was any good, nothing would ever be any good again. But the air was too heavy. It was piled up all round her, pushing in on her chest, even against her eyes and her nose and her mouth. Soon it would be too late even to remember.

"There *was* someone!" she shouted, somehow forcing her voice through the thickness. "I know there was someone!"

And then she was in bed with the sheets and blankets twisted all round her and a pillow half over her face, and Richard saying, "It's all right, love. It's all right."

For a moment she could only lie there, feeling him close and letting the horror flow out of her. She half-saw, half-felt the familiar room, the shapes of a chair, a chest of drawers, the faint glint of a mirror in the darkness.

"I had a dream," she said at last.

"I know. You nearly blew me out of bed."

"It was that awful one when I can't remember you."

His arms were round her. "I'm here."

"I know."

In the glow from the street lamp outside the window, she could just see his face, tired and concerned.

"It's such an awful dream," she said. "Why do you suppose I have it? It's like being caught in some awful shift of time and not being able to get back."

"Maybe some trick of the brain. You know – one lobe remembering and the other not picking it up till a fraction of a second later. Like déjà vu, only the other way round."

It did not comfort her.

"Suppose one got stuck."

"You couldn't get stuck."

"But if I did. If I really couldn't remember you. Or if I got stuck even earlier, before I'd learned to speak English. We wouldn't even be able to talk to each other."

"Yes, well," he said, "in that case we'd have other problems as well. You'd be about eleven years old."

At this she laughed and the dream, already fading, receded into harmlessness. She could feel herself aching from lack of sleep and remembered clearly, for the first time, about the previous day.

"Oh God," she said. "Mama."

His arms tightened about her. "I suppose all this worry has stirred up things you'd almost forgotten. About losing people – people and places – when you were small."

"Poor Mama. She was awfully good then, you know."

"I know."

"I wish to God I'd written to her." Through the gap between the curtains the sky looked black. "What time is it?"

"Only six o'clock." She could see him peering at her anxiously in the darkness. "I'm sure it would have made no difference whether you'd written or not. There must have been quite other reasons. She must have been worried about something, or terribly upset."

"D'you think so?" She wanted to believe him.

"And then, maybe, she thought of your father – how he had died – and she thought, why shouldn't she do the same?"

No, it wasn't right.

"Papa was different," she said. "He was old, and he'd had two strokes. Whereas Mama . . . Oh God," she said, "I suppose some people have parents who die naturally." She stared into the darkness. "The trouble is, you see, I don't suppose Max has written either, or if he did, the letter may not have got there from Greece."

"It still wouldn't be a reason to commit suicide."

Outside in the street there was a clinking of bottles followed by a clip-clop of the milkman's horse as it walked on to the next house. A car started up in the distance.

"We were all so close, you see, all those years," she said. "We couldn't help it, moving from country to country with everything against us. Mama used to say, if it weren't for Max and me, it wouldn't be worth going on – and she did get us through, she kept the family together."

"I know."

"I wish I'd written to her," she said.

Richard came with her on the bus to the airport. They said goodbye in the echoing lounge which smelled of paint and she left him, calmly, as she had planned.

But then, quite suddenly, as she pulled out her passport ready for inspection, despair swept over her. To her horror, she found tears pouring down her face, soaking her cheeks, her neck and even the collar of her blouse. She could not move but only stood there blindly, waiting for him to catch up with her.

"What is it?" he cried, but she didn't know either.

"I'm all right," she said. "I really am." She was horrified at having frightened him so. "It's not having slept," she said. "And I'm getting the curse. You know I always weep when I'm getting the curse."

Her voice came out quite loud, and a man in a bowler hat turned and looked at her in surprise.

"I could still come with you," said Richard. "I could get a flight later today or tomorrow."

"No, no, of course not. I'm really all right." She kissed him. Then she took her passport and ran. "I'll write to you," she shouted back to him.

She knew it was stupid, but she felt that she was leaving him for ever.

Once on the plane, she felt better.

She had only flown twice before and still found it exciting to look down on a world of toy-sized fields and houses and tiny, crawling cars. It was a relief to be out of it all and to know that Berlin was still some hours away. She looked out of the window and thought only of what she could see. Then halfway across the North Sea, clouds appeared, and soon there was only a blanket of grey below and bright, empty sky above. She leaned back in her seat and thought about Mama.

It was curious, she thought. Whichever way one imagined Mama, it was always in movement: the blue eyes frowning, the lips talking, Mama clenching her hands with impatience, tugging her dress into place, dabbing violently at her tiny snub nose with a powder puff. She did not trust anything connected with herself to function properly unless she kept tabs on it, and even then she always felt it could be improved.

Anna remembered how, during one of her visits from Germany, Mama had once brought Konrad round to her digs for lunch. Anna had cooked the only dish she knew, which was a large quantity of rice mixed with whatever happened to be on hand. On this occasion the ingredients had included some chopped-up sausages, and Konrad had said, politely, how nice they were. At once Mama had said, "I'll find you some more," and to Anna's irritation she had snatched up the bowl and rootled through it, to toss a succession of small sausage pieces on to his plate.

How could anybody so obsessed with the minutiae of every day suddenly want to stop living? Not that Mama hadn't often talked about it. But that was in the last years in Putney when she and Papa had been so utterly wretched, and even then it had not seemed like anything to be taken seriously. Her cries of "I wish I was dead!" and "Why should I go on?" had been so frequent that both Anna and Papa had soon learned to ignore them.

And the moment things improved, the moment the endless worry about money was lifted from her, her enthusiasm for life had returned – both Anna and Papa had been surprised how quickly. She had written long excited letters home from Germany. She had gone everywhere and looked at everything. She had translated so well for the Americans in the Control Commission that she had soon been promoted – from Frankfurt to Munich, from Munich to Nuremberg. She had wangled lifts home on American troop planes to arrive with presents for everyone – American whisky for Papa, nylon stockings for Anna, real silk ties for Max. And she had been thrilled when at last the British Control Commission had decided that Papa, too, should make an official trip to Germany.

Hamburg, thought Anna. Did the flight to Berlin pass over it? She peered down at the flat country which showed every so often through gaps in the cloud. It was strange to think that somewhere down there might be the place where Papa lay buried. If Mama died, she supposed she'd be buried with him. If Mama dies, she thought suddenly with a kind of impatience, I'll be the child of two suicides.

There was a click as something was put down on the folding table in front of her, and she became aware of the stewardess standing nearby.

"I thought you might like some coffee," she said.

Anna drank it gratefully.

"I was so sorry to hear of the illness in your family," said the girl in her American voice. "I do hope that when you get to Berlin you will find everything better than you expected."

Anna thanked her and stared out at the brilliant sky and the melting clouds below. But what do I expect? she thought. Konrad had only told her that Mama's condition was unchanged, not what that condition was. And in any case, that had been last night. By now . . . No, thought Anna, she's not dead. I would know if she were.

As the time of arrival approached, she tried to think what it would be like meeting Konrad. One thing, it wouldn't be difficult to find him, because he was so tall and fat. She'd see him over the heads of the other people. He'd be leaning on his walking stick if his back was giving him trouble as it so often did, and he'd smile at her with his curiously irregular features and say something reassuring. He would be calm. Anna imagined him always having been calm. You'd have to be calm to stay on in Germany under Hitler as a Jewish lawyer defending other Jews, as he had done.

He had even remained calm when they sent him to a concentration camp. By being calm and unobtrusive, he had survived several weeks, until his friends managed to get him out. Nothing too terrible had happened to him, but he would never talk about what he had seen. All he would say was, "You should have seen me when I came out," and he would slap his paunch and grin his lopsided grin and say, "I was thin – like a Greek youth."

He would certainly have made sure that Mama had the best possible treatment. He was very practical. Anna remembered Mama telling her that in England he had supported a wife and two daughters by taking a job in a factory. The daughters were grown up now, but he seemed not to care too much for any of them and seldom went home.

"We are now approaching Tempelhof airfield," said the stewardess, and all the lighted messages about seat belts and cigarettes flicked on.

She looked out of the window. They were still quite high and the airport was not in sight. I suppose all this is still East Germany, she thought, looking down at the fields and little houses. They looked like anywhere else and presumably would have looked just the same under the Nazis. I only hope we land in the right place, she thought.

The last time she had landed in Berlin had been with Richard. They had arrived at short notice, to tell Mama that they were getting married. It had been a curious, edgy visit, even though she'd been so happy – partly because she so hated being in Berlin and only partly because of Mama. Not that Mama had been against the marriage – on the contrary, she had been delighted. Only Anna had known that for years Mama had secretly dreamed of her marrying someone quite different.

In Putney, when Papa's health was failing and everything seemed hopeless, Mama had had a kind of running fantasy about this marriage. It would be to a lord – a very grand kind of lord with a big estate in the country. Anna would live with him at the castle, and Mama would live at the dower house (there always was a dower house, she had explained to Anna). There would be an apple-cheeked housekeeper to cook muffins for Mama to eat in front of the fire, and on fine days Mama would ride about the grounds on a white horse.

Of course she hadn't meant it. It had just been a joke to cheer them both up and, as Anna had frequently pointed out, Mama couldn't ride. Even so, when she told Mama about Richard, she knew that somewhere in her mind Mama was regretfully relinquishing the image of herself prancing about on this great bleached beast, surrounded by grooms or hounds or whatever she'd imagined for herself, and it had made Anna nervous.

Another thing that had made her nervous was that Mama did not really understand Richard's work. She got most of her information about England from Max who, as a rising young barrister, seemed to her a more reliable source than Anna with her art, and Max had told her that he did not have a television set, though they were considering buying one for the au pair girl. This had made Anna nervous of what Mama might say to Richard, or even when Richard was anywhere near, because Mama's voice was so loud.

It was silly because Richard was quite able to take care of himself. But she had been grateful to Konrad for steering Mama away from dangerous subjects. As soon as Mama got started on literature or drama (she tended, in any case, only to quote Papa's views, and not always correctly) he had looked at her with his nice, ugly smile and said, "It's no use talking about these things in my presence. You know perfectly well that I'm illiterate."

The plane tilted to one side. Anna could see Berlin, suddenly close, above the wing, and the airport beyond it. We'll be down in a minute, she thought, and all at once she felt frightened.

What would Konrad tell her? Would he blame her for not having written to Mama for so long?

Did he even know why Mama had taken the over-dose? And how would she find Mama? Conscious? In an oxygen tent? In a coma?

As the ground came towards her, it was like the first time she'd jumped off the high diving board at school. I'm going into it, she thought. Nothing can stop it now. She saw with regret that there was not even a veil of cloud to delay her. The sky was clear, the midday sun blazed down on the grass and tarmac of the airport as it rushed up towards her, then the wheels touched, they roared briefly along the runway and stopped with a shudder. There was nothing to be done. She was there.

Konrad was standing near the door of the arrival lounge, leaning on his walking stick as she had expected. She walked towards him through the blur of German voices, and when he caught sight of her he came to meet her.

"Hullo," he said, and she saw that his large face looked worn out and somehow skimpy. He did not embrace her, as he normally did, but only smiled at her formally and shook her hand. She was at once apprehensive.

"How is Mama?" she asked.

He said, "Exactly the same." Then he told her flatly that Mama was in a coma and had been ever since she had been found on Saturday morning and that there had been some difficulty in treating her because for a long time no one knew what she had taken. "I cabled Max this morning," he said.

She said, "Shall we go to the hospital?"

He shook his head. "There's no point, I've just come from there."

Then he turned and walked towards his car, slightly ahead of her, in spite of his bad back and his walking stick, as though he wanted to get away from her. She hurried after him in the sunshine, more and more distressed.

"What do the doctors say?" she asked, just to make him look round, and he said wearily, "The same. They simply can't tell," and walked on.

It was all much worse than anything she had imagined. She had thought he might blame her for not having written to Mama, but not to the extent of wanting nothing to do with her. She was appalled at the thought of coping with all the horrors to come alone, without his support. (If only Richard were here, she thought, but cut the thought off quickly, since it was no use.)

When he reached the car, she caught up with him and faced him before he could put the key in the lock.

"It was because of me, wasn't it?" she said. "Because I hadn't written?"

He lowered the hand with the key in it and looked back at her, utterly astonished.

"It would certainly be a good idea if you wrote to your mother more often," he said, "and if your brother did too. But that is not the reason why she tried to kill herself."

"Then why?"

There was a pause. He looked away from her,

over her right shoulder, as though he had suddenly seen someone he knew in the distance. Then he said stiffly, "She had grounds to believe that I was no longer faithful to her."

Her first reaction was, impossible, he's making it up. He was saying it to comfort her, so that she shouldn't blame herself if Mama died. For heaven's sake, she thought, at their age! Well, she supposed that if she had ever thought about it, she would have assumed that Mama's relationship with him had not been entirely platonic. But this!

Very carefully, she said, "Are you in love with someone else?"

He gave a sort of snort of "No!" and then said in the same stiff voice as before, "I had an affair."

"An affair?"

"It was nothing." He was almost shouting with impatience. "A girl in my office. Nothing."

She tried to think of a reply to this but couldn't. She felt completely out of her depth and climbed into the car in silence.

"You'll want some lunch."

He seemed so relieved to have got the bit about the affair off his chest that she thought it must really be true.

As he started the car, he said, "I want to make your stay here as pleasant as possible. In the circumstances. I know it's what your mother would wish. If possible even like a little holiday. I know you didn't get away in the summer."

For God's sake, she thought.

He made a gesture of impatience. "I understand, of course, that you'd give anything not to be here but at home with Richard. I only meant that when you're not at the hospital – and at the moment there is not much you can do there – you should have as pleasant a time as can be arranged."

He glanced at her from behind the steering wheel and she nodded, since he seemed so anxious for her to agree.

"Well," he said, "we may as well start by going somewhere pleasant for lunch."

The restaurant was set among the pine trees of the Grunewald, a popular place for family outings, and on this fine Sunday it was packed. Some people were even drinking at small tables outside, their overcoats well-buttoned against the chilly air.

"Do you remember this place?" he asked.

She had already had a faint sense of recognition – something about the shape of the building, the colour of the stone.

"I think I may have come here sometimes with my parents. Not to eat, just for a drink."

He smiled. "*Himbeersaft*."

"That's right." Raspberry juice, of course. That's what German children always drank.

Inside, the dining-room was steaming up with the breath of many good eaters, their coats hung in rows against the brown panelled walls, and mounted above them, two pairs of antlers and a picture of a hunter with a gun. Their voices were loud and comfortable above the clinking of their knives and forks, and Anna found herself both moved and yet suspicious as always, at the sound of the Berlin accents so familiar from her childhood.

"This thing with your mother has been going on for nearly three weeks," said Konrad in English, and the voices with their complicated associations faded into the background. "That's how long she had known."

"How did she find out?"

"I told her."

Why? she thought, and as though he had heard her, he went on, "We live in a very narrow circle. I was afraid she might hear from someone else."

"But if you don't really love this woman – if it's all over?"

He shrugged his shoulders. "You know what your mother is like. She said that things could never again be right between us. She said she'd had to start again too many times in her life, she'd had enough, that you and Max were grown up and no longer needed her –" He waved his hand to indicate all the other things Mama had said and which Anna could only too easily imagine. "She's been talking about killing herself for nearly three weeks."

But he hadn't actually said that it was all over between himself and the other woman.

"The affair, of course, is finished," he said.

When the food arrived, he said, "We'll go to

the hospital after lunch. Then you can see your mother and perhaps talk to one of the doctors. In the meantime, tell me about yourself and Richard."

She told him about Richard's serial, about the flat and about her new job.

"Does this mean that you'll eventually become a writer?"

"Like Richard, you mean?"

"Or like your father."

"I don't know."

"Why don't you know?" he asked almost impatiently.

She tried to explain. "I don't know if I'd be good enough. Till now I've really only tinkered with other people's plays. I've never done anything of my own."

"I could imagine you being a good writer." But he added at once, "Of course I know nothing about it."

They tried to talk about general subjects: Hungary, but neither of them had listened to the radio that morning, so they did not know the latest news; the German economic recovery; how long it would take Max to get a flight from Greece. But gradually the conversation faltered and died. The sound of the Berliners eating and talking seeped into the silence. Familiar, long forgotten words and phrases.

"*Bitte ein Nusstörtchen*," a fat man at the next table told the waiter.

That's what I always used to eat when I was

small, she thought. A little white iced cake with a nut on top. And Max had always chosen a *Mohrenkopf*, which was covered in chocolate and had cream inside. They had never wavered in their preferences and had both come to believe that the one was only for the girls and the other for boys.

"*Ein Nusstötchen*," said the waiter and set it down in front of the fat man.

Even now, for a fraction of a second, Anna was surprised that he let him have it.

"You're not eating," said Konrad.

"I'm sorry." She speared a bit of potato on her fork.

"Try to eat. It'll be better. The next few days are bound to be difficult."

She nodded and ate while he watched her.

"The hospital your mother is at is German. It's just as good as the American for this kind of case, and it was nearer. Also I thought that if your mother recovered, it would be easier for her if the Americans didn't know about her suicide attempt." He waited for her to agree, and she nodded again. "When I found her –"

"You found her?"

"Of course." He seemed surprised. "You understand, I've been afraid of this happening. I stayed with her as much as possible. But the night before, she seemed all right, so I left her. Only next day I had such a feeling . . . I went round to her flat and there she was. I stood and looked at her and didn't know what to do."

"How do you mean?"

"Perhaps . . ." he said, "perhaps it was really what she wanted. She'd said again and again that she was tired. I don't know – I still don't know if what I did was right. But I thought of you and Max, and I felt I couldn't take the responsibility."

When she could eat no more, he stood up.

"Come along," he said. "We'll go and see your mother. Try not to let it distress you too much."

The hospital was a pleasant, old-fashioned building set in a wooded park. But even as they approached the front door, past a man raking leaves and another shovelling them into a wheelbarrow, her stomach tightened on the lunch she had not wished to eat, so that for a moment she was afraid she might be sick.

Inside the hall, a very clean nurse in a starched apron received them. She had a tight expression and seemed to disapprove of them both, as though she blamed them for what had happened to Mama.

"Follow me please," she said in German.

They went, Anna first with Konrad behind her. It was more like a nursing home than a hospital – wood panelled walls and carpets instead of tiles and lino. It's more like a nursing home than a hospital, she said to herself, so as not to think about what she was going to see. Corridors, stairs, more corridors, then a large landing crowded with cupboards and hospital equipment. Suddenly the nurse stopped and pointed, and there, behind a piece of dust-sheeted machinery, was a bed. There was someone in it, motionless. Why was Mama not in her room? Why had they put her here, on this landing?

"What's happened?" she shouted so loudly that she frightened all three of them.

"It's all right," said Konrad, and the nurse explained in disapproving tones that nothing had happened: since Mama had to be under constant observation, this was the best place for her. Doctors and nurses crossed the landing every few minutes and were able to keep an eye on her.

"She's being very well looked after," said Konrad, and they went over to the bed and looked at Mama.

You could not see very much of her. Just her face and one arm. All the rest was covered with bedclothes. The face was very pale. The eyes were closed – not just closed normally but closed tight, as though Mama were keeping them shut on purpose. There was something sticking out of her mouth, and Anna saw that it was the end of a tube through which Mama's breath came thinly and irregularly. Another tube led to the arm from a bottle suspended from a stand near the bed.

"There doesn't seem to be any change," said Konrad.

"It is necessary to bring her out of the coma," said the nurse. "For this we must call her by her name." She leaned over the bed and did so. Nothing at all happened. She shrugged her shoulders. "*Na*," she said, "a familiar voice is always better. Perhaps if you speak to her she will hear."

Anna looked down at Mama and the tubes.

"In English or in German?" she asked, and immediately wondered how she could have said anything so stupid.

"That you must decide for yourself," said the nurse. She nodded stiffly and disappeared among the dustsheeted equipment.

Anna looked at Konrad.

"Try," he said. "One doesn't know. It may do some good." He stood looking at Mama for a moment. "I'll wait for you downstairs."

Anna was left alone with Mama. It seemed quite mad to try and talk to her.

"Mama," she said tentatively in English. "It's me, Anna."

There was no response. Mama just lay there with the tube in her mouth and her eyes tightly shut.

"Mama," she said more loudly. "Mama!"

She felt oddly self-conscious. As though that mattered at a time like this, she told herself guiltily.

"Mama! You must wake up, Mama!"

But Mama remained unmoving, her eyes obstinately closed and her mind determined to have nothing to do with the world.

"Mama!" she cried. "Mama! Please wake up!"

Mama, she thought, I hate it when your eyes are shut. You're a naughty Mama. Clambering on Mama's bed, Mama's big face on the pillow, trying to prise the eyelids open with her tiny fingers. For God's sake, she thought, that must have been when I was about two.

"Mama! Wake up, Mama!"

A nurse carrying some sheets came up behind her and said in German, "That's right." She smiled as though she were encouraging Anna in some kind of sport. "Even if there is no reaction," she said, "your voice may be getting through."

So Anna went on shouting while the nurse put the sheets into a cupboard and went away again. She shouted in English and in German. She told Mama that she must not die, that her children needed her, that Konrad loved her and that everything would be all right. And while she was shouting, she wondered if any of it were true and whether it was right to tell Mama these things even when she probably could not hear them.

In between shouting, she looked at Mama and remembered her in the past. Mama tugging at a sweater and saying, "Don't you think it's nice?" Mama in the flat in Paris, triumphant because she'd bought some strawberries at half-price. Mama beating off some boys who had pursued Anna home from the village school in Switzerland. Mama eating, Mama laughing, Mama counting her money and saying, "We'll have to manage somehow." And all the time a tiny part of herself observed the scene, noted the resemblance to something out of Dr Kildare, and marvelled that anything so shattering could also be so corny.

At last she could bear it no longer and found the nurse who led her back to Konrad.

She felt sick again in the car and hardly saw the hotel where Konrad had booked her in. There was an impression of shabbiness, someone leading her up some stairs, Konrad saying, "I'll fetch you for supper," and then she was lying on a large bed under a large German quilt in a strange, half-darkened room.

Gradually, in the quiet, the sick feeling receded. Tension, she thought. All her life she had reacted like this. Even when she was tiny and afraid of thunderstorms. She had lain in bed, fighting the nausea among the frightening rumbles and flashes of lightning, until Max got her a freshly-ironed handkerchief from the drawer to spread on her stomach. For some reason this had always cured her.

They had slept under German quilts like this one, not sheets and blankets as in England. The quilts had been covered in cotton cases which buttoned at one end and, to avert some long forgotten, imaginary misfortune, they had always shouted, "Buttons to the bottom!" before they went to sleep. Much later, in the Hamburg hotel after Papa's death, she had reminded Max of this, but he had not been able to remember anything about it.

That had been the last time they had all been together, she and Max and Mama and Papa – even though Papa was dead. For Papa had left so many notes and messages that for a while it had felt as though he were still with them.

"I *told* him not to," Mama had said, as though it were a case of Papa going out without his galoshes on a wet day. She had not wanted Papa to write any farewell notes because suicide was still a crime, and she did not know what would happen if people found out. "As though it were anyone's business but his own," she said.

She had left Papa one evening, knowing that after she had gone he would take the pills she had procured for him, and that she would never again see him alive. What had they said to each other that last evening? And Papa – what would he think of all this now? He had wanted so much for Mama to be happy. "You are not to feel like a widow," he had written in his last note to her. And to Max and herself he had said, "Look after Mama."

There was a shimmer of light as a draught shifted the curtains. They were made of heavy, woven cloth, and as they moved, the tiny pattern of the weave flowed and changed into different combinations of verticals and horizontals. She followed them with her eyes, while vague, disconnected images floated through her mind: Papa in Paris, on the balcony of the poky furnished flat where they had lived for two years, saying, "You can see the Arc de Triomphe, the Trocadero and the Eiffel Tower!" Meeting Papa in the street on her way home from school. London? No, Paris, the Rue Lauriston where later, during the war, the Germans had had their Gestapo headquarters.

Papa's lips moving, oblivious of passers-by, shaping words and phrases, and smiling suddenly at the sight of her.

The boarding house in Bloomsbury on a hot, sunny day. Finding Mama and Papa on a tin roof outside an open window, Papa on a straight-backed chair, Mama spread out on an old rug. "We're sunbathing," said Papa with his gentle, ironic smile, but specks of London soot were drifting down from the sky, blackening everything they touched. "One can't even sunbathe any more," said Mama, and the bits of soot settled on Mama and Papa and made little black marks on their clothes, their hands and their faces. They got mixed up with the pattern on the curtains, and still Mama and Papa sat there with the soot drifting down, and Anna too was drifting – drifting and falling. "The most important thing about writing," said Richard, but the plane was landing and the engines made too much noise for her to hear what was so important, and Papa was coming to meet her along the runway. "Papa," she said aloud, and found herself in the strange bed, unsure for a moment whether she had been asleep or not.

At any rate it could only have been for a minute, for the light had not changed. It's Sunday afternoon, she thought. I'm in a strange room in Berlin and it's Sunday afternoon. The draught moved the curtains again, and little patches of light danced over the quilt, across the wall, and disappeared. It must still be sunny outside. She got up to look.

Outside the window was a garden with trees and bushes and fallen leaves in the long grass. Near the dilapidated wooden fence something moved, flashing orange, leapt, clung to a wildly dipping branch, scrabbled the right way up and sat swinging in the wind. A red squirrel. Of course. There were plenty of them in Germany. She watched it as it sat washing itself, with the wind ruffling its tail. She no longer felt sick at all.

Papa would have liked the swinging squirrel. He had never known about Richard, or about Max's baby daughter, or that the world, after years of horror and deprivation, had once again turned into such a delightful place. But I'm alive, she thought. Whatever happens, I am still alive.

Konrad came to collect her at six o'clock. "We're spending the evening with friends," he said. "I thought it would be best. They'd originally invited your mother and myself for bridge, so they were expecting me anyway. Of course they only know that she has pneumonia."

Anna nodded.

As they drove through the darkened, leafy streets, she was filled again with the sense of something half-familiar. Yellow lights flickered through the trees, casting wavering shadows on the ground.

"This is all the Grunewald district," said Konrad. "Where you used to live. Do you remember any of it?"

She did not remember the streets, only the feel of them. She and Max walking home after dark, playing a game of jumping on each other's shadows as they slid and leapt between one street lamp and the next. Herself thinking, this is the best game we've ever played. We'll play it always, always, always . . .

"It was hardly touched by the bombing," said Konrad. "Tomorrow you might like to have a look round near your old home."

She nodded.

A group of shops, unexpectedly bright, throwing rectangles of light on to the pavement. *Apotheke*, a chemist. A newsagent. A florist. *Blumenladen* said the illuminated sign above it, and as she read the word she had a sensation of being suddenly very near the ground, surrounded by great leaves and overpowering scents. Enormous brilliant flowers nodded and dipped above her on stems almost as thick as her wrist, and she was clutching a huge hand from which a huge arm stretched up into the jungle above her. *Blumenladen*, she thought softly to herself. *Blumenladen*. Then the shop vanished into the darkness and she was back in the car, a little dazed, with Konrad beside her.

"Nearly there," he said in English, and after a moment she nodded again.

He turned down a side street, through a patch of trees, and stopped outside a white-painted building, one of a number placed fairly close together among scrappy lawns.

"Purpose-built American flats," he said. "The Goldblatts have only just moved in here."

They climbed a flight of stairs and as soon as Hildy Goldblatt opened the door Anna felt she was back in wartime England, for with her frizzy hair, her worried dark eyes and her voice which sounded as though someone had sat on it, she seemed like the epitome of all the refugees she had ever known.

"There she is," cried Hildy, opening her arms wide. "Come all the way from London to see her sick Mama. And how is she today?"

Konrad replied quickly that Mama's pneumonia was fractionally better – which was true, he had telephoned the hospital before leaving – and Hildy nodded.

"She will be well soon."

Her husband, a slight man with grey hair, had appeared in the hall beside her. "Today pneumonia is nothing. Not like in the old days."

"In the old days – *na ja*." They raised their hands and their eyebrows and smiled at each other, remembering not only the intractability of pneumonia but all the other difficulties overcome in the past. "Things are different today," they said.

As Hildy led the way to a lavishly laid table ("We eat now," she said, "then it will be done,") Anna wondered how they had preserved their refugee accents through all the years in England and of working with the Americans in Germany. It must be a special talent, she decided. She could almost have predicted the meal Hildy served, as well. In wartime London it would have been soup with knoedel, followed by apple tart. In Berlin, with the American PX to draw on, there was an additional course of steak and fried potatoes.

While Hildy heaped her plate ("So eat – you must be tired!") the conversation slid from English into German and back again in a way which she found curiously soothing. Erwin Goldblatt worked with Konrad at J.R.S.O., the Jewish Restitution Successor Organization, where they dealt with claims from the millions of Jews who had lost their families, their health and their possessions under the Nazis. "Of course you can't really compensate them," said Erwin. "Not with money." And Konrad said, "One does what one can." They talked of work, of the old days in London ("I can tell you, Finchley in 1940 was no summer holiday!"), of colleagues in Nuremberg where they had all first met.

"And your brother?" asked Hildy. "What is he doing? Something in Greece, your mother said."

"He's got a big case for a Greek ship owner," said Anna. "He had to go there for a conference, and the ship owner lent him a house for a holiday with his family afterwards. The trouble is, it's so far away even from Athens, on a tiny island. It's bound to take him a long time to get here."

Hildy looked surprised. "Max too is coming to see his mother? Is it then so serious?"

I shouldn't have said that, thought Anna.

Konrad swept in calmly. "Pneumonia is no

joke, even today, Hildy. I thought it best to let him know."

"Of course, of course." But she had guessed something. Her shrewd eyes met her husband's briefly, then moved back to Konrad. "So much trouble," she said vaguely.

"Ach, always trouble." Erwin sighed and offered Anna some cake. "But this young man," he said, brightening, "such a young barrister, and already ship owners are lending him their country houses. He is making quite a career."

"You've heard her talk about him," cried Hildy. "The wonder boy. He got a big scholarship in Cambridge."

"And a law scholarship after that," said Anna.

Hildy patted her hand. "There, you see," she said, "it will be all right. As soon as the mother sees her son, no matter how ill she is, she will just get up from her bed and walk."

Everyone laughed, and it was quite true, thought Anna, Mama would do anything for Max. At the same time another part of herself thought, then what in heaven's name am I doing here? But she suppressed it quickly.

Hildy went into the kitchen and reappeared a moment later with a jug of coffee. "The girl looks tired," she said, passing Anna her cup. "What can we do for her?"

Erwin said, "A glass of cognac," but Hildy shook her head. "Cognac afterwards. First I know something better."

She beckoned, and Anna followed her out of the

room, feeling suddenly at the end of her tether. I don't want any cognac, she thought, and I don't want any more cake or coffee, I just want to be home. She found herself standing beside Hildy in the hall. There was nothing there except a telephone on a small table. Hildy pointed to it.

"So why don't you ring up your husband?" she asked.

"Really?" said Anna. She felt tears pricking her eyes and thought, this is really ridiculous.

"Of course."

"Well, if you're sure." She blinked to stop the tears from running down her face. "I don't know what it is – I feel so –" She couldn't think what it was she felt like.

Hildy patted the telephone.

"Ring him up," she said and left Anna alone in the hall.

When she went back into the living room, they were all drinking cognac.

"Look at her," cried Erwin when he saw her, "she has another face already."

Konrad patted her shoulder. "Everything all right?"

"Yes." Just hearing Richard's voice had made her feel different.

Out of respect for Hildy's telephone bill, they had only spoken a few minutes. She had told him that she had seen Mama – but nothing about Konrad, it would have been impossible with him in the next room – and he had told her that he was trying to get on with the script and that he had cooked himself some spaghetti.

Halfway through she had suddenly asked, "Am I speaking with a German accent?" but he had laughed and said, "Of course not." Afterwards she had felt reconnected to some essential part of herself – something that might, otherwise, have come dangerously loose.

"I'm sorry," she said. "It's all been a bit disorientating."

They gave her some cognac which she drank, and suddenly the evening became very cheerful. Erwin told various old refugee jokes which Anna had known since her childhood but which, for some reason, she now found hilarious. She saw that Konrad, too, was leaning back, laughing, in his chair.

"Ach, the troubles we've had, the troubles we've had." Hildy had produced another cake, a chocolate one, and was pressing it on everyone. "And in the end, somehow, it's all right, and you think, all that worrying – better I should have spent the time learning another language."

Everyone laughed at the thought of Hildy attempting another language on top of her refugee English, and she pretended to threaten them with the chocolate cake.

"You can laugh," she said, "but all the same it's true what I say. Most things are all right in the end." She glanced at Erwin. "Not everything, of course. But most things."

Erwin looked back at her fondly. "*Na*," he

said, "at least they're better than they used to be."

When Anna got back to her hotel room she felt almost guilty at having enjoyed the evening so much. But what else could I have done? she thought. Lying under the German quilt in the darkness, she could hear a cat wailing in the garden. Somewhere in the distance a train went chuntering across some points.

She suddenly remembered that when she was small, too, she had listened to distant trains in bed. Probably it's the same line, she thought. Sometimes when she had found herself awake while everyone else was asleep, she had been comforted by the sound of a goods train rumbling interminably through the night. After Hitler, of course, goods trains had carried quite different cargoes to quite different destinations. She wondered if other German children had still been comforted by their sound in the night, not knowing what was inside them. She wondered what had happened to the trains afterwards, and if they were still in use.

The cat wailed and the chugging of another train drifted over on the wind. Perhaps tomorrow Mama will be better, she thought, and fell asleep.

Monday

When she woke up in the morning, it was pouring. She could hear the rain drumming on the window and dripping from the gutters even before she opened her eyes on the grey light of the room. In the garden, most of the leaves had been washed off the trees, and she hoped that the cat had found some shelter.

As she made her way downstairs, across worn carpets and past ancient, fading wallpapers, she noticed for the first time that what she was staying in was not a real hotel, but a private house, half-heartedly converted. There did not seem to be many other guests, for the breakfast room was empty except for an elderly man who got up and left as she arrived. She sat down at the only other table which had been laid, and at once a small bow-legged woman whom she dimly remembered from the previous day hurried in with a tray.

"Had a good sleep?" she asked in broad Berlinese. "You're looking better today. When I saw you yesterday I thought to myself, that one's had all she can take."

"I'm fine now, thank you," said Anna. As usual, she emphasized her English accent and spoke more haltingly than necessary. She had no wish to be thought even remotely German.

"I'll bring you your breakfast."

The woman was middle-aged, with pale hair so lacking in colour that it might have been either fair or grey, and sharp, pale eyes. As she scuttled in and out on her little legs, she talked without stopping.

"The gentleman phoned to say that he'd be calling for you at nine. It's dreadfully wet out. String rain, we call it in Berlin, because it looks like long pieces of string, d'you see? I really dread going out to do the shopping, but I have to, there's no one else to do it."

As she talked, she brought Anna a small metal can of tea, butter, jam and bread rolls.

"Thank you," said Anna, and poured herself some tea.

"I don't do suppers, but I can always fix you up a boiled egg or some herrings if you should want them. Or a bit of cauliflower."

Anna nodded and smiled in a limited way, and the woman, defeated by her English reserve, retired.

She looked at her watch. It was only a little after eight-thirty, she had plenty of time. She wondered how Mama was. Presumably the same, otherwise Konrad would have asked to speak to her when he rang. She buttered one of the bread rolls and took a bite. It tasted much as she remembered from her childhood.

"There are more rolls if you'd like them," said the woman, peering round the door.

"No thank you," said Anna.

When she was small, there had never been more than one roll each for breakfast. "If you want more, you can eat bread," Heimpi who looked after them always told them while she and Max wolfed it down before school. She had been so convinced of the infallibility of this rule that once, pondering upon the existence of God and also feeling rather hungry, she had challenged Him to a miracle.

"Let them give me a second roll," she had told Him, "then I'll know that You exist," and to her awed amazement Heimpi had actually produced one.

It had been a poor bargain, she thought. For months afterwards she had been burdened by the knowledge that she alone in a family of agnostics had proof of God's existence. Though she found it exciting at first (standing talking to Mama and Papa, her hands secretly folded in prayer behind her back, thinking, "Little do they know what I'm doing!"), eventually it had become such a strain that Mama had asked her if she were worried about anything. She remembered looking at Mama in the sunlight from the living-room window, trying to decide what to answer.

As always in those days, she was worried not only about God but about several other things as well, the most urgent being a book of raffle tickets she had recklessly acquired at school and had found impossible to sell. Should she tell Mama about the raffle tickets or about God? She had carefully examined Mama's face – the directness of her blue eyes, the childish snub nose and the energetic, uncomplicated mouth, and she had made her decision. She had told her about the raffle tickets.

As she sat chewing her roll in the shabby breakfast room, she wished she had told her about God instead. If it had been Papa, of course she would have done.

"I'm going now," said the woman. She had put on a long, shapeless coat which concealed her legs, and was carrying an umbrella. On her head was a hat with a battered veil.

"*Auf Wiedersehen*," she said.

"*Auf Wiedersehen*," said Anna.

For a moment she had a glimpse of Mama in a hat with a veil. The veil was blue, it just reached the end of Mama's nose, and it was crumpled because Mama was crying. When on earth was that? she wondered, but she could not remember.

Konrad arrived punctually, shaking the water from his hat and coat.

"Your mother's pneumonia is a little better," he said. "Otherwise she's much the same. But I managed to speak to the doctor when I rang, and he said they were trying a different treatment.

"I see." She did not know whether that was good or bad.

"Anyway, he'll be at the hospital, so you can speak to him yourself. Oh, and Max rang up from Athens. He's hoping to get on a flight to Paris this afternoon, in which case he'll be here either tonight or tomorrow."

"Oh good." The thought of Max was cheering.

"He only knows about the pneumonia, of course."

"Not about the overdose?"

"He didn't ask me, so I didn't tell him," said Konrad stiffly.

Watching him drive through the pouring rain, she noticed again how worn he looked. There were dark circles under his eyes, and not only his face but even his large body looked a little collapsed. Of course, he's been coping with all this far longer than me, she thought. But as they approached the hospital, her stomach tightened as it had done the previous day at the prospect of seeing Mama, and she felt suddenly angry. If Konrad hadn't had an affair with some wretched typist, she thought, none of this would have happened.

Unlike the previous day, the reception hall was full of bustle. Nurses hurried to and fro, the telephone kept ringing while a man in a raincoat stood dripping patiently at the desk, and immediately behind them an old lady in a wheelchair was being manoeuvred in from the rain under several black umbrellas. Of course, she thought, this was Monday. Yesterday most of the staff would have had the day off.

The nurse behind the desk announced their arrival on the telephone and a few minutes later a slight, balding man in a white coat came hurrying towards them. He introduced himself as Mama's doctor with a heel-clicking little bow and plunged at once into an analysis of Mama's condition.

"Well now," he said, "the pneumonia no longer worries me too much. We've been pumping her full of antibiotics and she's responded quite well. But that's no use unless we can bring her out of the coma. We've made no progress there at all, so we've given her some powerful stimulants in the hope that these may help. You'll find her very restless."

"Restless?" said Anna. It sounded like an improvement.

He shook his head. "I'm afraid the restlessness does not mean that she's better. It's just a reaction to the drugs. But we're hoping that it will lead to an improvement eventually."

"I see," she said. "What –?" She was suddenly unsure how to put it in German – "What do you think is going to happen?"

He spread-eagled the fingers of both hands and showed them to her. "Fifty-fifty," he said in English. "You understand? If she comes out of the coma – no problem. She'll be well in a few days. If not . . ." He shrugged his shoulders. "We're doing all we can," he said.

At first, when she saw Mama, in spite of what the doctor had told her, she thought for a moment that she must be better. From the far side of the landing, with Mama's bed partly obscured by a large piece of hospital equipment, she could see the bedclothes move as though Mama were tugging at them. But there was a nurse standing by the bed, doing something to Mama's arm, and as she came closer she saw that it had been bandaged on to a kind of splint, presumably to stop Mama dislodging the tube which led to it from the bottle suspended above the bed.

Tethered only by her arm, Mama was lurching violently about in the bed, and every so often a strange, deep sound came from her chest, like air escaping from an accordion. She no longer had the tube in her mouth, but her eyes were tightly shut, and she looked distressed, like someone in a nightmare, trying to escape.

"Mama," said Anna, gently touching her face, but Mama suddenly lurched towards her, so that her head almost struck Anna's chin, and she drew back, alarmed. She glanced at Konrad for comfort, but he was just staring down at the bed with no expression at all.

"It's the drugs," said the nurse. "The stimulants acting on the barbiturates she's taken. It causes violent irritation."

Mama flung herself over to the other side, dislodging most of the bedclothes and exposing a stretch of pink nightdress. Anna covered her up again.

"Is there nothing you can give her?" she asked the nurse. "She looks so – she must be feeling terrible."

"A sedative, you mean," said the nurse. "But she's had too many of those already. That's why she's here."

Mama moved again and her breath came out in a kind of roar.

The nurse gave the bandaged arm a final pat where it was connected to the tube. "In any case," she said quite kindly, "your mother is unconscious. She is not aware of anything that is happening."

She nodded to Konrad and went.

Anna looked at Mama and tried to believe what the nurse had said, but Mama did not look unaware of what was happening. Apart from the fact that her eyes were closed, she looked, as she had so often looked in the past, as though she were railing at something. Death, or being kept alive. There was no way of telling which.

She hoped that perhaps Konrad would try to speak to her, but he just stood there leaning on his stick, with a closed face.

Suddenly Mama gave a tremendous lurch, her legs kicked the bedclothes right off and she fell back on to the bed with one of her strange moans. Her pink nightie which Anna remembered her buying during her last visit to London was rucked up round her waist, and she lay there, shamefully exposed on the rumpled sheets.

Anna jumped to tug down her nightdress with one hand, while trying to replace the bedclothes with the other. The nurse, reappearing from somewhere, helped her.

"Look at those legs," she said, patting Mama's thigh as though she owned it. "Marvellous skin for her age."

Anna could not speak.

Once, in the Putney boarding house, Mama had rushed into their joint bedroom in great distress. It seemed she had been sitting in the lounge, her legs outstretched towards the meagre fire, trying to get warm, and a dreadful, crabby old man sitting opposite had suddenly pointed to somewhere in the region of his navel and said, "I can see right up to here." Mama had been particularly upset because the old man was one of the few English residents, which seemed to make it much worse than if he had just been a refugee. "It was horrible," she had cried and had collapsed on the bed to burst into tears. Anna had been filled with rage at the old man, but, while she comforted Mama with a kind of fierce affection, she had also wished quite desperately that Mama had just sat with her knees together like everyone else, so that none of it could have happened.

Now, as Mama threw herself about and they all stood looking down at her, she felt the same mixture of rage and tearing pity. She tried to tuck in a sheet, but it became dislodged again almost at once.

"I really think there is no point in your staying here at the moment," said the nurse. "Come back this afternoon, when she'll be calmer."

Konrad touched her arm to guide her away from the bed. She pulled away from him, but she could see that what the nurse had said was true, and after a moment she followed him across the landing. Her last glimpse of Mama was of her face, eyes closed, the mouth emitting a wordless shout, as it rose into view behind some shrouded piece of equipment and then fell back again out of sight.

The reception hall was full of people in wet coats, and the smell of steaming cloth made her feel sick again. It was still pouring: you could see the water streaming down the windows. Konrad stopped near the door, where a little fat woman stood peering out, waiting for a break in the downpour.

"Look, I'm sorry," he said, "but I have to go to my office." His voice sounded hoarse and unused, and she realized that he had hardly spoken since they had arrived at the hospital. "There's a meeting this morning, and everybody would think it very odd if I didn't turn up."

"It doesn't matter," she said. "I can look after myself."

"Don't be silly. I'm not going to leave you here in this weather. I can just imagine what your mother would think of that."

The little fat woman flung herself out into the

rain, shooting her umbrella open at the same time, and disappeared down the steps. A cold breath of wet air reached Anna before the door closed behind her and she breathed it gratefully.

"I thought if I could find you an occupation for this morning, we could meet for lunch. There's been a small exhibition here in memory of your father – your mother must have written to you about it."

"Is there?" She did not want to see any exhibition, least of all one that would remind her of Papa.

He looked at her. "You're feeling awful."

"I think I'd just as soon go back to the hotel. Perhaps when Max comes tomorrow –"

"Of course." He glanced at his watch. "I'll drive you back."

Her coat was not particularly waterproof, and even the short distance to the car was enough almost to soak her. He looked at his watch again as she sat dripping on to the upholstery.

"You'll never get dry in that hotel. The woman probably turns the heating down during the day. It's a miserable place, but it was all I could find. Everywhere else was full."

She shook her head. "It really doesn't matter."

"Well, I don't want two invalids on my hands." He started the car. "I'll take you to my flat. At least I know it's warm there."

As they drove through the downpour, water blurred the windscreen in spite of the wipers, and she could hear it beating on the roof of the car above the sound of the engine. Every so often she caught a glimpse of streaming pavements, dripping awnings, bent figures running under shiny umbrellas. Konrad sat leaning forward over the steering wheel, trying to see the road ahead.

"What time is your meeting?" she asked.

He glanced down at his watch. "Five minutes ago. They'll just have to wait."

His flat was in a side street like that of the Goldblatts, and as he stopped the car outside it, water from a huge puddle in the gutter shot over the curb and over the feet of an old man who shouted something and shook his umbrella at him. He insisted on holding the car door open for her, standing in the rain with water dripping from his hat, and then they both hurried across the pavement into the dry.

"I'll be all right now," she said as soon as he had ushered her into his hall, but he stayed, fussing over a hanger for her coat, telling her to make herself some coffee, and checking that the radiators were turned up.

"Till lunch, then," he said, and then hesitated in the doorway. "By the way," he said, "you will find a number of feminine possessions lying about. They are of course all your mother's."

"Of course," she said, astonished. It would not have occurred to her to think anything else.

"Yes, well –" He waved awkwardly. "See you later."

For a moment after the door had shut behind him, she stood in the dark little hall, wondering what to do. Then a trickle of water ran down her neck and she went into the bathroom to rub her wet hair with a towel.

As in the Goldblatts' flat, everything was very new and modern. There was a shower, a big mirror and a bath mat with flowers printed on it. On the shelf above the basin were two blue tooth mugs, each with a tooth-brush in it. She supposed that one of them belonged to Mama.

Konrad had put some instant coffee and biscuits ready for her in the kitchen, and she was just pouring hot water into the cup, when she was startled by the ringing of the telephone. At first she could not remember where the telephone was. Then she found it in the far corner of the living-room. She ran over to it, picked up the receiver and discovered that her mouth was full of biscuit. Swallowing frantically, she could hear a German voice at the other end ask with rising insistence, "Konrad? Konrad, are you all right? Are you all right, Konrad?"

"Hullo," she said through a mouthful of crumbs.

"Hullo." The voice – a woman's – sounded put out. "Who is that, please?"

She explained.

"Oh, I see." The voice became very business-like. "This is Dr Rabin's secretary speaking. Could you tell me what time Dr Rabin left his flat, please? Only he is rather late for a meeting at his office."

Anna told her.

"Oh, thank you, then he will soon be here."

There was a little pause, then the voice said, "I am sorry to have troubled you, but you understand, his colleagues were getting rather worried."

"Of course," said Anna, and the voice rang off.

She went back to her coffee in the kitchen and drank it slowly. That must have been her, she thought. The girl in his office. She had sounded quite young. Somehow, it had not occurred to her that she would still be there, working with him. It seemed to make everything more uncertain. Poor Mama, she thought. But another part of her examined the situation in terms of plot and thought angrily, how corny.

When she had finished her coffee, she wandered round the flat. It was tidy, well furnished and impersonal. The curtains in the living-room were almost exactly the same as the Goldblatts' – obviously it was all American Army issue. There was a bookshelf with a few paperbacks, nearly all detective stories, and a desk with a framed snapshot of a middle-aged woman and two girls in their twenties – his wife and daughters she supposed. The woman was wearing a flowered dress with a home-made look. Her hair was swept back neatly into a bun and she had a sensible, faintly self-satisfied expression. A real German *Hausfrau*, thought Anna.

The bedroom was not quite as tidy as the living-room. Konrad must have had a bit of a rush getting up. The cupboard door was slightly open and inside it she could see one of Mama's dresses among his suits. Her pale blue bathrobe hung beside his on the door and her hair brush lay on his dressing table. Next to it and half-surrounded by the cord of his electric shaver was a small glass dish in which nestled some of Mama's beads, a safety pin and half a dozen hairgrips.

She picked up the beads and ran them through her fingers. They were iridescent blue glass – Mama loved them and wore them all the time. Then she suddenly thought, but she doesn't use hairgrips. Mama's hair was short and curly. There was nothing to grip. Unless of course she had been washing her hair and had wanted to pin it in a particular way. That must be it, she thought. The fact that she had never seen Mama do this did not mean that it never happened. The hairgrips must be hers.

All the same, as she went back into the living-room, she felt suddenly very much alone. It occurred to her that she really knew very little about Konrad. After all, he had presumably abandoned his wife for Mama. Might he not be ready now to abandon Mama for someone else? And what would Mama do then, even if she got better? She relied on him so much, not only for his love but for his help. After years of trying to cope alone with the family's practical problems (and though Mama was more practical than Papa, thought Anna, she was still unpractical by most people's standards) she had found it almost incredible that Konrad should be prepared to look after her.

"He is so good to me," she had once told Anna.

Anna had waited to hear in what way and Mama, too, had evidently found it difficult to describe. "Do you know," she had said at last with a kind of awe, "he can even wrap parcels."

It was still raining, though not nearly so hard. Outside the window, across the road, she could see the wet roofs of other American blocks of flats, one of them Mama's.

She wondered what Mama had thought about when she took the barbiturates. She wondered if she had looked out of her window, if it had been wet or fine, if it had been dusk or already dark. She wondered if she had not had any regrets for the sky and the street lamps and the shadowed pavements and the sound of the passing cars. Clearly she must have felt that without Konrad they were not worth having. But perhaps she had not thought at all. Perhaps she had just been angry and had swallowed the pills, thinking, that will show him. Unlike Papa, she had left no notes for anyone.

There was some writing paper on Konrad's desk, and she spent the rest of the morning writing to Richard. It was a relief to be able to tell him everything that had happened, from Konrad's affair to her own reactions. When she had finished the letter she felt better. She stuck it down, put on her coat which had completely dried out on the radiator, slammed the front door as Konrad had told her, and went to meet him for lunch.

Probably because of the hairgrips and the telephone call, she felt uneasy as soon as she saw him. What shall I say to him? she thought. He was waiting for her in a small restaurant off the *Kurfürsten Damm*, newly rebuilt against a background of ruins still awaiting demolition. He rose at once to greet her.

"You found it," he said. "I'd have come to pick you up in the car, but the meeting went on and on. And as the rain had stopped –"

"It was no trouble," she said.

"I rang the hospital before I came out, and they think you should go and see your mother some time after four. They think she'll be in a better state by then."

"All right."

"I can get away before five. I could drive you there."

"There's no need," she said. "I'll make my own way."

There was an awkward little silence, then he said, "Anyway, you got dry."

"Yes, thank you."

"Good news today about Hungary. Have you seen it?"

She shook her head.

"They've told the Russians to get out."

"Really?"

"Yes." He produced a folded newspaper from his coat pocket, but was suddenly hailed by a small man with rabbity teeth who had appeared at their side.

"My dear Konrad," cried the little man, "I was hoping to see you."

"Hullo, Ken," said Konrad.

Was he pleased or annoyed at the interruption? It was impossible to tell. He introduced him, politely as usual, as Ken Hathaway from the British Council.

"Looking after the poetry side," said Mr Hathaway, smiling through his teeth and looking disconcertingly like Bugs Bunny. He pointed to the paper. "Isn't that amazing?" he cried. "Just told them to leave. Scram. Skedaddle. Vamoose. Back to Mother Russia. Mind you, I'm not surprised. Very fiery people, the Hungarians."

"Do you think the Russians will really go?"

Konrad shrugged his shoulders. "It would be a very remarkable thing if they did."

Mr Hathaway appeared to have sat down at their table, and after a moment – it must be because he, too, was finding it difficult to be alone with her, thought Anna – Konrad asked him to join them for lunch.

"I was so very sorry to hear of your mother's illness," said Mr Hathaway, and Konrad produced his usual vague phrases about pneumonia. Mr Hathaway managed somehow to make his teeth droop in sympathy. "Do give her my love," he said. "I admire her so much." He turned to Anna. "She has such enthusiasm, such a feeling for life – for living it to the full. I always think that's a very continental quality."

Anna agreed a little sadly about Mama's enthusiasm for life, thinking at the same time how cross it would make her to hear herself described as continental. There was nothing Mama was quite as proud of as her British citizenship. She always referred to herself and the British as "we" (whereas Anna would go to infinite trouble to circumvent such phrases) and had once even talked, in her slight but unmistakable German accent, about "when we won the First World War," to everyone's confusion.

"And her feeling for the arts," cried Mr Hathaway. "Her love of the theatre – I suppose that must have been nurtured by your father. But her music was her very own. To me, she stands for a very special kind of flowering, a special European –" He suddenly ran out of words and said, "Anyway, we're all very fond of her here," with such genuine feeling that Anna decided he was really quite nice, in spite of his teeth and his foolishness.

It was odd, she thought, but she had quite forgotten about Mama's music. When she was small, the sound of the piano had seemed as much part of Mama as the way she looked. Every day while Papa wrote in his study, Mama had played and even composed. She'd been good, too, people said. But with the emigration, it had all stopped. If she had continued, would she have had something to hang on to in the present crisis instead of swallowing a bottleful of pills? And had she stopped because of the endless, crushing worries, or had the music never, really, been essential to her – only part of the romantic image she had of herself? There was no way of knowing.

"We'll miss her on Wednesday," said Ken

Hathaway, and it transpired that he was giving a party to which both Mama and Konrad had been invited. "Perhaps you would consider coming in her place?" He smiled hopefully over a forkful of schnitzel.

"Oh, I couldn't possibly," said Anna.

She was appalled at even thinking about Wednesday. Suppose Mama was still in a coma by then? Suppose she was worse? Then she saw Mr Hathaway's face and realized how rude she must have sounded.

"I mean," she said, "it must depend on how my mother is."

"Let's say I'll bring her if her mother can spare her," said Konrad, making everything normal again.

She knew that he was doing it for Mama's sake, to make life easier for her if she recovered, but it still worried her that he should be so good at covering up.

"Was there something you wanted to talk to me about?" he asked Ken Hathaway, who at once launched into an account of a poetry reading he had arranged, at which he hoped as many people as possible would turn up.

By Wednesday Mama may be dead, thought Anna.

A small German boy at the next table was eating cherry cake, and his mother was nagging him not to swallow the stones.

"What happens to people who swallow cherry stones?" he asked.

"What happens to people when they die?" Anna had once asked Mama in German, long ago when she was still a German child.

"Nobody knows," Mama had said. "But perhaps when you grow up, you'll be the first person to find out," and after that she had been less frightened of death.

She must have eaten without noticing, for suddenly Konrad was paying the bill.

"Can I drive you anywhere?" he asked. "It's still too early to go to the hospital. What would you like to do?"

"I thought perhaps I'd just walk about."

"Walk about?"

"Where we used to live. It's the only bit I remember."

"Of course."

He dropped her off where she asked him, having first provided her with a street map, as well as detailed instructions for getting to the hospital and then back to her hotel.

"I'll ring you after six," he said. "Look after yourself."

She waved and watched him drive off.

It was not the first time she had been back to this part of Berlin. Two years before, she had walked here with Richard and Mama. She had pointed out to Richard all the places she remembered, and Mama had explained various changes which had happened since. They had chatted all the way – it had been a lovely day, she remembered – and she had been so happy that Richard and Mama were getting on so well that she had little time for any other emotions. Now, as she stood alone in the gusty wind, it felt quite different.

Konrad had dropped her at the end of the street where she had lived as a child. How ordinary it looked. She had to check the nameplate at the corner to make sure it was the right one.

When she was small, the street had always seemed to her very dark. The pavements were lined with trees planted at short intervals, and when Mama and Papa had told her that they were going to live there instead of their old flat in a perfectly good light street with no trees at all, she had thought, they're mad, and had wondered dispassionately whatever foolishness they would get up to next. That had been in the summer – she must have been four or five – when the leaves had made a kind of awning right across the road. Now most of the leaves were on the ground, swept into piles in the gutter, and the wind blew through bare branches.

She had expected the house to be quite a long way down, but she reached it almost at once. It was hardly recognizable – she knew it wouldn't be from her previous visit. Instead of their small family villa, it had been extended into a building containing three expensive looking flats. The gabled roof had been flattened and even the windows looked different.

Only the garden still sloped down to the fence as it had done in the past, and so did the little paved drive where Max had taught her to ride his bicycle. ("Isn't there an easier way to learn?" she had asked him when, unable to brake or reach the ground with her feet, she had repeatedly crashed into the gate at the bottom. But he had told her there wasn't, and she had believed him as always.)

Then she noticed that something else was unchanged. The steps leading up to the front door – now the entrance to one of the flats – were exactly as she remembered them. The steepness, the colour of the stone, the slightly crumbly surface of the balustrade, even the rhododendron bush wedged against its side – all this was exactly as it had been more than twenty years before.

She stared at it, remembering how, after school, she had raced up there, pulling at the bell, and, as soon as the door was opened, shouting, "Is Mama home?"

For a moment, as she looked at it, she remembered exactly what it had felt like to do this. It was as though, for a fraction of a second, she had half-seen, half-become the small, fierce, vulnerable person she had once been, with her lace-up boots and socks held up by elastic bands, her fear of volcanoes and of dying in the night, her belief that rust caused blood poisoning, liquorice was made of horses' blood, and there would never be another war, and her unshakeable conviction that there was no problem in the world that Mama could not easily solve.

The small person did not say, "Is Mama home?" She said, "*Ist Mami da?*" and did not speak a word of English, and for a moment Anna felt shaken by her sudden emergence.

She walked a few steps along the fence and tried to peer round the side of the house. There had been some currant bushes there once, and beyond them – she thought she could still see the beginning of it – a kind of wooden stairway leading to the terrace outside the dining-room.

In the hot weather she, or the small person she had once been, had sat on that terrace to draw. She had had a round tin filled with crayons of different lengths, old pencil shavings and other odds and ends, and when you opened it, these had emitted a particular, delightful smell.

Once, during her religious period, she had decided to sacrifice one of her drawings to God. First she had thought of tearing it up, but then that had seemed a pity – after all, for all she knew, God might not even want it. So she had closed her eyes and thrown it up into the air, saying – in German, of course – "Here you are, God. This is for You." After allowing plenty of time for God to help himself, if He were so minded, she had opened her eyes again to find the drawing on the floor, and had put it calmly back into her drawing book.

Afterwards – or it might have been some other time altogether – she had walked through the French windows into the dining-room, to find Mama standing there in a big white hat. As her eyes adjusted to the indoor darkness and the colours returned to the curtains, the tablecloth and the pictures on the walls, she had thought how beautiful it all was, especially Mama. She had looked at Mama's face in surprise because she had never thought about her in that way before.

Beyond the terrace, out of sight at the back of the house, was the rest of the garden, probably neatly planted now, but in those days a grassless waste which Mama had sensibly handed over to Max and herself. There they had played football (herself in goal, vague about where the goalposts were supposed to be, uninterested in stopping the ball), they had wrestled and built snowmen and dug holes in the ground, hoping to reach the centre of the earth.

Once in the summer she had sat in the shade of the pear tree with Heimpi and had watched her embroider new eyes on her favourite stuffed Pink Rabbit in place of the glass ones which had fallen out.

When they had fled from the Nazis, Pink Rabbit had been left behind, embroidered eyes and all, with all their other possessions, and so had Heimpi whom they could no longer afford to pay. She wondered what had happened to them both.

The wind sang in the branches above her head and she walked on, past the place where she used to retrieve her tortoise as it tried to escape from the garden, past the place where a man had exposed himself to her on a bicycle ("On a bicycle?" Papa had said in amazement, but Mama had said – she could not remember what Mama had said, but whatever it was, it had made it all right, and she had not been worried about it).

At the corner of the street, where she and Max's gang had always met to play after school, she stopped in surprise.

"Wo ist denn die Sandkiste?"

She was not sure whether it was she who had said it or the small person in boots who seemed, suddenly, very close. The sandbox, containing municipal sand to be scattered on snowy roads in winter, had been the centre of all their games. It had marked the dividing line between cops and robbers, the starting point of hide-and-seek, the place where the net would have been when they played tennis with a rubber ball and home-made wooden bats. How could anyone have taken it away? She and the small person in boots could not get over it.

But the rowan trees were still there. *Vogelbeeren*, they were called in German, and once Mama, seeing the red berries ripening, had cried regretfully, "Already." When Anna had asked her why, Mama had said that it meant the end of summer.

A car passed, trailing petrol fumes, and the street seemed suddenly empty and dull. She walked back slowly towards the main road.

There was the paper shop where she had bought her drawing books and crayons, her exercise books and the special blue paper with which they had to be covered. She had gone inside it with Mama on her previous visit, but it was under different management and no one had remembered her. The greengrocer next door had gone, but the kiosk at the old tram stop was still there and still sold burnt sugared almonds in tiny cardboard boxes, even though there were no more trams, only buses.

Next came the café and, round the corner, the general shop, still two steps down from the pavement, where Heimpi had sometimes sent her on errands. *Bitte ein Brot von gestern.* Why had Heimpi always insisted on yesterday's bread? Perhaps because it was easier to cut. The numbers of the trams were 76, 176 and 78. There was something unreliable about the 78, it did not always stop long enough. Once, as it passed him Max had put his gym shoes on the step – *Turnschuhe*, they were called – and had not got them back for two days.

Hagen Platz. Fontane Strasse. Königsallee.

This was where she had turned off to go to school. She had walked with her best friend Marianne who was older and could draw ears front view. "*Quatsch!*" she had shouted when they had disagreed, and Marianne had called her *ein blödes Schaf*, which was a silly sheep.

A flurry of leaves – *Herbstblätter* – blew along the pavement, and she felt suddenly disorientated. What am I doing here? she thought in German. *Was tue ich eigentlich hier? Die Mami wartet doch auf mich.* But where was Mama waiting? At home, beyond the door at the top of the worn stone steps, waiting to hear what had happened at school today? Or groaning and struggling under the covers of her hospital bed?

Something seemed about to overwhelm her. The clouds, piled huge and grey in the sky, seemed to press down on her head. (*Die Wolken*, she thought in slow motion, as in a dream.) The pavement and the leaves rose treacherously under her feet. There was a wall behind her. She leaned against it. Surely I'm never going to faint, she thought. And then, out of the shifting sky, an unmistakable voice addressed her.

"My dear, you look as pale as cheese," it said, and a face surrounded by frizzy hair blocked out the rest of the world. She recognized the kindness before she remembered the name. Hildy Goldblatt, from the previous night. Of course, she thought, they live near here. A hand supported her arm. Another slipped round her shoulder. Then pavements and trees were swimming past and Hildy's voice, like God's, came out of nowhere. "What you need is a cup of tea," she said. "Not, of course that they can make it properly here." There was a sudden rush of warmth with the opening of a door, and then Anna found herself settled behind a table in the café with some hot tea before her.

"Now then," said Hildy, "I hope you're feeling better."

She drank the tea and nodded.

Had she once sat at this table, eating cakes with Mama? But the whole place, flooded in yellow neon light, had changed too much for her to remember.

"I'm sorry," she said. "It's all been a bit overwhelming."

"Of course." Hildy patted her hand. "And worrying about your poor Mama. Mothers worrying about their children, that's nothing, they're used to it. But the other way round is always bad." There was some cake on a plate before her and Anna watched her put some in her mouth. "Are you going to the hospital later?"

"Just for a moment." She was afraid that Hildy would want to come with her, but Hildy only nodded.

"Good," she said. "You will have your tea, and perhaps a cake – No? Are you sure? – And I will try not to talk like a chatterbox as Erwin always tells me, and then, when you are feeling better, I will put you in a taxi. All right?"

Anna nodded gratefully.

Behind Hildy, through the café window, she could see the pavement of the *Königsallee*. She and Max had passed that way each day on their way to school. Funny, she thought, you'd think it would have left some kind of a mark. All those times. On their own . . . with Mama and Papa . . . with Heimpi . . .

The waitress hovered. Hildy filled up her cup. "*Ach ja, bitte noch ein Stückchen Kuchen,*" and there was another piece of cake, apple this time, and Hildy was eating it.

"I saw your mother only two weeks ago," said

Hildy. "She showed me some pictures of her summer holidays," and suddenly they were at the seaside, she was quite small and Mama's face was above her, huge and smiling against the summer sky.

"*Mami, Mami, Mami!*" she squealed.

There was sand between her toes, and her woollen bathing suit clung to her wet legs and to her sandy body where Mama was holding her.

"*Hoch, Mami! Hoch!*"

She flew up into the sky. The sea was like a great wall at the end of the beach, and Mama's face, suddenly beneath her, laughed up from the shining sand.

"She always enjoys everything so much," said Hildy.

"Yes," said Anna.

She could still see Mama, the brilliant blue eyes, the open, laughing mouth, and the blazing beach behind her. Like a vision, she thought. And then it faded, and there was Hildy at the other side of the table, looking concerned.

"I don't want Mama to die," she said childishly, as though Hildy could arrange it.

"Well, of course you don't." Hildy refilled her cup and stirred more sugar into it. "Drink," she said.

Anna drank.

"I think your mother won't die," said Hildy. "After all, however it may seem just now, she still has very much to live for."

"Do you think so?" The hot, sweet tea had warmed her and she was beginning to feel better.

"Of course. She has two nice children, a grandchild already, perhaps more to come. She has a job and a flat and friends."

Anna nodded. "It's just – she had a bad time for so many years."

"Listen!" Hildy peered at her across the teacups. "My Erwin worked at Nuremberg. I know what happened to the Jews who stayed behind: *They* had a bad time." And as Anna looked at her in surprise, "When you've finished your tea, you go to the hospital, and I hope your mother – I hope the pneumonia will be not so bad. And if she can hear you, you tell her it's time she got better."

"All right." For the first time she found herself laughing, because Hildy made it all sound so simple.

"That's right." Hildy finished the last crumbs on her plate. "People," she said, without explaining exactly whom she meant by them, "people shouldn't give up so easy."

At the hospital she was received by the nurse who had been on duty that morning. "Your mother is calmer now," she said in German, and led Anna up the familiar corridors and stairs. For a moment, after her vision of Mama on the beach, it was surprising to see her grey-haired and middle-aged. She was lying quietly under the covers, her breathing almost normal, so that she might have been asleep. Only once in a while

674

her head turned restlessly on the pillow and the untethered hand twitched.

Anna sat down on the bed and looked at her. She's fifty-six, she thought. Mama's eyes were tightly closed. There were deep frown lines between them, and two further lines ran to the pulled-down corners of her mouth. The chin had lost some of its firmness, it was pudgy now rather than round. The hair straggled on the pillow. But in the middle of it all was the nose, tiny, snub and incongruously childish, sticking up hopefully from the ageing face.

When I was small, thought Anna, I used to have a nose like that. Everyone had told her that her nose was just like Mama's. But then, some time during her adolescence, her nose had grown and now – though it certainly wasn't a Jewish nose, Mama had said – it was straight and of normal length. Somehow Anna always felt that she had grown up past Mama along with her nose. Hers was a more serious nose, an adult nose, a nose with a sense of reality. Anyone with a nose like Mama's, she thought, was bound to need looking after.

Mama stirred. The head came a little way off the pillow and dropped back again, the closed eyes facing towards her.

"Mama," said Anna. "Hullo, Mama."

Something like a sigh escaped from the mouth, and for a moment she imagined that it had been in reply to her voice, but then Mama turned her head the other way and she realized that she had been mistaken.

She put her hand on Mama's bare shoulder, and Mama must have felt that, for she twitched away very slightly.

"Mama," she said again.

Mama lay motionless and unresponsive.

She was about to call her again when, deep inside Mama, a sound began to form. It seemed to rise up slowly through her chest and her throat and finally emerged roughly and indistinctly from her half-open lips.

"*Ich will*," said Mama. "*Ich will.*"

She knew at once what it was that Mama wanted to do. Mama wanted to die.

"*Du darfst nicht!*" she shouted. She would not allow it. She was so determined not to allow it that it took her a moment to realize that Mama had actually spoken. She stared down at her, amazed and with a kind of anger. Mama tried to turn her head away, and the strange sound rose up in her again.

"*Ich will*," she said.

"*Nein!*"

Why should she remember, now of all times, about the pencil sharpener that Mama had stolen from Harrods? It was a double one in a little pig-skin case, and Mama had given it to her for her fourteenth or fifteenth birthday. She had known at once, of course, that Mama could not possibly have paid for it. "You might have been caught," she had cried. "They might have sent for the police." But Mama had said, "I just wanted you to have it."

How could anyone be so hopelessly, so help-lessly wrong-headed, stealing pencil sharpeners and now wanting to die?

"Mama, we need you!" (Was it remotely true? It didn't seem to matter.) "You must not die! Mama!" Her eyes and cheeks were wet and she thought, bloody Dr Kildare. "*Du darfst nicht sterben! Ich will es nicht! Du musst zurück kommen!*"

Nothing. The face twitched a little, that was all.

"*Mami!*" she shouted. "*Mami! Mami! Mami!*"

Then Mama made a little sound in her throat. It was absurd to imagine that there could be any expression in the toneless voice that came from inside her, but to Anna it sounded matter of fact, like someone deciding to get on with a job that needed to be done.

"*Ja, gut,*" said Mama.

Then she sighed and turned her face away.

She left the landing in a state of confused elation. It was all right. Mama was going to live. Your little brother will play the violin again, she thought, and felt surprised again at the corniness of it all.

"I spoke to my mother and she answered me," she told the nurse. "She's going to get better."

The nurse pursed her lips and talked about the Herr Doktor's opinion, but Anna did not care. She knew she was right.

Even Konrad was cautious.

"It's obviously an improvement," he said on the telephone. "I expect we'll know more tomorrow."

He had heard from Hildy Goldblatt about her moment of faintness in the *Königsallee* and was anxious to know if she were all right. "I'll come and pick you up for supper," he said, but she did not want to see him and told him that she was too tired.

Instead, she ate scrambled eggs served on a not-very-clean tablecloth in the deserted breakfast room and thought about Mama.

The bow-legged proprietress hovered nearby and talked – about the Nazis (she had never been one, she said), about the concentration camps of which she had known nothing, and about the bad times just after the War. No food, she said, and such dreadfully hard work. Even the women had to clear the rubble.

Her Berliner voice, a bit like Heimpi's, like all the voices of Anna's childhood, went on and on, and, even though Anna believed little of what she said, she did not want it to stop. She answered her in German and was surprised to find that when she really tried, she could speak it almost perfectly.

"Is' doch schön, dass es der Frau Mutter 'n bischen besser geht," said the woman.

Anna, too, was glad that Mama was a little better.

"Sehr schön," she said.

Tuesday

Tuesday began with a telephone call from Konrad. Anna was still in bed, when she was wakened by the knocking at her door, and she had to run down to the telephone in the hall with her coat thrown over her nightdress, the crumbly lino chilling her bare feet as she said, "Hello? Hello, Konrad?"

"My dear," Konrad's voice sounded much more positive, "I'm sorry I woke you. But I thought you'd like to know straightaway that I've just spoken to the doctor, and he says your mother is going to be all right."

"Oh, I'm so glad." Even though she had been sure of it, she was surprised by the wave of relief which flooded over her. "I'm so glad!"

"Yes – well – so am I." He gave a little laugh. "As you can imagine."

"Yes."

"Well, I just thought I'd tell you. So you could

have your breakfast in peace. I'll meet you at the hospital at nine-thirty."

"All right." It felt like an outing, a party, a celebration. "And thanks, Konrad. Thanks for letting me know."

She hurried back to her room to put on her clothes, and had hardly got them on before she was called to the telephone again. This time it was Max, from the airport.

"Max," she cried, "it's all right. Mama is going to be all right."

"I know." He sounded in control of the situation, as always. "I've just spoken to the hospital."

"Did they tell you –?"

"The overdose. Yes." There was a pause. "It's funny," he said. "I've been sitting in planes and at airports for two days with nothing to do but think about Mama, but that possibility never occurred to me. I just kept wondering whether she'd be alive when I got here."

"I know." She could hear his breathing through the telephone – fast, shallow breaths. He must be dead tired.

"Do you know why she did it?"

"Konrad," she said. "He had an affair."

"Konrad? Good God." He was as amazed as she had been. "I thought it was something to do with us. I hadn't written for a bit."

"I know. I hadn't either."

"Good God," he said again, and then became very practical. "Look, I don't know what sort of transport I can get from here, but I'll get to the hospital as soon as I can. You meet me there."

"All right." The odd feeling of it being a celebration returned to her as she said, "See you then."

"See you then," he said and rang off.

She rushed through her breakfast with only the briefest replies to the proprietress who was determined to continue the conversation of the previous night. Even so, when she arrived at the hospital, Max was already there. He was talking to the nurse behind the desk and she recognized not only his back, but also the expression on the nurse's face – that special smile, denoting pleasure and eagerness to help, which he had been able to induce in almost everyone he met since he had been about seventeen.

"Max," she said.

He turned and came towards her, looking tired but unrumpled in his formal suit, and most of the visitors and patients looked up to watch him.

"Hello, little man," he said, and in answer to the old endearment, left from their joint childhood, she felt a glow spread through her, and smiled back at him much as the nurse had done. "What a lot of trouble," he said as he kissed her, "Bringing up our poor Mama."

She nodded and smiled. "Have you spoken to Konrad?"

"Just for a moment. He gave me your number. He said something about taking full responsibility. I couldn't think what he meant."

"He feels very badly about it."

"Well, so he should. Though perhaps . . . Mama isn't easy." Max sighed. "Oh, I don't know. Has he said anything about what he's going to do?"

"Not exactly. But he said the affair meant nothing to him – that it's all finished."

"I suppose that's something."

"Yes."

There was a pause. She was conscious of the other people and the nurse behind the desk watching them. "He's coming here at nine-thirty," he said. "Do you want to wait for him or go and see Mama first?"

"Let's go and see Mama," he said, and she thought how much easier it would be to face going up to the landing now that Mama was better, and with Max beside her.

As they started along the corridor which smelt of disinfectant and polish as usual, she did not feel the least bit sick. "I'm all right today," she said. "Always when I've come here before I've felt sick."

He smiled. "You should have put a clean hankie on your stomach," and she was surprised and touched because he did not usually remember much about the past.

"I think it only worked if you got it out of the drawer," she said.

They had reached the stairs and she was about to go up, but he steered her past them, towards another passage.

"Room 17," he said. "The nurse told me."

"Room 17?" Then she realized. "They must have moved her now that she's out of danger. They must really be sure."

He nodded. "The nurse said she'd be very sleepy. She said only to stay a minute."

"She's been on a kind of landing till now." For some reason it seemed important to explain. "Where everyone could see her. And of course she'd throw herself about and groan and I was shouting and trying to get through to her. It was rather horrible."

But they had come to the door of Mama's room and he was not really listening. "All right?" he said with his fingers on the handle, and they went in.

The first thing that struck her was how pretty the room was. It was full of light, with pastel-coloured walls and a big window which overlooked the park. There were flowered curtains, an arm-chair and a furry rug on the floor. Mama was lying in a neat white bed, untethered, without tubes, one hand tucked under the pillow, the other relaxed on the covers, as Anna had so often seen her in the Putney boarding house, and seemed to be peacefully asleep.

Max was already by the bed.

"Mama," he said.

Mama's eyelids fluttered, sank down again, and finally opened quite normally. For a moment she stared in confusion and then she recognized him.

"Max," she whispered. "Oh, Max." Her blue eyes, the same colour as his, smiled, half-closed, and then opened again full of tears. "I'm so sorry,

Max," she whispered. "Your holiday . . . I didn't mean . . ." Her voice, too, was just as usual.

"That's all right, Mama," said Max. "Everything is all right now."

Her hand moved across the bedclothes into his, and he held it.

"Max," she murmured. "Dear Max . . ." Her eyelids sank down and she went back to sleep.

For a moment, Anna did not know what to do. Then she joined Max at the bed.

"Hello, Mama," she said softly, her lips close to the pillow.

Mama, very sleepy now, hardly reacted. "Anna . . ." Her voice was barely audible. "Are you here too?"

"I've been here since Saturday," said Anna, but Mama was too sleepy to hear her. Her eyes remained closed, and after a while Max disengaged his hand and they went out.

"Is she all right?" he asked. "Is this very different from the way she's been?"

"She's been in a coma for three days," said Anna. "She only came out of it while I was with her last night." She knew it was childish, but she felt put out by the fact that Mama seemed to remember nothing about it. "They told me to keep calling her, so I did, and finally she answered."

"I'm sorry," said Max. "Was it awful?"

"Yes, it was. Like one of those dreadful, corny films."

He laughed a little. "I didn't know they still did that – making you call her. I thought these days it was all done with pills. You may have saved her life."

She was careful not to say so, but secretly she was sure that she had. "It was probably just the German instinct for drama," she said. "I can't imagine them doing it in England, can you? I mean, you wouldn't be allowed into the ward for a start."

They were walking back along the corridor and near the stairs they met the sour-faced nurse of the first day, carrying a bedpan. At the sight of them – or more probably of Max, thought Anna – her mouth relaxed into a smile.

"*Na*," she said in satisfied tones, "*die Frau Mutter ist von den Schatten zurückgekehrt.*"

In English this meant, "So your lady mother has returned from the shadows," and Anna, who had had time to get used to German phraseology, managed to keep a straight face, but, combined with the bedpan, it was too much for Max. He spluttered some kind of agreement and dived round the next corner, Anna following and hoping that the nurse would think he had been overcome with emotion.

"They all talk like that," she giggled when she caught up with him. "Had you forgotten?"

He could only shake his head. "*Aus den Schatten zurückgekehrt* . . . How does Mama stand it?"

She looked at him and began to laugh as well. "*Die Frau Mutter* . . ." she gasped, and even though she knew it was not as funny as all that, it was difficult to stop. She leaned against the wall, clutching his arm for support, and when the nurse came back, without the bedpan this time, they were still laughing so much that they had to pretend to search for something in Anna's bag until she had passed, only to explode again immediately afterwards.

"Oh, Max," cried Anna at last without knowing exactly what she meant, "oh, Max, you're the only one."

It was something to do with their childhood, with having grown up speaking three different languages, with having had to worry so much about Mama and Papa and to cheer themselves up with trilingual jokes which nobody else could understand.

"There, there, little man," said Max, patting her arm. "So are you."

They were still laughing a little when they emerged into the entrance hall, even more crowded now. Konrad and the doctor were already talking together in a corner, and the nurse behind the desk smiled and pointed them out to Max, in case he had not seen them. But Konrad who must have been watching for them, came to meet them and clasped Max warmly by the hand.

"It's good to see you, Max," he said. "I'm sorry we had to drag you away from Greece, but right until this morning it's been touch and go with your mother."

"Of course," said Max. "Thank you for coping with it all."

"*Nu*," said Konrad in tones reminiscent of the Goldblatts, "at my age you learn to cope with everything."

There was an awkwardness between them, and he turned to Anna with evident relief. "That's quite a change of expression you've got there."

"I told you Mama would be all right," she said happily, and by this time they had reached the doctor, and Konrad introduced him to Max, and Max thanked him for all he had done for Mama.

"I believe you've had a long journey," said the doctor, and Max told him a little about it, but quickly brought the conversation back to Mama.

"We were lucky," said the doctor. "I told your sister –" he spread his fingers as he had done the previous day. "Fifty-fifty, didn't I tell you?"

Anna nodded. It seemed a long time ago.

"Yes," said the doctor. "Fifty-fifty. Of course in such a case one does not always know what the patient's wishes would have been. But one has to assume . . . to hope . . ." He discovered his fingers, still in mid-air, and lowered them to his sides.

Behind him, Anna could see a very old lady walking carefully with a stick, and a small boy with his arm in a sling. She was aware of a woolly smell from Konrad's coat, the warmth of a nearby radiator and the babble of German voices all around her, and she felt suddenly tired and remote. Mama is going to be all right, she thought, nothing else matters. For some reason, she remembered again how Mama had looked that time when she had cried in her blue hat with the veil. The veil had been quite wet and had got more and more wrinkled as Mama rubbed her eyes with her hand. When on earth was that? she wondered.

Konrad coughed and shifted his feet. ". . . can't thank you enough . . ." said Max in his very good German, and Konrad nodded and said, ". . . deeply grateful . . ." "After a few days in the clinic to recover . . ." The doctor waved his hands and there seemed to be a question hanging in the air. Then Konrad said loudly and firmly, "Of course I shall be responsible for her." She glanced at him quickly to see if he meant it. His face looked quite set.

The doctor was clearly relieved. So was Max who, she noticed, now looked rather pale and suddenly said, "I've eaten nothing since yesterday lunch time. D'you think I could possibly get breakfast anywhere?"

At this the group broke up.

They all thanked the doctor again, and then she and Max were following Konrad down the steps to his car and Konrad was saying, "You must remember to shake hands with the Germans, otherwise they think you despise them for having lost the War," which seemed so eccentric that she thought she must have misheard until she caught Max's eye and quickly looked away for fear of getting the giggles again.

She stared out of the window while Konrad drove and made various arrangements with Max

– it was cold, but quite a nice day, she discovered – and did not really come to until she found herself sitting at a café table, with the smell of sausages and coffee all round her and Max saying, evidently for the second or third time, "Are you sure you don't want anything to eat?"

He himself was polishing off a large plateful of frankfurters and fried potatoes, and there was a cup of coffee in front of her, so she drank some of that and smiled and shook her head.

"Konrad is going to ring the theatre from his office," said Max, "so that they'll be expecting us."

"The theatre?"

"Where they've got the exhibition about Papa."

"Of course." She had forgotten all about it.

"It's really over. Konrad thought they might even have begun to dismantle it. But the stuff should still be there, and Konrad is going to ring the caretaker to make sure he lets us in."

He looked his normal self again, and she asked, "Are you feeling better now?"

He nodded, his mouth full of frankfurters. "Just reaction," he said. "No food and not enough sleep."

She felt very glad that they were going to see the exhibition together. Suddenly it seemed exactly the right thing to do. "It'll be good to see something to do with Papa," she said.

They had to travel on the *U-Bahn* to get there, but Konrad had explained the route to Max, and

689

he had also given him a map. If you stayed on the train too long, it took you right out of the Western Sector into the Russian Zone and Anna, who considered this a very real danger, watched the stations anxiously and was standing by the doors, ready to get off, when they reached the one they wanted.

"They warn you before you ever get near the Russian Zone," said Max as they climbed up the stairs to the street. "They have big notices at the previous station and announcers and loud-speakers. You couldn't possibly go across by mistake."

She nodded, but did not really believe him. Once, a few months after escaping from Germany, they had changed trains in Basle on their way to Paris with Papa, and they had discovered only at the very last minute that it was the wrong train.

"Do you remember in Basle," she said, "when we nearly got on a train that was going to Germany? We didn't even have time to get the luggage off, and you shouted until someone threw it out to us."

"Did I?" said Max, pleased with his past activity, but, as usual, he had forgotten it.

The theatre was in a busy, unfamiliar street, but then all the streets except the few round her old home and school were unfamiliar to her, thought Anna. There was some heavy bomb damage nearby, but the building itself had either escaped or had been carefully repaired.

They went up some stone steps to the entrance,

knocked and waited. For a long time nothing happened. Then, through a glass panel in the door, they could see an old man coming slowly towards them across the gloom of the foyer. A key ground in the lock, the door opened, and he became clearly visible in the light from the street – very old, very bent, and with a long, grey face that did not look as though it ever went out.

"*Kommen Sie rein, kommen Sie rein,*" he said impatiently, rather like the witch, thought Anna, beckoning Hansel and Gretel into the gingerbread house, and he led them slowly across the thick red carpet of the foyer towards a curving staircase.

As he tottered ahead of them, he talked unceasingly. "Can't put the lights on," he said in his heavy Berlin accent. "Not in the morning. Regulations don't allow it." He stopped suddenly and pointed to a chandelier above their heads. "Well, look at it. Set you back a bit to have that shining away, wouldn't it? Real gold, that is."

He tottered off again, muttering about the regulations which seemed to present a major problem, but resolved it to his satisfaction as, with infinite slowness, he climbed the stairs one step at a time. "Put the lights on *upstairs*," he said. "Nothing in the regulations against that."

On a small landing halfway up, he stopped again to get his breath. Anna caught Max's eye, but there was nothing to be done and they had to wait alongside him.

"Used to check the tickets," said the old man. "In the old days. Before it was all took over by them in brown." He flashed a look at Max. "You know who I mean, don't you?"

Max said, yes, he knew whom he meant.

The old man nodded, satisfied. "Used to stand down there at the entrance of the stalls, and see them all go in," he said. "All the gentlemen in their dinner suits and the ladies in their dresses. Quite grand, they was."

He sighed and started again on his slow climb, muttering to himself. A poster with Papa's name and "Exhibition" appeared in the half-darkness. "The great writer and critic", it said underneath.

"Used to see *him*," said the old man, jabbing a finger in its direction. "Come quite often, he did."

They looked at each other. "Did you?" said Anna.

He seemed to think that she was doubting him. "Well, of course I did," he said. "Used to check his ticket. Middle of the third row, he used to sit, never nowhere else, so he could write his little piece in the paper next day. And the others, they used to be real frightened of what he'd put. Once I fetch him a taxi to go home in after the show, and the manager, he come out of the theatre just as he drives off and he says to me, 'Herr Klaube,' he says, 'that man can make or break the play.' A real nice gentleman, I always thought, always thanked me and give me a tip."

Anna saw Max's face in the half-darkness. They both wanted the old man to go on talking about Papa at that time which they were too young to remember. She searched her mind for something to ask him.

"What –" she said, "what did he look like?"

He clearly thought it a stupid question. "Well," he said, "he look like they all look in them days, didn't he. He had one of them cloaks and a stick and a silk hat." Perhaps he sensed her disappointment, for he added, "Anyway, there's plenty of pictures of him in there."

They had arrived at a door with another, bigger, poster on it, and he unlocked it and switched on the lights, while Max pressed a coin into his hand.

"Thank you, sir. I'll drink to you with that," he said as, perhaps, he had said to Papa thirty-odd years before, and tottered back into the semi-darkness of the stairs.

The room he had opened for them was the circle bar, and now that the lights were on, she saw that the walls, not only in the bar but also in the passage outside it, were hung with photographs and reproductions. There was Papa with Einstein, Papa with Bernard Shaw, Papa making a speech, Papa and Mama in America with skyscrapers behind them, Papa and Mama on the deck of an ocean liner. Mama looked like herself, only younger and happier, but Papa seemed unfamiliar because of his habit, which Anna now remembered, of putting on a special expression for photographers.

There were framed newspaper cuttings with explanations beneath them. "The article which caused such controversy in 1927", "The last article to be published before he left Germany in 1933". There were drawings and cartoons, a magazine Papa had edited ("I didn't know he'd done that," said Anna), framed pages of manuscript with his familiar, spidery writing, endlessly corrected.

She looked at it all, touched and bewildered. "It's so strange, isn't it," she said. "All the time he was doing this, we hardly knew him."

"I remember people asking about him at school," said Max.

"And visitors coming to the house. There was a man who brought us some marzipan pigs. I remember Mama saying that he was very famous. I suppose it might have been Einstein."

"I think I would have remembered Einstein," said Max who had forgotten even the marzipan pigs.

Already half dismantled against the wall was a glass case with a complete set of Papa's books. They looked clean and almost unused – very different from his own shabby collection in the Putney boarding house. He had had to acquire the volumes piecemeal from friends who had managed somehow to smuggle them out of Germany.

"He never did get a full set together for himself, did he?" said Max.

"No." She touched the glass case gently with her hand. "No, he never did."

From the far end of the bar, steps led to another passage, and here, too, exhibits had already been taken down and were leaning in a corner, face to the wall. She picked one up at random. It was an enlarged reproduction of a recent article assessing Papa's work. She read, ". . . one of the most brilliant minds of his generation. The books, classics of their kind, are in every university library." In another case nearby were the two thick modern volumes with his collected writings which Mama had worked so hard to get republished the previous year.

"Look at this," said Max. He had found a photograph of the four of them in the garden in Berlin, Papa posing like an author as usual, Mama smiling radiantly, and herself and Max in matching striped woollies, Max with a Christopher Robin haircut on a scooter, herself on a tricycle.

"I remember that being taken," she said. "I remember I'd just got the tricycle, and I was trying to look like someone who could ride a tricycle round corners."

Max considered it. "It doesn't really come across," he said, and added, "actually, you look exactly like Papa."

Suddenly there were no more exhibits, and it seemed they had come to the end of the show.

"That's it," said Max. "It's not really very big, is it?"

They went to the end of the passage, through a door, and found themselves at the back of the circle, a curve of empty red seats sloping down on each side of them. In the vast dimness under the roof hung the usual theatre smell of glue and plaster, and from the well of the stalls came the hum of a vacuum cleaner. Peering down, Anna could see a foreshortened figure Hoovering along the aisle. She looked at the middle of the third row and tried to imagine Papa sitting there, but she couldn't bring him to life.

"It's really just something for people to look at in the interval," said Max, beside her. "But I think it must have been quite effective before they took half of it down."

She nodded and turned to go back the way they had come – and there, between two exits, like a saint in a niche, almost life-size and smiling, was Papa. He was wearing his old grey hat and the shabby winter coat which he had had as long as Anna could remember, and he seemed to be in the middle of saying something. His eyes were focused with interest on something or someone just to one side of the camera, and he looked stimulated and full of life.

She knew the picture, of course, though she had never seen it so enlarged. It had been taken by a press photographer as Papa stepped off the plane in Hamburg on that day long ago – the last picture taken of him before his death. Papa had not known that the photographer was there, so he had not had time to put on his special expression and looked exactly as Anna remembered him.

"Papa," she said.

Max, following her glance, stopped halfway up the steps, and they stood looking at it together.

"It's a perfect place to put it," she said at last. "Looking out over the theatre."

There was a pause. The whine of the Hoover continued to rise from the stalls.

"You know," said Max, "this is the one thing here that really means anything to me. Of course the rest is very interesting, but this, to me, is Papa. What I find so strange is that to everyone else he was someone quite different."

She nodded. "I haven't even read everything he wrote."

"Nor have I."

"The point about Papa –" For a moment she lost track of what the point was. Something to do with having loved Papa when he was old and unsuccessful and yet more interesting than anyone else she knew. "He never felt sorry for himself," she said, but it was not what she meant.

"The point about Papa," said Max, "was not just his work but the sort of person he was."

When they started back down the curved staircase, there were signs of activity in the foyer. The doors to the street were open, someone had taken over the glass-fronted ticket office, and an elderly man was trying to make a booking. They had reached the foot of the stairs, when a gaunt young woman appeared from nowhere, said something about *Kulturbeziehungen* and shook them warmly by the hand.

"Did you enjoy it?" she cried. "I'm so sorry I

wasn't here to meet you. I do hope the janitor – he remembers your father, you know. Your mother came when it opened, of course, and seemed quite pleased, but one always wonders. There is so little room, so one had to select."

"I thought it was excellent," said Max, and she lit up, as people always did when he smiled at them, and straightaway looked less gaunt.

"Did you?" she said. "Did you really? One hopes so much always to have got it right."

"I wish he could have seen it himself," said Anna.

Later, over lunch in a small bar, they talked about Mama.

"It rather hits one," said Max, "when one's seen this exhibition – the sort of person Papa was and the sort of life she used to lead with him. And now she tries to kill herself over someone like Konrad."

"He made her feel safe," said Anna.

"Oh I know, I know."

"I like Konrad," said Anna. "What I find so amazing is the way Mama talks about the things they do together. You know – 'we won three dollars at bridge and the car did eighty miles in an hour and a half' – it's all so boring and ordinary."

Max sighed. "I suppose that's why she likes it. She's never had a chance to do it before."

"I suppose so."

Max sighed again. "Papa was a great man. He took quite a bit of living up to. Being married to him *and* being a refugee – it would make anyone long for some ordinariness. I think in a way we all did."

Anna remembered a time at her English boarding school when she had wished for nothing so much as to be called Pam and to be good at lacrosse. It had been a short-lived phase.

"Not you so much, perhaps," said Max. "If one wants to paint or write, perhaps being different matters less. But me –"

"Nonsense," said Anna. "You've always been different."

He shook his head. "Only in quality. Best student, scholarship winner, brilliant young barrister tipped to be youngest Q.C. –"

"Are you?"

He grinned. "Maybe. But it's all conforming, isn't it? What I'm really doing is making damned sure that in the end I shall be indistinguishable from the very best ordinary people in the country. I've sometimes wondered, if we hadn't been refugees –"

"You'd always have done law. You've got a huge talent for it."

"Probably. But I might have done it for slightly different reasons." He made a face. "No, I can understand exactly why Mama wants to be ordinary."

They sat in silence for a while. At last Anna said, "What do you think will happen now?"

He shrugged his shoulders. "Konrad keeps saying he'll assume complete responsibility for her. I don't know whether that means he wants to pick up where they left off, as though nothing at all had happened. I suppose he may say something when we have dinner tonight."

"Yes." She suddenly saw Mama very clearly, with her vulnerable blue eyes, the determined mouth, the childish snub nose. "She'll be desperate if he doesn't."

"Well, I think he might. I think he means to. What I'm frightened of is that he might feel we're just taking him for granted, and that he'll be put off. I think he'll want some support."

"We could give him that, surely?"

He said nothing for a moment. Then he looked at her. "I left Wendy and the baby on a remote Greek island. I can't stay long."

"I see." It hadn't occurred to her, and she felt suddenly depressed. "Perhaps –" she said, "I suppose I could stay on a few days on my own –" But she hated even the thought of it.

"If you could, it would make all the difference."

"I'd have just to think about it. I've got this new job, you see. It's quite important." The new job and Mama were jumbled up in confusion. Back to Mama, thought part of her mind with the usual sense of panic, and another part thought of Richard, but he seemed far away. "I'd want first to talk to Richard about it."

"Well, of course," he said.

He looked white again when the waitress brought the bill, and said, "Do you mind if we go back to the hotel? I've had practically no sleep for two nights and I suddenly feel rather tired. Konrad said he'd fixed up a room for me."

While he slept, she lay on her bed and stared at the patterned curtains as they moved very gently in the draught. She wished that she had not mentioned staying on. Now it would be difficult not to do it, she thought, feeling mean. And yet, she thought, why should it always be me? Still, she hadn't actually committed herself, and at the worst it would only be a few days. I simply wouldn't stay longer than that, she told herself. For a moment she considered trying to ring Richard. But it would be best to talk to Konrad first. After all, now that Mama was out of danger, he might not even want anyone to stay.

The patterned curtains moved and flowed. She felt suddenly sharply aware of herself, of the shabby German house around her and of Max resting in the next room. There was Konrad in his office and his secretary watching him, and Mama waking up properly at last from her long anaesthesia and Richard trying to write his script and waiting for her in London, and in the past, behind them all, was Papa.

This, she thought, is what it's like. She felt that she could see it all, every bit of it in relation to the rest, and she knew everybody's thoughts and all their feelings, and could set them off against each other with hair-trigger precision. I could write about it all, she thought. But the thought was so cold-blooded that she shocked herself and tried to pretend that she had not had it.

*   *   *

They went to the hospital in the late afternoon,
and when they opened the door of Mama's room,
they found Konrad already there. He was sitting
on the bed, and Mama, who looked tense and
on the edge of tears, was holding his hand. Her
blue eyes were fixed on his and she had put on
some lipstick, which looked strangely bright in
her exhausted face.

"*Nu*," said Konrad, "here are your children
who have come from all the corners of the earth
to see you, so I'll leave you."

"Don't go." Mama's voice was still a little faint.
"Must you?"

"Yes, ma'am, I must," said Konrad. He heaved
his bulk off the bed and smiled his asymmetrical
smile. "I shall go for a walk, which is good for
me, which is why I so rarely do it, and then I shall
come back and buy your children some dinner. In
the meantime, you behave yourself."

"Don't walk too far."

"No, ma'am," he said, and Anna saw Mama's
mouth quiver as he went out of the room.

"He always calls me ma'am," she said tremu-
lously, as though it explained everything.

They had brought some flowers, and Anna
inserted them into a vase which already contained
some rather more splendid ones from Konrad,
while Max took Konrad's place on the bed.

"Well, Mama," he said with his warm smile.
"I'm very glad you're better."

"Yes," said Anna from behind the vase. They

were both afraid that Mama would begin to cry.

She still seemed rather dazed. "Are you?" she said, and then added with more of her normal vigour, "I'm not. I wish they'd just left me alone. It would have been much simpler for everyone."

"Nonsense, Mama," said Max, and at this her eyes filled with tears.

"The only thing I'm sorry about," she said, "is that I dragged you away from your holiday. I didn't want to – I really didn't. But it was so awful –" She sniffed through her little snub nose and searched for a handkerchief under her pillow. "I tried not to," she cried. "I tried to wait at least until you'd be back in London, but each day – I just couldn't bear it any longer." She had found the handkerchief and blew into it, hard. "If only they'd just let me die," she said, "then you needn't have come until the funeral, and perhaps you could have finished your holiday first."

"Yes, Mama," said Max. "But I might not have enjoyed it very much."

"Wouldn't you?" She saw his face, and her voice warmed to something almost like a giggle. "After all, what's an old mother?"

"True, Mama. But I just happen to be attached to mine, and so is Anna."

"Yes," said Anna, through the flowers.

"Oh, I don't know, I don't know."

She lay back on the pillow and closed her eyes, and tears damped her cheeks from under the closed lids.

"I'm so tired," she said.

Max patted her hand. "You'll feel better soon."

But she seemed not to hear him. "Did he tell you what he'd done?" she said. "He got another girl."

"But it didn't mean anything," said Anna. She had squatted down near the bed, and at the sight of Mama's tear-stained face on a level with her own, as she had so often seen it from her bed in the Putney boarding house, the familiar feeling rose up inside her that she could not bear Mama to be so unhappy, that it must somehow be stopped.

Mama looked at her. "She was younger than me."

"Yes, but Mama –"

"You don't know what it's like," cried Mama. "You're young yourself, you've got your Richard." She turned her face away and cried, to the wall, "Why couldn't they have let me die? They let Papa die in peace – I arranged that. Why couldn't they have let me?"

Anna and Max exchanged glances.

"Mama –" said Max.

Anna discovered that she had pins and needles and stood up. She did not like to rub her leg, in case it looked callous, so she went over to the window and stood there miserably, flexing and unflexing her knee.

"Look, Mama, I know you've had a bad time, but I think everything is going to be all right. After all, you and Konrad have been together a long time." Max was talking in his reasonable lawyer's voice.

"Seven years," said Mama.

"There you are. And this affair, whatever it was, meant nothing to him. He's said so. And when people have had as good and as long a relationship as you two, you can survive a lot more troubles than that."

"We did have a good relationship," said Mama. "We made a good team. Everybody said so."

"There you are, then."

"Did you know that we were runners-up in the bridge tournament? With lots of American and English couples competing, all very practised players. And we should really have tied with the couple who won, only there was a stupid rule –"

"You've always been terribly good together."

"Yes," said Mama. "For seven years." She looked at Max. "How could he smash it all up? How could he?"

"I think it was something that just happened."

But she was not listening. "The holidays we had together," she said. "When we first got the car and went to Italy. He drove and I map read. And we found this lovely little place by the sea – I sent you photographs, didn't I? We were so happy. And it wasn't just me, it was him, at least as much. He told me so. He said, 'Never in all my life have I been as happy as I am now.' His wife was very dull, you see. They never did anything or went anywhere. All she ever wanted to do was to buy more furniture."

Max nodded, and Mama's blue eyes, fixed on some distant memory, suddenly returned to him.

"This girl," she said, "The one he had an affair with. Did you know she was German?"

"No," said Max.

"Well, she is. A little German secretary. Very little education, speaks very bad English, and she's not even pretty. Only –" Mama's eyes became wet again – "only younger."

"Oh, Mama, I'm sure that's nothing to do with it."

"Well, what else is it to do with, then? It must have been something. You don't smash up seven years of happiness just for no reason!"

Max took her hand. "Look, Mama, there was no reason. It was just something that happened. It was never important to him, except for the way you reacted. Anyway, he's been here. Didn't he tell you so himself?"

"Yes," said Mama in a small voice. "But how do I know it's true?"

"I think it's true," said Anna. "I've been with him for two days, and I think it's true."

Mama glanced at her briefly and then looked back at Max.

"I think so too," said Max. "And I'll be seeing him tonight. I'll talk to him and find out what he really thinks, and I promise I'll tell you exactly what he said. But I'm sure it'll be all right."

Mama, her eyes finally brimming over, sank back into the pillows.

"Oh, Max," she said. "I'm so glad you're here."

Later, in the car, Anna stared out at the rubble and the half-made new buildings flying past in the light of the street lamps and wondered how it was all going to end. Konrad was driving, carefully and efficiently as usual, and she suddenly felt she had no idea what he was thinking. He seemed to be taking them on a tour of the city and, with Max on the front seat beside him, was pointing out various landmarks.

"Kurfürsten Damm . . . Leibnitz Strasse . . . Gedächtnis Kirche . . . Potsdamer Platz . . ."

She could see soldiers, some kind of a barrier and above it, carefully lit, a sign saying, "You are now leaving the American Sector". It looked cold and dark. Some young people, gathered in a group, were flapping their arms and stamping their feet. Most of them were carrying placards and, as she watched, they suddenly moved closer to the barrier and all shouted together, *"Russen raus! Russen raus! Russen raus!"*

Konrad caught her eyes in the driving mirror. "Supporters for Hungary," he said. "I can't see it having much effect, but it's nice to see them try."

She nodded. "There are a lot of them in London, too."

The *Potsdamer Platz* faded behind them.

"Do the Russians ever retaliate?" asked Max.

"Not by shouting slogans. There are more effective ways, such as doubling the checks on the road in and out of Berlin. That means everything takes twice as long to get through."

The shouts of *"Russen raus!"* could still be faintly heard in the distance. A group of American soldiers marching in step, steel-helmeted and armed, flickered momentarily into vision, to disappear again into the darkness.

"Doesn't it ever bother you, being surrounded like this? I mean," said Anna, "suppose the Russians attacked?" She tried to sound detached, without success.

Max grinned at her over his shoulder. "Don't worry, little man. I promise they won't get you."

"If the Russians attacked," said Konrad, "they could take Berlin in ten minutes. Everyone who lives here knows this. The reason they don't attack is because they know that if they did, they would find themselves at war with the Americans."

"I see."

"And even to get you, little man," said Max, "they won't risk starting a third world war."

She laughed half-heartedly. It was cold in the back of the car and as Konrad turned a corner, she suddenly felt queasy. Not again! she thought.

Konrad was watching her in the driving mirror.

"Supper," he said. "About three streets from here. I've booked at a restaurant you've been to before – I hope you don't mind, but you enjoyed it last time."

It turned out to be the place where they had celebrated her and Richard's decision to get married, and as soon as she recognized it – the warm, smoky atmosphere, the tables covered with red cloths and separated from each other by high-backed wooden benches – she felt better.

"*Etwas zu trinken?*" asked the fat proprietress.

(Last time, Mama having proudly told her what was being celebrated, she had given them schnapps on the house.)

Konrad ordered whisky, and when she brought it she smiled and said in German, "A family reunion?"

"You could call it that," said Konrad and, ridiculous though it was, that was exactly what it felt like.

Konrad sat between them and, like a fond and generous uncle, helped them choose their food from the menu, consulted Max about the wine, worried about their comfort and refilled their glasses. Meanwhile he talked about impersonal subjects – the dubious Russian promise to leave Hungary if the Hungarians laid down their arms, the trouble in Suez, where the Israelis had finally attacked Egypt. ("I hope Wendy won't be too worried," said Max. "After all, Greece isn't very far away.") Then, when they had finished the main course, Konrad sat back as far as it was possible for such a large man to sit back on a narrow wooden bench, and turned to Max.

"Your sister will have given you some idea of what has been happening," he said. "But I expect you'd like to know exactly."

"Yes," said Max. "I would."

"Of course." He placed his knife and fork neatly side by side on his plate. "I don't know if your mother happened to mention it in her letters, but she recently went to Hanover for a few days. It was a special assignment and rather a compliment to her. While she was away I – became involved with someone else."

They both looked at him. There seemed nothing suitable to say.

"This – temporary involvement was not serious. It is now over and done with. I told your mother about it, so that she should not hear about it from anyone else. I thought she would be mature enough to see it in its proper perspective . . ."

(Hold on, thought Anna. Up to now she had been with him, but if he really believed that . . . How could he possibly believe that Mama would take it calmly?)

". . . After all, we're neither of us children."

She looked at him. His kind, middle-aged face had a curious closed expression. Like a small boy, she thought, insisting that taking the watch to pieces could not possibly have damaged it.

"But, Konrad –"

He lost some of his detachment. "Well, she *should* have understood. It was nothing. I told her it was nothing. Look, your mother is an intelligent, vital woman. She has an enormous enjoyment of life, and that's something she's taught me, too, during the past years. All the things we've done together – the friendships, the holidays, even some of the jobs I've held – I would never have done without her. Whereas this other girl – she's a little secretary. She's

710

never been anywhere, never done anything, lives at home with her mother, does the cooking and the mending, hardly speaks . . ."

"Then – why?" asked Max.

"I don't know." He frowned, puzzling it out. "I suppose," he said at last, "I suppose it made a little rest."

It sounded so funny that she found herself laughing. She caught Max's eye, and he was laughing too. It was not just the way Konrad had said it, but that they both knew what he meant.

There was an intensity about Mama which was exhausting. You could never for a moment forget her presence, even when she was content. "Isn't it *lovely*!" she would say, daring you to disagree. "Don't you think this is the most *beautiful* day?" Or place, or meal, or whatever else it was that had made her happy. She would pursue what she believed to be perfection with ruthless energy, battling for the best place on the beach, the right job, an extra day's leave, with a determination which most people could not be bothered to resist.

"It's not your mother's fault," said Konrad. "It's the way she is." He smiled a little. "*Immer mit dem Kopf durch die Wand.*"

"That's what Papa used to say about her," said Anna.

She had tried to translate the expression for Richard. It meant not just banging your head against brick walls, but actually bursting through them head first, as a matter of habit.

"Did he really?" said Konrad. "She never told

me that. But of course she used to do it to very good purpose. Getting you both educated when there was no money. Getting a job without qualifications. I don't suppose that without her habit of bursting through brick walls, either of you would have come through the emigration as well as you did."

"Well, of course." They both knew it and felt it did not need pointing out.

There was a little pause. "But this other girl – the secretary," said Max at last. "What does she feel about it all? Does *she* think it's over?"

Konrad had his closed, little-boy expression again. "I've told her," he said. "I've made quite sure she understands."

Suddenly, out of the smoke and the muddle of German voices, the proprietress bore down on them with coffee and three small glasses.

"A little schnapps," she said, "for the family reunion."

They thanked her, and Konrad made a joke about the burdens of a family man. She burst into laughter and drifted back into the smoke. He turned again to Max.

"And now?" said Max. "What will happen now?"

"Now?" The little-boy look had disappeared and Konrad looked suddenly what he was – a rather plain, elderly Jew who had seen a lot of trouble. "Now we pick up the pieces and put them together again." He raised the little glass and put it to his lips. "To the family reunion," he said.

Afterwards Anna remembered the rest of the evening like a kind of party. She felt happily confused
as though she were drunk, not so much with
schnapps as with the knowledge that everything
was going to be all right. Mama would get over
her unhappiness. Konrad would see to it, as he
had always seen to everything. And between them
they had all – and especially Anna – saved Mama
from dying stupidly, unnecessarily, and in a state
of despair for which it would be difficult to forgive oneself.

Max and Konrad, too, seemed in a much more
relaxed state. They swapped legal anecdotes without any of the awkwardness that normally came
between them, and once, when Anna returned
from the Ladies (a very functional place almost
entirely filled by one large woman adjusting a hard
felt hat over her iron grey hair) she found them
roaring with laughter together like old friends.

The mood only began to fade while Konrad
drove them home. Perhaps it was the cold, and the
sight of the half-built streets with their patrolling
soldiers. Or, more likely, thought Anna, it was
the realization that it was nearly midnight and
too late for her to ring Richard. Whatever it
was, she found herself unexpectedly homesick
and depressed, and she was horrified when, at the
door of the hotel, Konrad suddenly said, "I'm so
glad you'll be able to stay on for a while in Berlin.
It will make all the difference."

She was too taken aback to say anything in

reply, and it was only after he had gone that she turned angrily to Max. "Did you tell Konrad that I was going to stay on?" she asked.

They were in the little breakfast room which also served as reception area, and a sleepy adolescent girl, no doubt a relation of the owner, was preparing to hand them their keys.

"I don't know – I may have done," said Max. "Anyway, I thought you said you were going to."

"I only said I might." She felt suddenly panicked. "I never said definitely. I said I wanted first to talk to Richard."

"Well, there's nothing to stop you explaining that to Konrad. I don't see why you should be in such a state about it." Max, too, was clearly suffering from reaction, and they stood glaring at each other by the desk.

"Rooms 5 and 6," said the girl, pushing the keys and a piece of paper across to them. "And a telephone message for the lady."

It was from Richard, of course. He had rung up and missed her. The paper contained only his name, grotesquely misspelt. He had not even been able to leave a message, because no one in the hotel spoke English.

"Oh damn, oh damn, oh damn!" she shouted.

"For God's sake," said Max. "He's bound to ring again tomorrow night."

"Tomorrow night I'm going to a bloody party," she shouted. "Konrad arranged that. Everybody here seems to decide exactly what I should be doing at any given time. Perhaps just once in a while I might be consulted. Perhaps next time you make long-term arrangements for me, you might just ask me first."

Max looked confounded. "What party?" he said.

"Oh, what does it matter what party? Some awful British Council thing."

"Look." He spoke very calmly. "You've got this whole thing out of proportion. If you like, I'll explain it to Konrad myself. There simply isn't any problem."

But of course it was not true. It would be much more difficult to tell Konrad that she was not staying, now he believed that she was.

Alone in bed, she thought of London and of Richard, and found to her horror that she could not clearly visualize his face. Her insides contracted. The familiar nausea swept over her, and for a long time she lay under the great quilt in the darkness and listened to the trains rumble along distant tracks. At last she could stand it no longer: she got up, dug in her suitcase for a clean handkerchief, climbed back into bed and spread it on her stomach.

Wednesday

Max could not have slept well either, and they were both bad-tempered at breakfast. They had to wait for their coffee, for the little breakfast room was filled with six or seven guests who must have arrived on the previous day, and even with the help of the adolescent girl, the proprietress was too disorganized to serve them properly.

"When do you expect to leave then?" Anna asked Max coldly.

He made an impatient gesture. "I don't know. But I've got to get back to Greece soon. For God's sake," he said, "nobody there speaks a word of English, Wendy doesn't speak a word of Greek, and she's got a ten-month-old baby."

She said nothing for a moment. Then resentment rose up irresistibly inside her and she said, "It's just that I don't see why it should always be me who has to cope."

"It isn't always you." He was trying to attract the proprietress's attention, without success. "You know perfectly well that even during the war when I was flying, and later when I was working my guts out in Cambridge, I always came home. I came whenever there was a crisis, and I came whenever I could, apart from that, just to lend moral support."

"You came," she said. "But you didn't stay."

"Well, of course I didn't stay. I was supposed to be flying a bloody aeroplane. I was supposed to be getting a First in law and make a career and be a prop to the family."

"Oh, I know, I know." She felt suddenly tired of the argument. "It's just – you can't imagine what it was like being there all the time. The hopelessness of doing anything for Papa, and Mama's depressions. Even then, you know, she was always talking about suicide."

"But she didn't actually do anything, did she?" said Max. "I mean, this *is* a bit different."

She had a sudden vision of Mama in her blue hat, her face wet with tears, saying, "I couldn't go on. I just couldn't go on." In a street somewhere – Putney, she supposed. Why did she keep remembering it? And was it something that had really happened or something she had imagined?

"Anyway," said Max, "if you really want to go back to London, you'll just have to go. Though I wouldn't have thought a few days would have mattered either way."

"Oh, let's wait and see," she said wearily. "Let's see how Mama is this morning."

Max had finally managed to catch the proprietress's eye, and she hurried resentfully over to their table.

"All right, all right," she said. "You're not at war here, you know."

While he ordered the coffee and rolls, Anna made a mental note of the expression – a bit of Berlin dialect which even Heimpi had never used. A German at the next table tittered at the sound of it. Then he smiled at Anna and pointed to his newspaper. "Rule Britannia, eh?" he said. She looked at the front page and read the headline: *Englischer Angriff in Suez.*

"For God's sake, Max," she said. "Look at that. We're at war."

"What?"

"*Bitte, bitte,*" said the German and handed the paper over to them.

It was true. British paratroopers were supporting the Israelis in Egypt. There was not much beyond the headline – clearly few details were known as yet – but a longer article speculated on the effect this new development might have on the Hungarian situation. A headline almost as big as the one about Suez said, "Russians offer to withdraw troops from Hungary, Romania and Poland".

"What does it mean?" said Anna, trying to control the panic rising inside her.

Max had his alert lawyer's look, as though in

the few moments since reading about it he had already weighed up the situation.

"One thing is certain," he said. "I've got to get Wendy home."

"What about me? What about here in Berlin?"

"I don't think it'll make any difference here. At least not at the moment. But you'd better ring Richard tonight. He may have a better idea of what's going on."

"The Russians –?"

Max pointed to the paper. "They seem quite conciliatory at the moment. I think they've got their hands full. Look, you hang on for the coffee, I'll just try and ring BEA. God knows how long it'll take to get me to Athens."

She sat at the grubby little table by herself and nervously drank some of the coffee when it came.

"*Bitte?*" said the German, pointing to the paper, and she gave it back to him.

Then Max returned, all energy and bustle. "They said to call in before lunch," he said. "There may be a connecting flight tomorrow. If I can get on that, and if I can contact my ship owner, perhaps he'll arrange transport for me at the other end."

"Max," she said, "couldn't I try and ring Richard now?"

He sat down. "No good, I'm afraid," he said. "I just checked. There's a three hour delay on all calls to London."

"I see."

"Look, there's no question of your staying here in case of any danger. At the smallest hint of anything you get on a plane home. Konrad will see to that, anyway. But I honestly think it's probably as safe here at the moment as it's ever been."

She nodded without conviction.

"Anyway, talk to Richard tonight. And talk to Konrad. If we hurry, we may catch him at the hospital."

However, Konrad had left a message that he had an urgent meeting and would visit Mama in his lunch break. They found her looking physically much like herself but in a desperate state of tension. The nurse was just removing her breakfast tray (anyway, she'd eaten it all, Anna noted with relief) and Mama did not even wait for the door to close behind her before she asked, "Well? What did he say?"

"What did who say?" Max knew perfectly well, of course, but was just trying to slow her down.

"Konrad. What did he say to you last night? What did he say about me?" Her blue eyes stared, her hands drummed nervously on the edge of the sheet. The whole room was filled with her tension.

Max managed to sound easy as he answered. "Mama, he said exactly what I expected, and what he'd already told you. The affair is finished. He wants you back. He wants to forget everything that's happened and to start again where you both left off."

"Oh." She relaxed a little. "But then why didn't he come this morning?"

"He told you. He had a meeting. Perhaps something to do with this Sucz business."

"Suez? Oh, that." The nurse must have told her, thought Anna. "But that wouldn't have anything to do with Konrad."

Max's irritation was beginning to show. "It may have nothing to do with Konrad, but it's got something to do with me. I have to get back to Greece as soon as possible and bring Wendy and the baby home. Probably tomorrow. So just for today, can we stop worrying about his every thought and gesture, and talk properly?"

"Wendy and the baby? But why do you have to bring them home? Why can't they just catch a plane on their own?"

They're going to have a row, thought Anna.

"For heaven's sake, Mama, they're on a remote island. Wendy doesn't speak a word of Greek. She couldn't possibly manage."

"Couldn't she?" Mama's anger was mixed with a certain triumph. "Well, I could. When you and Anna were small, I got you both out of Germany without any help from anyone. And before that, for two weeks after Papa had already fled, I kept it a secret and I got you to keep it a secret too – you were only twelve and nine at the time. I packed up our house and all our belongings, and then I got you both out, twenty-four hours before the Nazis came for our passports."

"I know, Mama, you were terribly good. But Wendy is different."

"How different? I'd have liked to be different too. I'd have loved to be different, so that everybody would look after me. Instead, I had to look after everybody else."

"Mama –" But it was no good.

"I cooked and cleaned when we lived in Paris. And then, when Papa could no longer earn anything, I got a job and supported us all. I got you into your English public school –"

"Not quite by yourself, Mama. I must have had something to do with it too."

"You know what I mean. And then, when we could no longer pay the fees, I went to see the headmaster –"

"And he gave me a scholarship. I know, Mama. But it wasn't easy for the rest of us either. It wasn't much fun for Papa, and even Anna and I had our problems."

Mama's hands clenched on the sheet. "But you were young," she cried. "It didn't matter. You had all your lives to come. Whereas I . . . All those years I spent in dreary boarding houses worrying about money, I was getting older. It should have been the best time of my life, and instead I spent it scraping pennies together and worrying myself sick over Papa and Anna and you. And now at last when I'd found someone who looked after me, with whom I could do all the things I'd missed, he had to go and – he had to go and have an affair with a stupid, feeble little German typist." Her voice broke and she wept again.

Anna wondered whether to say anything, but decided not to. Nobody would have listened to her anyway.

"It wasn't like that, Mama. It's never as simple as that." Max looked as though he had been wanting to say this for years. "You always over-simplify."

"But I did do those things. I did keep everything going. When we first came to England and still had some money, it was I who decided that we should send you to a public school, and I was right – you'd never have done so well if we hadn't."

"It might have been more difficult."

"And your headmaster told me – I always remember what he said about you. He said, 'He's got a first-class brain, he's hard-working and he's got charm. There's nothing he won't be able to do. He can be Prime Minister if he wants."

"He couldn't really have said that," Max was quivering on the edge of a grin. "I mean, old Chetwyn – it wasn't his style."

"But he did, he did! And he said what a good mother I was. And I remember at Christmas, when I still had that good job with Lady Parker, and she asked me what I'd like for a Christmas present, and I said, 'I'd like a radio for my son,' and she said, 'Wouldn't you like something for yourself, a dress or a coat?' and I said, 'It's the one thing he wants, if I can give him that it'll be better than anything,' and she said –"

"Oh, I know, Mama, I know –"

"And during the war, when you were interned, Papa just wanted to let matters take their course, but I *made* him write to the papers, it was me who got you out, if it hadn't been for me you'd have been there much longer. And it was me who found the secretarial school for Anna, and then, when you were in the Air Force and you had trouble with that girl, I coped with it, I went to see her –"

"I know, Mama, it's all true –"

Mama's face was red and tearful like a very small child's. "I *was* a good mother!" she cried. "I know I was! Everybody said what a good mother I was!"

"Well, of course you were," said Max.

It was suddenly quiet.

"But then, why," said Mama, "why is everything now so awful?"

"I don't know," said Max. "Perhaps because we've grown up."

They looked at each other with their identical blue eyes, and Anna thought how often in Putney, in Bloomsbury, even in Paris, she had sat through scenes like this. The arguments had been different each time, but always there had been, amidst the shouting and the anger, the same sense of closeness between them, something which left no room for anyone else. As now, she had sat silent on the edge, watching Mama's face, noting (even then?) the exact words of her accusations and of Max's replies. In those days, of course, there had been Papa to stop her from feeling entirely left out.

"You see," said Max, "in a way it was all exactly as you say. But it was also quite different."

"How?" cried Mama. "In what way? How could it have been?"

He frowned, searching for the right phrases. "Well, it's quite true, of course, that I've been a success, and that without you, it would have been much more difficult."

"Very much more difficult," said Mama, but he ignored her.

"But at the same time, it wasn't all for me. I mean, in a way, perhaps because everything was so awful for you, you needed me to be a success."

Mama drummed irritably on the sheet. "Well, why shouldn't I? For God's sake, do you remember how we used to live? I'd have done anything – anything – for Papa to have had even a little bit of success in those days."

"No, you don't understand. What I mean is – because you needed it so much, every little thing I did had to be, somehow, a triumph. I used to hear you talking about me. You used to say, 'He's going to stay with friends, they've got an estate in the country.' Well, it wasn't. It was a boy in Esher, I liked him very much, but he lived in a semi-detached. The only time I went anywhere grand while I was at school, my suitcase burst when the butler tried to unpack it, and the father, Sir Something-or-other, had to give me one of his, which he hated. It was all very embarrassing, but the way you told it, it was, 'And this lord took such a fancy to

Max that he insisted on giving him some of his own luggage.'"

Mama looked puzzled and upset. "Well, what does it matter – little things like that? And anyway, he probably did like you. People always do."

Max sighed impatiently. "But it was other things as well. You used to say, 'Of course he'll get a scholarship, of course he'll get a first.' Well, I did get them, but there was no of course about it. I had to work very hard, and I often worried about whether I'd make it."

"Well, perhaps – it's possible." Mama's mouth was pulled down obstinately at the corners. "But I still don't see that it matters."

"It matters because it made it difficult for me to see my life as it really was. And it matters now because you're doing the same thing to yourself. Re-shaping things if they don't fit. Everything black and white. No uncertainties, no failures, no mistakes."

"Nonsense," said Mama, "I don't do that at all." She was getting tired and her voice rose. "You don't know how I live here," she cried. "Everybody likes me, they all like talking to me and even ask me for advice. *They* don't think I see everything in black and white. I've got quite a reputation for solving people's problems, love affairs, all sorts of things." She finally burst into tears. "You don't know anything about me!" she cried.

Sooner or later it always came to this, thought Anna. She was relieved to see a nurse appear at the door with a cup of soup.

"Zur guten Besserung," said the nurse, and they all watched, Mama sniffing and blowing her nose, while she crossed the room and put the soup on the bedside table and went out again.

"Anyway, I was quite right," said Mama almost before she had left. "It's all happened just as I said. You do know all sorts of lords and people like that, and you *are* making a great career."

"Yes, Mama." Max was tired too. He patted her arm. "I must go soon," he said. "I've got to do something about my ticket."

She clutched his hand. "Oh, Max!"

"There, there, Mama. You're a very good mother, and everything will be all right." They smiled at each other, cautiously, with their identical blue eyes.

Anna, smiled too, just to be companionable, and wondered whether she should leave with Max when he went or stay with Mama and wait for Konrad. It would be difficult to know what to say, she thought. After the excitement of Max, anything she might think of would come as an anti-climax. On the other hand, if she stayed, she might be able to talk to Konrad about going home.

Mama was still holding Max's hand. "How was it in Greece?" she said.

"Absolutely marvellous." He began to tell her about the case he was doing, and about the ship owner's seaside house. ". . . right on the beach of this tiny island, with a cook and God knows how many servants. He owns it all – the whole place.

He's got olive groves and his own vineyard, all incredibly beautiful, and we had the run of it. The only trouble was, Wendy was a bit worried about the greasy food for the baby."

"Did you swim?"

"Three times a day. The sea is so warm and so clear —"

But, unexpectedly, Mama's eyes had filled with tears. "Oh, Max, I'm so sorry," she cried. "I didn't mean to interrupt your holiday. I didn't mean to drag you away to Berlin."

Anna suddenly felt childishly angry.

"What about me?" she said, startling all three of them, since she had said nothing for so long. "What about dragging me to Berlin from London?"

"You?" Mama looked surprised and upset. "I thought you might quite like to come."

"Quite like . . . ?" She was almost speechless.

"I mean, you weren't doing anything special, and I knew you hadn't been away in the summer."

There was a trace of a query in Mama's voice, and Anna found herself answering, in spite of herself, "I've got a new job, and Richard is in the middle of writing a serial." It sounded so feeble that she stopped, and fury overcame her. After all I've done, she thought. After sitting on her bed and dragging her out of her coma. But even while she was thinking it, another part of herself was coolly noting Mama's exact words, as it had already noted much of the conversation. If one were really going to write about this, she thought guiltily, they would make a marvellous bit of dialogue.

In the end she left the sickroom with Max and waited for Konrad in the reception hall. Through one of the windows, she watched him park his car in the drive, hesitate whether or not to bring his stick, and finally walk up towards the entrance without it. He manoeuvred his bulk through the swing doors and smiled when he saw her.

"Hullo," he said. "How's your mother?"

"I'm not sure," she said. "We had a row."

"*Nu*," he said, "if she could have a row, she must be feeling better." He looked at her. "Was it serious?"

"Not really, I suppose. It was mostly with Max, and I don't think she minds that so much. I only came in at the end."

"I see. And is that why you waited for me here?"

"No." She decided to take the bull by the horns. "It's this Suez business. Max is worried about Wendy and the baby, and he's gone to try and book a flight to Athens. And I just wondered –"

"What?"

A woman with a bandaged hand said, "*Verzeihung*," and pushed past them, giving her time to choose her words.

"What do you think?" she said. "Might there be trouble here? I mean, I suppose all this is bound to affect the Russians." She added quickly, before he could answer, "Richard rang me last

729

night, but I missed him. I expect he may be worried."

"Yes," he said, considering her. "Yes, I suppose he may be."

"Of course I don't mean that I want to rush off at once or anything. It's just that – it seems impossible to get through to London in the daytime," she said. "D'you think I could ring Richard from the party tonight? Just to know what he thinks?"

"Well, of course," he said. "There'll be no difficulty about that."

"Oh, good."

There was a pause.

"I don't think the Suez business represents any kind of threat in Berlin at the moment," he said at last. "But I can see that for you there may be other considerations."

"It's really Richard," she said. "I wouldn't want him to worry."

He nodded, looking tired. "I'd better go and see your mother. You ring Richard tonight, and then we'll talk."

She felt guilty while she sat on the bus to the *Kurfürsten Damm* where she was to meet Max for lunch. But it's not as though I'd said I was leaving, she told herself, I was only asking his advice.

Even so, the memory of his tired face stayed with her. As she waited for Max, she stood staring into a newly-built shop window filled with garishly checked materials. "Genuine English Tartans" said a sign in German, and they had names like

Windsor, Eton and Dover. One was even called Sheffield. Richard would enjoy that, she thought, but instead of feeling amused she found herself fretting about Konrad. I'll see, she thought. I'll see what happens tonight.

Max arrived, full of energy and confidence as always, and swept her off to a nearby café.

"I've booked a flight," he announced before they had even sat down. "It connects with a flight from Paris to Athens. I also got them to let me use their telephone and got through to my ship owner, and he's arranging for someone to meet me at the airport."

"I'm glad," said Anna.

"Yes." He added as an afterthought, "My ship owner also thought it was urgent to get Wendy and the baby out of there."

She nodded. "When do you go?"

"At one o'clock in the morning."

"What – tonight?"

"That's right. Well," he said, "it really makes no difference. I couldn't have seen Mama tomorrow anyway, unless I'd stayed till the afternoon, and that would have been too late. I thought I'd see her again later today and stay a long time, however long one is allowed, till she goes to sleep. And then – well, I could come to the party and go straight to the airport from there."

"Yes, I suppose so." As so often with Max, she was left far behind, still feeling her way round a situation which he had long assessed. "Have you told Konrad?"

"Not yet, but he'll know from Mama that I'm probably leaving. Did you have a chance to speak to him?"

"Only for a moment." She did not want to go into details. "He said we'd talk tonight."

"Good. And you're going to ring Richard?"

"Yes."

He smiled his confident, warm, affectionate smile. "Well," he said, "I'd better go and pack my things."

Max's last evening with Mama was very harmonious. Mama looked pink and relaxed. She had been reassured by Konrad's visit at lunch time – he had stayed almost two hours and they had obviously talked things out – and afterwards she had slept. When Anna and Max arrived, she had only just woken up and was still nestling deep in the pillows, looking up from beneath the big white quilt like a baby from its cot.

"Hullo," she said, and smiled.

Her smile was as warm as Max's, but without his confidence. No grown-up person, thought Anna, should look so vulnerable.

She was less upset than they had expected by the news of Max's departure, and quite pleased with the dramatic manner of it. "You're going to the party first?" she kept saying admiringly, and when a nurse looked in to collect a dirty towel, she insisted on introducing him and saying, "He's flying to Athens tonight."

"And how was Konrad?" asked Max after the nurse had gone.

"Oh –" Mama's smile softened and she sniffed

a little with emotion. "I really think it's going to be all right. We talked for ages. He explained it all to me again, about this girl. It really didn't mean anything to him. It was just because I was away and he missed me. Frankly, I think it was largely her doing. She sounds," said Mama, "a rather predatory creature."

"I'm so glad it's all right."

"Yes, well, of course we'll have to see." But her eyes were bright. "He wants us to go away on a holiday together," she said. "As soon as I'm better. The doctor thinks I should stay here for a few days, and then maybe a week in a convalescent home." She made a face. "God knows how much it'll all cost. But after that – we thought, not Italy at this time of year, but perhaps somewhere in the Alps."

"It sounds a very good idea."

"Yes." Her lip quivered for a moment. "I think I probably need it. It's all been quite a shock."

"Of course."

"Yes. The doctor says I'm lucky to have come through it. He says I nearly died." She shrugged her shoulders. "I still think it might have been best."

"Nonsense, Mama," said Max.

Mama looked suddenly very pleased.

"It seems," she said, "that anyone less strong than me certainly would have done."

Later the conversation drifted to the past. "Do you remember?" said Mama: How she used to buy bruised strawberries in Paris for almost nothing and cut off the bad bits to make a delicious Sunday pudding. The bomb that wrecked their Bloomsbury boarding house. The last years in Putney.

"You had a blue hat with a veil," said Anna.

"That's right. I got it at C and A, and everyone thought it came from Bond Street."

"That woman who ran the boarding house – she used to put a camp bed up for me when I came to visit and never charged me," said Max. "She was a very decent soul."

"She ended up by marrying one of the guests, a Pole. Do you remember, the one who made the bird noises? We used to call him the Woodpigeon."

"It was all quite funny, really," said Anna, but Mama would not have it.

"It was awful," she said. "It was the most awful time of my life."

When the nurse brought her supper, she ate it in their company, trying to press various bits upon them. "Wouldn't you like just a little bit of meat?" she would say. "Or at least a carrot?"

They both assured her that they would be able to eat at the party, and she seemed to regret not being able to go. "There'll be a lot of interesting people," she said. "Just about everyone from the British Council."

But when it came near the time for them to leave, all her new-found composure collapsed. She clung to Max and tears ran down her cheeks.

"I'll wait in the entrance hall," said Anna. She kissed Mama. "See you in the morning," she said as cheerfully as she could manage. Mama gazed at her distractedly through her tears. "Of course," she murmured. "You'll still be here, won't you, Anna." Then she turned back to Max, and the last thing Anna heard as she left the room was her unhappy voice saying, "Oh, Max – I don't know if I can go on."

Outside, the lights in the corridors were already dimmed down. There was no one about and, although it was not yet nine o'clock, it felt like the middle of the night. In the entrance hall, only a shaded lamp shone on the desk where the porter sat writing figures in a book, and he did not look up when Anna came in. The heating must be turned down as well as the lights, she thought, for she felt suddenly cold.

She found a chair and sat there, listening to the scratching of the porter's pen and thinking about Mama. Mama weeping, Mama saying, "I can't go on," Mama in the blue hat . . .

A car drove past outside, scraping the gravel. The waiting-room chairs threw leaping shadows across the walls, and in the glass kiosk where flowers and chocolates were sold during the day, a tinselly bird on a box of sweets was momentarily picked out and sparkled in the darkness.

And then she suddenly remembered. She remembered the time Mama had cried while wearing her blue hat with the veil. Not gradually, but all at once, completely, as though it had just that minute happened, and her first feeling was one of amazement that she could ever have forgotten.

It had happened – if anything had happened at all – during her first year at art school. Everyone had thought that, once the war was over, things would be better, but for Mama and Papa they had got worse. Papa's health was failing and, since so many young people had returned from the fighting, Mama could no longer get even the third-rate secretarial jobs which had, until then, kept them afloat.

Anna still shared a room with Mama and had felt full of compassion. But she was also doing what she wanted for the first time since she was grown up. She had only three years in which to do it, and she was determined that nothing was going to stop her. She still had long conversations with Papa about painting and writing – things which interested them both. But when Mama started on her money worries and the hopelessness of the future, there was a point beyond which she would not listen. She would nod her head deceitfully and escape into thoughts of her work and her friends, and Mama who always knew, of course, what she was up to, would call her cold and unaffectionate.

And then one day – it must have been a Saturday, because she had been shopping in Putney High Street – this curious thing had happened.

She had just caught a bus home and was still standing on the platform, when she had heard her name called by what seemed to be a disembodied voice. She was tired and nervous after pretending to listen to Mama late into the previous night, and for a moment the sound had really frightened her. Then she had seen Mama's face, white and tense, looking up at her from the pavement as the bus swept by, and she had jumped off at the traffic lights and hurried back to her:

"What is it?" she had asked, and even now she could clearly see Mama standing there, outside Woolworth's, shouting, "I don't want to go on! I can't!"

She had felt angry and helpless, but before she could say anything, Mama had cried, "It didn't work. I really tried and it didn't work."

"What didn't work?" she had asked, and Mama had said, "The Professor's pills." Then she had looked Anna straight in the eye and said, "I took them."

At first, she remembered, she had not known what Mama was talking about. She had just stared at Mama as she stood there in her blue hat with a windowful of Woolworth's Easter chicks behind her. And then, suddenly, she had understood.

The Professor, a friend, had given Papa the pills in 1940, as a last resort in case he and Mama were captured by the Nazis. They were instant poison.

She had stared at Mama in horror and cried, "When did you take them?" and Mama had said, "Last night, when you were asleep. I took one, but nothing happened, and then I took the other, and still nothing happened, and then I thought perhaps there was a delayed effect and I waited, but nothing happened, nothing happened at all!" She had begun to cry, and then she had noticed Anna's horrified face and said, "I took them in the bathroom, so that you wouldn't find me dead in bed."

Anna had suddenly felt very old – perhaps that was when it all began, she thought – and angry that Mama should have made her feel like this, and yet dreadfully, overwhelmingly sorry for her. She had been conscious of the pavement under her feet and of the shoppers pushing past her in and out of Woolworth's, and she had looked at Mama crying with the Easter chicks behind her, and at last she had said, "Well, of course it would have made all the difference to me, finding you dead in the bathroom instead."

Mama had sniffed and said, "I thought perhaps the maid might find me."

"For God's sake," Anna had shouted, "the maid, me, Papa – what difference does it make?" and Mama had said in a small voice, "Well, I knew it would upset you, of course." She had looked so absurd, with her snub nose and her blue hat with the veil, that Anna had suddenly started to laugh. Mama had asked, "Why is that funny?" But then she had laughed as well, and they had both become aware of an icy wind blowing down Putney High Street and had gone inside Woolworth's to get warm.

She could not remember exactly what had

happened after that. They had walked round Woolworth's – she rather thought Mama had bought some mending thread – and they had talked about the extraordinary fact that the Professor's pills had been completely innocuous. ("I might have known they wouldn't work," Mama had said, "I always thought he was a charlatan.") She remembered wondering what the Professor would have done if there had really been a Nazi invasion. Would he then have replaced them with proper ones? But perhaps, said Mama, the pills they had were really effective, only they had lost their strength over the years. From what she could recall of her chemistry lessons at school, she seemed to believe that this was possible.

They had ended up drinking tea at Lyons and, with Mama sitting hale and hearty on the other side of the table, it had seemed as though, after all, nothing had really happened.

And had it? wondered Anna in the half-darkness of the hospital, while the sound of the car slowly faded, someone, somewhere, shut a door, and the porter's pen went on scratching.

There had been so much talk, in those days, of suicide. For Mama, just talking about it might have been a kind of safety valve. Perhaps she never even took the pills, thought Anna, or else she knew all along that they wouldn't work. If Mama had really tried to kill herself, she thought, surely I could not have forgotten. She could not remember ever talking about it to Max or Papa. But perhaps she had just not wanted to think about it, so as to get on with her own life.

She was still trying to work it out, when she jumped at a touch. It was Konrad, reassuringly large and patient.

"Your brother's just coming," he said. "Let's go to this dreadful party, so you can ring up your Richard."

Ken Hathaway lived in an old-fashioned flat full of heavy German furniture. He seemed inordinately pleased to see them and welcomed them with a delighted, rabbity smile.

"So nice to see new faces," he cried. "The old ones do get rather used in such a small community – don't you agree, Konrad?"

There was a large silver bowl containing a pale liquid with bits of fruit afloat in it, and a fair-haired young German was ladling it into glasses.

"German cold punch," said Ken proudly. "Günther's own concoction. God knows what he puts in it."

Judging by the happy sounds of the guests, thought Anna, it was probably plenty.

As Ken was about to sweep them off and introduce them, Konrad put a restraining hand on his arm. "Just before we join the festivities," he said, "do you think Anna could ring her husband in London?"

"Only very quickly," she said.

Ken waved a generous hand. "My dear," he

said, "help yourself. It's in the bedroom. But you'll be lucky if you get through. There've been delays all day – this wretched Suez business, I suppose."

She found the bedroom filled with everybody's coats, and sat on the edge of the bed in a gap between them. The operator took a long time to answer and then gave a disapproving snort when asked for London. "Up to two hours' delay," he said, and was persuaded only with difficulty to book the call.

When she emerged from the bedroom, Konrad and Max had already been absorbed by the party. Konrad was talking to a bald man in a dark suit, and Max had got a middle-aged blonde who was gazing at him with the stunned delight so long familiar to Anna, as though she had just found a lot of gold at the bottom of her handbag. Then Ken bore down on her with a glass and an earnest-looking man who turned out to be some kind of academic.

"I'm interested in medieval history," he shouted over the mixed English and German voices, "though here I'm working on –" But she never discovered what he was working on, for a grey-haired woman next to her gave a little scream.

"Suez! Hungary!" she cried. "What a fuss they make about these things. Here in Berlin we're used to crises. Were you here during the Airlift?"

Her partner, a small clerkish person, had carelessly been elsewhere, and she abandoned him with contempt, but a fat German with glasses smiled his agreement.

"Berlin can take it," he shouted, with difficulty, in English. "Like London, *nicht wahr*, in the bomps?"

Anna could think of nothing to reply to this, so she looked vague and thought of Richard, while the voices rose another decibel.

". . . trigger off World War Three," cried an invisible strategist, and the academic's measured tones rose momentarily above the rest. "One old and one new empire, each clinging to its conquests . . ."

"More punch," said Günther and filled up the glasses.

Someone had closed the bedroom door and she wondered if she would still be able to hear the telephone. Out of the corner of her eye, she could see Ken lead Max away from the blonde who followed him sadly with her eyes, and introduce him to a tall man with a pipe.

"They could take Berlin in ten minutes," said the grey-haired woman, and someone replied, "But the United States of America . . ."

Then Ken was upon her and propelled her to another part of the room, where various people asked after Mama and expressed pleasure at her recovering from pneumonia. Clearly Konrad had done a good job in explaining her illness.

"We really miss her," said an American colonel, meaning it. "In a tight little community like ours . . ." A woman with a fringe said, "She's the best translator we've got," and a girl with freckles and a pony tail said, "Somehow you can always tell when she's *there*."

More punch – Ken pouring this time. A sudden burst of laughter from a group nearby, followed by a ringing sound, so that for a moment she thought it was the telephone, but it was only all of them clinking glasses.

"Excuse me," she said.

She wove her way through the crowd, went into the bedroom and came out again, leaving the door ajar. On her way back she passed Max who had been rejoined by the blonde and several other people and she heard one of them say admiringly, "Really? To Athens? Tonight?" Konrad saw her and waved, and she was just wondering whether to fight her way through to him, when she heard herself being addressed in German and found Günther beside her.

"I must tell you," he said, "I've read your father's works."

"Really?" She wondered what on earth was coming.

"Yes." He gazed at her ardently over the half-empty jug of punch. "I think they're –" He searched for the words. "Terribly relevant," he managed at last, triumphantly.

"Do you?" His fresh face shone under the blond hair. He couldn't be more than eighteen, she decided. "I'm so glad you liked them."

He put down the jug, so as to concentrate better. "I think everyone should read them," he said.

She was touched. "Did you like the poems?" she said.

"The poems? Oh yes, the poems too. But his political awareness at that time – that's what I really find incredible."

"Well, it was rather forced upon him," said Anna. "By circumstances. His real loves were the theatre and travel –" but he was not listening. In his excitement he had advanced upon her and she found herself wedged in between him and the table holding the jug.

"Terrible mistakes have been made," cried Günther. "Our parents made them, to Germany's shame, and it is up to my generation to put them right." He brought his hand down sharply on the table and the jug trembled.

She looked for a way of escape but there was none.

"How?" she asked. If my call comes through now, she thought, I'll have to dive through under the table.

"Very simple," said Günther confidentially. "We shall discuss. My comrades and I discuss everything."

"Do you?"

He nodded and smiled. "Every Tuesday. Yesterday we discussed the Nazi ethic, and next week we shall discuss the persecution of the Jews."

"Really," she said. "On Tuesday."

He beamed at her. "Would you like to come?"

At that moment, to her relief, she saw Hildy Goldblatt, only a little way behind him, gazing round the room. She caught her eye and waved, and Hildy waved back and moved towards her.

"Excuse me," she said, as Hildy reached them, and he stepped aside reluctantly.

"My dear," said Hildy after a brief nod at him, "isn't this dreadful? I have seen some food on a table next door. Let's go and talk quietly in there."

Anna followed her, making sure that all doors remained open so that she could hear the telephone, and they sat down near the depleted buffet.

"Well then," said Hildy, tucking into some bread and sausage, "your Mama is quite better. I told you everything would be all right. But your husband must be worried about you: the Suez business now as well as Hungary. When are you going home?"

She looked at Hildy, her frizzy hair sticking out untidily from her clever, affectionate face, and wondered how much she had guessed.

"I don't know," she said carefully. "I'm waiting for a call from him now."

Hildy nodded and chewed.

"I want to go home," said Anna. "Only Max has to leave tonight, and I'm not sure . . ."

"If your Mama can manage without both of you."

"Yes."

"Yes," Hildy polished off the sausage with one bite. "I can't stay long," she said. "My Erwin is not well – something with his stomach. In any case, one should never give advice. But if it's any use –" She hesitated. "It's only what I think," she said. "But I think that Konrad . . . will do what needs to be done. I think – I think one can trust him. You understand what I mean?"

"Yes," said Anna.

"He is a kind man. And anyway," said Hildy, "you should be home with your husband now. I know we have had a lot of frights and always, at the last minute, the politicians draw back, but at such times it is no good for people to be apart." She heaved herself out of the chair. "I really must go. My poor Erwin. He has vomited, you know, and that is something which, for him, is not at all normal."

As they entered the other room, the party appeared to have quietened down. A number of guests must have left, and the rest were sitting rather than standing, some of them on the floor, and talking in undertones.

"Always the same faces," said Hildy. "What can they find to talk about?"

Konrad hurried towards them. "Are you going, Hildy? We ought to go as well, to get Max to the airport."

"But I'm still waiting for my call from Richard," said Anna, and at that moment the telephone rang. She cried, "That'll be him," embraced Hildy quickly, and ran to the bedroom. Someone had closed the door again. She threw it open and found herself looking straight at a girl with her dress unzipped and pulled halfway down off her shoulders. Immediately behind her, a man with a handlebar moustache was making great play of adjusting his tie over his unbuttoned shirt. The telephone was still ringing.

"Excuse me," she said, edging past both of them, and answered it.

At first there seemed to be no one there, then there was a buzzing sound and an unidentifiable voice saying something a long way off.

The man and the girl – her dress now pulled up again – were watching her uncertainly.

"Hullo?" she said. "Hullo?"

The voice faded, but the buzzing continued.

"Hullo," she said more loudly. "Hullo. Hullo. Hullo."

Nothing happened, but the handlebar moustache suddenly appeared very close to her face, exuding alcoholic fumes.

"Just-look-ing-for-her-hand-bag," its owner explained, pronouncing each syllable with great care and lifting up one of the coats to show what he meant.

She nodded impatiently and waved him away.

"Hullo?" she shouted into the telephone. "Hullo? Richard, is that you?"

Somewhere infinitely far away, she heard Richard's voice. "Hullo, love. Are you all right?" and at once all her anxieties and tensions melted away.

"Yes," she shouted. "Are you?"

He said something she could not catch, and she shouted, "Mama is out of danger."

Richard's voice suddenly came through loud and clear.

"What?" he said.

"Mama is out of danger. She's going to be all right."

"Oh, I'm glad."

Out of the corner of her eye, she could see the girl self-consciously straightening her hair and leaving the room, followed by the man. Thank God, she thought.

"Richard, it's lovely to hear you."

"And you. When are you coming home?"

"Well, what do you think? What do you think about this Suez business?"

"It's difficult to –" The buzzing began again and drowned the rest of his words.

"I can't hear you," she cried.

He repeated whatever he had said – she could tell he must be shouting – but all she could catch were the words "if possible".

"Do you want me to come home? Richard? Would you like me to come home straight away?" She was shouting at the top of her voice.

There was a little click. The buzzing stopped, and a German operator said loudly and clearly, "*Charlottenburg* exchange. Can I help you?"

"You cut me off!" she shouted. "I was talking to London and you cut me off. Please reconnect me at once."

"I'm sorry," said the voice. "There is a three hour delay to London and we are accepting no more calls."

"But I was talking to them. I was talking to them, and you cut me off in the middle."

"I'm sorry, but there is nothing I can do."

"Please!" cried Anna. "I've waited all day for this call. It's really important."

But of course it was no use.

After she had put down the receiver, she stayed sitting among the coats for a moment, fighting an overwhelming urge to break something, to be sick, to walk straight out and catch the next plane to London. Then she stood up and went back to the party.

"All right?" said Konrad. He was waiting for her with Max's briefcase in his hand. "Come on, Max," he called before she could answer. "We really must go."

Max was having some difficulty in disentangling the blonde who appeared to be offering to come to Athens with him. Behind him, someone had rolled back the carpet and a number of people, mostly middle-aged, were dancing to the radio.

"Coming," said Max, managing to ditch the blonde at last. Ken handed them their coats and they hurried towards the door. "So sorry you have to leave. . . regards to your Mama. . ." Teeth bared in smiles, handshakes, *auf Wiedersehens*, and then they were outside in the dark, and Konrad was driving very fast towards Tempelhof.

"Did you get Richard?" asked Max, turning back in his seat, while shadows of trees and lamp posts raced across them.

She shook her head. "I couldn't hear him, and

then we were cut off." If I'm not careful, she thought, I'm going to weep all over the car.

He made a face. "Don't worry. Any sign of trouble and you go straight home. All right?"

"All right."

Konrad was leaning forward over the steering wheel, and the car was tearing along through the night. "I hope we'll make it," he said without taking his eyes off the road.

Max glanced at his watch. "Christ," he said. "I didn't know it was so late." He began to drum with his fingers and stare tensely into the darkness ahead.

She sat in the back, her coat wrapped round her for warmth, feeling alone. Her chin tucked into her collar, her hands thrust deep into her pockets, she tried to think of nothing. Then she felt something under her fingers, something thin and rustly – a piece of paper. She pulled it out and, by holding it very close to her eyes, could just distinguish the word "Heals" printed across the top. It must be the bill for the dining-room rug.

It seemed like something from another world, from the infinitely distant past which had gone and would never come again. She clutched it in her cold hand and suddenly felt desperate. I've got no business to be here, she thought, surrounded by Russians when there might be a war. I don't belong here. I should be home with Richard. Suppose I never get home? Suppose I never see him again? She stared at the dark, unfamiliar landscape racing past the window and thought in terror, I might be here for ever.

At last there were lights. The car swerved and braked.

"See you in London, little man," said Max and scrambled out before it had properly stopped.

She watched him run to the airport entrance, his shadow leaping wildly beside him. There was a dazzle of light as he opened the door, and then he was gone.

"I think he'll just catch it," said Konrad.

They waited in case he didn't and wanted to come back, but nothing happened. The door remained closed. After what seemed like a long time, Anna climbed into the front seat and they drove slowly back to the centre of town. It was one o'clock in the morning and very cold.

"I'm sorry you couldn't speak to Richard," said Konrad after a few kilometres.

She was too depressed to do anything but nod. It suddenly seemed a familiar feeling. Of course, she thought. All those times in Putney when Max had gone back to the Air Force or to Cambridge. This was how she had felt then. It did not seem so very long ago. Back with Mama, she thought. Trapped. She could almost sense the Russians all around.

"I entirely agree with Max, you know," said Konrad. "At the first hint of trouble, you get on a plane to London."

She could see his face, greenish-grey in the glimmer from the dashboard. Behind it, indistinct dark shapes fled through his reflection in the glass.

"I wish –" she said.

"That you were at home with Richard instead of driving round Berlin in the early hours of the morning."

"Not just that. I wish Mama lived in a house. I wish she liked cooking and made large meals which nobody could eat, and fussed about people's appetites and the cleaning." For a moment she could almost persuade herself that it was possible.

"Where?" said Konrad.

"Somewhere." She knew it was nonsense. "Not in Berlin."

They were off the main road now, into lamplit side streets – the beginning of the suburbs.

"She's never been keen on domesticity," said Konrad. He added loyally, "Thank God."

"Well, if she could just take life as it comes. Make the most of what there is, even if it isn't perfect. Rather than this awful romanticism, this rejection of everything that isn't exactly as she's dreamed it. After all, there are other ways of solving one's problems than by committing suicide."

His eyes left the road for a moment and flickered towards her. "Aren't you being rather hard on her?"

"I don't think so. After all, I've lived with her a lot longer than you have." The anger and frustrations of the day suddenly boiled over inside her. "You don't know what it was like," she said, and was surprised how loud her voice sounded.

They had reached a familiar arrangement of shops and houses. The car turned a corner, then another, and there was the street with her hotel.

"I think I can imagine," he said. "She's often told me about it. The worst time of her life, as she calls it. I know how she talks, but it must have been quite difficult for her as well as you."

He stopped the car outside the hotel, switched off the engine, and they sat for a moment without talking. In the silence she could hear a faint, distant tremor. Thunder, she thought, and her stomach contracted.

"That's one of the things I feel worst about," he said.

"What?"

He hesitated. "Well, look at me. I'm not exactly a film star. With my paunch and my slipped disk and my face like the back of a bus. Hardly the sort of man for whom women commit suicide. And yet, somehow, I've driven your mother . . ."

The thunder was getting closer. She could see the drawn expression on his face, very pale in the light of a street lamp.

". . . I've driven her to do something which, even during the worst period of her life, she was never tempted to do."

"How do you know?"

"That I drove her to it?"

"No." Part of her was too angry to think, but another part knew exactly what she was saying. "That she was never tempted to do it before."

He stared at her in the dimness of the car, and she stared back. There was another rumble of thunder – strange in November, she thought – and then she suddenly realized that it was not thunder at all.

"Listen!" She could hardly get it out. "It's gunfire."

His mind was still on what she had been saying, and he did not seem to understand.

"It's the Russians!" For a moment it was like water closing over her head. Then she felt quite calm. Goodbye, she thought. Goodbye, Richard. Goodbye, everything she had ever wanted to do. Mama and Berlin for always. It had caught up with her at last, as she had always known it would.

"The Russians?" said Konrad, very surprised.

She was struggling with the window and finally got it open. "Can't you hear it?"

"My dear," he said, "my dear, it's nothing, you mustn't be so frightened. That's not the Russians, it's the Americans."

"The Americans?"

He nodded. "Artillery practice. Every other Thursday – though usually not quite so early in the morning."

"The Americans." She couldn't have breathed for a while, for she felt as though her lungs had stuck together. Now she opened her mouth, and a lot of air rushed in. "I'm sorry," she said and felt herself blush. "I don't normally get so panicked."

"It was perfectly natural." His face was even more drawn than before. "I ought to have warned you. But living here, one forgets."

"Anyway, I'm all right now. I'd better go to bed." She made to get out, but he put out his hand.

"I've been thinking," he said.

"What?"

"Various things. First of all, I think you should go home."

Her heart leapt. "But what about Mama?"

"*Nu*, she is no longer seriously ill. Of course I should have been glad of your support a little longer, but I had not realized how difficult all this has been for you. Could you still stay over tomorrow?"

"Well, of course."

"Good. Then we will book you a flight for Friday, and I'll send a cable to Richard that you're coming."

Suddenly she no longer felt cold. She could feel the blood rushing into her toes and fingers, warming them. Her whole body was aglow with relief, and she looked at Konrad's pale, heavy face, filled with an almost physical affection for him.

"Are you sure?" she asked, knowing that it was quite safe to do so.

"Absolutely."

The day after tomorrow, she thought. Tomorrow, really, for they were already well into Thursday. Then she realized that Konrad was still talking.

"I hope you don't mind my asking," he said. "But you understand that it's important for me to know. After all, I am very much concerned."

To know what?

He hesitated how best to put it. "Has your mother ever, previously . . . Did she ever, before, try to kill herself?"

What did it matter, now that she was going home? She wished she had never brought it up. "I don't know," she said. "I really don't."

"But you were saying earlier –"

She could simply deny it, she thought, but he was looking at her with his worried eyes, blaming himself. She did not want him to feel so guilty.

"There was something," she said slowly at last. "But I don't honestly think it was very serious. In fact I'd forgotten all about it until today."

"What happened?"

So, as lightly as possible, she told him about the Professor's pills. "I think she knew they wouldn't work," she said. "I think she just had to do something, and so she pretended. After all, if she'd really tried to kill herself, I wouldn't have forgotten."

"Wouldn't you?"

"Well, of course not. It would have been too awful to forget."

"Or too awful to remember."

Nonsense, she thought.

"Look," he said, "I've seen as many bad psychological thrillers as you have. I have no wish to act like an amateur – headshrinker, isn't it called? But those pills were supposed to be poison, and your mother did take them."

"I'm not even sure of that."

"I think she took them," said Konrad.

She had wanted him to feel less guilty, but he seemed almost exultant. There was an edge to his voice which she had not heard before, and she suddenly wondered what on earth she had done.

Thursday

During what was left of the night, she slept only fitfully. She dreamed endlessly of Mama – Mama wandering on a mountainside, in the streets, through the rooms of an ever-expanding house, and always searching for Konrad. Sometimes she found him and sometimes she only glimpsed him for a moment before he disappeared. Once Anna found him for her, and Mama hugged her on the beach and laughed delightedly with the sun on the sand behind her. Another time he slipped away from them in Woolworth's while Anna was buying Mama a hat.

She woke uneasy and depressed, much later than usual, and found the breakfast room deserted, with only a few dirty cups and plates still cluttered on the tables. The proprietress, engaged half-heartedly in clearing them away, stopped at the sight of her.

"Have you heard?" she said. "The Russians are leaving Budapest." As Anna looked at her, uncomprehending, she repeated it in her thick Berlin accent. *"Sie gehen,"* she said. *"Die Russen gehen,"* and produced a newspaper to prove it.

Anna read it while the woman scurried about, clattering the used crockery and turning the stained table cloths. Incredibly, it was true. She could hardly believe it. Why? she wondered. The West must have acted. A secret message from the White House, leaving no room for doubt. All the free countries together, united as they had never been against the Nazis until it was too late. She looked for news of Suez, but only found a small paragraph. Nothing much seemed to be happening there.

"They'll be happy today in Budapest," said the woman, putting down some coffee and rolls before her. "Dancing in the streets, it said on the radio. And they've pulled down a great statue of Stalin – whatever will they do with it, do you suppose? And they're going to change everything and have things just the way they want them."

Anna drank her coffee and felt suddenly better. It was all going to be all right. Unlike the Nazis, the Russians were not going to get away with it. Mama was alive and almost well again. She was going home – Konrad had said so. Just as long as nothing happens to stop it, she thought.

"I can just imagine how they're feeling in Hungary," said the woman, lingering by the table with the empty tray in her hands. "When I think of what the Russians did here . . ." And she embarked on a long rambling story about a soldier who had fired six shots into a stone gnome in her front garden. "And he was shouting, 'Nazi! Nazi!' all the time," she said in a shocked voice. "After all, the gnome was not a Nazi." After a moment's thought she added, "And nor, of course, was I."

Anna struggled to keep a straight face and stuffed herself with the rolls and butter. She did not want to be late for her visit to Mama, especially if she were leaving the following day. Even so, she missed her usual bus and had to wait ten minutes for the next.

It was cold, with dark, drifting clouds which every so often erupted into drizzle, and when at last she arrived at the hospital, the warmth of the entrance hall enveloped her like a cocoon. The receptionist smiled at her – I'm beginning to belong to the place, she thought – and Mama's little room, with the rain spitting on the double windows and the radiator blasting away, was welcoming and snug.

"Hullo, Mama," she said. "Isn't it good about Hungary?"

"Incredible," said Mama.

She was looking much brighter, sitting up in bed in a fresh nightie, with a newspaper beside her, and began at once to ask about the party and about Max's departure. "So Konrad drove him straight from the party to the airport," she said when Anna had described it all. It was the bit that pleased her most.

There were new flowers on her table, as well as a lavish box of chocolates from her office and a coloured card with "Get well soon, honey" on it and a lot of signatures. Konrad had rung up earlier, while she was in her bath, but had left a message that he would ring again. She leaned back into the pillows, relaxed for the first time since she had got better.

"By the way," she said in the warm, no-nonsense voice which Anna remembered so clearly from her childhood, "the nurse told me what you did when I was in a coma – about you being here so much of the time and sitting on my bed and calling me. I'm sorry, I didn't know. One doesn't remember, you see." She added with curious formality. "She says you may have saved my life. Thank you."

Anna found herself unexpectedly touched. She cast about for something to answer, but could think of nothing adequate so she grinned and said, as Max might have done, "That's all right, Mama – any time," and Mama giggled and said, "You're dreadful – you're just as bad as your brother," which, coming from Mama, she supposed was the nicest thing she could have said.

She looked so much more like herself that she decided to broach the question of leaving.

"Mama," she said, "I've been here nearly a week. I'd really like to go home. Do you think, if I could get a flight tomorrow, you'd be all right?"

She was about to add various qualifications about keeping in touch and not going unless Mama was absolutely sure, when Mama said, in the same sensible voice, "I'm much better now, and after all it's only ten days till I go away with Konrad. I think I'll be all right." Then she said, "But I'll miss you," and touched Anna's hand gently with her fingers. "I've hardly talked to you."

"You were talking to Max."

"I know," said Mama. "But I see him so seldom." She said again, "I'll miss you."

"I'll write every day," said Anna. She had decided this in advance. "Even if it isn't very interesting. So that if you're feeling low or Konrad is busy or anything, at least you'll know that *something* will happen."

"That'll be nice," said Mama. She thought for a moment. Then she said, "I'm sorry – I realize now that all this has been a lot of trouble to everyone, but, you know, I still can't see any reason why I shouldn't have done it."

Anna's heart sank.

"For God's sake, Mama –"

"No, listen, let's not pretend. Let's talk about this honestly." Mama was very serious. "I'm fifty-six, and I'm alone. I've done all the things I had to do. I brought you and Max up and got you through the emigration. I looked after Papa and I've got his books republished, which I promised him I'd do. Nobody needs me any longer. Why shouldn't I die if I want to?"

"Of course we need you," said Anna, but Mama gestured impatiently.

"I said, let's be honest. I don't say that you wouldn't be pleased to see me occasionally, say at

761

Christmas or something, but you don't *need* me."
She looked at Anna challengingly. "Tell me," she
said. "Tell me honestly, what difference would it
have made if I had died?"

Anna knew at once what difference it would
have made. She would have blamed herself for
the rest of her life for not having, somehow,
given Mama enough reason to go on living. But
you couldn't ask people to stay alive just to stop
you feeling guilty.

"If you had died," she said after a moment, "I
would have been the child of two suicides."

Mama disposed of that in a flash. "Nonsense,"
she said. "Papa's suicide didn't count." She glared
at Anna, daring her to disagree.

"One suicide, then," said Anna, feeling ridiculous.

They stared at each other, and then Mama
began to giggle.

"Honestly," she said, "can you imagine anyone
else having a conversation like this?"

"Not really," said Anna, and somehow they
were back in Putney, in Bloomsbury, in the
cramped flat in Paris, in the Swiss village inn –
a close, close family surrounded by people different from themselves. As the familiar sensation
enveloped her, she suddenly knew what to say.

"I'll tell you what difference it would have
made," she said. "Though you may not think
it enough of a reason. But whenever anything
happens to me, anything good like a new job
or even something quite small like a party or

buying a new dress, my first thought is always, I must tell Mama. I know I don't always do it. I don't always write, and when we meet I've maybe forgotten. But I always think it. And if you were dead, I wouldn't be able to think it any more, and then the thing that happened, whatever it was, wouldn't be nearly as good."

She looked at Mama expectantly.

"That's very sweet of you," said Mama. "But it's not a reason to go on living." Then she sniffed, and her eyes were suddenly wet. "But it's very sweet of you, just the same," she said.

After this neither of them knew quite what to do, until Mama grabbed hold of the box on the table and said, "Would you like a chocolate?"

Anna made a great fuss of choosing one, and Mama told her, as she had often told her before, about a governess she had had as a child, who, for reasons of daintiness, had insisted on always eating chocolates in one bite. "So you never found out what was inside them," said Mama indignantly, as always when she remembered the story.

They were just choosing another chocolate each when the telephone rang on the bedside table.

"That'll be Konrad," said Mama, and as she put the receiver to her ear, Anna could hear him saying, "Good morning, ma'am."

"Give him my regards," she said, and went over to the window, so as not to look as though she were listening.

It was still raining outside, and she could see the tops of the trees, now almost bare, blowing in the wind. Someone had tried to sweep the carefully laid out paths, but already the leaves were drifting back across them from the grass.

"Oh yes, I'm much better," said Mama behind her, and went on to talk about what she had eaten and what the doctor had said. Some birds – sparrows, she thought – had found an old piece of bread and were pecking at it, jostling each other and pushing each other away. She could see their feathers glistening with the rain, but they did not seem to mind.

"Have you fixed up about your leave?" said Mama. "Because, if we're going to book the hotel –"

The piece of bread, pecked by one of the birds, rose up into the air to land a foot or so away, and all the rest half-hopped, half-flew to follow it.

"What do you mean?" Mama's voice suddenly sounded different. "What do you mean, see what happens in the office first?"

Anna tried, without success, to keep her mind on the sparrows who had now pulled the bread in half.

"But you said – you promised!" Mama's voice was rising. Stealing a glance at her, Anna could see that her face was flushed and upset.

"Well, I've been ill as well. Don't I deserve some consideration? For heaven's sake, Konrad, what do you think I'm going to do?"

Oh God, thought Anna. She took a step towards Mama with some idea of offering support, but at the sight of her face, closed to everything except the crackle from the telephone, abandoned it.

"Yes, I know the work is important, but this is the one thing that's kept me going. Surely Erwin could manage. Why are you suddenly so concerned for him?" Mama was biting back her tears, and her voice was almost out of control, "Well, how do you know it is serious? Are you sure it's really Erwin you're worried about and not someone quite different?" The telephone crackled, and she shouted, "No, I don't believe you. I don't know what to believe. For all I know, she's there with you now, or listening on the extension."

"Mama –" said Anna, but there was no stopping her.

"I'm not hysterical," yelled Mama. "I've been ill, and I nearly died, and I wish to God I had." She was crying now, and angrily wiping the tears away with her hand. "I wanted to die. You know I wanted to die. Why on earth didn't you let me?"

The telephone spat, and her face suddenly went rigid.

"What do you mean?" she cried. "Konrad, what do you mean?"

But he had rung off.

Anna went over to the bed and sat cautiously on the edge. "What's happened?" she said in as matter of fact a voice as she could manage. She suddenly felt very tired.

Mama took a trembling breath. "He hasn't applied for leave," she brought out at last. "He doesn't know if he can get away." She turned her head away. "I always knew," she said indistinctly into the sheets. "I always knew it was no good – that it could never come right."

"Mama," said Anna, "what exactly did he say?"

Mama looked at her with her hurt blue eyes. "I don't know," she said. "Something about Erwin being ill. And then, at the end –"

"Erwin *is* ill," said Anna. "He was sick yesterday. Hildy told me." But Mama was not listening.

"He said something about it not being the first time. I said I wanted to die, and he said – I couldn't quite catch it, but I'm sure he said, 'Well, it isn't the first time, is it?'" She stared at Anna, her face working nervously. "Why on earth should he say that?"

Anna felt as though a huge stone were rolling slowly towards her and there was no way of escape. "I don't know," she said. "Perhaps he was just upset."

"It didn't sound like that."

"Oh, God, Mama, how do I know what he meant?" She suddenly wanted nothing further to do with it, not with Mama, not with Konrad, not with any of them. "It's not my business," she shouted. "I came here because you were ill, and I've done my best to make you better. I can't do anything more. It's too complicated for me. I can't tell you how to run your life."

"Nobody asked you to." Mama was glaring at her and she glared back for a moment, but could not keep it up. "What's the matter with you?" asked Mama.

"Nothing," she said, and then, to her relief, there was a knock at the door and a nurse came in.

"Excuse me," she said. (It was the friendly one.) "I'd like just to take a peep at your telephone."

They both watched her walk across to the bedside table, and heard the tiny ping as she adjusted the receiver on its support. "There,' she said. "The cord had caught under it." She smiled at Mama. "Dr Rabin telephoned for you. We couldn't get through to your room, so he left a message with the switchboard. He's on his way to see you."

"Now?" said Mama.

"That's right. I told him he mustn't stay long because it's nearly time for your lunch, and then you must have your rest. All right?"

"Yes," said Mama, looking confused. As soon as the nurse had gone, she turned to Anna and said, "It's no distance in the car. He'll be here in a moment."

"I'll go."

"Could you just – I'd like to wash my face."

"Of course."

She climbed out of bed, looking as she had looked in the mornings in Putney, the pink night-dress clinging to her middle-aged legs (they were short and chubby like Anna's), the childlike eyes tense. While she poured water on her face with her hands and nervously combed her crisp grey hair,

Anna straightened the sheets. Then she helped Mama back into bed and tucked the bedclothes round her.

"All right?" she said. "You look very nice."

Mama bit her lip and nodded.

"I'm sure it'll all be fine." She tried to think of something else to say – something that would give Mama courage, that would make her say all the right things to Konrad and at the same time, somehow, exonerate herself – but there was nothing.

"See you later," she said. Then she smiled hypocritically and left.

As she passed through the entrance hall, she saw Konrad coming up the steps outside. For a moment she thought of intercepting him – "Please don't tell Mama that I told you . . ." But what was the use? Instead, she went and stood behind a group of people buying flowers at the kiosk, and he stumped past with his stick without seeing her. She did not dare look up until after he had passed. From the back, with his thinning hair disarranged by the wind, he looked old – too old, she thought, to be involved in a love affair, let alone a triangular one.

Outside, the cold stung her face and she walked as fast as she could down the wide, windswept road. It was no longer raining, but the temperature must have dropped several degrees, for her coat seemed suddenly too thin. The wind blew right through it, round her shoulders and up her sleeves, and since she had no idea, in any case, where she was going, she turned down a side street to escape from it.

Here it was more sheltered, and she slowed down a little, though still keeping her mind on her surroundings and on putting one foot in front of the other. She had no wish to think of Mama's room in the hospital, or of what she and Konrad might now be saying to each other.

"I can't cope with all that," she said aloud.

There was no one to hear her except a dog loitering in the gutter. No people. They were all at work, she supposed, rebuilding Germany. She passed only two or three cars, a boy on a bicycle and an old man swathed in jackets and scarves, snipping away in one of the overgrown gardens which edged the pavement.

What shall I do? she thought, sinking her chin into her collar against the cold. She couldn't go on walking about for ever. Sooner or later she would have to go back to Mama – and what would happen then? I'll have to find out from Konrad what he said to her, she thought, but her heart sank at the prospect.

At the end of the street, the view became more open. A main road led to a square with shops and buses and a taxi rank. *Roseneck* said a sign, to her surprise. When she was small, she had come here once a week for her dancing class. She had come on the tram, the fare money tucked inside her glove, and when the conductor called out the stop, she had jumped off and run across – where?

The trams were gone, the square had been

rebuilt, and she recognized nothing. She stood disconsolately in the icy wind, trying to work out where the tram stop would have been, so as not to think, instead, how Mama was probably feeling about her at this moment, but it was no use. It's all gone wrong, she thought, meaning both the business with Mama and her unrecognizable surroundings. She longed for somewhere familiar and reassuring. A sign in the road said, *Richtung Grunewald*, and she suddenly knew what she wanted to do.

It felt strange, giving the taxi driver the old address, and she half-expected him to look surprised. But he only repeated, "number ten," and drove off.

Hagen Strasse, where buses now ran instead of trams, *Königsallee*, with the wind bending branches and tearing through the awnings outside the shops. Turn right into the tree-lined side street, and there they were. It had taken no time at all.

"That's the house," said the driver, as she lingered on the pavement. He seemed anxious to see her actually go in, and only left her there reluctantly. She watched him drive away and disappear around the corner. Then she walked a few steps along – there was nobody about. She found a tree to lean against and stared across at the house, waiting for some kind of emotion.

The house stared back at her. It looked like anywhere else, and she felt put out. There are the steps I used to run up, she told herself. That's where the currant bushes used to be. That is the slope where Max taught me to ride his bicycle.

Nothing. The house stood there like any other. There was a crack in one of the windows, some yellow chrysanthemums were shivering in a flower bed, and a dog was barking shrilly somewhere inside.

But I remembered it all the other day, she thought. She wanted to feel again as she had felt then, to sense with the same ghostly clarity what it had been like to be small, to speak only German and to feel utterly secure in the knowledge of Mama's existence. It seemed to her that if only she could do this, everything would come right. Everything between Mama and herself would be the same as before.

I wore brown lace-up boots, she thought. I had a satchel on my back and I used to run up those steps after school and shout, *"Ist Mami da?"*

"Ist Mami da?" she said aloud.

It sounded merely silly.

On the other side of the road a woman had come out of a house with a shopping bag and was staring across at her. She began to walk slowly down the street. The house next door had been completely rebuilt. Funny, she thought, that she hadn't noticed it the other day. The one beyond that she could not remember at all. Then she came to the corner and stopped again.

At least this still looked the same. There were the rowan trees, now quite bare, and there was the place where the sandbox had been. There was even the lamp post, unnoticed by her before, which Max had once climbed in a game of pirates. She stood looking at it all for a long time. Someone had played here once, she thought, but it did not feel as though it had been her.

As last she became aware of the wind in her back and her feet which were almost frozen. Well, that's over, she thought without knowing exactly what she meant by it. She turned and walked briskly back up the street, a young Englishwoman in a thin tweed coat. It was really cold, as though it might be going to snow. In the *Königsallee* she found a cruising taxi, and asked the driver to take her to Konrad's office.

J.R.S.O. – the Jewish Restitution Successor Office – was housed in a brand-new building not far from the *Kurfürsten Damm*. There were two receptionists, one American and one German, presiding over a mass of forms and pamphlets which explained how to claim restitution for anything of which you might have been robbed by the Nazis, including your nearest and dearest. A few people sat round the walls, waiting for appointments. There was a plan showing the various departments, and arrows pointing the way to go.

She noticed that the mention of Konrad's name was received with respect, and it was not until she was actually going up in the lift that she remembered about his secretary. Christ, she thought, I suppose she'll be there. What on earth will she say? Somehow, she imagined a whole gaggle of girls – I might not even know which one it is, she thought – but when she opened the door to his outer office, there was only one. She was sitting behind a typewriter, talking to a man in a shabby coat, and seemed relieved at the interruption.

"*Guten Tag*," she said with the formal bow of the head that even women practised in Germany. "Can I help you?"

She was only a few years older than herself, thin, with a slightly spinsterish quality, her face plain but not unpleasant. Was this Mama's deadly rival? Anna introduced herself, and it was clear at once that she was. The girl tensed up and said stiffly, "I believe I spoke to you the other day on the telephone." Then she said, "I am glad that your mother is better," and added, "it has all been a great worry to Dr Rabin."

It appeared that Konrad was not yet back.

"He had to go out unexpectedly to attend a meeting," said the girl, apparently believing it, and Anna settled down uncomfortably to wait, while the girl went back to the old man in the coat.

She had never been in Konrad's office before, and while the man mumbled what sounded like a long list of names, she took in the filing cabinets covering the walls to the ceiling – Abrahams, Cohen, Levy, Zuckerman, read the labels on the drawers – the piles of letters on the girl's desk, the sound of typing through a half-open door.

"I know," said the girl in her slight Berlin accent. "But there is really no need. You gave Dr Rabin all this information earlier this morning."

The old man seemed troubled but insistent. He had a big brown envelope and kept putting a shaky hand inside it to feel for something.

"It's the spirit, you see," he said. "The names – well, they're just names, aren't they? Name, age, last-known address – I thought they ought to see . . ." He lost touch with what he was saying, and Anna saw that his hand with its bony knuckles and wrinkled skin now held a sheaf of ancient photographs.

"It's the faces," he said. "You can't understand without the faces." He suddenly put the photographs on the desk in an untidy spread, disarranging a pencil and some papers. The girl drew back slightly.

"My cousin Samuel," he said, pointing. "He was an electrician with the Post Office. Age 36. Last-known address Treblinka. My brother-in-law Arnold, 32. My young niece Miriamne and her brother Alfred –"

"I know, Herr Birnbaum." The girl was clearly put out. "But you see, it isn't necessary. As long as we have the information on the forms, there is no problem about compensation." Her hand moved towards the photographs, wishing to return them to him, but did not quite dare. "We have all the facts we require," she said. "The matter is being dealt with."

Evidently she liked things tidy.

774

The old man looked at her with his tired eyes. "The gentleman I saw this morning –"

"He's not here," said the girl, but he went straight on talking.

"I think he understood. Please –" He touched one of the pictures with his hand – "I should like him to see."

The girl hesitated. Then, perhaps because she remembered Anna's presence, she gathered them up in a pile. "I'll put them on his desk," she said.

He watched her while she opened the door to the inner office and put them inside. "It really isn't necessary," she could not help saying when she returned. You could see it had upset her. But the old man's face had spread into a quavering smile.

"Thank you," he said. "I shall be easier now." He still seemed to feel that he had not properly explained. "It seems the least you can do," he murmured, "that they should be seen." Then he clutched the empty envelope to his coat and shuffled out of the door.

The girl glanced at Anna after he had gone. "He was here for an hour this morning, talking to Dr Rabin," she said, perhaps fearing that Anna had thought her impatient. "And it isn't even Dr Rabin's job. There is a special department to deal with people like him, but he was so insistent . . ." She adjusted her hair in its neat bun which did not need adjusting. "Dr Rabin always helps people," she said. "But they wear him out."

"He's a very kind man," said Anna.

The girl lit up at once. "Oh, he is," she said. "He certainly is." She was clearly bursting with examples of Konrad's kindness but, realizing that Anna was hardly a suitable confidante, picked up some papers on her desk. "If you'll excuse me, I'll get on with my work." She put a sheet into her typewriter and began to type.

Anna watched her surreptitiously – the broad, competent hands moving efficiently across the keys (Mama could never type like that, she thought) the tidy blouse, the earnest, dutiful expression. She reminded her of someone, but she could not think who. It was hard to think of her as a rival to Mama, and yet, she thought, if one were very tired . . .

"Dr Rabin may have gone straight out to lunch," said the girl. "Would you rather come back later?"

But before Anna could answer, the door opened and Konrad stumped in. He looked startled at the sight of her, but quickly recovered his balance.

"I'm glad you've come," he said in what she supposed must be his official voice. "I wanted to speak to you." He added, "I see you've met my secretary, Ilse."

Ilse was already disposing of his coat and stick. "Did you have an interesting meeting?" she asked, as though it really mattered to her.

He avoided Anna's eye. "Quite interesting," he said, and plunged quickly into the list of messages which she had noted down for him. He sighed at her account of Birnbaum and his photographs. "All right," he said. "I'll think of something to do with them." Then he looked at his watch. "Time you went for your lunch. And perhaps you'd ask them to send us up some sandwiches. Oh, and Ilse, afterwards you might like to have a word with Schmidt of Welfare. I met him in the lift just now, and I was talking to him about the arrangements for your mother –"

Anna did not listen to the details, but whatever arrangements Konrad had suggested, they were obviously very welcome.

He waved Ilse's thanks aside. "Off you go," he said. "And don't forget the sandwiches."

She paused for a moment at the door. "Ham?" she said, blushing a little and smiling. It was clearly a joke between them. He did not catch on for a moment. Then he laughed loudly. "That's right," he said, "ham," and she went.

Once in his office, he waved Anna into a chair and sank into his own with a sigh. "I'm sorry," he said. "It's been a difficult morning. As you can imagine." He absently fingered the photographs on his desk. "You needn't worry about your mother," he said. "I've calmed her down. I've told her that, whatever happens, I'll take her away for a short holiday within a fortnight. She was quite happy with that."

She felt a great sense of relief. "What about Erwin's illness?" she asked.

"Oh –" He gestured impatiently. "Hildy rang me this morning in a great state. It seems they had to call the doctor last night, and he mentioned that it could be hepatitis. It probably isn't. Erwin sounds better already. But of course I'll have to cope with his work, and Ilse threw a small fit – about that and other things – and then poor little Birnbaum . . . I'm afraid it all got on top of me." He had picked up one of the photographs and showed it to her. A small, dark-eyed face, faded and blurred. "'Rachel Birnbaum, aged six.' No wonder he's a little crazy."

"Did he lose all his family?"

He nodded. "Fourteen relations, including his wife and three children. He's the sole survivor. The thing is, he doesn't want compensation. We've already sent him quite a large sum. He just put it in a drawer."

"What, then?"

He raised his eyebrows ironically. "He wants them to understand what they've done," he said. "Only that."

There was a knock at the door of the outer office, and a boy appeared with sandwiches. Konrad divided them between two paper plates with a napkin on each.

"Well, now," he said as they began to eat, "I've got your ticket. Your plane leaves at nine tomorrow morning. I'll drive you to the airport, of course."

She was taken aback. "But Mama – are you sure Mama will be all right?"

"I told you."

"But what about –?"

"If you mean the business of the Professor's pills which I so stupidly alluded to on the phone, I've persuaded her that she told me about it herself."

"And she believed you?"

He nodded, almost regretfully. "Oh yes," he said. "She believed me."

She felt confused and not entirely reassured.

"It's all right," he said. "Forget you ever told me. It didn't matter anyway. You've made me feel less guilty, and for that I'm grateful."

"And you'll look after her?"

"Of course."

"Because without you –" She still was not quite sure.

"Without me, she can't carry on. I make her feel safe." He sighed. "I make everyone feel safe. Her. Ilse. My wife and daughters. For heaven's sake," he said, "I even make Ilse's mother feel safe."

She laughed a little, uncertain what to say. "What will you do about her?" she asked at last.

"Ilse's mother?"

"No."

"Look," he said, "I can only do my best. I've found her another job. With more pay. She starts in a fortnight."

"And she'll be content with that?"

He was suddenly on the defensive. "It's as I told you," he said. "I can only do my best."

After they had eaten, he got a file from one of the drawers and said in his official voice, "You know of course that your family will be getting compensation. I advised your mother on the claim – perhaps you would like to see."

She had known, but forgotten, and now it seemed somehow incongruous. The file had Papa's name on it, and he saw her looking at it.

"I met him once, you know," he said.

"Really?" She was surprised.

"At a refugee function in London. Of course I didn't know your mother then. I admired him very much."

"Did you?" she said, touched.

"He was so witty and interesting. And the things he knew. And his enthusiasm – just like your mother. They were very good together. Both emotionally and intellectually," said Konrad ponderously, "I have never been in their league."

"But Konrad –"

"No," he said, "I haven't, and I know it. I have no feeling for nature, I'd rather see a Western than opera any day, and these days especially, I get tired."

"But she loves you."

"I know," he said. "I make her feel safe. And that's the most confusing thing of all because, as you may have noticed, I'm really a rather unreliable fellow."

Somehow the words "unreliable fellow" sounded very odd, pronounced in his refugee accent.

"You're not," she said, smiling to make it all into a joke.

He only looked at her.

"But you will look after her?"

"I told you," he said, and opened the file.

They looked at the papers together. There were claims for her and Max's interrupted education and a string of things for Papa: loss of property, loss of earnings – he explained it all, why he had claimed in this way rather than another, and how much money they could expect to get.

"Is there nothing for Mama?"

He bristled slightly, thinking that she was criticizing. "She claims in your father's name," he explained. "As his widow, all this money will come to her. It should help her quite a bit. Why? Should there be something? Is there something she should have claimed for that she didn't tell me?"

"I don't know." She felt suddenly silly. "Loss of confidence?"

"*Nu*," He threw up his hands. "If one could claim for that, we'd all be claiming."

He insisted on coming down in the lift with her to get her a taxi, and as they went out through the big glass doors of the building, they met Ilse coming in. She was carrying a Thermos flask and looked flustered when she saw them.

"You've already eaten," she cried. "And I'd got you this. It's from home – they filled it up with coffee for me across the road."

"Wonderful," said Konrad. "I'll drink it in a minute."

"You need it, this weather," said Ilse. "I've got some sugar in my pocket. And I know where I can borrow a proper china cup."

She smoothed the Thermos with her hand, looking house-proud and faintly self-satisfied, and Anna suddenly knew of whom she reminded her. Apart from being so much younger, she looked remarkably like Konrad's wife.

It was even colder when she got out of the taxi at the hospital, and she had to wait a few minutes before seeing Mama.

"Sister is with her," said the nurse, and when she finally went in, she found Mama sitting up in a chair. She was wearing the flowered dressing-gown she had bought soon after going to Germany and was making some kind of a list. Even though it was only early afternoon, the day had become very dark, and in the light of the table lamp Mama looked frailer than she had done in bed.

"They want to move me to the convalescent home next week," she said. "And then I'll be going away with Konrad. I must organize my clothes."

"So everything's all right."

"Oh yes." But Mama still looked jumpy. "It was just this silly business of Erwin's illness. And Konrad – I do realize all this has been a great strain on him. And of course he's having a lot of trouble with the German girl. He's found her another job, you know."

"Yes," said Anna.

"He's booking our hotel this afternoon. It's right up in the mountains. We've been there before – it should be lovely."

"That's good."

"And the sister thinks I should practise getting up a bit, especially as I'm going to the convalescent home." Suddenly her eyes had filled with tears and she was crying again.

"Mama – what is it, Mama?" Anna put her arms round her, finding her somehow smaller than she used to be. "Don't you want to go to the convalescent home? Isn't it all right?"

"Oh, I think it's quite nice." Mama blinked and sniffed. "It's just – the thought of the change. Of moving again. The sister says it's got a ping-pong table," she said through her tears.

"Well, you'll like that."

"I know. I'm just being silly." She rubbed her eyes. "I think this kind of poisoning – it is a kind of poisoning, the doctor said so – it leaves one rather confused. Do you know, Konrad was talking about something I once told him, and I could remember absolutely nothing about it. I mean, I couldn't remember telling him. Anyway –" She sniffed again – "It didn't really matter."

"I'm sure it didn't."

"No. Well, anyway, I'd better have some things washed and cleaned." She wrote something more on her list. "I thought I'd ask Hildy."

"Mama," said Anna, "when you come back from your holiday – if you're still not quite all right, or if you just suddenly feel like it – why don't you come to London?"

"To London?" Mama looked alarmed. "What should I do in London? Anyway, I'm coming to London at Christmas, aren't I?"

"Yes, of course. I only thought, if you suddenly got fed up –"

"Oh, I see. You mean, if things don't work out with Konrad."

"Not necessarily –"

"If things don't work out with Konrad," said Mama, "I'm certainly not going to hang round your and Max's necks."

There was a pause. Anna could see something drifting slowly down outside the window. "I think it's trying to snow," she said. They both watched it for a moment.

"Look, Mama," she said at last. "I'm sure everything will be fine with Konrad. But if by any chance it weren't, it wouldn't be the end of the world. I mean, you'd still have Max and me, and your job if you want it, or you could easily get one in another part of Germany. You've done it lots of times before."

"But it would be different now."

"Well, it's never quite the same, but – look, Mama, I'm not a child. I do know what it's like." Suddenly she remembered with great clarity how she herself had felt, years before, when she had been jilted by a man she loved. "You think that your life is finished, but it isn't. It's awful for a while. You feel that nothing is any good, you can't bear to look at anything or to listen to anything or even to think of anything. But then, especially if you're working, it gradually gets better. And you meet new people, and things happen, and suddenly, though life perhaps isn't as good as it was, it's still quite possible. No, really," she said, as Mama seemed about to interrupt, "for someone like you, with an interesting job, and no money worries, and us —"

"You've described it very well," said Mama. "But there is one thing you don't know. You don't know how it feels to be fifty-six years old."

"But I can imagine."

"No," said Mama. "You can't. It's quite true, I could do all the things you say. But I don't want to. I've made enough new starts. I've made enough decisions. I don't want to make any more. I don't even," said Mama, her mouth quivering, "want to go to that bloody convalescent home with the ping-pong table."

"But that's because you're not well."

"No," said Mama. "It's because I'm fifty-six, and I've had enough."

The snow was still drifting past the window.

"One of the doctors was talking to me yesterday," said Mama. "You know, they have all this awful psychology now, even in Germany. He thinks that when someone tries to kill themselves, it's a cry for help — that's what he called it. Well, all I know is that when I had swallowed those pills, I felt completely happy. I was lying on my bed — they take a while to work, you know — and it was getting dark outside, and I was looking at the sky and thinking, there's nothing I need to do. It no longer matters. I'll never, ever, have to make another decision. I've never in my life felt so peaceful."

"Yes, but now – now that everything's changed and you're going on holiday and –" Anna had a little difficulty in getting this out – "if everything is all right with Konrad, won't you be quite glad?"

"I don't know," said Mama. "I don't know." She frowned, trying to think exactly what she meant. "If I had died, you see, at least I should have known where I was."

It did not occur to her that she had said anything odd, and she looked surprised when Anna laughed. Then she understood and laughed too. "Why do you always think I'm so funny?" she said delightedly, like a child who has inadvertently made the grown-ups laugh. "I'm really very serious."

Her snub nose stuck out absurdly under her tired blue eyes and she sat there in her flowery dressing-gown, needing to be looked after.

Later the nurse brought them tea with some little cakes. (*"Plätzchen,"* said Mama. "Do you remember how Heimpi used to make them?") Konrad rang up to say that he had booked the hotel and also to remind Anna that he would pick her up early next morning.

After this, Mama went happily back to bed and, even though it was now quite dark outside, they left the curtains drawn back, so that they could watch the snow. It was too wet to stick, but of course, said Anna, it would be different in the Alps. Mama asked about her new job and, when Anna explained about it, said, "Papa always said that you ought to write." She only spoiled it a little by adding, "But this job is just for television, isn't it?"

Towards seven, the sister came back and said that Mama had had a very tiring day, and Anna shouldn't stay too long. After this, it became more difficult to talk.

"Well –" said Anna at last.

Mama looked up at her from the bed. "It's been so nice today," she said. "Just like the old days."

"It has," said Anna. "I've enjoyed it too."

"I wish you could stay longer."

Instant panic.

"I can't," said Anna, much too quickly. "I've got to get back to my job. And Richard."

"Oh, I know, I know," said Mama. "I only meant –"

"Of course," said Anna. "I wish I could stay, too."

She finally left her with the nurse who had brought in her supper.

"I'll write every day," she said as she embraced her.

Mama nodded.

"And look after yourself. And have a lovely time in the Alps. And if you suddenly feel like it, come to London. Just ring us up and come."

Mama nodded again. "Goodbye, my darling," she said, very moved.

Anna looked back at her from the door. She was leaning back in the bed as she had so often done in the Putney boarding house, her grey hair spread on the pillow, her blue eyes brave and appallingly vulnerable, her nose ridiculous.

"Goodbye, Mama," she said.

She was almost out of the room when Mama called after her, "And give my love again to Max."

She came out of the hospital for the last time and suddenly didn't know what to do next. The snow was trying to stick. It glistened patchily on the invisible grass and, more thinly, in the drive, making a pale shine in the darkness. A taxi drew up, white flakes whirling in the beam of its headlamps, and deposited a woman in a fur coat.

"*Wollen Sie irgendwo hin?*" asked the driver.

It was not yet eight o'clock, and she could not face going back to the hotel, "*Ja, bitte*," she said, and gave him the Goldblatts' address.

She found Hildy in a state of euphoria. Erwin was much better and the doctor, who had only recently left, had assured her that he was suffering not from hepatitis but the current form of mild gastric 'flu.

"So we are celebrating with cognac," she said, handing Anna a glass. "We are drinking to the hepatitis which did not catch him."

"And also to the brave Hungarians who have defied the Russians," Erwin called through the half-open door. She could see him sitting up in bed, a glass of cognac in his hand, the billowing quilt covered with newspapers which rustled every time he moved.

"Look at this," he cried. "Have you seen it?"

"Ach, poor Anna, from one invalid to the next," said Hildy, but he was holding out the illustrated paper so eagerly that she went in to see. It showed a fat, frightened man emerging from a house with his hands above his head. "Hungarian civilians arrest a member of the hated secret Police," said the caption. In another picture, a secret policeman had been shot and his notebook which, the caption explained, contained the names of his victims, had been left open on his chest. There were pictures of dazed political prisoners released from jail, of children clambering over captured Russian tanks, of the Hungarian flag, the Russian hammer and sickle torn from its centre, floating over the giant pair of boots which was all that was left of Stalin's statue.

"What they have done!" said Erwin. "What these wonderful people have done!" He raised the cognac to his lips. "I drink to them," he cried, and emptied his glass, which Anna felt sure could not be good for him. But she too was moved, and glad for a moment to think of something other than Mama.

She smiled and emptied her glass also. It was surprising how much better she felt almost at once.

"Wonderful," murmured Erwin and was refilling both of them from the bottle on his bedside table, when Hildy took over.

"So now it's enough," she said. "You'll only give her your germs."

She took the bottle and carried both it and Anna off to the kitchen, where she was in the middle of chopping vegetables for soup.

"And so," she said, as she settled Anna on a stool. "What's new?"

Anna was not sure where to start. "I'm going home tomorrow," she said at last.

"Good," said Hildy. "and how is your Mama?"

The fumes from the cognac mingled with the fumes from Hildy's chopped onions, and she was suddenly tired of pretending.

"I don't know," she said, looking hard at Hildy. "All right, I suppose, if Konrad stays with her. If not . . . I don't know what will happen if he doesn't."

Hildy looked back at her equally hard.

"So what are you going to do about it?" she said. "Stick them together with glue?"

"Of course not. But –" She wanted desperately to be reassured. "It seems awful to leave her," she said at last. "But I can't bear to stay. And I think I've really made it worse by being here. Because I told Konrad – I told him something about Mama. He says it didn't matter, but I think it did."

Hildy swept the onions into a saucepan and started on the carrots. "Konrad is old enough to know if it mattered or not," she said. "And your mother is old enough to know if she wants to live or die."

It seemed an absurd over-simplification, and Anna felt suddenly angry. "It's not as easy as that," she said. "It's easy to talk, but it's not the same as coping with it. I think that if your mother had tried to kill herself, you'd feel very different."

There was a silence because Hildy had stopped chopping. "My mother was not at all like yours," she said. "She was not so clever and not so pretty. She was a big woman with a big Jewish nose who liked to grow *Zimmerlinden* – you know, house plants. There was one that she'd grown right round the living-room window, she called it *'die grüne Prinzessin'* – the green princess. And in 1934, when Erwin and I left Germany, she refused to come with us because, she said, whoever would look after it?"

"Oh, Hildy, I'm sorry," said Anna, knowing what was coming, but Hildy remained matter of fact.

"We think she died in Theresienstadt," she said. "We're not quite sure – there were so many, you see. And perhaps you're right, what I say is too simple. But it seems to me your mother is lucky, because at least she can choose for herself if she wants to live or die."

She went back to chopping the carrots. Anna watched the glint of the knife as they collapsed into slices.

"You see, what are you going to do?" said Hildy. "Go to your mother each morning and say, 'Please, Mama, live another day?' You think I haven't thought about my mother, how I should have *made* her come with us? After all, she could have grown *Zimmerlinden* also in Finchley. But of course we did not know then how it would be. And you can't make people do things – they want to decide for themselves."

"I don't know," said Anna. "I just don't know."

"I'm a few years younger than your mother," said Hildy. "But she and Konrad and I – we're all the same generation. Since the Nazis came, we haven't belonged in any place, only with refugees like ourselves. And we do what we can. I make soup and bake cakes. Your mother plays bridge and counts the miles of Konrad's car. And Konrad – he likes to help people and to feel that they love him. It's not wonderful, but it's better than Finchley, and it's a lot better than Theresienstadt."

"I suppose so."

"You don't suppose – you know. Anyway, what can you do about us? Make the Nazis not have happened? You going to put us all back in 1932? And if your mother, with her temperament, says this life is not good enough for her, you going to make her go on living whether she wants to or not?"

"I don't know," said Anna again.

"She doesn't know," said Hildy to the carrots. "Look, can't you understand, it's not your business!" She swept the carrots into the pan with the rest and sat down at the table. "You want something to eat?"

"No," said Anna. "I mean, thank you, I'm not hungry."

Hildy shook her head. "Pale green, you look."

She picked up the cognac and filled up her glass. "Here, drink. And then home to bed."

Anna tried to think how many glasses of cognac she had already had, but it was too difficult, so she drank this one as well.

"I would just like –" she said, "I would just like to know that she will be all right."

"*Nu*, that you know. Konrad is a good man, and they have been together so long. He will certainly stay with her, at least for a while."

"And then?"

"Then?" Hildy raised both hands in the age-old Jewish gesture. "Who can worry about then? Then, what do we know, everything will probably be quite different."

It was snowing more than ever as the taxi drove her home to the hotel. She leaned back, dazed, and looked out at the flickering whiteness racing past the window. It shone when caught by the light, broke up, whirled, disappeared, touched the window from nowhere and quickly melted. You could see nothing beyond it. You might be anywhere, she thought.

Her head swam with the cognac she had drunk, and she pressed it against the glass to cool it.

Perhaps out there, she thought, is a different world. Perhaps out there, as Hildy said, it really had, none of it, ever happened. Out there Papa was still sitting in the third row of the stalls, Mama was smiling on the beach, and Max and the small person who had once been

793

herself were running up some steps, shouting, *"Ist Mami da?"*

Out there the goods trains had never carried anything but goods. There had been no torchlight processions and no brown uniforms.

Perhaps out there Heimpi was still stitching new black eyes on her pink rabbit. Hildy's mother was still tending her plants. And Rachel Birnbaum, aged six, was safe at home in her bed.

Friday

She woke early and was out of bed and at the window almost before she had opened her eyes, to see what the weather was like. It had worried her, at intervals during the night, that the plane might not be able to take off in heavy snow. But when she looked out into the garden, most of it had already melted. Only a few shrinking patches were left on the grass, pale in the early morning light. The sky looked clear enough – grey with some streaks of pink – and there seemed to be little wind.

So I'll get away all right, she thought. She wrapped her arms about her against the cold and suddenly became aware of feeling rather strange. I can smell the glass, she thought. I can smell the glass of the window. At the same time, her stomach gave a heave, everything rose up inside her, and she just managed a wild rush to the basin before she was sick.

It happened so suddenly that it was over almost before she knew it. For a moment she stood there shakily, letting the water run from the taps and rinsing her mouth in the tooth-glass. This is not tension, she thought. Oh God, she thought, I've caught Erwin's gastric 'flu. Then she thought, I don't care – I'm still going home.

She was afraid that if she once went back to bed, she might stay there, so very slowly and methodically, she put on her clothes, opened her suitcase, threw in her things, and then sat down in a chair. The room was inclined to rise and sink around her, but she made a great effort and kept it steady.

Perhaps, after all, it was only the cognac, she thought. She kept her eyes focused on the curtains, mercifully still today, and concentrated on their intricate, geometrical pattern. Gradually, as she followed the interlocking woven lines on the dark background, the nausea receded. Down, across, down. Across, down, across. In a moment, she thought, I'll be able to go and have some breakfast.

And then she suddenly realized what she was looking at. The pattern resolved itself into a mass of criss-crossing right-angles. It consisted of nothing but tiny, overlapping swastikas.

She was so surprised that she got up and walked across to them. There was no doubt about it. The swastikas were woven right through the fabric. Her nausea forgotten, she was filled instead with a mixture of amusement and disgust. I always thought that woman was a Nazi, she thought. She had found swastika patterns in Germany before, of course – engraved on the cutlery in a restaurant, carved deep into the backs of chairs or into the newspaper holders in a café. But she was repelled by the thought that she had unwittingly shared a room with this one, that she had been looking at it while thinking about Mama and Papa.

It's just as well I'm leaving, she thought. She moved her eyes from the curtains to the window and, very carefully, turned round. Then she walked down to the breakfast room and drank two cups of black coffee, after which she felt better. But the table was grubby as usual, a German voice was shouting in the kitchen, and suddenly she could not wait to get out of the place.

She went to fetch her suitcase and put on her coat. The proprietress, to her relief, was nowhere about, so she did not need to say goodbye to her. She smiled at the adolescent girl who, she calculated, could not have been more than three or four at the end of the Thousand Year Reich and could not thus be held responsible. Then she carried her suitcase out into the street and, even though it was far too early, sat on it in the cold until Konrad arrived to collect her.

"You look terrible," he said as they stood together at the airport. "What's the matter with you?"

"I think I had too much cognac last night.

I felt awful when I first got up, but I'm all right now."

It was not strictly true. She was still troubled by nausea, coupled with the curious intensification of her sense of smell. The leather seats of Konrad's car had been almost too much for her, and she had ridden a large part of the way with her nose stuck out of the window.

"I'm quite well enough to travel," she said, suddenly afraid that he might somehow stop her.

"I wouldn't dream of daring to suggest otherwise," he said. "Especially as I've cabled Richard to meet you."

She smiled and nodded.

There was a pause. She could smell his coat, floor polish, a packet of crisps which someone was eating, and the wood of some seats nearby, but it was all right – she did not feel sick.

"Well," he said. "This is very different from when you arrived. At least we've got your mother through."

"Yes." She hesitated. "I hope it won't be too difficult for you now. With – with your secretary and everything."

"I'll manage," he said. "Obviously, one can't just – abandon people. But I'll manage."

"And I hope you have a good time in the Alps."

"Yes," he said. "I hope so too."

"And when you come back –" She suddenly needed, desperately, to hear him say it – "you will look after Mama, won't you?"

He sighed and smiled his tired, asymmetrical smile. "You should know me by now," he said. "I always look after everybody."

There was nothing more she could say.

The smell of crisps became suddenly overwhelming and nausea returned, but she fought it down.

"Good luck with the job," said Konrad. "I look forward to seeing your name on the television screen. And give my love to Richard."

"I will."

"Perhaps I'll see you both at Christmas. I'll be in London then to visit my family."

"That'll be lovely." The part of her not occupied with the crisps noted that it was ludicrous of him to mention his family at this point, but replied, even more ludicrously, "And Mama will be there then as well."

They looked at each other and then, to her relief, her flight was called.

"Goodbye," she cried and, on an impulse, embraced him. "Look after yourself. And thank you!"

"For what?" he called after her, and it was true, she did not know. For making Mama happy in the past? For promising, with no great certainty, to look after her in the future? Or just because she herself was at last going home?

She turned and waved to him from Passport Control and he waved back. Then she watched him thread his way through the crowd in the lounge – a tall, fat elderly man with thinning hair and a stick. The great lover, she thought and it seemed very sad.

She was almost sick again as the plane took off – but here at least, she thought, they'll just think it's air sickness. She got as far as feeling for the paper bag provided, just in case, but as the plane rose up into the sky, away from the rubble and the re-building, from the dubious goods trains and the even more dubious people who claimed to have known nothing about them, away from the threatening Russians and the ex-Nazis whom they so much resembled, from the Grunewald and the German language and Mama and all her problems, it seemed as though her nausea had been left behind with all the rest.

She looked out at the blazing sky and felt a huge sense of relief. Well, I've made it, she thought, as though it had been some kind of escape. She was suddenly hungry, and when the stewardess brought her some breakfast, she devoured a double portion, to the last crumb. Afterwards she wrote a note to Mama, to be posted at London Airport. This way, she thought, Mama would get it tomorrow and it would be something, at least, to stave off depression. When she had stuck down the envelope, she leaned back in her seat and stared out at the sky.

"We have now left the Eastern Zone of Germany and are flying over the Western Zone," said the stewardess through a little microphone. "In a few minutes you may see the city of Bremen on your left."

The man beside her, a middle-aged American, stirred and smiled. "I guess it's silly of me," he said, "but I'm always glad when we get to this bit."

She smiled back at him. "So am I."

Already, as she looked back, her time in Berlin was beginning to shrink into the past. I didn't do much good there, she thought, but with detachment, as though she were considering someone else. Small, fleeting images ran through her mind – Mama searching for a handkerchief under her pillow; the exact inflection of Konrad's voice as he said, "The affair, of course, is finished." Perhaps one day I'll really write about it, she thought, and this time the idea did not seem so shocking. If I did it properly, she thought – the way it really was. If I could really describe Mama.

But as she picked through everything that had happened, there was a sense of something missing. Something forgotten, or perhaps neglected – something quite ordinary and yet important, that should have happened but hadn't. If I could just remember that, she thought. But she was tired and it was lovely not to feel sick any more, and after a while she put it out of her mind.

What would Papa think about it all? she wondered. During his last years, when her German had faded and Papa's English remained inadequate, they had made a joke of addressing each other very formally in French . . . *Qu'en pensez-vous, mon père?* she thought, and only realized from her neighbour's astonished glance that she must have said it aloud.

"I'm sorry," she said. "I think I was dreaming."

She closed her eyes to make it look more convincing, shutting out everything except the throbbing of the engines. Of course if you wrote about it, you'd have to put all that in, she thought. The different languages and the different countries. And the suitcases. Packed and re-packed so many times. Stored in the lofts and basements of the various shabby boarding houses, counted and re-counted on the train journeys from one temporary home to the next.

"*Wir fahren mit der Eisenbahn*," said Mama. The iron railway. It even sounded like the noise the train made rattling across Germany. The compartment was dirty and Max had got his knees black from searching for his football under the seat. "Here comes the passport inspector," said Mama and put her finger to her lips, so that Anna would remember not to give them away to the Russians. She could see them standing all along the frontier in an endless line.

"Anything to declare?" said Konrad, and she forgot and told him about the Professor's pills, but Mama shouted, "I'm fifty-six years old," and the train moved on, across the frontier, right through the middle of Paris and up Putney High Street.

"I've got the children through," said Mama to Papa who was sitting by his typewriter in his shabby room. He smiled fondly, ironically, and without a trace of self-pity. "As long as we four are together," he said, "nothing else matters."

"Papa," cried Anna, and found herself looking at the face of a stranger. It was quite close to her own, carefully made up and surrounded by permed, blonde hair. Below it was a crisp, blue blouse and a tailored tunic.

"We are about to land at London airport," said the stewardess. "Please fasten your seat belt." She looked at Anna more closely. "Are you quite well?" she said. "You're looking very pale."

"Quite well, thank you." She must have answered automatically, for she was still too much hung about by the dream to know what she was saying.

"Is someone meeting you at the airport?"

"Oh, yes." But for one endless, panicky moment, she could not remember who it was. Papa? Max? Konrad? "It's all right," she said at last. "I'm being met by my husband."

"Well, if there's anything you need —" The stewardess smiled and moved on.

They dived down through the cloud, and below it was raining. Everywhere was wet, and there was mud on the airport floors from the passengers' feet.

UK passports to the right, others to the left. She went through the gate on the right with more than the usual feeling of having conned someone, but the man smiled at her as though she belonged. "Not very nice weather to come home to," he said.

The customs officers in their blue uniforms were easy and relaxed as usual. "What, nothing?" they said. "Not even a bottle of schnapps for the boy-friend?"

"Nothing," she said, and there, beyond the partition, she could see Richard.

He was looking past her at a group of people just coming in, and for a moment she watched him as though he were a stranger. A slight, dark-haired man, carelessly dressed with a quick, intelligent face. English. Well – more Irish really. But not a refugee. He looked alone and unencumbered. He's lived here all his life, she thought. He's never spoken anything but English. Papa died years before I even met him. She felt suddenly weighed down with past words and places and people. Could she really belong with anyone so unburdened?

The customs officer made a white chalk mark on her suitcase, and at the same moment Richard turned and saw her.

"Anna!"

She grabbed her case and ran towards him. As she reached him, she saw that he looked tired and worried. She dropped the case and fell into his arms. He smelled of coffee, paper and type-writer ribbons.

"Darling," she said.

He said, "Thank God you're back."

For the first time since she'd left him, she felt all of one piece. There were no more doubts. This was where she belonged. She was home.

"It's been getting a bit frightening," he said, as they sat together on the airport bus.

"The Suez business?"

"And Hungary."

"But I thought that was all right."

He looked astonished. "All right?"

"Settled."

"Haven't you heard? It's in all the papers. You *must* have heard."

"No." But she knew from his face what it was. "Did the Russians –?"

"Of course. When they said they were moving out, they were just waiting for reinforcements. Now they've got them and they've pounced. Tanks all round Budapest. They've grabbed the Hungarian leaders. They're closing the frontiers and chucking out the Western press."

She felt suddenly sick. "So all those people –"

"That's right," he said. "God knows what will happen to them now. Apparently thousands of them are getting out while they can."

Again! she thought, and was overcome by anger. "Surely someone must do something," she said. "They can't just be left."

He said nothing.

"Well, can they?"

He smiled wryly. "The Labour Party are having a huge protest rally in Trafalgar Square."

"About Hungary?"

"About us. How wicked we are, going into Suez like awful imperialists. And while we're busy with our own little fiasco, the real imperialists are doing what they like."

Outside the window of the bus, streets of identical red brick houses streamed past in the rain and were left behind.

"I think everybody's scared," he said. "You can see it in their expressions. It could so easily all blow up."

More houses, a factory, a horse in a scruffy field. What about Mama? she thought. "You think there'll be trouble in Berlin?"

He made a face. "If it did blow up, I suppose it wouldn't matter where you were. But I'm very glad you're back."

"So am I. Oh, so am I."

His coat was damp, and she could smell the tweed, mixing with the rubbery smell of other people's macs.

"Will your mother be all right?" he asked. "I mean, with Konrad?"

"I don't know." She wanted to tell him about it but suddenly felt too tired. "It's very complicated," she said.

"Konrad always seemed so responsible."

"That's the funny thing," she said. "I think he is."

At the air terminal in Kensington High Street the bus deposited them, and they stood on the curb with her suitcase, trying to get a taxi. As usual in the rain, these all seemed to be full, and she stood there in the wet, peering out at the cars and buses splashing past through the puddles, and felt utterly exhausted.

He looked at her in concern. "Are you all right?"

She nodded. "I think I had too much cognac last night. And very little sleep. There's one!" A taxi had appeared round a corner, empty, and she hailed it.

"Poor love," he said. "And you had the curse as well."

The taxi came towards them and she watched it approaching, infinitely slowly. So that's it, she thought – the thing that had been missing, the thing that should have happened in Berlin but hadn't. She could see the driver's face under his woolly cap, the wet shine of the metal, the water spurting from the wheels like a film in slow motion – she could almost count the drops – and she thought, good heavens, me! It's happened to me! The taxi stopped.

"No," she said. "I didn't."

He stared at her. "You didn't?"

"No." She could feel the happiness rising into her face and saw it echoed in his.

"Good God," he said.

The driver watched them from behind the steering wheel. "You do want a taxi?" he asked with heavy irony.

"Of course." Richard gave him the address and they scrambled in.

"Are you sure?" he said. "I suppose it could have been the strain."

"No," she said. "I was sick this morning, too. And there's something else that's funny – I keep smelling things." She felt for the words. "I'm with child."

She laughed with pleasure, and he laughed too. They sat very close together, thinking about it, while the taxi crawled through the traffic. Near Kensington Church Street a policeman stopped them to allow a small procession to cross the road. Middle-aged people, some with umbrellas, carrying placards. "Save Hungary" she read, but there were not many of them and they soon passed. Then up Church Street, down the side streets lined with trees, almost bare now, the sodden leaves clogging the gutters –

"I wonder what it will be," said Richard. "Do you mind which?"

"Not really." But she imagined a daughter. A little girl, running, laughing, talking . . . "I suppose it won't speak any German."

"You could teach it if you liked."

"No," she said. "No, I don't think so." Anyway, it wouldn't be the same.

Much later, when it was getting dark, she sat in the little living-room on the new striped sofa, listening to the news. She had unpacked, and telephoned James Dillon – though now, she supposed, she would only be able to do the new job until the baby was born – and had told Richard all about Mama. She had inspected the dining-room rug which looked just right but might not be suitable for a nursery, and they had decided on Thomas for a boy but had not been able to agree on a name for a girl.

The curtains were drawn, supper was cooking in the kitchen, and apart from the fact that the stack of typewritten sheets next to Richard's typewriter had grown taller, she might never have been away. She could hardly remember Berlin, or even a time when she hadn't known that she was pregnant.

The newsreader's careful accents filled the room. The Egyptian army had been routed, a British cruiser had sunk a frigate, British and French infantry were ready at any moment to move in –

"Are you sure you want to listen to this?" asked Richard anxiously. He had got some glasses from the kitchen and was pouring her a drink.

She nodded, and the careful voice went on. "In Hungary the Russians have swept back in force . . ." He gave her a glass and sat down beside her. ". . . no one knows what will happen now to the brave people of Budapest . . . the Secret Police, wreaking a terrible vengeance . . . refugees, many of them children, pouring across the frontier . . ."

She sipped her drink, but it didn't help.

". . . never again, said a spokesman, will the West be able to trust . . ."

She found that tears were running down her face. Richard reached out, there was a click, and the voice stopped.

"It makes one weepy," she said. "Being pregnant makes one weepy."

"Everything makes you weepy," he said. He raised his glass and said with fierce affection, "To our little creature."

"To our little creature." She wiped her eyes and sniffed. "It's just –" she said – "it's hardly the best time to start a baby, is it?"

"I don't suppose it ever is."

"No, I suppose it isn't."

He put his arm round her. "You'll be a lovely mum."

She was taken aback by the word. "A mum?" she said doubtfully.

He smiled. "A lovely, lovely mum."

She smiled back.

Somewhere very far away, a small person in boots was running up some steps, shouting, "*Ist Mami da?*"

I wonder how I'll do, she thought. I wonder how on earth I'll do.

"All my novels are based on things that happened to me a long time ago. I wrote them because I wanted to describe what it was like - what it was really like - to flee from the Nazis, go to schools where they don't speak your language, live through air raids and - in those days - grow up. (Most of it was much better than you'd imagine because, in spite of the hardships, it was also very exciting.)

I write slowly and with difficulty and have never yet got through a book without saying, 'Never again!' But then when the work is finished and one's got it more or less the way one wanted it, it seems like the most satisfying thing one has ever done."

Judith Kerr